HANGING ROCK REBEL

Lt. John Blue's War in West Virginia and the Shenandoah Valley

Edited by Dan Oates

This Burd Street Press publication
was printed by
Beidel Printing House, Inc.
63 West Burd Street
Shippensburg, PA 17257 USA

In respect for the scholarship contained herein, the acid-free paper used in this book meets the guidelines for permanence and durability of the Committee on Production Guidelines for Book Longevity of the Council on Library Resources.

For a complete list of available publications
please write
Burd Street Press
Division of White Mane Publishing Company, Inc.
P.O. Box 152
Shippensburg, PA 17257 USA

Library of Congress Cataloging-in-Publication Data

Blue, John, 1834-1903.
    Hanging rock rebel : Lt. John Blue's war in West Virginia and the Shenandoah Valley / edited by Dan Oates.
        p.   cm.
    Originally published as articles in The Hampshire review, between 1898 and 1901.
    Includes bibliographical references and indexes.
    ISBN 0-942597-62-1 : $24.95
    1. Blue, John, 1834-1903.   2. United States--History--Civil War, 1861-1865--Personal narratives, Confederate.   3. Shenandoah River Valley (Va. and W. Va.)--History--Civil War, 1861-1865.   4. West Virginia--History--Civil War, 1861-1865.   5. Soldiers--West Virginia--Hampshire County--Biography.   6. Hampshire County (W. Va.)--Biography.   I. Oates, Daniel P.   II. Title.
E605.B68   1994
973.7'82--dc20   93-39320
                                                                        CIP

PRINTED IN THE UNITED STATES OF AMERICA

Acknowledgements

Lana Bean
Madeline M. Blue
Frances Buckbee
Davis History House
Mrs. Ruth Grapes
Ralph Haines
Hampshire Co. Public Library
National Archives, Washington, D.C.
Paul Oates
Potomac Edison's Valley Echo (1959 - 1965)
Miss Mary Pugh
Melinda Blue Schantz
Lee Teter
West Virginia University Archives
Ranger Mike Brown, Point Lookout State Park

Dedication

To Beth, for her love, "patience and understanding"

Contents

LT. JOHN BLUE (1834 - 1903)
(MADELINE M. BLUE)

Foreword

I guess the story of Lt. Blue is something that I have been acquainted with ever since I entered my eighth grade West Virginia History class under Mrs. Catherine Long in 1964. The story has always been ingratiated with much heroism, but it wasn't until I stumbled onto the complete story that I became fully intrigued by this multi-faceted man.

In 1989, I was contacted by a writer from Virginia, Richard Armstrong, who was completing his research on the regimental history of the 11th Virginia Cavalry of the Confederate States of America. Armstrong needed information on the post-war activities of many of the soldiers of this regiment. In assisting him with his research, I came upon the "experience", as Blue titled his memoirs, in The Hampshire Review. Further research revealed that the account of John Blue's Civil War experience had not been made public since its original printing at the turn of the century.

The Review began publishing Blue's accounts in the spring of 1898, and the last installment was printed approximately three years later in 1901. During that time Blue took numerous leaves from writing. One break came on June 18, 1898 after the first sixteen installments. Blue writes, "...as soon as the dog days are over, if living and in health, you will hear from me again." He continued in the fall of 1898 for 51 weeks before stopping again after November 15, 1899. His last writings began April 18, 1900 and ended somewhat abruptly April 17, 1901.

John Monroe Blue was born March 25, 1834, four miles north of Romney, Virginia, now West Virginia, along the banks of the South Branch of the Potomac River. The area, then and now, is referred to as Hanging Rocks. The rock cliff extends over three hundred feet at a point where the South Branch slices through Mill Creek Mountain. Railroad tracks and a narrow road hug the edge of the river at the bottom of the "Rocks".

His parents were Garret I. and Sarah (Long) Blue, both of whom he mentions numerous times in his writings. His education was not like school as we know today. I feel certain he attended school until the eighth grade and then, probably, attended the Potomac Seminary in Romney for higher education. The amount of knowledge needed to write his memoirs would certainly lead one to believe he was highly educated for his time.

At the outbreak of the war, he had four sisters and one younger brother, age 11. Being the oldest son of the family, John's farming duties were obvious. Hunting and other survival skills were part of his everyday life. These skills, mixed with a keen intellect, created the perfect mix for a soldier and scout during the Civil War. The importance of a soldier with Blue's skills was immeasurable. Romney and its surrounding territories were a stronghold due to its location to the railroad, river and the Northwestern Turnpike (present day U.S. Route 50). Northern and southern troops alternated in and out of Romney, so much that historians have documented 56 times that Romney had changed hands.

As to why Mr. Blue waited thirty-five years to write his experiences of the war, one can only speculate. The loss of the war was considered a personal loss to him. While loss of life and property were unbearable, the Confederate veteran had to live with loss of dignity and cause. Possibly this served as a cleansing of his memories. The diary that is mentioned four times within the text of this book has never been discovered. Madeline Blue, wife of John Blue, grandson of Lt. John Blue, related that after the death of his wife, Lt. Blue lived with his two sisters, Rebecca and Sallie, and his brother, Ed. About the whereabouts of the diary, Mrs. Blue can only speculate, "My mother-in-law said that Rebecca and Sal were the darndest people to throw away things." Since his death was sudden, she wonders whether the diary was thrown out.

After the war, Lt. Blue returned to Romney but had little money or property to his name. The war had devastated the area both financially and politically. In a letter to a cousin dated June 3, 1866 Blue states, "I suppose that you have heard of the ratification of the late amendment to the Constitution of West Va. It disfranchises all rebbles and rebble sympathizers. They are hence forth and forever prohibited holding any property or doing any business; are to be treated as foreigners. So you see we will be compelled to fight again or emigrate. I think of going to South America this fall if I can raise the means and keep my health. I think it folly to remain longer in this state."

After further thought Blue decided not to go. In 1867, he married Eliza Ann Fox, daughter of Vause and Rebecca (Harness) Fox of Hampshire County. Soon afterwards, at the insistence of his prosperous cousins in Berryville, Virginia, Blue and his new wife moved away from Romney to try farming in the Shenandoah Valley. This was short lived because his wife missed her home and they soon moved back to Hampshire County. He began renting property and farming for the crops.

Blue entered politics in 1892 as the assessor for the first district and was serving in his second term when he died on June 30, 1903. He passed away quietly while rocking on his front porch of a heart attack. His obituary, which appeared in the July 1 <u>Hampshire Review,</u> says it best, "He was a plain, blunt man, of more than ordinary intelligence and sense."

Dan Oates, Editor

CHAPTER I

The Huckleberry Rangers

A little after sunrise on or about the 18th of May 1861, the Hampshire Guards, and the Frontier Riflemen, were in line in front of the Courthouse. It was a Sabbath morning clear and calm. Col. David Gibson gave them a short talk, in which he urged them to obey their officers, to be true to the cause they had espoused and if fall they must let it be doing their duty, with their face to the Heavens and their foot to the foe, or if they should be spared to return let it be in honor, but never in disgrace. It was a sad parting with dear ones, a parting never to be forgotten by those who witnessed it. They were conveyed in buggies, carriages and wagons to Green Spring Station on the B & O Railroad. Col. Isaac Parsons with about a dozen men rode in front. There was to be a train meet them from Harpers Ferry. The advanced guard had been there only a few moments, when the train backed up, with Col. E. H. MacDonald standing on the platform. It was reported that Jacob Cragon was trying to raise a crowd at Old Town to give trouble. We were ordered down to the Old Town ford to give notice of anything suspicious. Soon we heard the train moving off, we rode back to the station. The train had passed from sight, and Hampshire County had sent its first contribution to the front.

We turned homeward with feelings of sadness which refused to be shaken off, at least during our ride home.

The next company of Volunteers to leave the county was the Potomac Guards, raised at and in the neighborhood of Springfield, Philip Grace was their Captain. There was a volunteer company organized at New Creek, now Keyser. The company split up on the question of Secession. If I am not mistaken Col. E. M. Armstrong was their, Captain, and George Sheetz first Lieutenant, any way about the first of June the company reorganized under the name of the Hampshire Riflemen with Sheetz Captain.

Captain Sheetz moved to Blues Gap, a few days later Captain Grace arrived at the same place with the Potomac Guards. The Independent Greys a Moorefield company was at Romney, a few days later Captain Sheetz and Captain Grace came to Romney with their companies. Col. Cummins and Lieutenant Col. Leo had arrived at Romney for the purpose of organizing a regiment. They had been in town but a few days, when old uncle Jimmy Parker (as almost every one called him) dashed into town soon after sunrise one morning with the news that the yankees would be on them in a few moments. Uncle Jimmy Parker had been aroused in the early morning by the unusual barking of the house dog. He arose from

Col. Lew Wallace and his Eleventh Indiana Zouaves arrive west of Romney at the bridge crossing the South Branch of the Potomac. *(DAVIS HISTORY HOUSE, ROMNEY, WV)*

his bed and on approaching the window discovered a column of soldiers passing through Headsville moving towards Romney. He surmised their destination. (He then lived where Mr. Isaac Carskadon now lives) he knew that those three companies were in town and had no cavalry picket. They kept an infantry guard at the bridge a mile from town. Uncle Jimmy knew that the yankees would be at Romney shortly after sunrise, and more than likely surprise and capture the three companies at that place. He determined if possible to warn them of their danger. Dressing hurriedly with his shoes in hand he stepped out the back way, after going a safe distance stopped and put on his shoes and then started on foot to Romney. On crossing an old field several hundred yards from the road he was tired several times. He took a bee line for Mechanicsburg which place he reached about sunrise some distance ahead of the yanks. Uncle Jimmy was at that time was over sixty years of age and the speed at which he had traveled for several miles through the mountains had nearly exhausted him. Mr. William Taylor was up and quickly had him mounted. He rode into town perhaps a half hour ahead of the yankees. Had it not been for this timely notice in all probability the confederates would have been captured. Col. Cummins had them in line and marching to the bridge. Col. Cummins soon discovered that he was outnumbered at least five to one. His men being indifferently armed and with but little ammunition, except for Col. Sheetz's company which was armed with Mississippi rifles and at that time numbered about 30 men. This company remained at the bridge, but as the yankees advanced after exchanging a few shots at long range fell back along the ridge southeast of town. Col. Cummins with the other two companies passed through town in the direction of Winchester a few moments before the yankees entered at the lower end. They fired several shots as they marched up the street, old Mr. Buzby was struck in the hip who was the only person I heard of being hurt. Col. W. H. Harness was in town. He carried a fine large long range rifle and he gave the yankees several rounds before they entered town and thought he did some execution. With the exception of the destruction of the Intelligencer outfit, little harm was done in town. Mr. Gibson's house was raided. I was in it a few hours after the yankees had left. Bureaus and wardrobes had been broken open and contents scattered over the floor and many things of value carried away. The yankees were commanded by Col. Lew Wallace. The yankees only remained a few hours and then returned to New Creek. The Confederates fell back to Winchester, where the Potomac Guards and Hardy Greys were soon mustered into regular service. Capt. Sheetz's company mounted themselves and afterward came back to Romney with Col. Angus McDonald about the middle of June. Col. Hill with two or three regiments came to Romney. The Frontier Riflemen and Hampshire Guards were detached for the purpose and

3

came with them. In this way most of them had a chance to visit their homes. Several deserted on this trip.

Col. Hill started after dark one night for the purpose of destroying the bridge below Keyser. He reached there a little after daylight found it guarded by the home guards, who ran. It was soon ablaze (and we) captured one small cannon. A few days later marched back again to Winchester.

A short time after, about the 20th, Capt. Turner Ashby came to the county and camped on Mr. George Washington's farm about five miles north of Romney. He remained only a few weeks. During the time his brother Richard was mortally wounded while on a scout along the Baltimore & Ohio railroad above Greenspring station. He died a few days later. Soon after Ashby returned with his company to Winchester. This was about the 10th of July, 1861. About this time several regiments of State Militia had been gathered at Winchester to take the place of the Confederate forces soon to march to Manassas. Among others, was the Hampshire Militia, under Col. Alexander Monroe. Men subject to military service were now very scarce in the county.

Col. Isaac Parsons had been in Richmond and returned a few days after Capt. Ashby left the county, with the authority to raise an independent company of mounted men for border service. This now he under took to do, and in a short time had about 30 men enrolled and organized by electing Isaac Parsons, captain; John Blue, 1st lieutenant; Isaac Parsons, Jr., 2nd lieutenant. We had on the roll the names of Alexander Sanders, Benjamin Powell, Arch McDonald, John W. Poland, John Adams, John G. Monroe, William C. Newman, Isaac Blue, Isaac Dunn, Uriah Lees, Isaac Kuykendall, Charles Gates, W. D. Rees, J. M. Rees, S. Bane, C. Umstot, Silas Pancake, W. McBride, George White, Vause McNary, Herman Seniff, W. M. Parsons, T. Stuckslagle, Adam Parrish, John Seymour, W. V. Inskeep of Burk, Dan Seymour, Benj. McDonald, these are all that I can remember.

Our captain owned a mountain farm known as the Cheshire place, about two miles from Romney, here we first camped, quartermaster and commissary being furnished by our captain. Our arms were principally the home rifle. We had a few flintlock muskets which we found in the loft of the courthouse, also a dozen or so old sabers and perhaps as many horse pistols (flint locks) all of which had seen service in the Revolution. They were all built for service.

The flint lock musket would be quite a curiosity to many of the young men today. I will give a partial description of one of those ancient weapons that our forefathers gained their independence. The gun which I am about to describe was about 5 1/2 feet in length, 2 in. at the breech and 1 inch at the muzzle, the lock weighing about 1 pound. We used

Indian darts for flints. A charge for these guns was about 6 drachmas powder, an ounce ball and about 6 buck shot with about a tablespoonful of powder to prime the piece and then the gun was ready for action. When a man made up his mind to pull the trigger, if mounted, he had better dismount, and if ornamented with false teeth it was best to dispense with them for a time. If the first attempt to pull her off failed the only thing to do was to get your wind and try again. You would know when it went without being told. There would be a sharp flash dot unlike lightning, a puff of smoke, a shock resembling an earthquake, when the one at the breech of the piece would be apt to take about six steps backward and more than likely sit down sudden like, then a deafening roar resembling thunder, when a bolt had struck about ten feet away.

The horse pistol was like unto the musket only on a smaller scale.

It was no small job to clean the dust and rust from these ancient weapons and get them ready for service. About the time we had them ready for service we got the word that the yankees were advancing from the direction of Cumberland. We were ordered to saddle up and prepare to meet them. We were soon mounted and started down the road to meet them. When we reached the upper end of the gap at Hanging Rocks, the captain thought it would be better if we followed an old road back of the mountain until we reached the wire bridge and if the yankees had passed up, we would follow, fall on their rear and kill or capture the whole lot. When we reached the bridge we found that they had not yet crossed. We then concluded that they halted in Springfield. We again determined to make a flank move and if possible get in their rear. We forded the river at M. Blue's ford, and reached the pike again near Springfield, but found no yankees and could hear of none. After consulting we thought it not prudent to follow the pike to Frankfort knowing that if we met the yankees they would outnumber us 5 or 10 to one, so we determined to make another flank move after passing through Springfield. We left the pike and followed an old road to the left of the pike, again entered it near Frankfort. After examining the pike we found that neither infantry or cavalry had passed that day. We rode on to Frankfort, when we learned that there was only a company of Home Guards in Cumberland.

It was now near sunset. We got supper, fed our horses and then concluded to picket at the ford below town. Next morning all being quiet, we concluded to return to Frankfort, feed our horses, get breakfast and then return to Romney, as there was no show for a fight without going to Cumberland and then the yankees might come over from New Creek and capture Romney in our absence. We were riding along very leisurely, having reached the upper end of the gap, four miles below Romney, when we met Mr. James Hines, who had been up the road. He said Romney was full of yankees. We were halted at once and a council of war held to

5

determine what was to be done. We had ridden at least 20 miles looking for yankees and had found them where least expected; right at home.

We thought prudent to reconnoitre before doing anything rash. We left the pike following a mountain road for some distance then making our way across ridges and hollows, through woods and brush until we reached a point on top of the mountains, about one mile east of town where we had a good view of the country all around the town. After keeping a sharp lookout for sometime and discovering no yankees we began to think Hines had played a joke on us. He was about half Union anyway. He was threatened in language far more empathic than eloquent. Finally we sent a man into town on foot and in case there was no yankees to signal us. We soon saw the signal of no danger. In a few moments we were riding down Main Street as brave as lions, listening to the boys relate their hair breadth escapes. The yankees had marched from New Creek in the night and entered town early in the morning, remained a few hours and returned to New Creek again. They were under the command of Col. Cain.

We returned to our camp, outwardly sorry that we were away, inwardly glad we were. A few days after we concluded to have our flintlocks changed to percussions, there being a gunsmith on Jersey Mountain. We moved our camp to a grazing farm, belonging to the Captain, near the gunsmith's where we had the needed work done. We turned our horses in pasture and spent the next two weeks in hunting, game being plentiful. We had no trouble keeping ourselves in meat, the farmers nearby furnished us bread. Here some evil disposed person gave us the name of the Huckleberry Rangers. After having our flintlocks changed we found that it would be necessary to get army caps as our rifle caps were too small. These could not be had any nearer than Winchester. Our Captain made a requisition on the Ordinance Master at Winchester and detailed Adam Parsons and myself to get what we needed. When we arrived in Winchester we called upon the Ordinance Master to have our requisition filled. He said General Carson (who was there in command) would have to approve it before he could do anything for us. We then called on the general, he said he could only order ammunition issued to his immediate command. Then we were stuck but concluded to call on Col. Monroe who was there in command of the Hampshire Militia. After consulting him he said I will make a requisition for the Hampshire militia and have the general to approve it. In this way you can, I think, get what you want. This he did and we had no further trouble. We remained in camp one day viewing the forts, breast works, etc. near town. We found Dr. Canfield in charge of the heavy guns on the forts. Next day returned to camp, our guns being repaired and our horses in good plight, game and huckleberries getting a little scarce and more particular for the credit of

6

the command we thought it necessary to make a forward move and as there were no yankees nearer than New Creek we thought it would be safe to advance as far as the lower end of the gap at Hanging Rock. Early next morning we packed our baggage, consisting one blanket and one tin cup each, one pot one bucket, one skillet and one coffee boiler. By 8 a.m. we were mounted formed into a line, the roll was then called, after which the Col. wheeled us into column, placed himself at its head and gave the command to march. By 10 o'clock a.m., we had gone into camp on the west side of the South Branch, in an old vacant house, which had been used for a school house and church. Here again the Col. owned a farm. A field near by afforded abundant green grass for our horses. A detail was sent on the mountain for meat and returned late in the evening with two fine deer and a turkey. Our bread detail having returned sometime before, we soon had supper. The hams of our venison we make jerk by drying it over a bed of coals. When prepared in this way it would keep for a long time and was intended for use on a march or in case of emergency, as well as to preserve the fresh meat in warm weather. One of our hunters found a bee tree that evening and several of us went upon the mountain about two miles that night and cut the tree which proved to be a good one. We got over a 100 pounds of honey. We charged and were repulsed several times before we succeeded in capturing the fortress. Some of the boys complained more from an overdose of honey than the sting of the bee. We occasionally sent out a detail to gather huckleberries which we stowed in a half-bushel pot, when done were dipped out in our tin cups each having a cup of his own. When cooked this way they were not bad to eat. We slept in the house at night, some on the benches we put together some on the floor, a few over head on boards placed across the joist, the upper floor having been taken up for some purpose or other. Here we slept without camp guards or picket horses running loose in the pasture. A half dozen veterans would have captured the whole outfit. This was the beginning before the end came. Most of us had learned to be more cautious.

We remained here for about two weeks, hunting, fishing and made a little scout as far as Patterson's Creek once, but was not lucky enough to meet with any blue coats and was thus relieved of the trouble bringing them to camp. One night while camped at this place Lieutenant Ike Parsons and I went to a deer lick about a mile from camp. About midnight a deer came which we succeeded in killing. We tied its feet together then swung it on a pole and started for camp. We had about three hundred yards to go down a dark hollow through woods before we came to the field in passing under a leaning sycamore in the top of which was a thick cluster of grape vines. We heard the loose bark falling on the dry leaves and halted to investigate and came to the conclusion that there was a coon

7

up there getting grapes. There had been a potato patch chopped off and a brush pile or two made against the steep hillside just above, which had not been burned. One of those we set on fire, which made it almost as light as day for some distance around. We soon discovered what we took to be a half grown coon up among the vines. Parsons said he would go up and shake it down and I should throw my blanket over it and we would take it to the camp and slip it in the house and fasten the door on the outside and have some fun when the boys awoke. This I agreed to do. Ike took off his boots and commenced to climb the tree, the coons commenced to climb also and kept climbing until it was near the top. Ike followed on until well up, when he gave a vigorous shake at the same time said, "look out, he is coming!" About that time it struck the ground, I made a dash at it with my blanket but soon found that I had tackled the wrong coon. It proved to be full grown, and more than that had his war paint on. I soon found he meant business and did not purpose being captured without a struggle. I soon found that I had more on my hands than I had bargained for, the thing seemed to mad all over and fought like a bulldog. After waltzing around for some time, and by handling my feet the best I knew how, I finally succeeded in letting him go, but was in great fear of Ike loosing his hold and falling to the ground. He might have been heard laughing for a mile around. After he had somewhat controlled himself he said, there is another one up here, I know its a young one, try and capture it. I asked him to hold on until I procured a good club, as I did not care to capture any more coons. When I signaled my readiness he gave a shake and down came the coon. It hadn't more than struck the ground until I struck him a blow that settled him for all time. It proved to be a young one no larger than a cat. Now, said Ike, "there is another one up here and I know that it's a young one, I can see it plain. Try and capture this one without hurting it." I gathered up my blanket again, but kept my club under my arm ready for an emergency, and took a position indicated by Ike. It took several shakes before he struck the ground. I soon had him securely tucked up in my blanket.

We soon had him securely tied and swung on the pole along with our deer and in half hour were at camp. The night being warm the door had been left partly open, it had a chain and staple on the outside. The house stood within fifty yards of the river, where we had a boat in which we placed our deer, blankets and guns. Then Ike caught the coon by the back of the neck and the hind legs and after having untied him, carried it up to the house, slipped it in and closed the door hitching the chain over the staple, then sat down on the step to await developments. Pretty soon one of the boys, Sam Bane said to Uriah Lease, "Uriah, Uriah, what is this climbing over me. Uriah there is some kind of an animal in here and I believe it's a pole cat." Then there was a general scramble. In a very short

8

time the boys were all perched up on the joist holding consultation as to what it was and how it got in, the door being shut. Sam Bane declared in very emphatic language that it was fast on the outside as he had tried to get it open and couldn't. "Well boys," said the Colonel, who was almost dying from laughter, "we must have a light, who has a match." All seemed to have but they were all below and no know would volunteer to get them. Day was beginning to break in the east. We quietly slipped the chain from the staple and then ran to the boat and shoved out to a large rock in the river to await further developments as soon as it became light enough. They discovered the little coon "scrooched" up in a corner. Then some roared with laughter and some roared with anger and swore vengeance against Parsons and Blue. We were soon discovered and dire threats were made as to what our fate would be when they got us though most of the boys took it as a joke and laughed at those who did not see it in that light, when we told them he had a deer and they wouldn't get any of it unless they promised not to molest us. But they did not believe that we had a deer. Finally they agreed if we had a deer we could land without being disturbed, but if we had no deer then we must submit to a thorough ducking. So we pushed ashore, we had the deer, they settled the matter though we had to tell the boys all about the coon hunt. We soon had our deer dressed and frying for breakfast.

When we had satisfied the inner man, we again held a council of war and having heard that there was but one company of artillery at New Creek determined on an advance with a view of capturing that point. We further concluded that it would be better for various reasons to let our horses remain in the pasture and move on foot with the exceptions of perhaps a half dozen mounted men who would be expected to do picket duty when thought necessary. Also to move our camp equipage. Next morning bright and early we took up our line of march up Mill Hollow. The mounted men followed the road, the foot men deployed on each side for a hunt. Almost the entire distance lay through woods. It was understood that all should meet at a vacant house on top of Middle Ridge, belonging to M. Blue and brother. At not later than 12 a.m., when the boys got in they had one small deer, but two of the boys were missing. We concluded to camp here for the night and await the missing boys. In the meantime dressed and jerked the fleshy part of our deer and cooked the remainder so as to keep it from spoiling until used. The other two boys came in about 4 o'clock in the evening, said they had been lost and had found themselves near where they had started in the morning. They had found us by following the trail made by our horses. They were pretty well tired out. We camped here for the night and next morning after breakfast started for what is known as Cold Spring, on Patterson's Creek in the neighborhood of Mr. W. D. Rees', Mr. Abraham and Mr. Greenwell

Johnson's. Before the middle of the day we were in camp at Cold Spring. The ladies nearby soon had abundant rations for a regiment. The men had to keep their hands off for fear of a trip to Camp Chase[1]. The Captain thought perhaps we had better remain here for a few days and learn all we could as to the number of yankees at New Creek. We were now in a neighborhood where all were not favorable to the south, which made it necessary for us to be a little more cautious in our movements. We always moved our camp after dark for fear some union man who know of our whereabouts might pilot the yanks to our camp and disturb our slumber.

In making a move at night we always left a man or two some distance in the rear, who was acquainted with the route and who know where we would stop. In this way would know if we were followed by a spy or not.

One night we got word that there was a company of yankee cavalry camped for the night at Burlington. The rangers were soon astir examining their arms and ammunition and putting on fresh caps, and a little after midnight were on the march, over fences and ditches, through brush and briars for seven or eight miles. At length we came to a halt in the rear of and to the right of the old Vandiver Hotel at Burlington, just as day began to break. After consulting for a few moments we advanced to a sink or low place near the Northwestern Grade. Just then some one passed in front of the barn and commenced hollering. We supposed that he had seen us and was giving the alarm. Without a thought several of the boys raised their guns and fired. The man fell about the same time the bugle sounded to horse and the rangers took to their heels and were soon under cover in the timber. The yanks formed and marched down the Patterson Creek pike a short distance, then up into the field a short distance, but did not come into the range of the home rifle which we were mostly armed.

The yanks were soon in the saddle and were at a double quick toward New Creek. The rangers returned to our camp at Cold Spring, not well pleased with our expedition.

A few days after Col. Ed. McDonald joined us with a company of mounted militia from about Forks of Capon. They only remained with us a few days, during which time we made a scout or two along Knobley Mountain as far up as Ridgeville, but were lucky enough not to meet any yanks. Col. Ed. McDonald at the breaking out of the war was the Colonel of the 77th Regiment Virginia Militia. I was ordered to notify, as far as I could, all the militia belonging to the 77th Regiment to report at Romney on a certain day. The next day after our scout to Ridgeville Col. McDonald and his mounted militia returned to Romney.

We remained near Cold Spring for a day or two longer, and having

---

[1] Prison Camp for Confederates in Ohio.

heard that the yanks were in the habit of coming over on Cabin Run every few days in squads of half dozen, for butter, chicken, eggs , &c, we concluded to move over on George's Ridge, near John W. Taylor's, where we could have full view of the Knobley Mountain and Cabin Run roads. After we had been at this point a day or two without sighting any yankees, we concluded one night to go over to the top of Knobley Mountain where there is a high ledge of rocks, only a short distance below the village of New Creek, now Keyser. From this point we had a fair view of the town and all of its surroundings, by means of a good glass, which the Colonel carried with him. We arrived at the point named in the after part of the night. By daylight we had made ourselves secure from observation in case some one should point their glass in that direction. It did not take long for us to learn that there were several hundred yankees at New Creek station.

We lay here all day and returned to our camp at night with out accident. The Colonel left his glass on the rocks where we had been the day before and did not miss until nearly back to camp. I accompanied two others back for the glass next day. In crossing the Cabin Run road on our return we discovered that a company of cavalry had just passed up the run. We got back to camp all right.

The next day was Sunday. It commenced raining in the night and rained all day. We had no shelter, except for tents made by cutting small poles and leaning them against a larger one withed to two small saplings six or eight feet from the ground, then spreading a blanket over them. In this way we kept comparatively dry. About 4 o'clock in the evening a messenger came into camp with news that a yankee scout had come over to Headsville and had captured M. D. Sheetz and had come down the creek and taken old Mr. James Parker at Abraham Johnson's and had followed the road from there to Cabin Run on their way to New Creek Station. We were soon on a forced march, hoping to intercept them on the Cabin Run road, but we were a little too late. They were going out of sight when we reached the place where we expected to intercept them. It was getting late so we returned to camp. Some were disappointed that we had not been in time; others were glad that we were not in time. The rain had ceased. We gathered some pine knots and dry or dead wood and soon had a cheerful fire around which we arranged our blankets to dry. At the same time some were busy making coffee and preparing supper. We soon had ourselves and our blankets dry. Supper over, we held a council of war and concluded, as we were now among Union people, who would betray us and would not hesitate to pilot the yankees to our camp, if they knew where to find it. We thought that it would be better to move. Fifteen minutes later we were on the march. When we had gone about two miles the Colonel ordered a halt in some heavy timber, and said that we would

11

stop here for the remainder of the night. So went into camp, each man wrapping his blanket around him and squatting with his back against a tree, dozed until day began to break, when we again moved to our old camp at Cold Spring at which place we remained for a few days, watching the Patterson's Creek pike for a yankee scout by day and secreting ourselves by night in some vacant pine thicket. The Colonel thought it would be a favorable time to look up the militia. So one morning bright and early, Capt. Kuykendall who was at that time a ranger and I started up Beaver Run to look up the militia in that quarter. We found a few but they were as wild as rabbits, generally had the women and children on the lookout and generally got out of the way. At one place we came in sight of about a dozen men and boys threshing wheat. A little girl, who was on picket, saw us some distance away and gave the alarm. They left the machine running and broke for the woods a hundred yards or more distant. We only succeeded in over hauling three or four of them. The others all got to the brush. We notified perhaps a dozen during the day but I do not think more than three or four ever reported to Romney on the day appointed. On our return toward evening, we were riding leisurely along the Patterson's Creek pike talking over the events of the day, when near the top of the hill between where Samuel Umstot and David Rees resides, we heard someone hollering in the direction of Mr. Okey Johnson's. At first we paid no attention to it, but finally we halted and after looking in the direction from which the sound came from we discovered someone on top of a ledge of rocks on the opposite side of the creek, hallowing and waving his hat. Although we could not understand what he said we concluded from his gestures that he was trying to warn us of danger. So we concluded to ride back and see what was wanted. We rode at a lively rate until we reached the old Greenwall Church and on looking back we saw to our surprise a column of yankee cavalry on the very spot where we had left not five minutes before and if we had not been warned of our danger would no doubt have met on top of the raise, but both being well mounted no doubt have made our escape unless a stray bullet had over taken us. They did not follow us, we rode on to Mr. Okey Johnson's where we learned that it was he who had warned us of our danger just in time to save a little excitement and perhaps saved us from a trip to Camp Chase' or perhaps to another world. Any way we were glad that we did not meet them. We learned from Mr. Johnson that they had captured our camp and all our equipments consisting of one pot, one dutch oven and a few tin cups, also one coffee broiler. The yankees thought to surprise the rangers but failed and that night most of them reached our old camp at Hanging Rocks.

Thus ended our advance on New Creek. Several of our men never reported to duty again. Our Captain had a great deal of stock on hand and thought it unsafe to have them so near the enemy. His time was now taken up in moving and disposing of cattle and hogs. The remnant of the Huckleberry Rangers, about 20 in number, reported to Col. Ed. McDonald at Romney and was directed by him to retain our horses and do picket duty as mounted militia. We could thus draw rations for ourselves and horses. We went into camp at the old Stone Tannery a little way below town at which place Capt. Amos Robinson, with the remnant of the 77th Regiment of militia was encamped. About this time Col. Angus McDonald arrived at Romney, having three or four companies of cavalry under his command. The mounted militia were employed for several days trying to gather up the militia. After getting them to camp the Colonel would give them a furlough for a few days to go home and get a change of clothes and blanket; that was generally the last of them.

One day Capt. George Stump came to our camp and said that Col. Angus McDonald wished to find out as near as possible what number of troops were at New Creek and that he was going on a scout that evening and wanted me to go with him. This I agreed to do, provided he got permission of Col. Ed. McDonald. He said that it was alright as he had already seen the Col. After dinner we started on the northwestern grade until we arrived at Burlington. Here we halted until night and then started after dark. We quietly left the village leaving the impression that we would return to Romney at once. But instead of returning to Romney we turned down Patterson's Creek pike which we followed some distance. We soon came to a road leading off to our left in the direction of New Creek Station. This we followed for a mile or more and again turned to our left; all the while Stump was the pilot. I was altogether at sea without a compass. Soon we left the road or the road left us. We ran against a high fence and came to a halt, I asked the Captain if he had any idea where he was at and he replied in very emphatic language that all he knew was that we were somewhere between Patterson's Creek and New Creek, but just where he did not know and that he had lost his bearings and really did not know if we were going east or west. We opened a fence and passed through and in a short time found ourselves in a field near a house, which Captain Stump said belonged to Mr. Welch, and said, we are all right now, I know exactly where we are. After riding for some time we came to another house, which the Captain said was where Mr. Parris lived. Not long after we came to a halt in a pine thicket the Captain said we had better tie up here and take foot as he thought we were near the point we were aiming for. We dismounted, tied our horses and laid down on the leaves and one of us at least was soon asleep. When day began to streak in the east, the Captain awoke me and said, we must be moving.

We soon found ourselves on the top of a ridge east and nearly opposite New Creek station. Here I climbed a tall pine and made a blind by bending the limbs together to shield me from observation, for it really seemed to me that I was so close that the yanks would surely see me. It was now light enough to see the camp guards walking their beats or hear their challenge distinctly. Capt. Stump lay on the ground beneath, not long after daylight each company was in line ready for roll call. I could hear each name distinctly called, I think my estimate of cavalry, infantry and artillery, all told, was about one thousand. The question with me was how to get down without being seen, for it really seemed to me that any one looking in that direction could see me and an expert marksman could easily have picked me off. They were soon busily engaged in preparing and eating breakfast. This Capt. Stump said was my opportunity to get down, which I did as speedily as possible. We were soon mounted and after a short consultation, we determined to call on Mr. Parris and get breakfast and have our horses fed, as he was a Union man he would not likely be molested for feeding rebels. We rode up to the house, the old gentleman was in the yard and he knew Capt. Stump but did not know me. The Capt. told him, in answer to his many inquiries as to where we came from and where we were going, that we were trying to get information as to the number of troops at New Creek, and the location of the fortifications, if any. The Capt. said, I know you are a good southern man at heart but situated as you are of course you have to keep quiet. Now, said the Capt., we have been riding all night, wanting to get to your house before day and get a good view of New Creek station, but that we had lost our way and been delayed but now we know we were among friends who would like to get our horses fed and get something to eat ourselves". Oh yes, he said get down and the boys will take your horses to the stable and feed them. No said the Capt. we are in a hurry, bring them about a dozen ears a piece and we will feed them here in that trough, pointing to one nearby. The corn was brought and in a few minutes we were called to breakfast. The Captain kept the old man engaged in conservation to keep him from sending news of our whereabouts to the yankees at New Creek Station. When we were through with our meal and Capt. called the old man to one side and asked him to direct us to some suitable place where we could get a good view of the yankee camp and of course New Creek Station, also a good place to tie our horses, as we expected to remain all day and learn all we could and would be at his house again about dark and if there should happen to be any yankees about or should be any danger he was to have a candle in the east window. This he promised to do. Also he said his wife wished that he take some butter to the store and get some coffee that evening and that he would get what news he could for us by the time we got back. By this time our horses were done eating, the old man said he would walk up in the field with us and direct us where to go. When some distance from the house, he directed us to a thicket at the

14

lower side of the field where he thought we could get a good view of the yankee camp. Where he directed us to leave our horses was the place we had them tied and had taken them from, little more than an hour before. Capt. Stump said, I will bet two to one that old scamp will have the yanks here inside of two hours. Let us ride through this thicket over against that ridge where we can see his house, and I bet we will see either the old man or his boy go toward New Creek inside of ten minutes. We rode over and sure enough we saw the old man mounted and start in a fast trot toward New Creek station. Now said Capt. Stump the sooner we get out of here, the better that old scamp will have the yankees on our trail inside of an hour so we took the back track and arrived at Romney about 4 p.m., without an accident. We afterward learned through A. J. Parker, who was at New Creek at that time, that Capt. Stump's surmise was correct in regard to old Mr. Parris. He was at New Creek within an hour after leaving us and the yankees made a thorough search, but the game eluded them for that time.

Lew Wallace
(POTOMAC EDISON'S VALLEY ECHO)

Col. Angus W. McDonald
(POTOMAC EDISON'S VALLEY ECHO)

Lieut. Col. Turner Ashby
(POTOMAC EDISON'S VALLEY ECHO)

CHAPTER II

The Battle of Hanging Rock

A few days later about the 25th of Sept., 1861, about midnight, we were called out and ordered to double quick to the gap at Hanging Rocks. We had, if I remember right, about 25 men all told, under the command of Col. Ed. McDonald. We were soon on top of the Rocks at the upper end of the gap where the Rocks nearly overhang the road. At that time Col. Angus McDonald was raising a regiment of cavalry and was at Romney with 4 companies. Capt. Sheetz, Capt. Shans, Capt. Harper, Capt. Myres and Col. Alexander Monroe had been in camp at the lower end of the gap for a few days in command of perhaps 150 to 200 men of 111th regiment of Hampshire militia. The Col. had moved his camp the evening before to Jersey Mountain.

The yankees were reported advancing from New Creek. Col. Mc-Donald thought that in all probability they would make a feint at Mechanicsburg gap, which was picketed by a company of cavalry; whilst the main body passed down on the west side of the mountain, cross at Rock Ford and take the Confeds in the rear, when they would be expecting the Federals to make a dash through Mechanicsburg gap. When we reached our position, the first thing we did was to gather piles of rocks near the edge of the cliffs to be in readiness to cast over when the time came. The night being cool, we were allowed to build fires a little distance back; in the mean time we got word from Col. Angus McDonald that up to that time no enemy had attempted to pass through Mechanicsburg gap. He thought perhaps there had only been a scouting party from New Creek and it had returned and that he had sent a company of cavalry out to ascertain and if they found nothing in their way would pass around the mountain, cross the river at the lower end of the gap on their return and to be careful not to fire on them. Just before day the fog began to rise from the water and in a short time was so dense that we could not see nothing beneath us. About this time we heard very distinctly cavalry crossing at the ford below. Soon we heard them coming up the road, but could not tell whether they were friends or foe. We lay flat on the ground, our heads stretched out as far as possible trying to make out whether they were Confeds or Federals, but could not determine. To allow an enemy to pass us, rendered our position untenable at once and retreat impossible unless effected at once. But all doubt was soon dispelled by the whistle of a bullet and the report of a pistol below. A person looking up could readily discern an object between him and the sky. This a yankee had done, he saw a human head and fired his pistol at it. Unlucky shot for the yanks.

Site of the Battle of Hanging Rock. Picture taken c. 1897. *(FRANCES BUCKBEE)*

A second later it was raining rocks at a lively rate. The Ringgold Cavalry commanded by Capt. Keys was in front, closely followed by about 600 infantry. The cavalry had not advanced far enough to be much hurt by the falling rocks but were terribly frightened. At the first discharge from above they faced to the rear and dashed through the column of infantry, riding them down, many of which rushed into the river to escape from they knew not what. The water being deep many were drowned. When the cavalry charged to the rear at such break neck speed no doubt the infantry expected to see at least a thousand rebels at their heels, and were ready to throw down their arms and surrender unconditionally. But, no rebs appeared, only a few shots greeted their ears from the rocks above and three or four hundred yards in front of them.

They evidently began to recover from their fright and fired volley after volley at our position on the rocks. This was the first fire we were ever under and the wonder is that fright did not kill some of us. The way the musket balls rattled, spatted and hissed around us was a caution. Fortunately we were all sheltered behind the rocks. The fire only lasted for a time. The yanks got themselves back as quick as possible to the opposite side of the river. Soon a new danger presented itself. The yanks climbed the end of the mountain on the opposite side of the river until they were on a level or rather above our position from where they could easily reach us. The fog soon began to drift down river which left us exposed to view in good musket range of the yankees on the opposite side. They had long range rifles. We had no protection from this direction. Soon the Enfield musket balls began to plow up the sod on top of the rocks and cut off the cedar brush over our heads. This was getting too close for beginners. We did not wait for orders to fall back. Our position was flanked right in front, each man fell back in good order about as fast as his legs would carry him. Occasionally a man fell but as he never stopped running he was not supposed to be hurt and generally passed those in front of him in a very short time. The retreat was short but sharp. In a very short time we were out of range and halted to give the wounded time to come up, and to learn how many had been killed. When to our surprise and joy all were present and nobody hurt. We fell back to Romney but keeping all the while a sharp lookout to our rear.

When we reached town, we found Col. Angus McDonald had placed his two pieces of cannon in the cemetery. His men were between town and the bridge with a picket at Mechanicsburg gap. Shortly after, the middle of the day, the yankees advanced and drove the Confeds from the gap and showed themselves in considerable force between the Cummin's and Shull's mill, when a few solid shots was sent among them from the cemetery. The Confederate picket fell back and crossed the bridge. The yankees did not attempt to advance again that evening but kept a picket at the east end of the gap until dark.

The yankees were reported advancing again by the way of Hanging Rocks. Col. McDonald asked who would volunteer to go down the road and see if the report was true or false. As no one seemed to desire the honor, I offered my services which was accepted. I started on foot and alone, kept near the pike sometimes on one side and then on the other, ears strained to catch any and every sound, coming from the pike in the direction of the Hanging Rocks gap, which place I finally reached, without making any discovery. Here I halted and hesitated for some time before making up my mind to venture through the gap, nearly a mile in length. Finally I determined to make the attempt. To do so I would have to follow the pike with but little chance of escape, should I alarm a picket. However, after lying with my ear to the ground for several minutes without hearing anything unusual I started and proceeded very slow and cautious halting every few steps to listen for any sound that might indicate danger until I reached the lower end of the gap feeling very much relieved at discovering no yankees. I turned back and reached Romney about 1 o'clock, found all quiet, no one stirring. I went to the Keller house, found Mr. Paskal, who said the cavalry had all fallen back to Frenchburg and that there were no soldiers of any kind in town. Not having had any sleep or rest for nearly 48 hours I began to feel like I wanted rest and sleep, not knowing what would come to pass the next day. I went back toward town run and lay down in a fence corner and was soon in a sound sleep from which I did not awake until daylight. I arose and went over to the hotel.

In a short time David Lyn, of Cumberland, came in. He too having lain out near town. We were standing talking with Mr. Paskal and one or two others, when W. M. Parsons and a Mr. Bonifee rode in from toward Frenchburg. They had halted but a moment when breakfast was announced. They said they had had breakfast and would ride down to the cemetery and stand picket while Lyn and I ate. We had scarcely taken our seats at the table when we heard an unusual noise on the street and rushed out to learn the cause. As we reached the door, Parsons and Bonifee dashed past, shouting to us to get out, the yankees were coming up town hill. Lyn and I grabbed our guns, ran out the back way across by the Seminary and were soon in the brush on the ridge northeast of town. Each of us halted behind a good sized tree. Very soon a company of yankee cavalry rode up the pike and halted just above the Institution, perhaps three hundred yards from where Lyn and I stood. Lyn was armed with a double barreled shotgun. I had a Minnie rifle, captured from old John Brown at Harper's Ferry and presented to me by Col. Isaac Parsons. Lyn fired his shotgun at them, but the distance was too great for a gun of that kind. Some of them cursed him for a damn cowardly son of a bitch to be firing into town among your own women and children. Lyn fired again. In the meantime I had been measuring by my eye and arranged my sights accordingly. I took deliberate aim and fired an instant later. I heard the ball distinctly strike the fence. I knew at once that the distance was greater than I had supposed. My shot had made them a little uneasy. They kept moving a few paces every few seconds. I reloaded and raised my sight for fifty yards, took careful aim and said to Lyn, keep your eye on that iron gray horse. I think I will get the horse or the rider, one this time. When my rifle fired, the rider threw himself forward and clasp his horse around the neck. Lynn said you struck him for sure, I saw the dust fly off his jacket, load and give them another as quick as you can. They did not wait for another round, but counter marched and trotted back to town. Dr. Lupton was at home. They halted and had him dress a serious wound one of their men had received up the pike from a bushwacker.

Lynn and I then started up the run. When we came to the drain above the Toll House, we crossed over the top of the ridge on the opposite side of the pike. A high fence ran parallel with the pike on top of the ridge. We followed the fence on the outside where the brush was thick until about opposite Reed's shop, when we saw a company of cavalry coming up the pike. We dropped behind the fence and made ready to give them a round when they came opposite us. Before they came up, we heard some persons talking in a low tone down the fence a little ways from us. We came to the conclusion that it was yankee infantry sent out by the cavalry from being ambushed. We thought best to get away, so we crept down the opposite side of the ridge, some forty of fifty yards and concealed ourselves in some thick laurel. We could yet hear talking in a low tone which seemed to be about the same place. Soon we heard firing up the pike about Jersey Mountain road, but this did not last long. We finally came to the conclusion that it was some persons hiding from the Yankees, whom we heard talking and I proposed to Lynn that we try and get near enough to see who they were. He said well, there is no use for both of us to go. You find out and I will stay where I am until you whistle. I crept toward them as quietly as possible, until I discovered that they were citizens. I went up. There were two of them; Mr. Joseph Poling and Mr. J. J. Combs. They had left town at the first alarm and were lying behind the fence waiting for further developments. They said the firing we heard was up about the Jersey Mountain road; and that the Yankee cavalry had gone back to town. At that moment, we saw a piece of artillery attended by perhaps twenty men. They came up just opposite where we were lying and unlimbered and fired a shell up the pike toward Grassy Lick road. The cause for this was Col. Alexander Monroe had come in on the Jersey Mountain road with the 114th Regiment Militia and fired on the Yankee cavalry and driven them back. This piece of artillery had been ordered up

21

to shell the woods and drive the militia off; but they cut the fuse to short, the shells burst far short of the destination. The artillery was in good rifle range of where we lay. I could not resist the temptation to give them one round. So I slipped the muzzle of my rifle through the fence when Mr. Poling said, what are you doing? For God's sake, they will be all over this ridge in five minutes. I said, I am going to give them one round, anyway. Well, said he, if you must act the fool let us get away. They left at a lively gait. The Yankees had just fired a second time and were ramming home the third round when I fired into the bunch. They scattered like a bunch of sheep when something fell among them. They soon gathered around one of their number, led him back a few steps and eased him back a few steps and fired another shell. They then limbered up and started for town on doubled quick. By this time I had reloaded and gave them another regard, but they had raised such a dust I could not see if any damage had been done. I was at a loss how to account for this retreat and had about come to the conclusion that I had whailed the whole thing.

When the Yankees had passed into town I turned and looked up the pike. The hasty retreat of the Yanks was solved. Rising above the tree tops in the direction of Frenchburg I beheld a cloud of dust which appeared to be rapidly approaching. The Yankees had seen the same and understood its meaning. McDonald's cavalry was coming back. Soon the head of the column dashed through the gap into full view, led by Capt. Geo. Sheetz and Sergeant John C. Leps. Two as brave and chivalrous men as ever drew a sword or led a charge. Could they have lived through that four year strife, beyond a doubt, their names would have been written high on the scroll of time. Side by side with Jackson, Ashby and Steward. But an all wise Providence had ordered otherwise. In less than two months Sergeant Leps was accidently killed at Hanging Rock and on the 23rd of May 1862, Capt. Sheetz fell leading his men at Buckton Station between Front Royal and Strawsburg. But to my text. When I saw the approach of the cavalry, I ran down to the pike and gathered up perhaps a half dozen blankets and several canteens which had been left by the Yanks in their hurry to get away. Here the Confederate cavalry began to pass me at a quick trot. I trotted as fast as I could until I reached Dr. Lupton's where I threw my captured property over into the Doctor's yard. The doctor was standing in his door. He remarked that the Yankees had got three men pretty badly hurt up the road. They had halted a moment to have him to examine their wounds and concluded that they would not have time, said he asked what was up. A Yankee Lieutenant pointed up the pike, said, do you see that dust yonder, the road is full of Rebs for five miles and we will have to get into the gap before they overtake us. Don't you hear them yelling? Come on boys, no time to stop here. They were carrying their wounded in blankets.

Close on their heels of the cavalry came Col. Monroe with the 114th Virginia Militia, numbering some two or three hundred men. The Yankees made a stand on the opposite side of the bridge, lying behind the fill or bank and fence. Capt. Harper's company were from Brock's Gap, Rockingham County and were armed with long range guns. They were dismounted and crossed over the Gibson Mill Dam on the Gibson Island and thought to shelter themselves behind the brush and timber that grew along the river and drive the Yankees from the Bridge. I crossed over with this company. We soon found that the Yankees were better protected from us than we were from them. In a short time Col. Monroe had some of his militia along the bank of the approach to the bridge. They beat a hasty retreat, keeping along the foot of the mountain where the cavalry could not get at them. Some of Capt. Sheetz's men crossed over on to the island, mounted among them was Robert J. Tildon, mounted on a spirited gray mare. He was a conspicuous mark and soon had a broken arm. He could go no further and he proffered me his mare, which I gladly accepted and took his place with Capt. Sheetz.

The Yankees had fallen back to the west end of Mechanicsburg Gap and planted their artillery as to sweep through the gap. Col. McDonald then had his two pieces hauled up on Mill Mountain, opposite the gap, from which point he could shell the Yankee camp. The cavalry then moved through the gap. There was no Yankees in sight. We learned they had retreated on the direct road to New Creek Station by way of Headsville.

Pursuit was commenced at once. Capt. Sheetz with about a dozen men, a little ways in front; we saw no Yankees until we had crossed Middle Ridge and descended the other side. Some distance, when on passing through a piece of timber, we found ourselves in short range of the whole Yankee force. They gave us a volley which caused us to face to the rear without orders, and all got back to shelter except myself. The Tilden mare which I was riding had her leg broken and refused to retreat as the bullets continued to fly pretty thick. It did not take me long to make up my mind to dismount and hunt shelter. There was a steep bank on the lower side of the road over which I sprang and dropped behind a large tree that had fallen. The Yanks started again on double quick. They were passing through a lane just beyond the house in which Geo. Gilbert lived at the time. The lane was crowded. I gave them three rounds at good range and can't see why somebody was not hurt. At this time I was considered a good shot.

They were soon out of sight. Capt. Sheetz advanced again in a short time and although I was on foot again I kept along with the advance until we reached Mr. Isaac Carskadon's place, when we found the Yankees had made a stand at Headsville. Col. McDonald halted under cover and sent back to hasten up his artillery, but by the time it arrived and was placed in position, the Yankees were gone.

From Headsville there was an old road to the right and nearly parallel with the road on which the Yankees were retreating. This road, Capt. Sheetz thought, he could follow, head the Yankees off on top of a range of hills which lay between Knobley Mountain and Patterson's Creek and bushwack them. After consulting a few moments with Col. McDonald, Capt. Sheetz started his own and Capt. Shans' company to execute, if possible, the objective stated. Here again I had the good luck, through the kindness of Mr. Abraham Johnson, to be mounted, he having been in the chase from Romney to this point. Several of the mounted militia being along, Col. McDonald ordered me to take about a dozen men and keep about two hundred yards in front of the artillery. The cavalry followed the artillery. The militia had not yet arrived. The road lay principally through woods. We moved with great caution, expecting to be fired on at any moment. We had just reached the top of the ridge after passing up a deep hollow, when to our surprise a volley was fired from the right of the road and only a short distance from us. We supposed that the firing was from Yankees who had let us pass to let the main column come up. We wheeled out of the road to our left, rode back to the brush, some fifty yards, dismounted and leaving three or four men to hold our horses, we advanced to within a dozen paces of the road and halted each man behind a tree. Isaac Parsons stood a few feet to my right and W. V. Inskeep a little way to my left. We soon discovered, as we supposed, a Yankee creeping through a thicket toward us. I said boys don't fire, save your loads, I will settle this fellow. I had dropped on one knee and resting my elbow on the other, was waiting for him to step into an opening just in his front. I was looking through the sights with fingers on the trigger when he stepped from the dark shade to bright sunlight. I saw he wore gray. I recognized him as Capt. Kuykendall. I yelled out, don't fire boys, these are Sheetz's men. When I thought how near I had been to killing one of my best friends, I could scarcely stand.

It was Capt. Shans' company who had fired on our artillery, thinking it was the Yankee artillery by its being in front. One man was seriously hurt by this mistake, which caused a halt for a short time. We then pressed on until we reached the top of Knobley Mountain without sighting the Yankees again. They had evidently made a forced march from the time they left Headsville until they reached New Creek Station. We afterward learned that they went to Cumberland the same night, confidently expecting the Rebs to take possession next morning.

When we reached Knobley Gap it was in the dusk of the evening. We were ordered back to Romney. When we reached Headsville I turned down the Patterson's Creek pike for the purpose of returning to Mr. Abraham Johnson his horse. When I arrived at Mr. Johnson's house it was late. The family had retired. I put the horse in the stable and over a straw tick nearby and went into camp and was soon asleep. As soon as it was light, I went to the house, gave Mr. Johnson a history of the pursuit after leaving Headsville, ate a hearty breakfast, which I enjoyed, not having eaten anything for thirty six hours. After breakfast I started on foot across Middle Ridge. I reached home about the middle of the day and reported at Romney the next day.

Col. McDonald again established his command at Romney.

About the 1st of October, the 114 Regiment of Virginia Militia under command of Col. A. Monroe, was quartered at the Wire Bridge, about six miles below Romney. His command amounted to about three hundred men.

The 77th Regiment Virginia Militia was quartered in Buffalo Hollow numbering not over fifty men under the command of Col. McDonald, about twenty five of these mounted. The 77th Regiment was made up from the western end of the county, which at that time reached well up into the Alleghany Mountains. The citizens living in this end of the county were largely opposed to succession and many of them had gone into the Union army. Capt. Sheetz's, Capt. Sherrard's and Capt. White's companies were largely volunteers from the 77th Virginia Militia. The remnant were those quartered in Buffalo Hollow. Here we built comfortable quarters, expecting to occupy them all winter. We had two pieces of cannon on the hill in rear of Mrs. Foreman Inskeep's house. Around this elevation, we had dug a ditch a short distance from the top to protect our infantry when supporting the artillery. This was quite a formidable position if attacked in front or flank, but untenable if assaulted from the rear. During this time Col. Monroe had not been idle at the Wire Bridge. Although to hold the bridge for any length of time with the arms at hand, was an impossibility. Yet the Colonel had placed his men in as good as a position to hold, but a very bad one to let go. He had his men to build a breast work of stone on the upper side of the pike some two hundred yards from and directly in front of the bridge, with a steep rugged mountain immediately in the rear, up which his men would have to retreat if driven from their position in face of a victorious enemy and at point blank range. This would not have been a pleasant past time, but under the circumstances it was the only thing to do. Armed as his men were, with old Militia flint lock rifles, smooth bore muskets, shot guns and home rifle. To have placed them on the top of the ridge in their rear where retreat would be safe and easy to have done this, as far as holding the bridge was concerned, they had almost as well been armed with pop guns. They would have only been targets for the improved long range guns with which the Yankees were armed, without being able to reach them with their short range guns. To hold the bridge, the position selected was the only one a brave man would stay and a coward could not get away under fire.

This was the military situation in and around Romney on Saturday, October 27, 1861. The day was warm, calm and bright. Lieut. Ike Parsons, W. V. Inskeep and myself had crossed the river onto the mountain for a hunt. Game was rather plentiful at that time. About three o'clock in the evening we were on top of the mountain opposite town when to our surprise we heard the report of a cannon toward Moorefield Junction. Soon another and another. We crossed over to the south side where we could see into town. There seemed to be great excitement. We guessed the cause and started on double quick for camp. When we arrived there we found our baggage had been loaded up and sent to Romney so as to be ready for a retreat, if necessary. The artillery was in position and the militia in the breast works ready for action.

It was now between four and five o'clock p. m. We heard firing at or near the bridge at over town; also at the Wire Bridge.

We were momentarily expecting to see the Yankees push through the Hanging Rock Gap, but none came. All now seemed to be quiet. We could hear no firing in any direction. We supposed that the Yankees had been driven back. It was now sun down. Ike Parsons had rode down back of the mountain to the Wire Bridge and returned, reported a fight at the Wire Bridge. The Yankees had attempted to cross and had been driven back toward Springfield and Col. Monroe had fallen back to Jersey Mountain. Col. McDonald had sent a courier to Romney to learn what was going on. He had soon returned with news that the town was full of Yankees. It was now getting dark.

We hitched to the cannon and started up Buffalo Hollow and reached Rev. Harris' place about midnight. From there we crossed town hill to Little Capon. From Capon we followed the road from Robert Thompson's (now Tutwiler's) to Pleasant Dale. It was now nearly daylight. Here we found some of Sheetz's men, who reported our teams and all our baggage captured. Most of the cavalry and militia reported at Blue's Gap next day. I got permission of Col. McDonald to go home and get a change of underwear and a blanket.

I turned back at Pleasant Dale, kept off public roads as much as possible until I reached an old house in a hollow surrounded by a few acres of meadowland. Here I turned my mare loose, hid my saddle and started on foot to take a look at Romney. I was not long in reaching a favorable place on top of the mountain east of town from where I had a good view of the Yankee camp which was quite a show for me. Never before having seen so many men in one body.

After lying here looking at the Yankees for several hours, I started home thinking it would be dark by the time I reached there. I had reached the top of the ridge between Buffalo Hollow and Sugar Hollow, when I discovered a squad of some fifteen or twenty Yankee cavalry driving several of Foreman Inskeep's horses into a corner for the purpose of capturing them. I crept down as near as I thought prudent. Part of them had dismounted and were trying to halter the horses which they had run into a fence corner. I supposed that I was about four hundred yards away. I raised the sight of my minnie rifle and fired at the bunch. I saw the dust rise from a clay bank. The ball had passed over them. They no doubt heard it. At least they mounted and left in a hurry. I then pushed on, keeping in the woods all the way. I reached home an hour after dark. After getting something to eat, I procured a blanket and some clothing, not knowing when I would get home again and started back to where I left my mare. When I got back, day had begun to show in the East. I found my mare all right, saddled up and started, reached George Thompson's in time for breakfast and reached Blue's Gap before the middle of the day, where I found most of my militia and cavalry which had been driven away from Romney and vicinity.

The cavalry had not lost a man, except Jim Johnson, a colored teamster, who refused to stop his team when ordered to do so and received a sabre cut on the side of the head. Our baggage was all captured, including a half dozen wagons and as many horses, most of the horses having been cut loose and ridden away.

Col. Ed. McDonald had got away from Buffalo Hollow with his two cannon and would have saved his baggage, if he had kept it with him.

Col. Monroe received notice of the approach of the yankees in time to get his men in position after having first taken up part of the flooring of the bridge. The yankees came on at double quick and soon reached the place where the flooring had been removed. When they received a volley which sent them to the rear faster than they came, leaving one man dead on the bridge. How many dead and wounded were carried off was not known. They did not attempt to cross again, but sent some sharp shooters on top of the rocks, who with their long rifles could easily reach the rebs. Whenever one showed his head he was sure to hear a minnie whistle. However they did not tarry long but fell back to Cumberland from whence they came. Col. Monroe having heard the cannon above Romney in the afternoon and not getting any news from there, was fearful that he might be attacked in the rear and retreat cutoff and not knowing that the yankees in his front had gone, and feeling that he could not hold the bridge with a body of men on the top of the rocks on the opposite side of the river under the circumstances, thought it the part of wisdom to fall back to Jersey Mountain. Which he did without loss of a man or baggage. A new base was now formed along North River. If I remember right, Col. Monroe with the 114th was quartered at the Hammack Factory; Capt.

Sheetz at Blue's Gap; the 77th Militia was quartered a mile or so up the river above the gap, except the few mounted militia which were quartered with Sheetz company in a large mill, which stood where the present mill now stands. Capt. Sheetz's had his pickets thrown out as far as Pleasant Dale. We had been in our new quarters several days when one morning about 10 o'clock a courier dashed into camp with news that the yankees were advancing and would be up in a short time. Capt. Sheetz had us mounted at once and started to meet the Yankees. We soon met Sergeant Leps, who had fallen back with his pickets and crossed the North River Bridge, behind which his men were sheltered. The yanks came into view a half a mile back and appeared to be in force. Soon came the boom of a cannon and the bursting of a shell, though too high and too far to our right to do any harm. Capt. Sheetz then ordered his men back through the gap, the yankees sending another shell after us, which fell short, bursting between Col. Blue's house and the bridge. Capt. Sheetz, being too weak to make a fight, fell back out of range and halted. The yankees did not attempt to pass through the gap but halted on the opposite side, at Col. Blue's house. Sergeant Leps, Samuel High, Ike Parsons and myself had secured a safe position on the point of a ridge back of the mill and above the pike. We could see some distance into the gap. About 4 o'clock, we discovered what we supposed to be a yankee coming through the gap at a very slow cautious gait. He was dressed in dark clothes; we thought yankee blue. He soon stepped into an opening when Leps and High each fired. The supposed yankee fell. All was quiet again except for an occasional groan from the wounded man.

Parsons said that he did not believe it was a yankee and if I would go with him, we would go and see. We cautioned Leps and High to keep a sharp lookout through the gap and started. We soon reached the fallen man when to our horror we found it was old Wm. Vance (father of the late John T. Vance of this county), who was coming through the gap to let us know the yankees had gone. We carried him back to the house where he died in a short time.

The yankees had been gone an hour or two before Mr. Vance had left the house to inform us of the fact. It will never be known which fired the fatal shot; Leps or High, but one ball struck him. This was a sad accident and very much regretted by the whole command. A few days later Leps was accidently killed within a hundred yards of the spot where Mr. Vance was shot. High was killed not long after by a union man (whom he had arrested without any authority) by the name of Spencer. High had laid his gun on the bed, Spencer was getting ready to go, watched his opportunity, grabbed the gun and shot High. The yankees did little mischief aside from capturing a few chickens and helping themselves to what grain they wanted. On their return they burned a few vacant houses which stood near the road.

28

CHAPTER III

First through the Lines

A bout the 15th of November, Col. Parsons, who had been to Richmond with cattle, returned to our camp and was very anxious to hear something definite from home and, if possible, to get a change of clothes and a blanket. He thought by using proper precautions that he might possibly get home and determined to make the attempt. He asked Adam Parrish and myself to go with him. This we agreed to do. We started that afternoon, left the northwestern grade near Pleasant Dale and by following roads and paths, we reached a point in Sugar Hollow, perhaps two miles north of Romney, an hour before night. Here we tied our horses in a pine thicket and started on foot. We soon reached the top of a hill on the line between Col. Isaac Parsons and Foreman Inskeep. Here we halted again. Col. Parsons was an influential man in the county, which he had represented in both branches of the Legislature and was known throughout the State.

He was an extreme states right man and did as much, perhaps as any man in the State toward having an ordinance of secession passed. The first year of the war he fed more soldiers at his table and more horses from his cribs, gratuitously, than any five men in the county. This I know from personal observation. For these reasons we did not think it prudent or necessary for him to attempt to go to his house until he knew that it was safe to do so. Parrish proposed that he and I first go and see if the way was clear and that the Colonel remain where he was until our return. This he finally agreed to do and after he had given us careful directions how to approach the house, we started with Adam in the lead. It was very dark and cloudy and began to rain. We crossed the pike and struck up through the middle of the bottom as near as we could guess. It was rather a slow march, blundering over corn stubs and ditches.

We finally reached a run that passed near the house; this we followed until within fifty yards of the house. We halted to consider the next step to be taken. We had heard before we left camp that the yankees kept a guard at the Colonel's house day and night, but did not know certainly that was correct. The rain was now falling at a rapid rate. It was so dark that we could not see our hand before us. We thought that we heard footsteps approaching and fell back a short distance. Finally concluded that we were mistaken in thinking we had heard something. Well, said Adam, there is no use in us both going to the house, when one will answer every purpose. We agreed on the point but the question was which should go. Every vote was a tie, It looked as though the expedition had ended in failure.

Well, said Adam, this is too bad to go back as we came. I tell you what if I didn't have a wife and children to look after, I would get a blanket and a change of clothes for the Colonel or die trying.

Come on said I, let us both go. No said he, I don't think it would be right for me to run too much risk on account of my family. I said Adam, you stand here until I come back and if you hear firing and I am not here in one minute, you can report to the Colonel that the yankees are at the house and that I have been killed or captured.

I then started toward the house. Soon reached the yard fence, climbed over and moved very cautiously toward the house. It being so dark, though within 20 yards could not see it. I soon reached the window on the back part of the house by which I know that G. W. Blue's bed stood. I tapped on the window when I thought I heard someone turn in bed, tapped again when, "who's there" came in a shaky voice, which I recognized as that of Uncle Garrett. I had some trouble getting him to understand who I was. Finally he raised the window and said in a shakey voice, "my God boy, what had made you so imprudent as to come here; we are watched day and night. The yankees are on the front porch and may be around here anytime. If they find you here, we will all be burnt up". I told him what I came for and would not go back without them. He said, "I will see Susan." (Susan was the Colonel's wife) It was raining lively. I stood with my back against the house awaiting his return.

Soon I thought I heard footsteps coming around the end of the house. My first thought was to run. It flashed through my mind that if I did this, he would fire in the direction of the noise and might hit me. It occurred to me that I had better stand my ground and if discovered, it would be at close range, when I would try to get the first shot and then run with a better show of getting away. I squatted down as close to the wall as possible, cocked my revolver and waited. The steps came nearer though a little distance from the house. I began to think the yankee would pass without discovering me. I felt the danger past, when to my horror the window was raised and Miss Kate asked in low tone where her father was. I sprang to my feet and was about to make a dash for liberty, when to my joy the yankee coughed and it was a cow. But I didn't feel good. A bundle was passed out. Miss Kate wanted to make some inquiry about her father and brother, but Uncle Garrett said, get away from here as quick as possible and don't come here again. I started with the bundle under my arm to find Parrish. When I reached the place as I thought where I had left him, and gave the signal agreed on, but failed to get an answer. I started down through the bottom, after blundering over corn stubs and against corn shocks for something like a hundred yards, I again gave a whistle and this time was answered by the whoot of an owl at my right rear. After going in the direction of the sound for some distance, I whistled and was answered a little ways off. I soon found Adam, who had moved in a half circle and was heading straight for the Colonel's house. He said he was sure he had heard loud talking at the house and felt sure that I had been captured but the run and rain made such a noise he could not hear very distinctly and was glad that he was mistaken. I said that I was as glad as he was. That the yankees were on the front porch but that I had got away without being discovered, but came near being scared to death by an old cow. Well said he I will carry the bundle a while and let us get back. The Colonel will be uneasy at our long absence. We started, he up the bottom and I down. I said where are you going now? "To find the Colonel", said he. You will not find him at the house, I said. "I am not going to the house", he said, "I know exactly where I am, come on." I said Adam, you are bewildered, are turned around and if you continue the direction you are now going, it won't be fifteen minutes until the Yankees will have you. He now seemed to get out of humor and said, "you must think I am a fool."

No said I, but a night like this any one might move in a circle. This you have done. Don't you remember that this rain was in our face when we came up the bottom and the way you want to go, it would still be in our face. He thought for a moment and said, I think the wind has changed. Well said I one thing is certain; I am not going to follow you in that direction. But if you will follow me for a few moments, I will convince you that I am right. "Go ahead", said he, but I am satisfied that you are wrong. We started and in a short time, came to the line fence which crossed the bottom between Parson's and Inskeep's. I asked Adam if he was satisfied that he was wrong. "I can't understand," he said "how I got turned around". We soon found the Colonel who was quite fidgety at what he thought our long absence. We fell back to our horses, were soon mounted and with the Colonel in the lead. It continued to rain. Our course lay up a deep hollow with only a path to follow through a dense wood. The darkness could almost be felt. The Colonel was riding a colt which soon got out of the path. The Colonel said we would have to try and get some rich pine and make a torch before we would be able to get out of the hollow. The Colonel carried a small hatchet in his belt and having dismounted gave Adam the rein to hold and felt his way up the side of a ridge in search of a pine knot. Soon we heard him trying to split one. A moment later he said, "my God boys, I have ruined myself. I have sunk my hatchet into my knee and bleeding to death". I dismounted and made my way to him as quick as I could. He was sitting on the ground holding the cut together as best he could. He said I should get his hankerchief and wrap his knee as tight as I could. This I did and then tied my own around to keep it in place. I then tried to make a light but failed on account of the rain. The Colonel said he did not see what we could do but stay where we were until morning. By this time, we did not have a dry thread on and to sit there in the rain until morning, one of us, at least, felt it would be no pleasant past time. I said to the Colonel if he could get to his horse and get on, I thought my mare would follow the path and take us to the top of the mountain. After getting him to his horse and mounted, I took the lead, giving my mare the rein and let her follow her own course. In less than an hour, we saw a dim light and a few moments later was at a house where the Colonel said Fred Carter lived. We called but received no answer. Adam dismounted and opened the door. There was a good bed of coals in the fireplace but no one was home. We tied our horses and helped the Colonel in the house, found plenty of dry wood inside and soon had a good hot fire. We found two beds in the room from which we took blankets and hung over the windows to hide the light, took off our clothes and hung them around the fire to dry.

The Colonel thought best not to untie his knee as it had stopped bleeding. Our stomachs began to demand recognition. We began looking around to see what was to be found to satisfy them. We found in the cupboard some nice homemade cheese, plenty bread and butter, also a coffee broiler which we soon had boiling hot. After satisfying the inner man and being well dried, we went to bed and one at least, was sound asleep. About daybreak we were up. It continued to rain. We were soon mounted and reached Rev. Mr. Harris' by daylight. Here we parted with Adam Parrish. I saw him no more until after the close of the war. He going as he said to old Mr. John Patterson's. The Colonel and I crossed Town Hill and reached Mr. George Thompson's house in time for breakfast. Little Capon was almost past fording and rising. We felt safe with the creek between us and the yankees. Our horses were soon cared for and we enjoyed a good warm breakfast. When this was over, old mother Thompson dressed the Colonel's cut knee and applied some healing salve, after which he seemed to be easy. Old Mr. Thompson was a thoroughbred southern man and he never failed to look through the sights of his old home rifle at a blue coat whenever he got the chance. We stopped with Mr. Thompson and his wife for two days. By this time the rain had ceased and the creek had begun to fall. We thought it time to get a little further from the Yankees and by 12 o'clock we were at Blue's Gap again after an absence of three days.

While camped at Blue's Gap one morning, the latter part of November 1861, Col. McDonald called me aside and said he had just received a letter from Gen. Jackson desiring all the information to be had relating to the yankees in and around Romney, as to the number of infantry, cavalry and artillery. Also if fortified, how and any other important information to be had. The Colonel said, "you are better acquainted with Romney than any one I know of. Can you get the desired information?"

I said I would try.

"Well", said he, "take with you as many men as you wish, be as cautious and as expeditious as possible and of all things don't allow yourselves to be captured inside the yankees lines. Tell no one where you are going, not even those you take with you and start as soon as you can."

I took Lieut. Ike Parsons and W. V. Parsons aside, told them I was going on a secret expedition and would be away two or three days. I asked them if they would go with me. They wanted to know where I was going. I said that I was not at liberty to tell.

They said, "All right, we will go".

I selected them to accompany me because they were raised almost in sight of Romney and know the country well, could reach any given point the darkest night in case we were separated and more than all, I knew they could be relied on in any emergency. We had but little preparation to make and soon left camp following by roads and paths. We reached James B. Hear's house near Little Capon about 4 o'clock in the evening. Having got permission to turn our horses in a meadow nearby, we started on foot. Our objective point being my father's house, some 10 miles distant.

We had heard before starting that the Yankees scouted on the Jersey Mountain road as far as Three Churches. On arriving at a point near this road and nearly opposite where John Thompson, Sr. then lived, we halted for the purpose of reconnoitering. Parsons carried a good spyglass, on ascending a tall pine tree he could view the road in several places. He was not long in locating a squad of yankee infantry at Mr. Thompsons's house.

They soon passed on over the mountain in the same direction we were going. For them to reach Romney and for us to reach the place intended, our line of march would have to cross at some point where we could not tell. This made it necessary for us to advance quietly and cautiously. We lay in a thicket nearby until dark, then started and reached father's house about 9 o'clock at night. We only stopped long enough to get something to eat. Not knowing where the Yankees we had seen, might be prowling, we did not feel altogether safe to remain longer. Father had a small boat and put us over the river and said he would have the boat at the same place next night at 10 o'clock. We went down the river about a half mile to W. V. Herriott's house and stopped for the night.

After giving and getting all the news we could, we lay down on a bed to sleep for the first time in months.

We requested our host to call us not later than 4 o'clock in the morning. Being somewhat fatigued, we were soon asleep, although the yankee picket was little more than a mile away. Our host called us promptly at the hour named, breakfast was soon ready and after satisfying the inner man, we started again. This time our objective point being some place on the mountain west of Romney, where we could have a good view of the town and its surroundings.

By sunrise we were in position in the top of a tree about opposite where the railroad depot now stands and about two hundred yards from the top of the mountain. We now had a fine view of the yankee camp and could easily count their tents which were nicely arranged in rows or streets. By the aid of our glass, we could see the buttons on their coats. Parsons, who was fairly good with the pencil, commenced a drawing of Romney and its military surroundings. The weather for several days had been warm, dry and smoky. A regular Indian Summer. The Yankees had a regimental drill in the fields below town in the morning. We looked on with a good deal of interest and had a fine opportunity of estimating their number. About the middle of the day, we climbed down to the ground to eat our lunch, provided by our host that morning. When we had completed the job, Parsons again ascended the tree to complete his drawing. Inskeep and I stretched out on the leaves and was soon asleep. We had slept perhaps an hour when aroused by the call to fall in of the fife and drum. Parsons said there seemed to be an alarm in camp. The whole force appeared to be turning out. Inskeep and I scrambled up the tree to get a better view. We soon found out that it was a dress parade of the whole Yankee forces; Infantry, Cavalry and Artillery. Here was an opportunity of estimating almost to a certainty the strength of each arm of the service. We had dreamed of a chance like this. While Parsons was busy with his drawing, Inskeep and I were taking down the number of regiments, both infantry and cavalry; also the number of batteries and section of artillery.

This parade was quite a treat to me, never having seen anything like this before. We were so completely absorbed by the display below that we had not noted or was unmindful of flight of time, until the shades of evening had nearly reached the summit of the distant hills. The cavalry had gone to their quarters. The artillery poured into the lot just above the Institution and the infantry was marching back to their quarters.

Parsons said he would be through with his work in a few moments. A moment later we detected a noise or thing walking in the dry leaves a long distance away toward a low place in the mountain. After listening attentively, we concluded that it was either deer or turkeys. I climbed down, put on my boots and coat (or hunting shirt, rather), took up my rifle and walked up the mountain about forty yards and sat down on a log. The rustling in the leaves was more distinct. I was soon satisfied that it was neither deer or turkeys, but men and no doubt yankees. I said to Parsons and Inskeep come down at once, it's men we hear and no doubt yankees. Bear never backed down a tree quicker than they. I had risen and stepped behind a tree. By the time the boys had gotten their boots on, two yankees stepped from a bunch of pines, perhaps fifty yards away. Parsons and Inskeep each stepped behind a tree.

34

The yankees advanced directly toward them. When about thirty yards away, Parsons said halt.

One of the yankees said, "Oh, we saw you; it's getting late and we had better be getting to camp."

Parsons then showed himself at the same said, "halt".

The yankees sprang behind trees. Parsons slid back behind his tree. After a moment's silence on both yankees said, "who are you fellows anyhow?". Oh we live over the mountain, said Parsons, been having a little hunt. Now, who are you?

"We are federal soldiers, been hunting", said they, "come with us to camp. You will be cared for and tomorrow we will have a pig hunt."

Parsons said no we are expected home tonight.

"Well," said the yankees, "you are our prisoners and you will have to come with us."

Parsons said, "come and take us".

All parties now standing as straight as ramrods behind their tree.

At length Parsons said, "you fellows can't hurt us and we can't you, if we stand here a month. I propose that we set down our guns and meet half way and shake hands, then each go his way."

"Agreed", said the yankee. "The proposition is yours, you fellows come half way first and we will meet you".

Parsons said, "no, I will meet one of you half way without arms, then our friends will follow suit".

"Agreed again", said the yankee.

Parsons set his gun against the tree and walked out. One of the yankees doing the same.

Now said Mr. Yankee, "your friends next and mine will follow suit".

Inskeep set down his gun and walked to the side of Parsons. The remaining yankee now stepped out with his gun laying in the hollow of his arm.

"Hold", said Parsons. "We agreed to meet without arms."

"Oh", said the yankee, "you are caught in your own trap. I guess you will go to camp with us".

Parsons said, "this is not fair".

"All things are fair when dealing with Rebs and bushwackers", said he.

"But we are neither", said Parsons.

"Do hunters generally carry spyglasses when hunting", said the yank, who had halted perhaps 20 feet where the others stood.

I had detected the sound of footsteps approaching from the same direction and felt sure that it was more yankees and several of them. I felt that something must be done and quickly, too, or in ten minutes time we would be prisoners, if alive. To be captured this near a yankee camp, dressed in citizens clothes and carrying a spyglass, I well knew would fix our fate, but what was to be done? One of two things; that yankee must drop his gun and trot down the mountain without arms. If he refused to drop his gun, then our liberty would compel me to drop him. The thought was terrible, but there was nothing else to do that I could see. I stepped from the tree with my gun at my shoulder and said in as stern a voice as I could command, drop that gun or you are a dead man.

He hesitated, looked at me. I pressing the trigger when his gun dropped to the ground. An instant later a minnie ball would have pierced his heart. He walked up and shook hands with Parsons and Inskeep, who gave their names as Brown and Smith. The yankees gave their names as Freeman and Coles.

They said to me, "leave your gun and come down and shake."

I said no I don't want to shake. You fellows leave your guns and double quick straight down the mountain.

They said, "we don't want to go to camp without our guns".

I said, when you have gone two hundred yards you can come back and get them if you like, as we have no use for them, but go at once. One of them remarked that he did not see any necessity of being in such a hurry and did not see why they could not take their guns with them.

I again drew my gun to my shoulder and said' "go".

Inskeep said, If you fellows want to live, you had best go.

Parsons and Inskeep shook with them again and invited them around the mountain to take a hunt and turned to get their guns. The yankees started very slowly. I said, move quick and don't look back. They broke into a trot. The boys came up and we started for the top of the mountain without delay.

Approaching steps could now be heard uncomfortably nearer. We were soon over the top of the mountain and making the best time possible in order to reach the bottom, feeling thankful that we were safe once more, for the time at least.

We reached Mrs. Fox's house a little after dark, got supper, which we certainly enjoyed.

The family was southern to the core and were naturally anxious to hear all they could from their friends in Dixie. The elder brother David, being among one of the first who responded to Virginia's call, and marched with the Hampshire Guards to Harper's Ferry in May 1861.

After relating our experience of the day on the mountain, also the news from Dixie and gathering what news the family could give us as to the yankee doings, we declined an invitation to sleep in the house. The ladies offering to stand guard while we slept. But we declined with thanks to their kind offer, preferring, under circumstances, to sleep in the open air, but said we would, if agreeable, take breakfast with them next morning, provided we could get it not later than five o'clock.

36

We left the house, each having been presented with a blanket, which we promised to return next morning, if the way was clear. A lighted candle set in an upper window would denote danger. In that case, we would not return, but leave the blankets at W. V. Herriott's house.

We had talked the situation over before reaching Mrs. Fox's and come to the conclusion that it might not be altogether safe to attempt to get back to our horses that night.

We felt sure that the yankees had not been mislead as to our purpose on the mountain and would make the best possible time back to camp and report to headquarters. Then the roads, both up and down the river, would be strewn with yankees to prevent, if possible, our escape back to Dixie. We felt sure that every effort would be made to capture us, so we determined to find a safe place where we could have a good view of the roads and country, and not attempt to get through until next night.

On leaving the house, we went to the barn which stood some distance from the house and near the public road, but feeling unusually skittish. We concluded not to sleep in the barn, but crossed the hollow and camped in a thicket of pines.

Parsons placed his glass and drawing of the yankee camp in an old stump a little distance away and covered them up with leaves; not caring to have them in his possession, if accidently captured. Each rolled himself in his blankets and were soon asleep. When we awoke we discovered that the family were astir by the light passing through the house.

We arose, took up our blankets and started for the house separately and approaching from the different directions, in order to discover if the house was being watched. We had slept later than intended and found breakfast awaiting us of which we partook with a soldier's usual appetite, which is always good. Then with our hearts full of sadness and our pockets full of rations, we bade the family adieu, not knowing that we would ever meet them again.

Having selected Cedar Knob ridge as the point of observation which we reached shortly after daylight.

Having found a suitable place for our purpose in the top of a tree which had blown down during the summer and was covered with dry leaves. We crawled into this and were secure from observation, unless at very close range. From here we had a good view of the roads and country below Hanging Rock's Gap.

We soon discovered an unusual stir among the yankees. They seemed to be everywhere. There appeared to be a regular skirmish line on the mountain where we had been the day before. We knew well the game they were looking for. Toward evening they seemed to be mostly moving toward Romney.

When it had become too dark for our glass to be of further use, we

Union troops retreating across the bridge over the South Branch of the Potomac. Today this area is known as Blue Beach on U.S. Rt. 28. *(DAVIS HISTORY HOUSE, ROMNEY, WV)*

started again for W. V. Herriott's house, after spying until satisfied the way was clear. We went to the house. Herriott said there had been no yankees at this house since we were there, although he had noticed several squads prowling around the day. Had seen father that day, who had told him the yankees had placed a guard at his house. They said to protect his house.

This was important news to us as we had intended calling at father's house, but this news changed the program. We got supper, then Mr. Herriott put us over the river about 10 o'clock. An hour later we were lying behind a sharp knoll about 100 yards from the pike watching a squad of yankee cavalry passing toward the Wire Bridge.

The moon was about full and shone almost as bright as day and a person moving on the pike could be seen for quite a distance. As soon as the cavalry had passed from sight, we crossed the pike and once more felt that we were safe. We reached Mr. Hear's before daylight, climbed into the hayloft and were soon asleep. About daylight we crawled out, found our horses where we left them.

The family was all from home. We found our saddles all right, were soon mounted and on our way to Mr. Daniel Haines' on the Capon Mountain, where we got breakfast, had our horses fed and our canteens filled with something clear as water, but it wasn't water.

We reached camp about 10 o'clock well satisfied with the success of our expedition.

Capt. Sheetz had been ordered to Winchester and was forming in the pike in front of the mill, when one of the men by the name of Harrison, accidently let his carbine fall. It was discharged, the ball striking a rock, glanced upward and struck Sergeant John C. Leps under the left shoulder, ranged upward and killing him instantly.

This was a sad accident. No man in the company was better liked than he. No doubt he would have made his mark, could he have lived. All who knew him regretted his untimely death.

About the 1st of December 1861, in addition to the companies of Capt. Sheetz's, Capt. Shans and Capt. Harper; these were camped at Blue's Gap.

Several hundred militia gathered from Rockingham, Shenandoah and Hampshire counties. All under the command of Col. Alexander Monroe. At Capon Bridge there were about 50 militia under Col. E. H. McDonald; about 25 of them were mounted and used as mail carriers between Winchester and Moorefield.

About the last of December 1861, Gen. Jackson meditating an advance on Romney and desiring all the information he could get as the Yankee force as that place. Col. E. H. McDonald entrusted the task to W. D. Rees and myself.

The evening before we started Capt. Sheetz came to the bridge with two yankees, which he and some of his men had captured that morning near Frenchburg. They proved to be the same two that Parsons, Inskeep and I had met on the mountain west of Romney a few weeks before. They recognized me at once, called me a blue spy from a blue hunting shirt that I wore. They said that after we had gone from sight they went back to get their guns and met ten of their boys and if they would have kept us for five minutes longer they would have had us. Said they had a thousand men on that mountain next day and also had our names all right. One of them asked me to step a little to one side when he said (in a confidential way), "I will give you a piece of good advice; keep off that mountain. There has not been a day since we met there, that it has not been closely watched. Your father's house is also watched, but", said he, "if you ever go spying around Romney again, far better die fighting, no difference what the odds be never surrender".

Capt. Sheetz called to him and said they were ready to go. (He was taking them to Winchester.) He gave me his hand and said, "don't give me away, but remember what I have said."

I have never seen or heard of him since. His advice went in one ear and out the other. I afterward had reasons to think he was sincere.

Next morning early Mr. Rees and I started for Moorefield. We reached William Van Meter's early in the evening, got something to eat for ourselves and horses. After resting our horses for an hour or two. We again started and rode on until we reached a road leading over to Williamsport. When we reached the top of the mountain we left the road, turning to the right, followed the top of the mountain until we reached Barkville. (I think the mountain we followed was called Furnace Mountain.) We pulled up at the house of William Vest, who at that time lived at Pierce's Mill. We were nearly frozen on the mountain. The snow was 18 to 24 inches deep with no road or path to follow. We had to pick our way as best we could over and around fallen timber and ledges or rocks. Our progress was necessarily very slow. The night was bitter cold.

When we reached Mr. Vest's house it was about one o'clock in the morning. Mr. Vest soon had a blazing fire and then got a jug from a closet filled with something clear as water, but it wasn't water. It had the smell of ripe apples. Mr. Vest said it would help warm us. We asked no questions, but took a full dose and it was only a short time until the stuff began to act.

We remained here perhaps an hour, took another dose of fire water and started.

We kept down the creek through the fields until we were below where Archild Vandiver then lived. We crossed the creek and followed the creek pike until we reached the Samuel Davis' house. We had some Dixie mail to leave there. Mr. Rees being well acquainted with the family, soon had them aroused.

The family was intensely Southern and during the war gave the South much valuable information. We delivered our budget of mail, filled ourselves on cake, pie and cider, gave them what news we could from Dixie, then advised them of the time of expected return.

We again started, after having spent an hour and about fifteen minutes, (at least it seemed so, time flew so fast). It was with great reluctance that we again turned out to face the cold winter blast, but there was no other alternative. We were now near Headsville about midway between Romney and New Creek Station. Here a majority of the people were Southern, although many were for the Union and would have the Yankees on the track of a Southern soldier in a very short time, if seen by them.

This made it necessary for us to be under cover before daylight. We pushed on and reached Mr. Rees' house before day. Soon our horses were cared for and were warming by a hot fire. On learning that there was no Yankee Cavalry at New Creek, we felt tolerable safe and one of us, at least, was soon in bed and asleep, forgetful of every danger. When I awoke it was near the middle of the day. After dinner we saddled up and intended to cross Middle Ridge and stay overnight in Foxes Hollow and early next morning cross over the east side of the mountain opposite Romney and see what was to be seen. The snow in the valleys had nearly all melted off but on top of the ridge there was plenty of snow, though the weather had moderated somewhat. We reached what was known as the Spurling place on top of Middle Ridge. Here a man by the name of Hines lived. We felt safe to leave our horses with him until our return.

From here we only had about two miles to go where we expected to stay over night. There was a long ridge leading to the hollow on the South side. The snow had nearly all melted off. We followed this side of the ridge a short distance, when on looking across a deep hollow on the end of a high ridge on the North side of which there was plenty of snow, we discovered two persons whom we thought were Yankees, from their dress. We stood still until they had passed around the ridge from view, then made our way toward the hollow which we reached about sundown. The public road passed on the opposite side of the valley, some two or three hundred yards away. We sat down to wait until dark before going any farther. We had not been seated many minutes until we saw three Yankees ride up toward Mechanicsburg. We had determined that Mr. Rees would go to Captain Ephraim Herriott's house and get what news he could and I should go to Mr. Foxes and learn all I could and be at the Captain's before day next morning and we would try to be in a position on the mountain in time for roll call in the Yankee camp at Romney, and thus be able to make a fair estimate of their number. Soon as dark we

41

parted, each having about a half mile to his stopping place for the night. Our objective points were about one mile apart. When I reached Mr. Foxes house it was quite dark. After spying around for some time, I discovered there were more colored folks on the premises than belonged to the family but as the building which they occupied stood some 40 paces from the family residence to which I returned after satisfying myself that only the family were present. I walked in to the surprise of the family.

I inquired at once what strange darkies were there. Was informed that Parker's Jim and one of Mr. Washington's colored men were down at the lower kitchen. I then asked for the nearest picket. Was told there was one at the ford, one and one half miles distance. Well, I will not be safe here for two hours, if Jim finds me out, said I. The family thought I would be safe since the darkies would not be likely to leave their quarters again that night and would not know of me being there. I was shown to an upper room, the blinds lowered and cautioned not to speak above a whisper was then considered safe. The young ladies soon had supper prepared and brought it to my room which I certainly enjoyed. I believe anyone would have enjoyed that supper though not in the least hungry.

That supper came near to costing me my liberty, if not my life in preparing it. There had been occasion for going to the spring house for butter and cream, carrying a light about the house &c., raised the curiosity of the colored folks, who set about to investigate and by watching and listening at length found what caused the unusual stir. Jim and the other gentleman (it was afterward learned) watched around to see whether I would remain overnight or not or if I left, to find out where I was bound for. After getting all the news I could from the family in regard to the Yankees and giving them what news I could of interest from Dixie. It was now late, not caring to undress, I went down to the dining room and lay down on a lounge, having first bid the family good-bye, informing them that I would start about 4 o'clock and would get breakfast at Capt. Herriott's and not wishing to disturb anyone, I would take my departure as early as possible. On a clock in the room, I relied to awaken me at the proper time. I soon fell asleep.

Soon as the colored gentlemen were satisfied that the family had retired and that I had not left the house, one remained to watch the house, the other started to inform the pickets at the river. When they got the information, they concluded to send to Romney for more men so as to make sure this time of what they termed a spy.

I did not sleep sound, not feeling altogether safe. I heard the clock strike four and arose at once. In a few moments two of the ladies came down and insisted on my having breakfast before starting; at least a cup of coffee, said to do so would not detain me a half hour. I would then get up to Mr. Herriott's before they were up. I was feeling a little rough that morning and thought perhaps a cup of hot coffee would do me no harm and finally said I would stay.

The ladies went up stairs. Something seemed to urge me to go. I felt very uneasy and could not tell why. My will was to stay but I felt that I must go at once. This I determined to do and put on my overcoat, buckled on my revolver, took up my Minnie rifle and when the girls came down, I was ready to go.

They said, "You are not going?"

I said yes I feel that I am in some kind of danger here. They only laughed at the idea. I said all right I must go, bade them good bye and started.

The morning was very dark and windy. The house stands back something a hundred yards from the road. I started down the path leading to the road. When I had gone about half way I thought I heard something like a saber scabbard strike against a rock. Stopping at once, I listened for a moment but heard nothing more. The wind, which blew almost constantly made it impossible to distinguish sounds. I felt that precaution, in my case, might be a good thing, so I left the path I was following, climbed a fence into a meadow and crossed the main road, some distance above the gate lead into the highway, where I heard the suspicious noise. I kept away from the road and reached Capt. Herriott's as they were sitting down to breakfast. The captain said he thought it would be very imprudent for us to go on the mountain. Said he was satisfied that there had not been a day for the last month that the Yankees had not been on it hunting. Also said that he had been in town the day before and could tell us more than we could learn by going on the mountain. We concluded not to go any further, got all the Captain could tell us and started to back track.

We soon reached Mr. Hines', found our horses all right, arrived at Greenwell Johnson's and remained there until after dark. Then went to Mr. Rees' house and stopped for an hour or two, then started again, reaching Mr. Davis' house, found the Dixie mail ready. We only stopped long enough to get the news from New Creek and then pushed on.

The weather had moderated. It was much warmer than two days before. We reached Gabe Fox's house for breakfast.

After dinner we started again by crossing the river and bottom some distance below Moorefield. We saved a ride for several miles and soon reached the Wardensville grade. We reached Blue's Gap a little after dark and stopped for the night. Next day we reported to Capon Bridge before the middle of the day. We learned that Gen. Lander was in command at Romney, but do not remember what force he had. This was about the 1st of January 1862.

It was not until about two weeks later, after Gen. Jackson had come to

Romney, that I learned of my narrow escape. The morning I left Mrs. Fox's house, it was surrounded by Yankees a few moments after I left it. A company of cavalry had come down from Romney and had dismounted some distance below the house and was on foot when I heard the scabbard strike a rock. Had it not been for this sound my ear caught, I would have walked right among them and might have had trouble to get away, but fortune seemed to favor me again. The young ladies said that after daylight the Yankees searched the house from cellar to the garret. They would then consult with the colored folks and then go over the house and search again. Searching trunks, bureau drawers, wardrobes, between the bed-ticks, up the chimney, in barrels and boxes, in every place possible for a child two years old to hide. They had in the meantime ordered their breakfast. While some of them were eating, others were searching in every conceivable place.

The whites all denied when questioned that there were any Rebels there, but no doubt the darkies were confident that there was and, of course, they would believe the colored folks.

Finally they gave up near the middle of the day and departed, apparently not satisfied, believing no doubt, that the object of their search was secreted somewhere about the premises; and no doubt left spies at no great distance to watch the house. I met Jim six months later and made him own that he had gone to the pickets that night and told the Yankees. He did not live through the war.

CHAPTER IV

Battle of Blue's Gap

J anuary 1st, 1862, Col. Monroe had fortified his position at Blue's Gap by building breastworks not only in the Gap but on top of the ridge on each side of the Gap. In front of these works, the timber had been cut for some distance forming a network through which it would have been almost impossible to advance with a few cool determined men behind those breastworks.

The Gap was little more than wide enough for the pike to pass through. At the southeast end was placed two pieces of artillery. Upon the whole, Colonel Monroe's position at Blue's Gap was a strong one, if attacked from the front, but no good if attacked from either flank.

The men were comfortably quartered in long huts and were enjoying the good things brought them by their friends, who arrived during the holidays from Shenandoah and Rockingham counties, bringing with them several wagons loaded with holiday fixings, of which quite a quantity was done up in kegs and demijohns.

Most of the Hampshire Militia managed to get home for a short time during the holidays. Thus far, soldiering to us militia had not been such a bad thing.

A few militia under Col. McDonald at Capon Bridge, were doing equally well. When about 8 o'clock on the morning of the 7th day of January, 1862, we heard the roar of cannon in the direction of Blue's Gap. Some of the boys thought the firing was at Romney, others at New Creek. Col. McDonald thought it not farther than Blue's Gap and ordered the mounted militia to saddle up and we would ride up toward the Gap and see what was going on. By the time we were ready to mount, we discovered three or four men on horseback coming down the mountain from toward the Gap at a break neck speed, bearheaded and hair streaming to the rear. They proved to be the artillerymen from Blue's Gap. They reported being surrounded by anywhere from 5 to 10,000 Yankees. All killed or captured except them. They had attempted to bring the cannon away, but found they would be captured and cut the horses away from the guns just in time to make their escape. They said the Yankees were not more than a mile or two off, coming on, going straight to Winchester; said they must hurry on and let Jackson know or he would be captured. They dashed through the Bridge toward Winchester and for all I know, are going yet.

We mounted and rode to the top of the mountain west of the Bridge, where we met some of Capt. Sheetz's company, who had halted and were watching the Yankees on the opposite side of Park's Hollow, near the top of the mountain engaged in burning some three or four wagons, which they had captured. (The wagons were from Shenandoah and Rockingham counties.) We had a Confederate flag which the Yankees could plainly see for a short distance as we carried it over the top of the mountain. As soon as we passed from their view, Col. McDonald had it rolled up, taken back and carried over again. This was done several times, leading the Yankees to believe that they had seen several regiments cross the mountain top. Very soon we saw them turn back towards the Gap. We followed cautiously, having a few men on each side of the pike, a little in advance to prevent falling into a trap, if the Yankees should set one for us.

We reached Blue's Gap about three o'clock in the evening without seeing anything more of the Yankees.

At the entrance of the Gap, we found the large new mill in ashes. Also a dwelling house that stood near and the militia headquarters. Amid the smoking ruins of the dwelling house lay the charred corpse of the old shoemaker, whose name, I think, was Reed. He had been shot through a window and his house burned over him. By the side of the road, where the mill stood, lay a dead Confederate, an artilleryman. These were the dead or wounded found. On passing through the Gap, we found that Col. Blue's house, barn and out buildings had shared the same fate. All that remained was a charred smoking ruin. Perhaps as many as 25 houses were burned that day by the Yankees as they returned to Romney.

We gathered the particulars of the capture of Blue's Gap from those who were present. Col. Monroe had ordered the cavalry to picket Pleasant Dale, but they had only gone about half the distance and stopped at a vacant house with the reserve and picketed a few hundred yards further on. Early in the morning, firing was heard at the picket post. By the time the reserve was mounted, the picket dashed up, closely followed by the Yankee advance. Capt. Sheetz had his men in a favorable position and promptly gave them a volley which caused them to face to the rear and fall back, but they soon advanced again in force and Sheetz was compelled to fall back, at the same time sending a dispatch to Col. Monroe that the Yankee cavalry was advancing, but was unable to ascertain in what force. The Colonel supposed it to be a scout from Romney and gave it but little thought more than send an order to camp for the men to be held in readiness to march at a moments warning. The Colonel had his headquarters at Col. Blue's house, some distance in advance of the Gap, and of his command, one in command can generally be located in the rear of his men. (The Colonel chose the front). Capt. Sheetz soon discovered that there was a large body of infantry, also artillery in rear of the cavalry.

When the second dispatch reached the Colonel, he at once ordered the men to the positions assigned them.

The friends from Rockingham and Shenandoah had not all gone. A few yet remained with their teams. These were anxious to get away, and instead of obeying the order promptly to man the works, they wasted precious time in helping their friends to get off.

The Yankees were piloted by persons well acquainted with the country and with the location and extent of the fortified positions on each side of the Gap.

The Yankees, under cover of the timber, sent out strong flanking forces in advance of their main column, which advanced slowly to give the flanking forces time to reach the breastworks ahead of the militia, if possible, from the ridge, where the Yankees had halted a half mile or so west of the Gap). They could easily see their flankers ascend the ridge on which the militia had built their defences. When these were nearly reached, the main column moved out from the timber and threw a few shells into the Gap and then advanced at a double quick.

Capt. Sheetz had fallen back to the Bridge, now passed on through the Gap with his men. The militia had a steep rocky ridge to ascend for perhaps 200 yards, in order to reach their breastworks. When they reached them they found the Yankees ahead of them and at once faced to the rear and started at a two forty gate for the Blue Ridge.

When the militia on the left of the Gap gave away, it was necessary for the artillery and the militia on the other side to get away from the rear.

The Yankees had now reached the top of the ridge on the right and were in good musket range of the pike, which ran nearly parallel with the ridge on which the fortification had been built.

Mr. William Hass, who was a quartermaster, had been to the front two or three times and reported with the regular orthodox military salute, "Colonel, the yankees are advancing", at the same time suggesting the necessity of his getting away. The Colonel said he had some important papers that must not fall into yankee hands and hurried into the house to secure them. Just then Capt. Sheetz passed with his company at a break trot. The Yankee bayonet's were visible on the opposite side of the bridge. Quartermaster Hass became somewhat excited and forgetting the respect due to a superior officer, roared out, "G-d d—m it Alex, you must get out of here. The yankees are crossing the bridge." The Colonel rushed from the house, mounted his horse and dashed through the Gap amidst a shower of bullets. On passing the gap, he expected to find his cannon in position ready to sweep the gap with the grape and canister and those assigned to the breastworks in their places, ready for action. Seeing no one, the Colonel rode on until he turned on a short curve beyond the mill, when he discovered his cannon standing in the road and a dead man laying along the side of them. A moment later a volley was fired from the ridge opposite. The bullets whistled around him thick and fast. This

47

being the first intimation he had of his works being manned by Yankees instead of Rebs. At once throwing himself into position of a thoroughbred Commache, nothing being visible above his horses back but a number ten boot and one arm. The Yankees supposed he had fallen from his horse and raised a yell of triumph. "Frank" was not slow in carrying his master out of danger.

A few days later we were ordered to Bloomery. A day or two after, we started for Romney, having got word that the Yankees had left town. We arrived about 9 o'clock at night and found Capt. Sheetz already there. It seemed that Capt. Lander, who was in command, had heard from Jackson, in some way, and concluded not to wait until he could turn the town over to him but left in somewhat of a hurry, leaving a lot of the commissary and quartermaster stores behind. On the 14th of January, 1862, Gen. Jackson reached Romney, but the game was gone.

The Huckleberry Rangers (or mounted militia) were quartered at H. B. Dawson's house, now Mrs. Sallie Brady's. We were now among our friends. Nearly all of us could get to our homes. We had plenty to eat, good quarters and nothing to do.

One morning about 2 o'clock, Col. McDonald sent me an order to have my men saddle up and get ready to go on a scout with Capt. Harper's company toward New Creek. We were soon in the saddle and awaiting orders. In a short time Capt. Harper passed down street with his company. We were ordered to follow. On reaching Mechanicsburg, we left the grade and followed a county road, by which we again reached the northwestern grade, (at Zachariah Arnold's house, now John W. Arnold's), shortly after daylight. We halted and fed our horses and most of the men got breakfast. We had placed two men on top of the ridge in the pike, a few hundred yards toward Burlington. In a short time a Mr. Leatherman, (who lived a short distance below Mr. Arnold), sent his son, a boy of some 12 or 14 years of age, to Keyser with a basket of marketing.

The pickets stopped him and in looking over his marketing found a letter directed to the officer in command at New Creek Station, using very harsh and disrespectful language in reference to Col. Angus McDonald, Capt. Harper and Col. Ed. McDonald. We concluded to arrest Mr. Leatherman and take him back to Romney. We started back to Romney following the pike, when we came to the lane leading to Mr. Leatherman's house, which stood about 100 yards from the pike. Capt. Harper took three or four men and rode over to the house to arrest Leatherman. The remainder of the command, in all not more than 75 men all told, had halted opposite the house, and while awaiting Capt. Harper were gathered around Col. McDonald, who was reading aloud the captured letter. When he had finished he said, "Boys, one of you ride back to the turn until you can see up the ridge, the Yanks might run upon us." One of the men rode back perhaps 50 yards, when he wheeled and came back a the top of all speed, shouting, "My God boys, the road is full of Yankees!"

Every man started on a run, at the same time yelling to Capt. Harper to get away. He was on the opposite side of the house from the road and was waiting on Mr. Leatherman, who with one of the Captain's men had gone to the barn to get a horse. On seeing us going down the pike in such a hurry, he rode to the end of the house when to his surprise, he saw a regiment of Yankee cavalry coming down the pike from the direction of New Creek.

The column reached back to the top of the ridge. The Captain estimated them at less than 600. He called to his men and started down through a meadow on the opposite side of a ditch, parallel with and not over 75 yards distant from the pike. After going perhaps a hundred yards, he came to a high fence. After throwing off the riders, his men jumped their horses over. The Captain was mounted on a fine young horse of high mettle, which he had only ridden a few times. He refused to leap the fence. The Captain had to dismount and lay down the fence until his horse could step over. His men had left him. The Yankees were firing at them and yelling at them to halt.

The Captain's horse became unmanageable. He could not mount him and was running beside him. The Yankee's column had halted in the pike opposite. The Captain threw down the fence when a dozen or so Yankees rode over to him, who finding that he could not escape had halted. The ditch between them was wide and deep and was difficult to cross.

I had halted in front of a house (where I think a Mr. Ludwick then lived). Mr. James Whiteman, father of David C., was standing on the porch. I saw that the Captain was a goner unless I could get them to follow me. In case they did, he would still have a very slim chance for making his escape, provided he could mount his horse. He had not yet succeeded in getting his mare to cross the ditch. I asked Mr. Whiteman to hold my mare a moment, but he was afraid to do it for fear of the Yankees. I rode back a short distance to a stable that stood near the pike, in full view and not over 75 yards from the Yankees. I was mounted on a well-bred mare and felt sure that I could get away unless a stray ball should interfere. My mare was excited and would not stand. I dismounted holding the rein in my left hand, my Minnie rifle on top of the fence. The Yankees were facing the ditch and almost in a line with my position. I thought to wing about three, took careful aim and fired, then mounted, swung my rifle across my back and drew my revolver, fully expecting the Yankees to make a dash for me. Relying on the speed of my mare for safety, but in case any of them should be better mounted than I, my revolver might be of use (when not too bad scared, I was a fairly good shot). To my surprise the Yankees seemed to take no notice of me, but were gathered around one of their

49

companions. I fired two shots from my revolver and started toward them shouting, "come on boys, we've got them."

Samuel Bane had halted some little distance below, now rode back. The Yankees had left the Captain and were hurrying toward the pike. The whole column having faced about and were going at a brisk trot.

The Captain had led his horse farther down and crossed the ditch and come over to Bane and me. He mounted his horse and we rode through a gate to the top of the hill from which we had a good view of the pike to the top of the ridge beyond Mr. Arnold's house, also of the Beaver Run road down which we discovered the rear of the Yankees column just passing from sight on a full run. We turned and rode back to the pike, overtaking most of our men before reaching Romney. Capt. Harper rejoiced very much over what he considered a miraculous escape. If I had been a woman, no doubt he would have embraced me. The Captain's home was in Rockingham County. He was over age and soon after left the army and declared war against the Devil by preaching the Gospel. I had the pleasure of breaking bread with him at his home several times afterwards, and was really glad that it had been my good fortune to do the Captain a favor. I was always treated the greatest kindness. He had three rosy cheeked daughters, but of course, they had nothing to do with my visit to the Captain.

But I am getting away from my text, as far better men have done before. We learned a few days after that the Yankees went back to New Creek by way of Headsville and they reported having been bushwacked and had two men badly hurt. The same day they burned Sheetz's Mill, which no doubt was a great satisfaction to them.

Gen. Jackson only remained at Romney ten days. His chief object in marching to Romney was to capture the Yankee force at that place. Failing to do this, and fearful that General Banks might move up the valley in his absence, he returned to Winchester about the 20th of January, leaving Gen. Loring at or near Romney with three small brigades.

The weather was now warm with a great deal of rain and sleet. The Yankees were said to be collecting a heavy force both at New Creek and Cumberland.

On the 31st of January, 1862, General Jackson received an order from the Secretary of War to withdraw General Loring's command back to Winchester at once. It being thought by the War Department to be in great danger.

This order was complied with at once, but it came near losing to the Confederacy, a leader, who had no superiors and but few equals in the world's history, as a military chieftain.

The road between Romney and Winchester was in a fearful condition, artillery and wagons in many places, sinking to the axle in the mud. Often the whole train would be halted for a hour or two until a team in front, stuck in the mud, could be got out and the road repaired, which was soon done if there happened to be a fence nearby where rails could be had.

About two o'clock of the 2nd day of February, 1862, General Anderson's brigade, consisting of the first, seventh and fourteenth Tennessee regiments, which had been quartered near the Wire Bridge some six miles below town, came up, filed to the left and followed after the two brigades which preceded them.

A quantity of camp equipage that could not be moved on account of the roads was given to the citizens and such as they could not used; was burned. About dark the picket at Mechanicburg Gap, consisting of two companies of cavalry, under the command of Capt. Sheetz, passed through town. The mounted militia had come up from the Hanging Rocks, where they had been on picket and now joined Capt. Sheetz's command, which formed the rear guard of General Loring's division.

The South Branch was not fordable. General Loring had ordered the bridge above town burned as soon as the pickets were withdrawn. I was ordered to see that this order was executed. Lieut. Ike Parsons remained with me. The town was now held by only two Confederates. After the rush and hurry of the day, the town seemed almost as silent as a grave. It was a sad day to a large majority of the people of Romney and neighborhood. Many of whom would rather the Confederates had not come at all, than to come and leave them so soon again to the tender mercies of the Yankees. A report had reached town that the Yankees had camped at Mechanicsburg and had a picket at the bridge.

We were now at a loss to know what to do to carry out our orders. It was impossible if the bridge was guarded as reported. We finally concluded to go down to Ike's home and see what the Colonel thought about it. The Colonel had gone. We concluded to have supper and then followed on after the command and report the advance of the Yankees. Miss Kate Parsons thought that we had better try and learn to a certainty that the Yankees were really at the bridge before we reported such to be a fact. We concluded to take her advice and investigate as far as possible. We had with us a colored Confed, now a resident of Romney, who had volunteered to go with us. About 10 o'clock we started on foot, each carrying a bunch of hay under his arm and a supply of matches.

The night was very dark and windy. In reaching the foot of town-hill, we left the road and went up through the bottom until we reached the upper end near the bridge. Here we halted and listened for perhaps a half hour. We finally came to the conclusion that there was no one at that end of the bridge and ventured over the fence and onto the bridge. Here we stopped again and lay down with an ear to the floor, but the wind kept the bridge squeaking so that we could not have heard a person walking on the other end. Our colored brother was directed to climb up to the roof and stuff his hat between the roof and joist or binder and as soon as he saw a blaze start over the middle pier to strike a match and set his hay on fire, but in case he heard a shot fired at the other end of the bridge, to get away as fast as his legs would carry him, without setting fire to the hay.

Ike and I then advanced cautiously until we reached the middle pier. Here we again placed our ear to the floor, but heard nothing that sounded like the tread of a sentinel. Ike climbed to the roof, in order to place his kindling into position. After considerable persuasion, I prevailed on my legs to carry me to the farther end. Every puff of wind, rattle of a loose board or creak of the timber, my cowardly legs wanted to turn back. I knew that if they ever turned back, they would take me back to the other end of the bridge, something like a shot from a cannon. But after reaching the farther end, listening some little time, I mounted the roof, stuck my bunch of hay in a corner against the roof, stuck a lighted match into it, waited a second to see that it caught, jumped down and let my cowardly legs go. By the time they reached the middle pier, Ike had completed his work, jumped to the floor and being a little fresher, led me by a neck. When we reached the end of the bridge, our colored brother had done his work on time and disappeared. We soon came up with him, and hurried on until we reached the cemetery, where we waited and viewed, with regret, the ruin we had wrought. The bridge was built wholly of pine timber and weatherboarded with shingle roof. In less than 20 minutes after being fired, it went down.

We, as soldiers, had done our duty, which was to obey the orders of our superiors. The destruction of this military bridgeway may have been a military necessity. Had General Loring been pursued next day by a superior force, he would have lost all his artillery and wagon train and perhaps, most of his army. But with high water and no bridge between him and his pursuers, he was safe.

The destruction of this bridge made Romney an unsafe place for a Yankee army, thus relieving its people, to a great extent, from the worry and annoyance of having a standing army in their midst.

After leaving the cemetery, we went back to Ike's home and remained until morning, then followed on and overtook the rear guard at Frenchburg.

This fall back was very slow and tedious, on account of the bad roads. On reaching Back Creek, Captain Sheetz met an order to proceed with his command to Moorefield. The mounted militia went with him.

On reaching that place, we were quartered in vacant house and both men and beast were well provided for. After being in Moorefield a week or two, Capt. Sheetz concluded to take a scout by the way of the "Trough" road to Romney. The river being generally to full to ford at this time of the year and there being no bridge at Romney, there was but little danger of meeting with blue coats, unless a scout camp came up from Green Spring, at which place there was a company of cavalry and a few infantry guarding the railroad.

I thought that this was a good opportunity to make a visit home provided the way was clear. We found all quiet at Romney. No Yankees having been there for quite sometime.

Capt. Sheetz only remained in Romney a few hours and returned to Moorefield. Capt. Kuykendall, who was at that time a member of Capt. Sheetz's company, got leave of absence for a few days. (The Captain's father lived in Springfield.) He thought it safe to venture as far as his uncle Michael Blue's and get word home from there. I went to father's house. We expected to remain over a day or two. The Captain was to call for me when ready to return. I had just finished breakfast next morning, about daylight, when someone hallowed at the gate. I recognized the voice at once as that of the Captain and knew at once that the Yankees had something to do with his being there. I hurried out to learn the trouble. He greeted me with, "Get your horse, the Yankees are coming."

I asked no questions, but by the time I got ready to mount, father had my horse saddled. The Captain said that we could not reach the pike without meeting the Yankees and would have to try to cross the river at a ford a half mile or so below, which we soon reached. The river was flush but could be rode on a tall horse by keeping well down on the ripple. The Yankees had seen us and were now coming down the bottom. There was no time no lose. We were cornered and had to take water. There was nothing else to do. We plunged in. The Captain was mounted on a rather tall horse. I rode on the lower side, my mare being rather small. Some of the time she was on the bottom and part of the time she wasn't. When we reached the shore I was wet to the second story. The Captain had fared better. The Yankees came to the ford but did not venture in and soon turned back. We stopped at Mr. H's house and dried our clothes.

The captain had heard the Yankees crossing the Wire Bridge and by following a route back of the mountain and crossing a near way, reached father's house a short time ahead of the Yankees. No doubt someone had carried news to the Yankees at Green Spring of our being in the neighborhood. This was the 22nd day of February, 1862. The way I came to know the exact time was the firing of the cannon at New Creek to honor General Washington's birthday.

We went to Capt. Herriott's house and remained over night. Next morning started back to Moorefield and reached there early in the evening.

About 10 days later, Captain Sheetz's picket stationed at the ford below town, reported the Yankees on opposite side of the river at that place, before day on the morning of either the 2nd or 3rd of March, 1862.

The river was too deep to ford. As soon as it was light enough the Yankees drove the pickets from the ford, but could not cross. About 8 or 9 o'clock they made their appearance opposite the town on the other side of the river (at what I think was called Whiting's Ford). They had marched from New Creek expecting to surprise and capture the few cavalry at that place.

Their force consisted of infantry, cavalry and artillery. The river was too deep for infantry or artillery to cross, (but if I remember right) the cavalry crossed after we had left. The Yankees threw a few solid shots into town, one of which passed through the courthouse.

Capt. Sheetz was out numbered 20 to 1 and not caring to give the Yankees an excuse for shelling the town, moved out with his command, amounting to, perhaps, 75 men all told and took the road leading to Wardensville.

I had not been well since my ducking, but kept going. But now was scarcely able to ride. Col. Parsons had moved part of his family to Shull's Gap of Lost River. When we reached there, I stopped and laid down. Dr. Lupton and wife were staying at the Colonel's. Next morning the doctor said that I had measles. I did not get out again for two weeks. At one time, 4 doctors stood around my bed, but failed to kill me. They gave up the job, said they could do nothing more and advised letting my home folks know my condition. Next day father and one of my sisters reached my bedside.

When the doctors gave up the case, John Shull, brother of James S. and Thomas, said there was an old woman out in the ridges that knew more than all doctors together. He would go and bring her to see me. She came, looked at me, said nothing and went away, but came back in an hour or two, bringing several kinds of roots, from which she soon had a quantity of tea, and commenced dosing, by giving me a teaspoonful at a time. Increasing the dose until I could take several swallows.

The trouble had been that nothing would lay in my stomach. The old lady said that I would be alright in the morning and left. I have not seen her since. Next morning the measles were out about three deep, there was not room for more. I soon got better but was very weak for several days. There being no Yankees nearer than Green Spring on the B. & O. railroad. The Colonel concluded to take his wife and smaller children home. The two elder daughters, Miss Kate and Miss Sallie, and Ike, who had come from New Market, at which place the militia were quartered, Mrs. Dawson. Dr. Lupton and his wife, were also there. A few days later we were all shocked by the sudden death of Miss Kate. She and Mrs. Dawson occupied the same bed. Mrs. Dawson had risen about daylight and was dressing. Miss Kate was sitting up in bed, as usual, when Miss Kate fell back on the pillow. Mrs. Dawson alarmed the inmates at once. Before the doctor, who slept in a lower room, could reach her she had breathed her

54

last.

Although scarcely able to ride, I started to carry the sad news to her parents. About halfway to Romney, I met the Colonel. He was surprised to meet me, knowing that I ought not be out in such damp weather, and said: "What is wrong, what has happened?"

The Colonel had heart trouble and had not been well for sometime. I feared to break the sad news to him. I finally said, "Kate was taken very ill this morning and is in great danger, the doctor thinks. I was coming to let you know."

He said, "You are keeping something from me. Tell me the worst. I can hear it now. Is Kate living?

I said, no, she died about daylight this morning. For a moment or two I thought he would fall from his horse. He soon rallied and said, "You go on and break the news, as gentle as you can, to Susan, and tell her to have Vause McNary hitch up the carriage and bring her and the children out. I will go on. I am needed there. Vause McNary was staying at the Colonel's. I met him before I reached the house and delivered the Colonel's orders and left him to tell Mrs. Parsons of her loss. I went home and attended the funeral two days later. Ike and I returned to Shull's Gap, took our meals at Mr. Shull's and slept in the house, lately occupied by the Parson's family.

Ike only remained a few days and then returned to New Market, where the mounted militia, or Huckleberry Rangers, were quartered. By this time, the river has fallen and was fordable.

The Colonel did not think it safe to remain longer at home and came over to the gap a few days after his son, Ike, had left.

He had concluded to go to Harrisonburg and insisted on me going with him. This I consented to do. We started next morning and had a very disagreeable trip of two days: it snowing and raining most of the time. On reaching Harrisonburg, we learned that the Confederate Congress had passed a conscript act, requiring all male persons, between the ages of 18 and 35 years, to enter the Confederate Army. Those over 35 were discharged, nearly all of which, who could do so with safety, went home. The militia subject to the conscript act were organized into new companies or went into those already in the service from their respective counties.

Col. E. H. McDonald had organized the mounted militia (numbering, perhaps, 25 men) into a cavalry company. Others had enlisted principally from Hampshire County. The company, all told, numbering about 40 men. Col. E. H. McDonald had been elected captain, and William Taylor, 1st Lieutenant. No more commissioned officers being allowed for that number of men in a newly organized company.

This company was D, of the 17th Virginia Batallion, which was composed at that time of four companies and was commanded by Capt.

W. H. Harness, he being senior captain. The 17th Batallion, afterwards became the 11th Virginia Cavalry, which was commanded by Col. Funsten.

The militia of Shenandoah, Rockingham and Hampshire Counties, who less than three months before had ran from Blue's Gap at sight of the blue coats, without firing a shot, had been now mustered into regular Confederate army and followed Stonewall Jackson from Kernstown (where many of them fought like Veterans on the 23rd of March, 1862) to Chancellorsville, where sank the morning star of Confederacy. Yet many of the same militia followed lesser lights to Appomatox and was never known to turn their backs on a blue coat after that memorable morning at Blue's Gap.

Maj. E.H. McDonald
(POTOMAC EDISON'S VALLEY ECHO)

Maj. Oliver R. Funsten
(POTOMAC EDISON'S VALLEY ECHO)

CHAPTER V

First Capture and Escape

A fter remaining at Harrisonburg a few days, the Colonel being anxious about his family, concluded to return to Hampshire. And not feeling yet able to stand the exposure of a camp life. I returned with the Colonel. We reached James McDonald's house on Piney Mountain. The Colonel was very anxious to hear from home. I concluded to try and get to my father's house, some 4 miles north of Romney and in rear of the Yankees at that place. As soon as dark came, I started and reached home about 10 o'clock. I found at my father's house an old man by the name of John Smith, (an old Rebel who did some bushwacking at the commencement of the war), also a man who was working for father on the farm. There not having been any Yankees at father's after Gen. Lander left Romney, I concluded after getting all the news that I could take a few hours rest and was soon asleep, intending to start back at an early hour in the morning.

The Colonel had accompanied me a short distance and cautioned me time and again not to run any unnecessary risk, or close my eyes inside the Yankee lines, for said he, "They would hang you for a spy without a trial". I said catching comes before hanging but promised to be very careful. I promised to be at Mr. McDonald's house the next morning by 10 o'clock. The Colonel bade me good-bye and seemed to be a good deal excited, said he felt something was going to happen before I got back.

I had been asleep perhaps two hours when I was aroused by the bark of the house dog. After listening a moment, I heard a sound unusual to me. I sprang from the bed and looked from the window. The moon was shining bright almost as day, the ground frozen and covered by a heavy frost. To my horror, I discovered a column of Yankees just entering the yard. I grabbed my clothes and my revolver and rushed downstairs, hoping to make my escape by a back way, but when I opened the door I was met by a Yankee bayonet. I was trapped. I went back up stairs, stuck my Minnie rifle behind a bureau and put my revolver in bed with my brother, who was 12 years old. Then went to the garret loft and hid myself the best I could under some old clothes and sacks.

Pretty soon I heard someone ascending the steps with a lighted candle. I heard him order Smith, Dike and my brother to get up and dress themselves. He came on to the garret. After searching around for sometime, went downstairs. I began to hope they would not find me. I could hear them talking in the yard below. Heard one of them say, "We have found his horse and cavalry saddle and are sure that he is some-

The Wirgman building, site of Lt. Blue's first escape. Razed 1965 for The Bank of Romney. *(CLARK ALEXANDER. PHOTO 1959)*

where in the house." In a short time I heard someone again ascending the stairs; consumed sometime searching the second floor and then came to the garret floor.

There was a quantity of old plunder stored on the upper floor. After searching around for sometime, he spied one foot that was exposed, gave it a kick, said, "Hello James, wake up, you will take cold. Some of your friends heard you were at home and have called to see you".

I said alright and arose and followed him downstairs. My captor was a Liet. Cole. The company belonged to the 3rd Maryland Regiment, then stationed at Romney and was commanded by Col. Downey.

The company making the capture consisted of about 40 men, and was commanded by a Captain Shearer, who with three or four of his men, were in the room. The family had all risen, also Smith and Dike.

We were soon on the march for Romney. The prisoners were four in number, father, John Smith, Wesley Dike and myself.

We reached Romney shortly after daylight. After being searched, I was escorted by the corporal and two privates to a room immediately over that now occupied by Mr. Hart, druggist and locked in. The guard remained in the hall. The room was vacant not even a chair. The only moveable object in the room, that I could see, was a two-pound weight lying on the mantle. This I slipped into my pocket of my sack coat, though without any definite object in view. The fact is, I was too much rattled to think. After walking about the room for sometime, I seated myself on the floor in one corner of the room to try and arrive at some conclusion in regard to my future prospects. I bitterly regretted not having taken the Colonel's advice to not close my eyes in sleep inside the Yankee lines. Had I followed his advice, I would now be free, but regrets would never set me free.

I soon came to the conclusion that it looked rather doubtful about my meeting the Colonel at the place or at the appointed time.

To make my escape from an upper room of a strongly built brick building, well guarded, in a small town filled with Yankees, no other aid than a two-pound weight, was not a problem easily solved. At least it looked that way to me. The door opened and old man Smith entered the room. The door was closed and bolted again.

I learned from Smith that father and Dike had been set at liberty by the Provost Marshall, but he had held him until the arrival of Col. Downey, who was away at that time.

This was early in April, 1862. The day was bright and warm. We were allowed to raise the window and talk with lady friends on the street. They soon learned that we had nothing but the floor to sit on, when Mrs. John O. Heiskell sent up two chairs and a small table for our accommodations, which was appreciated very much and were grateful but this was not all.

61

The same lady sent us a nice warm dinner, which was enjoyed, especially so by not having had any breakfast. This was Tuesday. Our meals were sent us morning, noon and night by the ladies of the town, and were so tempting that, though prisoners, we never failed to enjoy them.

The ladies also furnished us with blankets and quilts to make us comfortable at night. The evenings being cool. The Yankees would make a fire and stay inside at night; a corporal and three men.

We were doing well for prisoners, being kindly treated by our guards and well supplied with newspapers, such as the Baltimore American and the Philadelphia Press. If the copies of these papers published during the war be in evidence against them at the final judgment day, I fear the verdict for living will be perfect.

One day the corporal assigned to duty, came in with a basket of provisions, quite enough for a half dozen men, when we had placed it on the table. The corporal said, "I almost wish that I too was a Confederate prisoner if I could be fed as you fellows are."

He was a real nice young man. We invited him to take dinner with us, which invitation he accepted. But our feasting was short lived.

On Friday Col. Downey reached town and did himself the honor of calling on us at once. Introduced himself by saying that he was Col. Downey and was in command of the post.

The Colonel was small in stature and young in years. I would not have taken him be be over twenty years of age. He wore the regulation uniform of a colonel in the regular army. He was rather a good looking youth, very pompous and conceited. At least this was the way I sized him up.

He looked at me for a moment and then said, "been spying around again have you and got picked up this time?"

I said, "No, I have not been spying."

"How is it that we find you in our lines, dressed in civilian clothes?"

I said, "I have never worn any clothes except those of a citizen. I was in the neighborhood and thought to visit my home and perhaps remain at home without being molested."

He says, "I know you by reputation to be a spy and to have had a hand in burning the bridge near town."

I said, "Colonel, those are serious charges, but there is nothing in them."

Says he, "I know what I am talking about, now listen to me. You are charged with being a spy and a bridge burner and your life is not worth the name. Now if you will answer truly such questions as I ask you, I will see that you are liberated, provide you take the oath of allegiance to the United States and if necessary take up arms in defense thereof."

Said I, "Colonel, any question that I can answer conscientiously, I am willing to answer."

62

"Well", says he, "to what command do you belong."

I said, "I don't belong to any."

"When were you last in the Valley, near Harrisonburg and what is the amount of the Rebel forces now in the Valley to the best of your knowledge."

I said, "Colonel, I cannot purchase freedom at such a price. I might be a spy or a bridge burner, but never a traitor to a cause I believe right."

"Then, he said, "Your fate is sealed, your days are numbered. On Monday you will be sent to Wheeling, hobbled and handcuffed. The evidence I can produce would convince any court of your guilt in fifteen minutes time and inside of ten days, instead of life and liberty, which I can offer you on easy terms, your worthless carcass will fill a disgraced and dishonored grave."

The Colonel had become a good deal excited and I, for once, had lost my head. For a few moments the language used was far more emphatic than eloquent and ended in the Colonel drawing his sword and said he would run me through, were it not for robbing the gallows of its rightful victim.

I said, "Colonel, you seem to be a very brave man, especially when faced by an unarmed prisoner."

He made no answer, but pointed with his sword to the windows, said to his orderly, "close those shutters and see that they are not opened until so ordered." And without another word, left the room.

After the Colonel had left the room, I sat down and tried to determine some line of action by which I might escape; what seemed to be my certain doom. Old man Smith was so deaf that I could not hold a conversation with him, without being over heard by the guard at the door. Our rations from that time were cold bacon, dry bread and a cup of water, which were scarcely touched.

The guards noticed and spoke of our treatment as being cruel and unnecessary.

Our guard was doubled at night. Instead of a corporal and three men, we had a corporal and six privates in our room each night. I could not sleep or eat, in fact, was not enjoying myself very much.

I looked my situation over, perhaps, a thousand times and always reached the same conclusion; that I was in a right bad fix; and could see no way out of it. No scheme that I could devise seemed to give any hope of success. I might make an excuse for hoisting the window after night and then jumping out only to cripple myself or I might make a rush for the door as the guard entered, but with little or no chance of escape. To hope to escape on the road to Green Spring, hobbled and handcuffed, was not to be thought of.

On Sunday morning, father came up to town (having heard that I would be sent away next day) brought me a sachel, containing a change of underwear. He had seen the Colonel, who promised that if I would agree to take the oath of allegiance and give him all the information I could, that no charges would be brought against me. Father advised me to do this and take no more risk of losing my life.

The corporal now opened the door and said, "Time is up." Father arose to go and bade me good bye and do as the Colonel desires. I said I would consider the matter, and though that matter had not already been settled in my mind. I said, "Take the sachel over and leave it with Mrs. Heiskell. I can get it from there." This he did.

It commenced sleeting on Saturday evening and now began snowing. By night three or four inches had fallen. It was so dark in the room that a person could not see to read. Soon after father left, I lay down and closed my eyes and tried to sleep, but no sleep for me; I could only think. I had no confidence in Col. Downey's word and could not trust him. When our supper came up, I arose and remarked that I had no idea that it was so late, tried to eat a little.

The guards, a corporal and six privates were now in the room. I tried to be as cheerful and lively as possible, remarked, "I guess the best thing I can do will be to take the oath of allegiance and go home." The guards all thought so, too. About nine o'clock, we all lay down, except the corporal and two guards, who were on duty two hours and off four. The corporal's duty was to relieve them every two hours. He sat by the little table, which stood near the centre of the room, on which a candle was burning, his revolver and watch lay by his side.

On the right hand, on entering the room near the fireplace with their heads to the wall, lay four soldiers. Their muskets stood in the corner behind the door. One of the guards sat on the floor with his back against the door. The other sat on a chair near the fire.

Smith and I lay on the opposite side of the fireplace with our feet toward the door. The door was opposite the fireplace.

This was the situation in the room named, on Easter Monday, about 6 o'clock a. m., 1862.

I awoke and arose at once. The fire had burned out, only a few coals remained. I complained of being cold, put on my coat and began walking the floor. I had very little hope of getting away. My plan was to get near enough to the guard who sat with his back against the door, strike him a stunning blow with my weight, which I held in my hand, then grab his musket and use it as a club and brain as many as I could before they downed me. I thought I could dispose of the corporal and other guards before they could use their arms.

The corporal was resting his head on his arm, which lay on the table. The guard sitting on the chair was asleep. I could not tell certainly if the corporal was asleep or not. All seemed to be sleeping except the one against the door. He was fingering with the lock of his musket, the breech sat on the floor. I had walked several times across the room, each time getting a little nearer my intended victim, when in reach I struck him on the side of the head at the same time, grabbed his musket by the muzzle, wheeled around clubbed it; ready to brain the first man that moved, all hope of escape had been abandoned.

The morning of Easter Monday, April 1862, was not a desirable one by any means. I stood ready to die, ready but not willing, although I felt that the time appointed had come and that there was no use of trying to dodge the question. A moment of lively work and all would be quiet again. One of the guards turned on his side, I thought he was about to rise, I grasped the barrel a little tighter and raised the musket a little higher, had he attempted to rise an instant later and he would have been on his last march. The guards all seemed to be sleeping, the guard whom I had struck had drawn himself up in a heap when struck; now straightened out and rolled away from the door. His overcoat which had been thrown over his shoulders had dropped to the floor, his cap lay by his side. All was now still as death in the room, except the breathing of the sleeping guards.

It now occurred to me that if I could get out before there was an alarm given, disguised in blue overcoat and cap, and carrying a musket, I might escape. I stepped quietly and lightly to the door, picked up the coat and cap, opened the door and with it shoved the insensible guard aside until I could get out, then closed and locked the door and put the key in my pocket. The key being in the lock outside, I leaned the musket against the door, slipped the coat on and cap and was ready either to run or fight. I was surprised to find that it was daylight when I stepped into the hall.

The shutters being closed and a candle burning in the room which I had just left, I was under the impression that it was yet dark out side. But I had no time to consider; the guards might awake at any moment. I took up my musket and at a "shoulder arms" descended the steps. To outward appearance, a thorough-bred Yankee, but beneath that overcoat and cap, if anyone attempted to investigate that morning, they would have found a fair sized animal, vulgarly called a Reb, who was not inclined to be very sociable. I thought on reaching the hall to try and make my escape by the rear of the house.

Col. Downey had his headquarters to the left of the hall on entering from the street, and immediately under the room which I had just left. For the last hour or two persons had been passing in and out. On turning down the main stairway I discovered a guard marching back and forth in the hall below. This discovery caused me to abandon my plan of retreat from the rear. The guard passed to the rear of the hall as I reached the last step. He only glanced up at me and passed on. I had turned up the wide

65

collar of my overcoat and was so well disguised that I doubt if my own father would have known me.

Without halting I marched straight to the front door. When in a step or two of the door, two Yankee officers passed by, I could have touched them with the bayonet. I stepped out behind them in fear that at any moment the shutters might be thrown open, a window hoisted and the alarm given, I walked across the street at an ordinary gait, hopping from one stone to another to keep out of the mud and water as much as possible. The snow had melted and the cavalry had tramped the street to a thin batter. On reaching the opposite side of the street I halted a second and pretended to be stamping the mud from my feet, but the object was to look the situation over a little. I glanced at the window of my late prison, all seemed quiet. A glance at the court house showed me perhaps fifty soldiers washing and combing their heads, and a lot more at the Keller Hotel.

I came to trail arms and turned into the alley leading to the D. H. Heiskell's store and was lost from view from persons on Main street. There was no fencing around, all had been burned by the soldiers for fuel. From the window of our prison before they were closed I had noticed that Captain Firey kept a very fine black horse in Mr. John C. Heiskell's stable, it occurred to me that if I could get mounted on that horse I would not care a fig for all the Yankees in town. I was soon on the opposite side of the stable from the hotel, but to my disappointment found some one in the stable grooming the animal I was after. So had to abandon the idea of escaping on horse-back. In full view of at least a score of Yankees at the Keller Hotel, I crossed the street, shaping my course rather toward the Gilkeson corner, and as I thought in regular military style, fearful that something in my movements or actions might cause suspicion and lead to an investigation.

Too much haste or a dodging nervous gait might attract attention and betray me, but then who would have thought for a moment that a full grown Rebel would have cheek enough to march through the streets of Romney in broad daylight, it being occupied by at least a thousand Yankee soldiers. These thoughts passed through my brain whilst crossing the street and I felt comparatively safe, until that dread alarm should be sounded from my late prison, and be echoed and reechoed through every street in town. This unwelcome sound my ear was strained to catch and only wondered why it did not come. On reaching the opposite side of the street, I was soon hid from view by the Gilkeson store house. I turned to the right, passed in rear of the house now owned by Mr. Seedars and reached the back street with the intention of making my escape up the hollow, then called Whippoorwill Hollow, near where Robert Fisher, colored, now resides.

I had only taken a few steps in this direction when it occurred to me that there were fortifications in that direction and may be a guard in them.

I took a hasty survey of the ridge in rear of the old church. No living thing was in sight, this seemed to be the shortest route to liberty, though in good musket range if discovered.

I determined to risk it. I now moved at a little quicker gait and soon had the old church between me and the town and undercover from it was making the best time I could for the top of the ridge. I covered half the distance when that much dreaded sound fell on my ear. The rattle of the drum, the bugle call was not to be mistook. They told too plainly that my escape had been discovered and the alarm given, although I had been making the best time possible as I thought I now felt as though I hardly touched the ground.

Just as I reached the top of the ridge I heard a musket ball whistle past. A moment later and perhaps twenty went singing over and around me. I had now passed over the top of the ridge from sight, and fallen on the ground completely exhausted, scarcely able to breathe. However, it was not long until I was creeping through the brush trying to reach a point directly opposite the public square, then crawled through the bushes to the top of the hill and took a peep into town, I wanted to see what the next move would be. There seemed to be a good deal of excitement and loud talking, mixed with quite a streak of profanity. It appeared to me they were making a great ado about so small a matter.

I supposed, or rather hoped that after talking the matter over they would go back to their quarters and finish their breakfast. But no. Soon a company of cavalry started at a brisk trot toward Winchester, another down toward the bridge. At same time I discovered a squad of fifteen or twenty infantry coming up the street toward me.

Their object now seemed plain. They thought to track me up with the infantry and cut my retreat off with their cavalry. I felt very much like scattering that crowd by emptying my musket among them, then giving one long, loud Rebel yell, but I didn't. Though perhaps I might have use for my ammunition before the day was over. These thoughts passed through my brain like a flash.

I had seen enough and thought I understood their plans and believed that my safety depended on getting outside of the line of cavalry intended to be thrown across my line of retreat before the way was closed. I was soon on my feet, dropped my overcoat and was sailing south at a rate of speed that if kept up on an air line and no collisions would have landed me in the Confederate capitol before sundown. The morning was dark and cloudy, the ground covered with snow to a depth of three or four inches, my trail could be easily followed. I had not gone far until I found that my progress would be slow and difficult on account of the undergrowth being loaded and lapped together by the weight of the snow. I did not fear those in my rear unless kept back by something in front until they could come up with me. I feared that the cavalry might form a skirmish line along the Gibson house. I pushed forward as fast as possible, shaping my course to cross the hollow a good distance from the river road. I was not long in reaching the hollow named, up which there was an old road that I expected the Yankees to follow; I approached it with great caution, after having examined my musket to see whether it would go if called on. Although the cap proved to be a water proof yet I felt doubtful about it, although I had done the best I could to keep the lock dry.

It so happened that at the point where I reached the road there stood several large white, or spruce pine trees which had kept the snow from reaching the ground leaving it bare, beneath which enabled me to cross without making any tracks which I was careful to do. I had not gone more than forty yards when I heard the rapid approach of cavalry coming up the hollow. Dropping among the laurel and low brush I was completely concealed and was thankful that I had succeeded in crossing the road without leaving a trail behind.

There was over a half dozen in the party. One of them said keep a sharp lookout for his tracks, he will likely cross here. If we can find his trail we will soon pick him up. Another said something about the Reb's having wind like greyhounds. They now had passed from hearing. I imagined there would be another squad along shortly and would keep riding up and down until the infantry came up when they would be sure to find my trail, and put a fresh pack in the chase would soon run me down. Again pushing forward I soon reached the top of the next ridge where I halted for a few moments to get my wind, and considered what best to do.

The cavalry once on my trail I felt that it would be only a question of time when I would be run down and trotted back to town a prisoner to be hooted and grinned at, or shot to death like a dog. The thought was not a pleasant one. Far better it seemed to me at that moment, it would have been had I not attempted to escape, but died in my prison. After having dispatched a half a dozen Yankees to answer the last roll call on the other side of the river. It seemed that this would have been satisfaction, had I possessed the whole world and could have exchanged it for my Minnie rifle and fifty rounds of ammunition, the exchange made right then and there, could I have had my Minnie rifle and ammunition more than one Union soldier's blood would have stained my trail that day. I am now thankful that I was unarmed.

Over thirty-six years have come and gone since thoughts like those passed through my brain, yet they seem almost as fresh in my mind as the morning when I stood on top of that ridge behind a tree watching with strained eyes the top of the ridge which I had lately crossed, to see, if possible, whether my trail was being followed. Hoping all the time that the chase had been given up by those of my track. Only a few moments had passed when I discovered my pursuers creeping over the ridge.

I started at once. Sight of the blue coats seemed to revive me. I felt almost as fresh as when I first started. When I reached the next hollow down which quite a stream of water was running, entering the stream I followed its upward course until I come to a smaller stream that came down from the ridge on my left, this followed perhaps a hundred yards when I again came to a thicket of pines where the ground was bare of snow. Here I left the water, being careful to make no sign more than I could possible help. A heavy mist has been falling for sometime.

It now began to rain lively, the snow was melting rapidly a dense fog had come down so that it was now impossible to see a man fifty yards in the timber. This made it necessary for me to proceed with great caution.

The snow melting and falling from the timber kept up such a racket that a person could hear but little else. I could not have been more completely soaked if I had swam the river. I continued to go forward wading in the little drains which was now rushing down every little hollow. The south side of the ridges were now getting bare. The snow was melting rapidly. I had but little fear of my trail being followed, and felt pretty sure there was no Yankees in my front, I had as I supposed been traveling about parallel with the river for several hours, and concluded that I must be near Lockender place, twelve or fourteen miles from Romney and felt that at last was once more free.

In a short time I came to a road that seemed to be traveled a good deal. In fact it looked as though a company of cavalry had passed a short time before. I crossed the road, climbed a steep ridge, when near the top I stopped. That road bothered me, I could not locate it, couldn't think of any such road in the direction I had been going. The rain had ceased, the snow was nearly gone, the clouds and fog looked as though the sun might break through at any moment. It flashed through my brain that I was lost and no idea where I was. I sat down at the root of a pine tree, tired, wet and hungry. To say I was discouraged would be putting it very mild. Soon I began to get drowsey, leaning back against the tree I was soon asleep. How long I had slept I could not tell, perhaps an hour. When I awoke, shivering with cold. The fog and clouds had disappeared and the sun shining brightly, from a clear sky and right before me, not more than a mile or two away was the town of Romney.

I will not attempt to express my feelings; I was in a kind of a dazed condition, thought I must be dreaming, but no, the discovery was real, and it nearly took my breath. I had lost my bearings and now found myself, after several hours of hard wearysome travel, almost at the starting point, instead of being, as I believed, at least ten miles away. I tell you I felt real bad about that time, sure. I was afraid to move for fear of being seen by some blue coat scouting through the ridges. My first thought was to hide in the top of a fallen tree near by until dark and then try to make my way to father's house, which was not over five miles distant, get some dry clothes, something to eat, a horse and my revolver, which I knew they had not gotten, then I would be in fair shape again. A second thought convinced me that to go home would be risky business as they would more than likely be watched, and again I was so wet and chilled that if I lay hid until dark I would not be able to move. I knew or rather had heard that on Big Mountain, at what was known as "Biggie's Shanty" or near there was the camping place of a few men who were keeping out of the way of the Yankees. It was my object from the start to try to reach this camp.

There were several houses within a mile or two where I could have gotten something to eat with safety as far as the inmates were concerned. But was afraid these houses might be watched, for this reason steered clear of them.

It was between one and two o'clock. I determined to make one more effort to reach the Big Mountain. To travel a distance of not far from fifteen miles in my condition, in space of about four hours when night and darkness would come was not a pleasing thought to me. The whole distance must be traveled through a wooded country over steep ridges and deep hollows. I was wholly unacquainted with the route, only knew the direction with the mountain west of the river as my guide and a good prospect of wandering through the night in the Mountains. I started and after many hairbreath escapes from being scared to death by black stumps, which I mistook for Yankee soldiers, reached Mrs. David Parsons' house now Mr. Jos. S. Pancakes, about dark. Boys you may think I was tired, but that was no name for my feelings, I was the worst done for boy you ever heard of. I determined to go to the house and ask for a piece of bread for I felt like I might starve before morning.

After shying around for a few moments I walked in and found Doctor Bowen sitting by a bright wood fire, a colored girl was in the room also. The Doctor said "hellow Rudolph where did you come from?" Been hunting and got lost said I. The Doctor asked the girl to bring him a drink. Soon as she left the room the Doctor, who knew me well but called me Rudolph that colored girl might not know who I was said "my God boy you are in great danger here. The Yankees have not been from here ten minutes. Have been riding up and down the road all day looking for you and may be again at any moment." One of the young ladies now came into the room. The Doctor said it would never do for me to stay there, I said I have been wandering in the woods all day and am very tired and hungry give me a piece of bread and I will go to the barn and sleep. The young lady, I think it was Miss Jemima, said to the Doctor, you saddle your mare and Tomp's and I will take him up to Mr. Murphy's and Mr. Murphy will take him to Joe Archies, where he will be safe until morning. The Doctor said suppose the Yankees come along about time you start. She said they could not catch us mounted on those horses. Said she was willing to risk the ride if I was. The Doctor soon had the horses at the door, in the meantime I had destroyed I don't know how many pies. We mounted at once, on two well-bred Boston mares and in a short time was at Col. Murphy's house. The Col. had several grown daughters, all seemed delighted to know that I was safe. They had heard of my escape from the Yankees, who had been riding up and down the road all day, who said it would be impossible for me to get away as every house in ten miles around was watched and almost their entire force was scouring the mountains. A reward of five hundred dollars would be paid for my body, dead or alive. That they were on my trail within ten minutes after I left town, which the snow made it easy to follow, and they had no doubt that I had been run down and killed or captured before ten o'clock. Col. Murphy said that from what he could gather from the Yankees I was tracked by the Infantry, with Infantry and Cavalry thrown across and around my line of retreat, in his opinion made my escape impossible and had said to his family that when they heard of me again he feared the worst. The old man wrung my hand again and again, while tears of joy rolled down his cheeks. The Col. had been at father's house often and I was one of his pets from a child. Some of the ladies seemed to have their feelings hurt and were using their hankerchiefs freely. I too could have shed a few tears, through politeness, but was too tired. To make a long story short, I almost felt that I would be willing to go through the same ordeal again for the sake of another such reception. Supper which had been delayed on account of the Yankees, was announced. Two of the ladies went to picket. We seated ourselves around the table, which was loaded with all the heart could wish, and whilst the ladies were planning for the safety of their guest, he was busy taking on ballast sufficient to carry the craft for an indefinite time through sunshine and storm.

The feast (to me) over, the ladies had decided that I must go to bed and get a good nights rest, and they would see to it that no Yankee entered the house that night. Then in the morning the Col. would show me the way to the refugee camp on the mountain. I protested against sleeping in the house, felt that I had gone through too much to take any unnecessary risk if I could avoid it. They insisted that they could and would protect me; I don't remember that they said with their lives, but I know that they talked very patriotic. It began to look as though I must give in or be rude, when Miss Parsons who had been on picket entered and after listening to their plans for my comfort and safety, declared that it would never do to take

71

such risk. Said that I was her prisoner and must go to Joe Archies house that night and if uncle Frank would not take me there she would. Col. Murphy agreed that he would go with me to the camp on Big Mountain that night, if I felt able to go that far. But thought I would be safe at Archies until morning, at least. After thanking all for their kind reception, good wishes and promised prayers, for my safety, all seemed to regret that prudence made it necessary for my safety, that I must go, none regretting it more than I. When I arose to go I could scarcely take a step I was so sore and stiff from being so over heated, then wading in almost ice water several times during the day, sometimes blundering or stepping in a hole and going head foremost, but it was the only thing to do to confuse and throw my pursuers off my trail. The ladies seemed almost ready to shed tears at what they termed my pitiful condition. It was quite an effort for me to mount again. Col. Murphy mounted the horse which Miss Parsons had rode. We soon reached Mr. Archie's house, some two miles back toward the mountain, I am guessing at the distance, from the length of time taken to reach the place. I never traveled the road before or since. Mr. Archie was not at home, but Mrs. Archie agreed to take me in. Col. Murphy promised to be there by sun up in the morning and take me to the camp on the mountain. Mrs. Archie's little son showed me the way to my sleeping apartment in the loft and carried my wet clothes down and hung them up by the fire to dry, while I tumbled into bed minus every stitch of clothing, hoping for a good nights rest. Vain hope, my tired, aching limbs forbade me sleep, until late in the night my eyes closed and I got an hour or two of half sleep. Daylight had come again, my clothes were sent up. I arose and attempted to get on my feet but it was no go, my limbs seemed to be of no use and refused to act, would not bear my weight. I finally succeeded in dressing, then crawled to the stair feet foremost. By the aid of a chair I reached the table where breakfast was waiting. A pan of water was placed on a chair, I washed and had just finished eating when Mr. Murphy rode up. He led a horse to the door and with no little effort and Mr. Murphy's help I succeeded in mounting, and by ten o'clock reached what was known as the home brigade situated on the top Big Mountain, very near where the line of Hampshire and Hardy crosses the mountain.

CHAPTER VI

Skirmish at Grassy Lick Run

W e found several persons here, who had no particular wish to meet the Yankees, among the number was Lieut. Ike Parsons, who had reached the camp the evening before, after having come near being captured at a school house on Grassy Lick Run. A man by the name I think of Humbaugh, was trying to organize a company, some twenty-five or thirty men being present. Some of them were armed with the home rifle but a majority of them had no arms. Not expecting any Yankees as there had been none on that road so far from town, and the morning being so raining and disagreeable that no one thought for a moment that Yankees could be found nearer than Romney, no pickets had been thrown out. The first intimation they had of Yankees being within ten miles of them they were nearly surrounded by near a hundred Yankee cavalry. The recruiting officer and his men rushed from the house and scattered in every direction under a heavy fire from both carbines and revolvers. All succeeded in making their escape without a scratch, but I imagine some of them at least were almost scared to death, it being the first time under fire. Col. Isaac Parsons was present, having just ridden up and if I remember right was sitting on his horse when the Yankees made the charge.

The Colonel carried a double barreled shotgun which he emptied among them at short range, then putting spurs to his horse, (which was a fast goer) was soon out of danger. Looking back as he rode rapidly away he saw a Yankee fire at his son, Lieutenant Ike, who was running across the road and was climbing a steep bank, saw him fall when the Yankee fired, and supposed that he had been killed. The Colonel rode onto Mr. Hott's house and was telling him of the surprise and of what he supposed to have been the death of his son, Ike. Mr. Hott, who came to the camp shortly after we arrived with the news of the Colonel's death, said that he seemed to be very excited, turned very pale and would have fallen from his horse had not he and his boys helped him down. In a few moments he was dead.

Mr. Hott was surprised to find Ike alive and well, believing him to have been killed the day before. Ike said that Capt. Firey had rode close up to him when climbing up the bank and fired at him. At the same instant he slipped and fell, the ball passing over him. Ike said he sprang to his feet, wheeled around with his double barreled shot gun at his shoulder. The Captain saw danger in the muzzle of those barrels, wheeled his horse around and rode away as rapidly as possible. Ike tried each barrel and

The academy today is used as a dining room by students at the West Virginia School for the Blind. *(FRANCES BUCKBEE)*

each missed fire. Ike thought that if his gun had fired he certainly would have killed him at such close range. Although several shots were fired at him as he ran up the hill. He escaped with one ball having cut the sole of his boot and scorching his foot across the bottom. He accompanied Mr. Hott to his home.

I would have gone with him and looked on the face and form, though lifeless, of the best friend I ever had, my own father excepted, but this sad pleasure was denied me. I was so sore and stiff that I could scarcely move one foot before the other. Col. Murphy remained a short time and returned home.

Col. Parsons' body was sent home for burial in the family burying ground. The Yankees thought that he had died from the effect of wounds received in the scrimmage on Grassy Lick Run and claimed the right to examine the body, hoping, no doubt, to find one or more wounds which would be a sufficient excuse for them to destroy his property. A professor Nelson who lived and taught school in the Academy in Romney at the beginning of the war, never having taken the oath of allegiance to the United States, claimed to be an English subject and claimed the property as his own, threatening to appeal to the English crown for protection if molested. In this way he no doubt saved from destruction, the building since enlarged and now occupied by the Deaf and Blind as a State Institution.

Mr. Nelson was a Presbyterian minister and was very much admired by the Parsons family. When the Yankees demanded the right to examine the body of the Colonel, Mr. Nelson said no, Col. Parsons was a friend of mine, no Union soldier would have dared touch him while living, and you shall not touch him now, though he is dead. Said he, if this thing must be done, I will have the corpse carried to another room and will there examined it in the presence of one or more Federal officers. No wound of any kind being found, the body was laid to rest in the family burying ground, there to await the last trumpet assembling the nations of the earth to answer the last roll call and render an account of the deeds done in the body.

For several days after I reached Fort Defiance, it was afterward known by this name. I could not take step without something to steady myself with and began to think that I would never have the use of my limbs again, but at the end of the week or ten days I peeled off like a snake and was again on the war path, with no weapon of defense other than my hickory cane. My object this time was to get home and make some arrangements by which I could get a horse, change of clothes, blanket and my revolver, which I knew they had not gotten.

At the commencement of the war navy revolvers were very scarce in Dixie. Toys of this kind were hard to get and cost as much as a horse. I got one from a friend at a reduced price. It cost only fifty dollars, not in gold but in money that was at that time as much as gold. My friend said he had got it very low and I believe he did; I always thought he stold it, but that did not stop me from running some risk to get possession of it again. I had, in the last few days, held a council of war several times and had at length come to the conclusion that in and around Romney was not the place for me to do business for the present, and determined to try to mount and arm myself the best I could and then go to the Valley and enlist for the war, or for life, in Capt. McDonald's Company. To do this it was necessary for me to go home to get a horse. I left Fort Defiance about two o'clock in the afternoon, and reached the river road, a short distance below Glebe, before sundown and laid in the brush until dark, then crossed the road and bottom of the river, then down the river bank in search of a boat in which to cross to the other side; I finally found one some distance below Mr. Joseph Pancake's house.

The boat was secured by a chain around a large root, the chain made fast by a padlock. I took a stout rail from the fence near by and got a hitch in the chain, broke a link and was soon on the other side of the river. The night was very dark and my progress along down the bank of the river in search of a boat had been slow. It was ten o'clock when I reached the W. J. Poland house, a short distance above where George Johnson now resides. There was a light in the house and after spying around a short time I concluded that there was no one in the house other than the family. I rapped on the door, no answer. I rapped a second and third time, when a trembling female voice asked, who is there? I said a friend. Who are you? was the next question. I gave my name and asked if Mr. Poland was at home. Mrs. Poland said there was no man about the house, that she, her sister-in-law, now Mrs. Isaac Van Meter, and the children were alone and she could not let me in. I then asked for a piece of bread and a blanket that I would camp on the mountain side and would return the blanket next morning.

After questioning me about my whereabouts since my escape, my answers seemed to satisfy Mrs. Poland and Miss Marthy that I was not an imposter and after a widespread consultation for a few moments, opened the door very cautiously when Mrs. Poland holding a lighted candle above her head peeped out. I saw that she was very much frightened and stepped back a few steps. I said Mrs. Poland you surely know me. She said come nearer that I may see your face. I removed my Yankee cap and advanced a few steps, when she threw the door open and said come in, I know you.

Mr. Poland was from home I don't remember where, but I was at home. As soon as recognized, Mrs. Poland said she had no baked bread, but plenty of good milk and soon have a pot of mush. I told her nothing she could give me would be enjoyed more. I don't think I ever enjoyed a meal more. While my meal was being prepared I gathered all the information I could as to the movements of the Yankees camped at Romney, whether or not they scouted on that side of the river or had ever been at the house. On learning that they had never been seen nearer the house than when in the road on the opposite side of the river, and river not being fordable I concluded to accept Mrs. Poland kind invitation to sleep in the house.

After having given Mrs. Poland and Miss Marthy a short history of my escape and my whereabouts to the present time, (it was now near midnight) I retired and was soon in a sound sleep, from which I did not wake until daylight. I arose at once, dressed and went below and found breakfast awaiting me. I sat down and ate a harty breakfast, not knowing when I would get another square meal. After thanking my hostess for her hospitality, which was all I could do, being dead broke financially, I started up the mountain.

On reaching the top I followed it toward Mechanicsburg gap, slow and with great caution, not knowing but what I might meet with Yankees, hunting, at any time.

The day was warm, bright and calm. The leaves were very dry and a person could be heard walking a long distance. I made good use of my ears and eyes, and moved with as little noise as possible. I had ample time to reach the gap where I would have to lay concealed until dark before attempting to cross the pike, which I would have to do to reach the mountain on the opposite side of the gap. I reached a point on Mill mountain where I had a good view, both through the gap and toward the bridge.

There seemed to be a move on hand of some kind. Several empty teams had passed toward Romney from the direction of New Creek, others had come down river loaded with corn and hay: As soon as darkness began to appear I started and on reaching the creek, heard a wagon coming from the direction of Romney, I stepped into a bunch of bushes until it had passed. I thought it was a farm team, but it was too dark to tell certainly. After lying here for perhaps a half hour, I ventured across the creek and pike and reached the top of the mountain below the gap, a good deal battered and bruised from the numerous blunders and falls over the rocks and logs. Let any one climb the end of that mountain of a dark night and if they don't see more stars than they ever saw before, in the same length of time, then I am very much mistaken. ·

Following the top of the mountain until I reached the low place opposite the Williams farm, when I made my way to the foot of the mountain on the west side, when I reached the road leading from the Rock ford to Mechanicsburg, the chickens were crowing for day. I had been about 8 hours going not over 4 miles. Pushing on I reached W. V.

Herriott's house by daylight. I remained at Mr. Herriott's house all that day and at night crossed the river and went home.

Father was not at home. The Yankees had pressed his team to haul a load to Moorefield the day before. They had all left Romney, except one company. I remained at home until evening and went back to Mr. Herriott's, but left word for father to come to Mr. H.'s as soon as he returned, which he did the next evening. I arranged with him to get a horse if possible up to Col. Murphy and have him bring or send it to the top of Big Mountain known as the Lockender path on either the next Wednesday or Thursday and I would be there to meet him. This was on Sunday. That night I made a call or two and crossed the mountain about 2 o'clock in the morning at the gap opposite the Williams farm.

My intentions was to go up through the fields until I reached a point opposite the mouth of Mill Creek, then cross the pike and creek between Shull's mill and the river, then follow the mountain until I reached Jack Pancake's, get breakfast, then continue my course up the river until I reached the boat in which I had crossed three days before. After considerable delay in blundering across the mountain. I at length reached the fields on the east side, then made my way as rapidly as possible until I reached the point where I proposed crossing the pike.

My suspicions had been aroused by what seemed to be dim lights from burned down fires at different places in the hill, or approach to the bridges, or where the bridge had been. I approached the pike very cautiously. On reaching the fence I halted for several moments to listen, thinking I had heard talking near by in a low tone, but come to the conclusion that I was mistaken. Streaks in the eastern sky warned me of the approach of day and that I had no time to lose. In attempting to climb the fence I put my foot on a rotten rail which broke making considerable noise. "Halt," followed by the sharp click of musket locks, caused me to drop to the ground.

"Who comes," was the challenge in very much of a Dutch tune. I knew at once that I had stumbled on a Dutch picket. A bunch of calves that was lying between me and the picket frightened and ran along the fence toward the picket. I heard them say something about "tam cow scare them," and shoot next time.

I was now making my way back to the mountain as fast as I could, lying flat on the ground snaking it the best I knew how until I had gotten some little distance, ventured to crawl on my hands and knees, but was soon on my feet and climbing the mountain, hoping to reach and cross the pike at the east end of Mechanicsburg gap before daylight had come and small squads of Yankees were passing toward Mechanicsburg. They were being ferried across the river at the bridge, or rather where the bridge had been and as soon as a load was landed they moved off carrying their cooking utensils on poles. These squads were almost in sight of each other, so close at least that I was afraid to attempt crossing the road and creek. I had supposed the last Yankees had left Romney the day before and had no thought of meeting with them at this time. Could not imagine where they come from.

I afterward learned it was part of General Schenck's command on its way to re-inforce General Milroy at McDowell. I lay concealed behind a large rock, within fifty yards of the road, until near the middle of the day. I could see some distance toward town, but could only see a short distance through the gap. The last squad to pass was ten or a dozen cavalry. Perhaps a half hour after they had passed, there being no more in sight I determined to cross the pike and creek or try. I ran down to and across the road and was at the bank of the creek. When the command "halt," struck my ear. I looked up the gap and saw a squad of cavalry. I think the same I had seen a half hour before pass up the gap, coming on a charge. At the same time several balls whistled by, one or two striking in the water too close to be agreeable.

I didn't stop to see what was wanted. A few lengthy strides not far short of fifteen feet each landed me in the brush on the opposite side. After running a short distance up the hollow turned and ran up the mountain a little way and dropped in a sink made of roots of a fallen tree. In a moment the Yankees dashed up the hollow. As soon as they had passed I started and went fifty yards or so farther up the mountain lay down along side of a log. The Yankees soon came back riding very slowly. I could get a glimpse of them occasionally through the timber. In a few moments I saw them on the pike going toward Romney. I then started for the top of Mill mountain, knowing that I would have no time to spare if I would reach camp on Big Mountain before dark.

Not feeling sure I could find it after dark, I pushed forward and reached Isaac Pancake's house about sun-down. Mr. Pancake was at the camp on the mountain when I left it. Mrs. Pancake gave me a bite to eat and I pushed on, reached Mr. Murphy's house. It was getting dark. I made arrangements with Mr. Murphy to bring the horse to the top of the mountain at the time appointed and started again.

Mr. Murphy advised me to go to Joe Arches and stay until morning as it would be impossible for me to find the way to the camp that night. I concluded to take his advice, but when I reached Mr. Archies', the house was locked up, no one there. I sat down on a log at the wood pile to try and make up my mind what was to be done. This was the fifth day of May. The night was rather cool to lay out without fire, or blanket: I had neither and concluded to try and reach camp, although to do so I must follow a path, that I had never seen but once, for several miles through the mountains.

79

I had slept but little for two nights, been on the move most of the time and was feeling a little tired. To make matters worse I had put on a new pair of boots which hurt my feet so that I could scarcely walk, but there was no help for it. The night was clear, with the north star for a guide I started, following the path leading to what was known as Biggie's Shanty, but lost the path before I had gone a mile. With the north star to my back I pushed on as near a south course as possible, though my progress was slow, which anyone that ever traveled through a thick woods after night can understand. My great fear was of coming in contact with a rattler.

It was 5th of May 1862, so says my diary. Clouds began to bank up in the northeast and before I reached the top of the mountain my guiding star was hid from view. I now felt sure that I had reached the top of the mountain, but could not tell at what point. I soon came to a rail fence, and knew at once that it was the fence surrounding the lot in which Biggie's Shanty stood. I sat down on top of the fence for perhaps a half hour trying to make up my mind to stay in the shanty until morning. The shanty was built of logs, an acre or two had been chopped off and a fence erected around it, though weeds and brush had taken possession. If I could have made a fire would have stopped here until morning, but the fear of snakes kept me away from the shanty.

I knew the course from this point to camp which I had left 4 days before. I determined to try and reach it and started, after blundering and falling over rocks and logs for about two hours found the camp. It was deserted. No sign of having been occupied for several days, not a spark of fire, the ashes were cold in the fire place, I could not understand why all had left. They had not intimated anything of the kind up to the time I left camp.

Something unusual must have happened. I could not tell what. Here I had expected to find food and rest, both of which I began to feel the need of. A terrible disappointment to me. I sat down on a rock and tried to think what was best for me to do. A heavy mist now began to fall, with a strong cold east air, which soon began to chill me. To make it worse I heard a wolf howl a way down the mountain in the direction I had come, it struck me at once that he was on my trail. Soon I heard an answering howl down in what is called Devil's Hole.

What to do was the question. I could not stay there and defend myself successfully in the dark. If the rock on which I sat had been solid gold I would have given it freely for a box of matches. I thought of climbing a tree and staying there until morning, but the cold drizzly rain which threatened to turn to sleet would have soon chilled me so that I would tumble to the ground. The howling continued, I imagined much closer. There was living at the foot of the mountain, on the south side, a man by the name of Evans. I determined to try and reach his house. I felt round and got hold of a dry chestnut stick about 8 or 10 feet long, to feel my way down the mountain side. The direction I wanted to travel was almost due south. The distance I judged to be about two miles.

I got my course and kept it by feeling of the bark of the trees, against which it seemed to me I ran every few steps. The rough and mossy side always being on the north side. It was easy to know to what point of the compass I was traveling, although the darkness it seemed to me could not have been greater had I been bunged up a barrel. I made but slow progress, having to stop at almost every step to feel my way, being in danger of falling over ledges of rock that stretched along the mountainside. In many places when I could not touch bottom with my stick or pole, I make a flank move until the obstacle had been passed and then resume my course again.

The rain was now falling pretty lively. I had been feeling my way for perhaps an hour, when something started a rock to rolling, it started several others. I thought it must be a bear. There were said to be a good many on the mountain at that time.

I felt around with my stick until I touched a tree, which I got behind as quick as possible, where I stood trembling like a leaf for several moments. My hair kept raising my hat on my head. I imagined I could see something even blacker than the night, which was almost dark enough to be felt. I even imagined I could hear the thing breathe, notwithstand the pattering of the rain on the leaves, I thought I heard it coming toward me. I held my revolver ready cocked, and when I thought the bear was in the act of clamping me, I fired, at the same time gave a yell that no jack could have beat. I stood perfectly still for several minutes but could hear nothing. Can it be possible, thought I, that I killed the thing? I finally commenced feeling around with my stick but could feel, see nor hear anything except the falling rain.

This was certainly a night of horror to me, and one that will never be forgotten while memory lasts. I have read of a person's hair turning white from fright, but I don't believe a word of it. If the fear of falling over a precipice, or being bitten by some poisonous reptile, tore to pieces by wolves, or chewed up by a bear, would not turn a person's hair white, I can't imagine what would. All these evils that I thought was about to overtake me except, the rock ledges, may have been all imagination and no snake, bear or wolf within, five miles of me.

After feeling my way an inch, at as it seemed, I reached an old field grown up with brush and briars. After going a short distance farther I spied a dim light which appeared to be a long distance away and not larger than the light from a candle. I determined to keep my eye on it, feeling sure that it came from some house, or at least some one was near it. I had gotten below the rocks and ledges, the ground now being comparatively smooth.

I crept through the brush, careful not to lose sight of my star of hope. The rain had ceased. A thick fog hung about the mountain top and began reaching down toward the foot of the mountain. Already the light began to grow dim, because of the density of the fog, I was fearful of losing it altogether. I had not gone over 200 yards when to my joy and surprise I come to a shanty built by two large store boxes being turned facing each other, joined together. On one side by a door large enough for a man to crawl through. On the opposite side, built of stone, was a small fire place with chimney, some five or six feet high. It was through the back of this chimney that I had discovered the light.

Approaching without noise I peeped through a crack in the door and to my great satisfaction saw old man Evans sitting on the floor of his shanty, reading his testament by candle light. I gave the door a jar with my foot and said "we have caught you at last, old fellow, been looking for you for some time, crawl out."

"Give me time to put my shoes on," said he in a very shaky voice.

I now pulled the door open, stuck my head in and said don't mind your shoes, if you have room for two I believe I will stay with you until morning.

The old man looked in blank amazement, did not recognize me for a moment, then his countance lit up as though a great weight had been removed.

"Where did you come from?" said he. "I have a great mind to shoot you, you came near scaring me to death, crawl in."

I didn't wait for a second invitation, but crawled in, got Mr. Evans to pull my boots, asked if he had anything to eat. He said that he could give me some bread, butter and coffee. I was thoroughly tired out, while the coffee was being warmed I lay down and was asleep in a moment, and did not wake up until nine o'clock next day. Mr. Evans had been to his house and brought up a fresh supply of commissary stores. I ate a hearty breakfast and then tried to get my boots on but it was no go. My feet were blistered in a half dozen places, I was in bad shape for trampling that day.

Mr. Evans said he would go to the house and get some sheep tallow to grease my feet and bring some soft cotton rags to wrap them with and an old pair of shoes, which he thought I could wear. It was only a short distance to his house, he was soon back again and had my feet done up in tallow and rags in the most approved style. He brought an old pair if shoes about four sizes too large, but they were comfortable. Mr. Evans said he had some matters to attend to and would not be back until evening, that I had better keep quiet and rest up that day, as I would have to go on the mountain next day.

I took his advice and crawled back into the den, stretched out and was soon asleep. When I awoke again the sun was nearly to the tree tops. The sky was now clear, but the air was a little cool. I concluded to try my shoes, they proved to be the very thing I needed, didn't touch anywhere, I got out, gathered some sticks and soon had a cheerful little fire, and had the coffee pot on the coals warming up and was making preparations for supper, when my host made his appearance, bringing a warm supper which I need not say was enjoyed hugely. After I had satisfied the inner man he gathered up the fragments and started to his house, said that he would be back as soon as he had attended to his stock. In the mean time I gathered in some wood and pine knots to make a light, I was feeling pretty stiff and sore, sure, from my tramp of the day and night before.

About dusk Mr. Evans made his appearance. We entered our castle, and closed the door after spreading our bed, which consisted of three blankets and a sack of leaves for a pillow. Mr. Evans insisted that I must let him give my feet another good greasing and roast them well by the fire. To gratify him I submitted. We then lay down, I had to give him a short history of what I had been doing for the last few months. Then he entertained me for an hour or two, telling of the narrow escapes he had of being eaten by a bear and being gored to death by an old buck that he had wounded. Said that deer and bear were right plentiful, and thought no doubt but what it was a bear that I had heard rolling rocks down the mountain the night before, but that the bear was as bad scared as I was and that he had killed a great many but had never seen one show fight unless it had been wounded first. Said my great danger had been in falling over a rock ledge or being bitten by a rattle snake, which the few warm days had brought from their dens along the south side of the mountain, where they were quite numerous.

We talked until near midnight he then gave my feet another oiling, then bound them up and again lying down we were soon asleep. About daylight my host shook me and said he thought I ought to be about square now on sleep, and said that if I was able to walk down to the house, he had told his wife that I would come down for breakfast. I put on the old shoes and we started for the house, which we soon reached found breakfast awaiting us. About 10 o'clock I borrowed a horse of Mr. Evans and started to go on the mountain to meet Mr. Murphy, in case father succeeded in getting a horse to him.

I found the path and followed for some distance down the west side of the mountain until I had a good view of the Lockender place. I hitched my horse and took a seat at the root of a tree, anxiously watching the Lockender house, near which a person in crossing the mountain, by what was known as the Lockender path, would have to pass. After sitting here for several hours, began to feel very despondent and had almost given up all hope of getting a horse. Finally about four o'clock, I discovered a man pass the house I had been watching, leading a horse, which I was sure was Mr. Murphy. I started at once to meet him, which I soon did. I was truly thankful to have a horse once more that I could call my own.

Mr. Murphy said that Miss Sallie Parsons, now Mrs. Sallie Brady, and one of my sisters had brought the horse to his house. Miss Sallie having procured a pass from the Provost Marshall for them to go up to her Uncle David Parsons. They had with them a colored boy who rode the horse intended for me, then rode back behind one of the girls. Mr. Murphy said there was a good many Yankees in Romney, and passing through on their way to re-inforce Gen. Milroy at McDowell.

After thanking Mr. Murphy for his kindness bade him good bye telling him that I had made up my mind to go to the Valley and enlist for the war, which he advised me to do. I reached Mr. Evans' again about dark. After caring for the horse, had supper and then went to our lodging place for the night. Next morning tried to get my boots on but found I could not wear them Mr. Evans made me a present of the shoes. After breakfast I tied my boots to my saddle, bade Mr. Evans and family adieu and started for John Shull's at Shull's Gap, on Lost River, where I arrived about the middle of the day.

Mr. Shull was a brother to James and Thomas Shull, of Shull's Mill, on Mill Creek. It was here I had come near passing over the river with measels but my time had not come. Mr. Shull and family were very glad to see me, and to get a history of my movements since they last saw me. I turned my mare in a lot near the house, around which there was a good plank fence I knew she could jump, but thought a deer could scarcely get over that fence.

Mr. Shull had a small farm a short distance from where he lived, on which was a comfortable little house, in which he had a bed, and slept there at night for fear of being picked up by the Yankees. After dark we went over to his camping place to sleep. We had to cross the river, he rode his horse I left mine in the lot and rode over the river behind him. We soon had a cheerful fire burning in the fire place. After talking of different things until perhaps 10 o'clock we lay down, it was then raining right lively, I was asleep in a few moments. I don't know how long I had been asleep when I was aroused by a dig in the ribs from Mr. Shull's elbow at the same time came a heavy thump on the door.

"Yankees," whispered Mr. Shull.

We lay still scarcely breathing. Soon came another thump on the door.

"Who's there?" said Mr. Shull.

"A friend," came from the outside.

"What is your name," said Mr. Shull.

"Henson, from Wardensville," came from the outside.

"What do you want," asked Shull.

"Let me in and I will tell you."

"Who is with you?" asked Shull.

"No one," came from the outside, "General Blenker and his staff came to Wardensville about dark and I left."

Mr. Shull and I had arisen and dressed ourselves. Mr. Shull unbolted the door, with doubt and trembling. A man stepped in and Mr. Shull closed the door again.

There was only a dim light from some coals in the fire place. Shull struck a match and lit a candle, then recognized the man as one Henson, a saddler and harness maker, living in Wardensville. Henson was pretty well soaked through. We had dry wood in the house and soon had a good fire, and had him hung up to dry.

CHAPTER VII

Guerilla action near Wardensville

He told us why he was there. He said that about sundown Gen. Blinker and his staff arrived in Wardensville and had stopped at the McKeever House. That after dark he took a peep at them through the window. They were playing a game called "bluff," and had loads of gold piled on the table. Said there were 19 in all, including one negro.

"Now," said he, "if we can get together a half dozen good men and get a good position and pitch into them when they come along in the morning, I believe we can kill or capture the whole outfit."

They are on their way to Moorefield to meet the command which had gone by the way of Romney. Shull said he thought he could raise 6 or 7 men in what he called the Hulver Settlement. Shull mounted his horse and started, although the rain was falling in torrents. I went to bed and in a short time Henson turned in also.

I afterward learned that it was General Blinker, which I doubted at the time, who had been with General Banks in the Valley, but had been detached and were in their way to reinforce General Freemont and Milroy at McDowell. General Blinker's Command had passed through Romney on Sunday and Monday the 4th and 5th May. It was his men I came near capturing before day. If that rail had not broke and gave them notice of my coming the whole thing might have been surprised.

About 5 o'clock old man Shull returned with 5 young men whom he had drummed up. They were armed with the home rifles. Henson had a double muzzle loading shot gun. I had no gun except a navy revolver. Mr. Shull had a small bored rifle which he loaned me. We started an hour before day, down the Wardensville pike. After going some distance, perhaps two or three miles, we halted just before reaching one Landaker's saw mill. The place selected from which to make the attack was on the side of a very steep, rugged, rough mountain. Below the pike was a stone wall several feet high. On the upper side the bank was almost perpendicular for several feet which made it difficult for a man to reach us from the pike. On our left was a deep narrow ravine, down which water was rushing at a furious speed. In our rear was the steep mountain side, covered with rocks and small scrubby timber.

The position was a strong one, if held, but very bad one to get away from in case a retreat should become necessary. We took position about 15 yards above the pike, on the side of the mountain, and commenced at once to strengthen it by rolling large rocks together and filling in between them with smaller ones, leaving a hole to fire through, then placing a few brush in front to hide our breast works from view as much as possible. All the while the rain was falling lively. We had placed our arms and ammunition under a ledge some 10 or 15 paces in our rear, where we now sheltered ourselves the best we could from the rain, from our position looking toward Wardensville.

The pike ran nearly in a straight line with cleared land on either side, and with a gradual ascent for several hundred yards until it reached the top of the ascent. To this point we had a good view of the road the whole way.

Towards Moorefield the ascent was more abrupt, yet we could see the pike most of the way for three or four hundred yards. Old Man Shull, or old Keg, as he was called by most of his neighbors, had taken a position some two hundred yards to our right, toward Moorefield, in a pine thicket near the pike.

He commanded the expedition and selected the battle ground. Old Keg was mounted on a little bay racker, that was hard to beat. When he turned to leave us, after having cautioned us to take good aim, no two to fire at the same man, thereby waste our ammunition. One of the boys, called to him and said, "General, if we have to run how are we to get away from here?"

"Run h—l, do you suppose I have been riding in the rain all night to find some one to run? Stay right here and fight like h—l as long as there is any breath in you, if necessary."

It was, I would say, about 9 o'clock a.m., when Old Keg came riding down, swore he did not believe there a Yankee between there and Winchester; said he would ride to the top of the hill in the direction of Wardensville, and if he could see nothing of them, we would wait no longer for them.

The rain continued to fall. We could see Old Keg as he rode toward the top of the hill. When he had nearly reached the summit, we saw him wheel his horse and come back at the top of his speed. Without making any halt dashed past. Said boys they are coming, give them h—l. They were now in full view on the top of the rise. I had been elected commander in chief and had numbered men from right to left and charged them to remember their number. That the Yankees would be in column of twos, that No. 1 would aim at the first two, No. 2 at the 2nd file and so on.

They were directed to take good aim, not higher than the belt, and be ready but wait for the word to fire. These instructions I tried to impress on the men, while we lay under the ledge, waiting patiently, expecting every moment to see the Yankees appear on top of the hill. I was sure that the Dutchman, Henson, would stand fire, but was doubtful about the other five. I had overheard one of them say to another, "I wish I had stayed home."

The reply was, "more of us that way."

As soon as I saw Old Keg turn back I knew they were coming, and said now boys get your places, hold your hats over the locks of your guns and keep them dry. Remember your numbers and aim as directed. Henson and I crept to our places. The Yankees coming on at rather a slow pace. I was trying to count them as they came down the grade toward us, when Henson exclaimed, "look at them d—m cowards, gone and left us."

I looked around and sure enough there they went, a hundred yards up the mountain like a lot of turkeys.

I said Henson what will we do? If we would get away from here we must go at once, if we stay and fire on these fellows, there are ten to one, and ten to one we will never get away alive.

Henson said, "I am not afraid to die, and am determined to empty my gun among them once before I go away from here.

His face was almost white as a sheet. I will never forget his looks.

He said, "if you, too, are a coward, go. I will stay alone."

I said, "no, I will stay as long as you, but it looks like a very foolish thing to do.

The Yankees were now within fifty yards of us. First came 8 cavalry in front, then an ambulance followed by a two horse buggy, with a colored driver and the General. In the rear was 6 or 8 cavalry.

There was a stream of water running across the road some ten or fifteen feet wide, and in our immediate front. The cavalry in front halted to water their horses, when Henson yelled, "give it to them boys," and fired one barrel after the other in quick succession. I fired a second later, dropped back so as not to be exposed to the fire of the Yankees and loaded, then arose to my knees, and peeped through my port hole, and to my surprise was the ambulance had been turned around and two apparently dead Yankees were being shoveled in the hind end by five or six dismounted men. The buggy had turned and was 200 yards or more away going at break neck speed, with 4 or 5 cavalry close in the rear. The remainder were around the ambulance jabbering worse than a lot of geese. I could not understand one word they said. They all seemed to be Dutch.

It occurred to me now that there was no fight in that crowd and the best thing to do would be to kill one of the horses harnessed to the ambulance and in this way capture their baggage. I accordingly took careful aim at the head of the nearest horse, the cap burst but the rifle failed to fire. I tired a second and a third time with the same result, the powder had got damp and refused to burn.

Henson was having the same luck, bursting caps and cursing, but it was no go. Wet powder is not dangerous. I had forgotten my revolver when I took my place behind our breast works. After firing I was afraid to expose myself, which I would have had to do to get it. As soon as the

89

dead or wounded men had been placed in the ambulance, all hands left on double quick, and were soon out of reach on top of the rise several hundred yards away, where they had halted and seemed to be holding a council of war.

Henson and I were, in the meantime, trying to get dry powder in the tube. The rain had about ceased. We were keeping an eye on the Yankees, saw one of them turn his horse to us, take his gum coat off and lay it across the saddle front, tighten the strap of his cap under his chin, then drew his revolver from its scabbard and seemed to be re-capping it.

Henson said that darned Yank is going to try to run past and get to Moorefield. Just then he started. I ran back and got my revolver and hurried down and stood on the bank within fifteen feet of him when he passed. His horse was coming at full speed, when about 20 paces distant he raised his revolver and fired. I fired almost at the same instant. When opposite I stood, fired again, he threw his head back at the same time fired in the air. I thought for a moment that he would fall from his horse. I pulled the trigger the third time, but the cap failed to explode. He had now passed and straightening himself turned in his saddle and fired again. I returned the fire and saw his field glass fall to the ground. I gave him the fourth round when about forty or fifty yards away, but failed to bring him down.

When the Yankees went back Old Keg had started and ridden down to within a hundred or a hundred and fifty yards of our position. When he saw the Yankee coming, he pulled out in the bushes, but when he saw the Yankee had passed us he wheeled into the road about 50 or 75 yards in front of the Yankee and let Dock go. His coat tail stuck straight behind. We could see that he was widening the gap when he passed from sight over the hill. The other Yanks had gone from sight the other way. I now went down into the pike and picked up the field glass and gum coat, which the Yankee had dropped. On examination I found the strap which crossed his shoulder and carried his glass had been cut into by a pistol ball. The battle over, the victory won.

Henson started through the mountains for Wardensville, and I started back to Shull's Gap. On the way I had to pass a small house, occupied by an old lady. I think her name was Wetzel but I am not sure.

She said that a Dutchman, who said he was a doctor, had stopped there an hour before and asked for some rags to bind up a wound in his arm and a ugly cut in his face; also a slight wound on one shoulder.

The old lady said when she asked how he got hurt, he said he "got shooted by one tam sesash; he shoot from the bush."

When I reached Shull's house I found that my mare had jumped out and gone. I got a bite to eat and started after my mare. I knew she would try to find her way home, but hoped some one would hold her up before

90

she had gotten very far. She had evidently gotten out late in the night. Her track being plainly visible many places where the ground was soft. I followed on until I reached Kirby, but could hear nothing of her.

After passing Kirby the tracks seemed to take the first right hand road. After going a mile or so, some one had drove a bunch of cattle in the direction which the track lead. I could track her no further, but continued on until I reached Mr. Benj. Pugh's house, it was near sun down. Mr. Pugh had just unhitched his team from the plow and was starting to the barn. I asked to stay over night.

After caring for his horses, we went to the house. I was hungry and tired. We were soon invited to a bountiful supper. I rather expect the family thought that I was hollow to the knees before I let up eating.

This appeared to me to be most entertaining place that I had yet struck. I remained at Mr. Pugh's over next day. On the morning of the second day, having abandoned all hope of getting my mare, I once more turned my face toward the Sunny South very much discouraged at the prospect of having to foot it all the way to Harrisonburg, where Gen. Jackson was encamped, the last time I had heard of his whereabouts. But there seemed to be no help for it; I had no money for which to purchase another horse, and was, with a few exceptions, among comparative strangers.

I was walking along near the mouth of Grassy Lick Run, meditating on what I thought was right bad luck, not dreaming of any danger, I thought I heard some one talking; on raising my head I discovered that the North River pike was packed with blue coats. They had crossed North River and were standing in the road.

I think they saw me first. Somehow or the other my legs had got so timid, that at the sight of a Yankee, I lost all control of them.

They about faced and started to the rear, with me at the top of their speed, without giving me time to take any notes. A moment later and a shower of balls rattled around, mostly overhead. My running gear, which I thought already was doing its best, just seemed to sail through the brush and kept sailing until the top of Short Mountain. I suppose the Yankees thought it useless to follow after a streak of lightning, at least I saw them no more.

I reached Mr. Benj. Fry's house about dark. Here I learned that the Yankees had been at Wardensville looking after the bushwackers, who had caused Gen. Blinker to fall back two days before. The Yankee who had run the gauntlet that morning had reported to Col. Downey, who was then stationed at Moorefield.

The Colonel had come down the Wardensville pike and reached that village. Next day notice of their approach not having been received, their visit was a surprise.

Henson, my pardner, of the bushwacking expedition, lived in

Wardensville, was, I think, a saddler by trade, and was at work in his shop, when he discovered the Yankees, he attempted to reach the woods, but was fired on and killed. No braver man ever lived. I was shocked when I heard of his death, and thought how near I had come to sharing his fate from the same party, who had crossed the mountain from Wardensville and struck the North River pike at Rio, and were on their way back to Moorefield when I surprised them or rather they surprised me, at the mouth of Grassy Lick run.

I learned also from Mr. Fry that they were at the house of John T. Wilson, who lived a short distance above Rio, that morning four young men who did not discover the approach of the Yankees until they were near the house. The young men ran out the back way and attempted to reach the woods a distance of something like a hundred yards.

The Yankees discovered them and fired on them as they ran across a narrow meadow. A man by the name of Humbaugh was killed, John W. Poland was mortally wounded and died next day, another Poland, if my memory is not at fault, was wounded. Zack Wilson escaped being struck, but was overtaken by the cavalry and captured. A short distance further up the river they came on some boys fishing. When the boys saw them coming, the little fellows dropped their poles and ran for life, although they were nothing but children. Col. Downey and his famous 3rd Maryland regiment, fired on them. Two of the three fell seriously wounded, the third slightly. James Earl, of Romney, was one of the boys. He has never fully recovered from the scare, and if questioned about the matter, says some very ugly things about the Yankees.

I slept in Mr. Fry's barn that night. Before I closed my eyes that night, I came to the conclusion that it was getting a little unhealthy in that neighborhood and that possibly I might take my last sickness on very short notice, and for fear that such might be the case. I determined to start next morning for Harrisonburg, by the way of Brock's gap. The thought of making the trip on foot was not a pleasant one but there seemed to be no help for it. I was up early next morning and informed Mr. Fry of my intentions.

After breakfast Mr. Henry Fry, who lived with his brother, said "I have, I think, the best horse on North River. Only the fear of losing him, makes me willing to part with him at any price. I will sell him. You may have horse, saddle and bridle, for $200."

I said, "you had as well said $2000, for I have not one cent."

"Give me your note for two hundred dollars and the horse is yours," said he.

I said to him, as near as I can remember, "Mr. Fry, I am a stranger to you, you never saw me until last evening, and when I leave here this morning the chances are that you will never see me again, as the life of a soldier is very uncertain."

He said, "I know your father and have heard of you. If you are willing to risk your life in this cause I am willing to risk getting pay for my horse. Give me your note and the horse is yours."

He drew a note, I signed it. We then went to the stable and saddled up a neat, smooth, roan of fine size, five years old, of good blood and by far the best cavalry horse, it was my good fortune to mount during the war. He would clear a six rail fence, it seemed, without an effort. After many thanks to Mr. Benj. Fry and good wife for their hospitable entertainment and to Mr. Henry for the greatest favor possible to confer at that time, I started, intending to stop at John Shull's house that night.

I reached Mr. Shull's house early in the day, found Mr. Shull at home, also a Mr. Baker, who had just returned from the Valley. He reported Jackson having fallen back to Staunton, and Banks following him. I was now at a loss of what course to pursue, I didn't know of any way to get to Staunton except through Brock's gap. With Yankees at Harrisonburg, I hardly thought that route a safe one. I finally concluded to lay low for a few days and await further developments. I remained with Mr. Shull for several days, spent most of time fishing. During this time, we could get no reliable news from the Valley.

We had rumors of a fight at McDowell and again at Franklin, between Gen. Edward Johnson and Gen. Milroy, but these reports had not been confirmed. We had reports that Jackson had been reinforced by Gen. Ewell's division and had gone to reinforce Gen. Ed. Johnson at McDowell, who was in danger of annihilation by the combined forces of Milroy, Freemont, Blinker and Schenck. In short, we could hear all sorts of news, but nothing certain.

I determined to investigate a little on my own hook. Not being able to get any one to accompany me, I started to go alone, I knew not where. This was Wednesday, May 22, 1862. That night I stopped with Mr. Joseph Inskeep on Lost River. The next morning I started again and in the after part of the day, near where a man called Fishwaters, kept sort of a public house, well down in Brock's gap, on the north fork of the Shenandoah. I was agreeably surprised to meet Capt. Geo. Stump, Vause McNary, Herman Seniff and two or three other Hampshire boys.

They were on their way to Hampshire and Hardy counties for the purpose of blockading the roads leading from Pendleton county to Winchester and Strasburg.

Once more with old friends I felt at home again and turned back with them. As we rode along Capt. Stump gave me a short history of Gen. Jackson's movements of the last month, of which I knew but little, most of the time having been taken up with in contending with Col. Downey for the possession of Hampshire county. It was with great reluctance that

I had made up my mind to surrender my native county to the Yankees, more I will admit, because of feminine attractions than from a military necessity.

Capt. Stump said that General Jackson moved his command from Rude's Hill about 15th of April and went into camp at Swift Run Gap in the Blue Ridge. Gen. Banks had followed and halted his command in the neighborhood of Harrisonburg.

On or about the 1st of May Gen. Jackson left his tents standing and following the western base of the Blue Ridge until he reached Brown's Gap, then crossed over into Ablemarl county, then followed the Virginia Central Railroad to Staunton. The same day that General Jackson moved from Swift Run Gap, Gen. Ewell with his division crossed from the east side of the Blue Ridge through Swift Run Gap and camped on the same ground that Jackson had left only a few hours before. Gen. Banks being ignorant of the change, supposed it was the terrible Stonewall Jackson that he was still watching; at the same time Gen. Jackson was pressing forward with all the energy he could command, in order to reach Gen. Edward Johnson and thus with the combined force, strike Milroy a stunning blow at McDowell before re-inforcement could reach him. The blow had been struck and Gen. Milroy, who had been joined by Gen. Schenck's command, had retreated toward Franklin and no doubt had joined Gen. Fremont, who, it had been learned was hastening to their assistance.

Gen. Jackson had turned back and was then at Harrisonburg. As soon as Gen. Banks missed Gen. Jackson and found Gen. Ewell in his front, he became alarmed for fear that Jackson might get in his rear and fell back to Strasburg on quick time. But when he heard that Jackson had gone to reinforce Gen. Johnson at McDowell, he hurried Gen. Blinker, by the way of Romney, with 10,000 men to re-inforce Milroy and Fremont, but the assistance came too late. General Jackson had left them and was now after Banks.

Capt. Stump and his party had been sent out to obstruct the roads so as to keep Gen. Fremont from reaching Gen. Banks until Gen. Jackson had got through with him. Capt. Stump thought that General Fremont would either attempt to reach Winchester by way of Romney in time to re-inforce Gen. Banks, or endeavor to get in Jackson's rear at Strasburg, by way of Wardensville.

We stopped that night in Brock's Gap, near Fishwater's with an old gentleman. I think, by the name of Havener. Next day crossed the mountain, or to South Fork and stopped at Mr. James Stump's, a brother of the captain. Capt. Stump thought of crossing the mountain and striking the road above Petersburg. But Mr. James Stump thought this would be a risky business on account of bushwackers, which he said were quite plentiful, and were not very particular who they bushwacked. There would also be a possibility of our being in the rear instead of the front of the Yankees, who, for all we knew, had already reached Petersburg and might be at Moorefield, to which place the Captain finally determined to go provided there was nothing in the way to prevent our doing so.

We left Mr. Stump's with about three days rations for both man and beast. When within two or three miles of Moorefield we met a boy some 12 or 14 years of age, who said that a company of cavalry, dressed in blue, had come to Moorefield the night before. We left the road and took to the woods and reached the Wardensville pike below Moorefield that evening. It had now commenced to rain. Captain Stump and I rode toward Moorefield for the purpose of reconnoitering a little while the remainder of our party under the supervision of McNary prepared a shelter for us during the night in a deep hollow a short distance from the road. Capt. Stump and I rode up near town, but made no discoveries. It now began to get dark and we returned to camp, where the boys had constructed a shelter by peeling the bark from a large oak tree and using it for roofing then built a logheap in front of our shelter, then gathered a pile of leaves under our roof and by frequent stirring soon had them dry, then by placing pine brush on the ground and covering them with leaves and spreading our saddle blankets over the leaves, we had a comfortable bed, using our saddles for pillows. We then ate a bite, after having first fed and secured our horses for the night. The Capt. thought we ought to keep a picket on the road to see if any one passed in the night. Said he would take the first turn and started. It was now near 10 o'clock. We laid down.

The boys had two gum blankets which we spread over our other blankets. The boys had all gotten the start and kept me awake with their continuous snoaring, each seemed to be trying to out do the other. It was now raining heavy, our roof began to leak; I thought surely these drips will soon stop this snoaring, but no, when a leak struck one of them in the face, he would draw himself down under cover and in a moment or two was at it again with renewed vigor.

In about an hour Capt. Stump came back, swore there was no use of a man staying out in this rain when it was so dark a man could not see and could not hear for the rain. The captain pulled off his coat, laid down, spread it over himself and said he felt like taking a nap. The rain had put our fire. The captain had been very quiet for perhaps a half hour, when he sat up and said with an oath, "how can you sleep with all this commotion?"

I said that "I had not been asleep yet."

We then talked the situation over and tried to arrive at some conclusion as to the best course to pursue under the circumstances in which we then found ourselves.

Capt. Stump thought that if the rain continued to fall, as it was then doing, the South Branch would not be fordable next day, and there would be no bridge either below Moorefield or at the crossing near Romney, it would, in all probability, be several days before the river was fordable. Gen. Fremont thus being delayed, could not possibly reach Winchester in time to aid Gen. Banks. Then there would be no necessity for blockading the road leading from Moorefield to Winchester by the way of Romney. From Moorefield they would almost to a certainty follow the Wardensville grade and endeavor to reach the Valley at Strasburg, in the rear of Gen. Jackson.

Capt. Stump thought that there would be no question of doubt that Gen. Jackson would destroy Gen. Bank's army or force him to cross the Potomac he left him, and felt sure that he was at that moment below Strasburg and might be below Winchester. He declared in the most emphatic language that Fremont must not reach Strasburg in the rear of Gen. Jackson, if he did, Jackson would be in a trap, from which he could not escape. Said if this rain continues for twenty four hours the waters will not be fordable for several days, and all we will have to do will be to destroy the bridge across Lost river, then Gen. Fremont will have to halt until the streams are fordable. But in case the rain should not fall in sufficient quantities to raise the water, then we must get every man and boy in reach, who are able to handle an ax or roll a rock, to join us because, as the captain thought, to hold Fremont for a day or two was to rescue Jackson's army from certain destruction.

Said he, if Gen. Fremont reached Moorefield last evening which I feel certain he did, or should have done, we will find out early tomorrow morning, and as soon as we learn the route he is following, a carrier must go to Jackson at once and inform him of his danger.

Capt. Stump argued that Jackson's situation was, to say the least, very critical. With Gen. Banks in the front and Fremont in the rear, his supplies of every kind would be cut off. He could not retreat across the Blue Ridge, since there at Manassas, an army equal, if not superior in number to that of his own, and another under Gen. McDowell at Fredericksburg. The only thing for us to do was to try and keep Fremont from reaching Strasburg before Gen. Jackson got back to that point, in case he was below that place.

Capt. Stump thought that we had better remain where we were until we could learn something definite as to the movements of the Yankees, that he and I would go up on the mountain early in the morning where we could see the road in many places, both above and below the town. Capt. Stump was a man of more than ordinary intelligence and but seldom erred in his judgement, brave to a fault, but cautious at all times. I knew him well, had been with him on more than one scout, was always ready to submit to his judgement and follow his lead at any time.

After talking in a low tone for an hour or two, we concluded to try again to get a little sleep, which we finally succeeded in doing. About day light we arose, fed our horses and ate a bite, then the captain told the others to stay where they were for at least two hours and if they heard nothing from us in that time, to go to the nearest house and see if they could get a bundle of hay each for our horses.

We started up the mountain, but had not gone a mile when we discovered a number of tents, both above and below town. We also discovered, by the aid of the glass which I had captured on the Blinker raid, that the South Branch below town could not be forded. After watching them for perhaps a half hour, we discovered that they were striking their tents. This satisfied the captain that their objective point was Strasburg. Soon we saw them take the Wardensville grade, we waited to see no more but hastened back to our camp.

The captain said that McNary and I should get a position near junction of the Wardensville and North River turnpikes. It might be possible that they would attempt to reach Winchester by following the North River turnpike to Blue's Gap on the northwestern grade; while he and the other three men would proceed to Shull's Gap on Lost River and with what additional help he could gather, would endeavor to make the road as near impassible as possible from there to the Lost River bridge.

As soon as McNary and I had learned to a certainty which route the Yankees would take, the North River or the Wardensville; then McNary should start at once to find General Jackson and report, without delay, that the bridge across Lost River would not be fired until it was actually necessary, and that he had better follow the Wardensville grade until he reached the Valley and learned the whereabouts of Gen. Jackson.

McNary and I selected a position within the angle of the two roads, from which we had a good view of either. We had not waited long until the advance of Gen. Fremont's army came in sights and followed the Wardensville grade. The question was settled as to his intended route. McNary mounted and started to find Gen. Jackson. I remained where I was until about four o'clock in the evening.

The Yankees had been passing all day, but had halted and were preparing to camp at the junction of the two roads. I left my place of concealment and started to find rations for myself and horse, also a safe place to camp for the night. It had rained steadily all day long. Captain Stump had requested me to remain in the neighborhood and meet him at Biggie's Shanty in the Big Mountain on Tuesday, May 28th, it then being the 26th . Not knowing when he would have another opportunity, he wished to visit his farm before going to the Valley again. He then owned the Kuykendall property near the Glebe.

Shortly after dark I found myself at Mr. Reason Haines' house, now Mr. Abner Poland's. I stopped with Mr. Haines that night and next morning started for Biggie's Shanty, carrying with me commissary and quartermaster stores, sufficient to last a week in case of emergency, consisting of about 10 pounds of side meat, one and a half large sized loaves of bread baked in a large dutch oven and about one bushel of oats. I reached the Shanty before the middle of the day. Can't say that I found it in apple pie order. However I proceeded to make myself as comfortable as possible under the circumstances.

After unloading my provisions and hanging them on a nail to a joist, I then laid up the fence around the lot and turned my horse loose to fill himself on grass, which was abundant. Then building a fire fired some bacon by holding it over the fire on the end of a stick and soon had dinner; this over, saddled my horse and started up along the mountain top to see if there were any Yankees in view or not. After going several miles I discovered a number of tents and a good many wagons at the same place where I had left them the evening before. I could see them very plain by aid of my glass.

There did not appear to be more than one regiment. From appearance there must have been from three to five hundred head of cattle scattered around in every direction. I was satisfied that their march had been delayed by obstructions of some kind. I went back to the Shanty, turned my horse in the lot to graze, kindled up a fire and prepared supper in the same manner as I had dinner.

My mind was exercised more in regard to sleeping than anything else. The house was very open. Snakes could crawl in without any trouble. I soon determined on a plan which was to get some hickory bark and pass it around the joist at four different points, then tie each of the four corners of my blanket so that I would swing about three or four feet from the floor. I then tied my horse for fear he might leave me before morning, then climbed into my hammack, wrapped my gum coat about me and was asleep in a few moments and slept the night through without awakening until daylight next morning.

After feeding my horse and eating breakfast, I wrote on the door with a piece of charcoal, where I could be found in case Captain Stump came in my absence. Then started to see what had become of the Yankees. Found them in the same place. I watched them all day or until the latter part of the day. Their cattle seemed to be very much scattered, which they now appeared to get together. I had heard cattle on the mountain side below me a short time before and concluded to go down and see if I could assist in gathering them in. I led my horse some distance along the mountain and hitched him in a bunch of low pines, where he could not be seen at any great distance. I then went down in the direction I had heard the cattle.

After going in the direction of the camp for several hundred yards, I came on a bunch of ten head busily browsing. After satisfying myself that no one was near, quietly moved them along and toward the top of the mountain, passing near where my horse was tied, which I secured and then drove my captured herd along toward the Shanty until dark came on, when I left them and went to the Shanty. Soon had a fire started, then gave my horse a bit of oats, concluded not to tie him, believing that he would not leave me, and after roasting a slice or two of bacon on the coals, ate a bite and went to bed, slept sound until about daybreak.

On awakening my first thought was of my horse, I found him all right. Although it was now the 29th of May, the nights were chilly. I gathered some dry wood and prepared to make a fire, but to my regret found that the last spark of fire had disappeared, although I had as I thought, covered it secure. I had no more matches and had to be satisfied with a cold breakfast consisting of a slice of raw bacon and dry bread, followed by a hearty drink of pure water, from a drain near by. A slice of side meat streaked with lean is not bad eating, though raw, if the appetite suits the occasion, which it often did during the sixties.

I now noticed writing on the door that I had not put there, which read, "I will be here tomorrow morning early, meet me."   "S."

I knew that Capt. Stump had been there the day before and had gone to his farm. Although anxious to look after my recent capture, I concluded to await his coming. In about an hour he made his appearance, bringing with him an additional supply of provisions.

I told him of my capture the day before. He was a good deal tickled. Said if the Yankees stayed here much longer I would steal their General next. We started at once to look after the cattle and to see if the Yankees were still visible. As we rode along he gave me a history of what had done toward delaying the Yankees by cutting timber and making the road impassable in every way, but the most effectual check was the rise in Lost River and the burning of the bridge across that stream by which they were detained for nearly two whole days. We found the cattle on top of the mountain near where I had left them the evening before, and drove them down to the Shanty, then went to see what had become of the Yankees, but they had disappeared.

We rode down to where they had been camped; nothing remained except a few cracker boxes and barrels. We learned from Mr. Peter Bean that the Yankees had left early that morning. On our return to the Shanty we met Mr. William Fellow who had captured 20 head of cattle from the Yankees and drove them over the mountain.

It was now getting late in the day. Capt. Stump promised to meet him next day and try to buy the cattle, which he did paying him $50.00 per head. I agreed to put my 10 in at the same price, and pay for five head of his and divide the profit, if we succeeded in getting them to market. We kept them together for two or three days. On the 1st day of June I started and drove them by a back way through the mountains until we reached a Mr. Wilkins, on what was then called Wilkin's Run. Mr. Wilkins had plenty of good grass, we kept the cattle here for two days waiting to hear from the Valley, but could get nothing definite, although it was reported that Jackson and Fremont had a battle at Strasburg and that Fremont had been worsted and then at Winchester.

On the morning of the third day we started to drive to Harrisonburg by way of Brock's Gap. On reaching a kind of public stopping place well down the gap, kept by a man by the name of Fishwaters. This route, to us for the present, must be abandoned. It now began to look very much as though in our cattle deal would draw a blank and possibly Gen. Fremont get his own again. We were really at a loss to know what to do with our stock. Mr. Fishwaters advised us to drive them back several miles to a large cave at the base of Shenandoah Mountain where a man by the name of Whitacre had a fine grazing farm and leave them until we could get them away; this we finally concluded to do.

After disposing of our cattle, we remained in the neighborhood for a day or two, then ventured farther down toward the mouth of the gap. On learning beyond doubt that the Yankees were in the neighborhood of Harrisonburg, we left the main road and followed up a stream called Dry River with the intention of trying to reach Staunton. This was Sunday June 8th. We heard cannonading during the day, that night we camped in the woods without food for ourselves or horses. '

Next day we reached the top of the Shenandoah Mountain about the middle of the day and stopped at the house of a man by the name of Fouk, who had a small farm. We got some corn for our horses and a good square meal for ourselves, consisting of corn bread, bear meat, potatoes, butter and milk. Not having eaten anything for 24 hours, we had appetites ready to devour almost anything that was digestible. We had heard the roar of the artillery all morning, in the direction of Cross Keys. The old man we had stopped with said there must be a lot of rain over that way, he had heard it thundering for two or three days, in that direction. Several times as we ascended the mountain, we had halted and listened to the roar of artillery away in the direction of Brown's Gap at the western base of the Blue Ridge mountain. It was the battle of Cross Keys to which we had been listening.

Brig. Gen. R.H. Milroy
(POTOMAC EDISON'S VALLEY ECHO)

Maj. Gen. John C. Fremont
(POTOMAC EDISON'S VALLEY ECHO)

Gen. Louis Blenker
(NATIONAL ARCHIVES)

CHAPTER VIII

Blue Officially Joins

H ere seemed to me the highest point I had ever reached on this planet. We seemed to be above everything in reach of natural vision. Mr. Fouk, was if I remember right, about fifty years of age. Said his father had built the log cabin which stood at the end of the house in which he then lived, seventy five years and had stood in the cabin door and killed both bear and deer, of which he said there were still a good many within a few miles. That he and his son killed about 25 to 40 deer and several bear every year. Had killed several panthers, but they didn't often see one nowadays.

Here I saw more deer horns than I ever saw in all my life before or since. The sides and ends of the house were completely covered from the roof to the ground with horns until there was no room for more. Some of them were of immense size. After inquiries as to the route we must follow to reach Staunton, it now being well on in the afternoon, we concluded to accept our kind host's invitation and stay over night, which was the windiest I ever experienced. I thought sure the house would be blown down before morning.

Next morning Mr. Fouk said he would go with us a few miles as we would have to follow a path until we reached an old wagon road leading to a large grazing farm on top of the mountain, owned by a Col. Hopkins. He shouldered his rifle and started, the captain and I followed, Indian file. After going five or six miles, we came to the old road spoken of. Here, after directing us how to proceed and wishing us all the good luck possible, our kind host bade us good bye and turned back never to meet again on earth.

We traveled on as we thought some ten or twelve miles and about the middle of the day reached Col. Hopkins' farm and found, perhaps 150 or 200 persons camped on the premises, consisting of old men, women and children, who had left their homes in and around Harrisonburg on the approach of General Fremont's command, taking with them their teams loaded with rations and what valuables they could carry, driving their stock in front of them. We halted here and got something for ourselves and horses to eat. Here we learned something of General Jackson's movements during the last twenty days or since Capt. Stump left him between Harrisonburg and New Market. Since that time Gen. Banks had been driven from the Valley.

Gen. Fremont and Gen. Shields had attempted to unite their forces in Jackson's rear at Strasburg, but had failed, although Gen. Jackson had several thousand prisoners and a captured wagon train, near twenty miles long. He succeeded in passing Strasburg before Fremont, who was advancing toward the South Branch Valley or Shields from the Rappahannock could reach that point.

Since the 1st June, Jackson had been falling back slowly and on the 6th had passed Harrisonburg and gone toward Port Republic, with Fremont only a few miles in his rear. Since then they had heard the roar of the artillery every day until that day, but could hear nothing of the result. But said they had sent out "runners," as they called them, early that morning and was momentarily expecting news, either good or bad, and advised us to stay with them until we heard what the result of the engagement, which had evidently been going on for the last three days. We accepted an invitation to remain, at least, until next morning.

Some of the best people of the Valley were camped here and had plenty of rations for both man and beast. About 10 o'clock that night we were awakened from a sound sleep by loud hurrahing in the camp. We were on our feet in an instant believing that the camp had been attacked by the Yankees. We soon learned the cause of the commotion. News had just reached camp that Jackson had again been victorious, and that Fremont and Shields had been defeated and were now hastily retreating down the Valley. The rejoicing in the Hopkins' camp was so great that no more sleep could be had that night.

Tents were struck and preparations were being made for an early departure for their homes next morning. After an early breakfast the procession started, Capt. Stump and I joined the happy crowd. On reaching the Valley they began to scatter, going to their respective homes.

Capt. Stump and I found Gen. Ashby's cavalry brigade camped in a grove near Harrisonburg, but the gallant Ashby was no longer with them. Their trusted leader had fallen on the 6th of June 1862, near the spot on which his command was now camped. No more would his battle cry be heard leading them in charge and to victory. Here, too, we heard for the first time, the fall of one of our Hampshire's most gallant sons, Heriot Sheetz, who liked his famed leader, fell shot through the heart with his face to the heavens and his feet to the foe, while leading his men at Buckton Station on 23rd day of May 1862.

Here I also learned with regret of the serious, if not fatal, wounding of William Inskeep, brother of J. F. Inskeep, and of Mrs. J. T. Vance. He was then lying in the Hospital at Staunton. He had volunteered in Capt. Sheetz's company and was wounded in the battle of McDowell on May 8th 1862.

I was real glad to be with my old comrades and acquaintances once more. Capt. Sheetz's company, now commanded by Lieut. Baker, were nearly all Hardy and Hampshire county men. Capt. Harness' company were mostly from Hardy county. Capt. McDonald's company was made up principally of the Hampshire militia and of that wandering tribe known as the "Huckleberry Rangers."

These three companies belonged to Gen. Ashby's old brigade, now commanded by Gen. B. H. Robinson, and was composed of the 2nd, 6th, 7th, and 12th regiments and the 17th battalion, composed of two companies that of Capt. Harness' and McDonald's. Capt. Harness being the senior captain, commanded the battalion. General Jackson's infantry was camped at or near Brown's Gap. General Fremont with his command were reported in the vicinity of Strasburg.

The next morning Capt. Stump and I started to bring our cattle into camp. We found them all right and on the evening of the fourth day landed them at camp and sold them to Major Richardson, quartermaster, at one hundred dollars per head and that we had made a very fair profit.

I now had made up my mind to volunteer for the war or while life lasted, and on the 17th day of June 1862 wrote my name on the roll of Company D, 17th battalion, Confederate State cavalry, on the same day Gen. Jackson started with his division to take part in the seven days fight around Richmond. Gen. Robertson remained with the cavalry in the neighborhood of Harrisonburg, keeping all the roads well guarded, to keep the Yankees from getting news of Gen. Jackson's movements. We didn't know he had gone for several days.

Gen. Robertson remained near Harrisonburg, picketing on the different roads leading in the direction of Strasburg, drilling every day, when in camp. Gen. Robertson was a very strict disciplinarian and was not well liked by his men. About the 25th of June, Capt. Harness received reliable information from Moorefield, that some three or four hundred Yankees were camped at the ford below and on the opposite side of the river from Moorefield. Also that several hundred were camped near Petersburg. Capt. Harness asked permission to take his own, Capt. McDonald's and Capt. Sheetz's old company, now Co. F of 7th Virginia Reg., commanded by Lieut. Baker, and go over to the South Branch Valley and try to capture the Yankees near Moorefield. We started and on Saturday evening June 28th the vicinity of Moorefield and that night the captain gathered needed information as to the exact position of the Yankees, the location of their pickets &c., then the officers of the command held a council of war and determined on a plan of attack early next morning.

On Sunday morning June 29th before day the command was on the march, crossing forks of the South Branch some distance above the town and by a circituous route reached the Yankees' camp by day light and formed a line of battle at the edge of a large pasture field in a heavy piece of timber, while the line was extensive and visible in places it was impossible to estimate the number of Rebs from the camp, although only a level open field lay between.

The Confederates were out numbered more than two to one. The Moorefield Valley that morning was shrouded in dense fog a man could scarcely be seen fifty yards distant. Sargent Amos Roberson, of Captain McDonald's company, and four or five men had been left behind with orders to capture the picket at the toll gate below town on the east side of the river.

The Yankee's camp was situated on the east side of the river. I was with Sargent Roberson's squad. We reached the picket post about day light. I had been selected to advance, when we were halted by the picket, the others to follow with drawn revolvers concealed as much as possible. We rode on at a walk laughing and talking unconcerned, though we knew we were near friends, when with in fifty yards of the toll house we discovered a small fire by the side of the road and a single Yankee standing over it. When 30 or 40 yards from him he halted us with the usual challenge, "who comes there?"

I replied, "Jessey scouts," advance one and give the countersign, come next. I said as I rode forward, we have no countersign, we are just from Petersburg with dispatches and important—At that I was now along side of him, three others had come out of the house and were standing on the porch. I noticed their muskets sitting in the corner of the fence. I had my revolver struck under my arm. I whipped it out and stuck it in his face at the same time ordered him to drop his musket, said that we were Rebels and a thousand at that. The other boys had come up, the Yankees on the porch had gone into the house.

We took their muskets and ordered those inside to come out which they did very reluctantly. We then took their ammunition from them and pitched their muskets over in the field. They seemed at first to be a good deal cut down, but they soon brightened up when we told them that they were lucky in being on picket, that their camp was surrounded by a whole cavalry brigade and unless they surrendered would be cut to pieces in a very short time. This news seemed to reconcile them to their fate when they become more cheerful and quite talkative.

We were ordered to remain at the toll gate until we saw what result would be on the other side of the river. After the fog had scattered, about 8 or 9 o'clock we saw a horseman riding rapidly across with a white hankerchief on a stick, toward the Yankee camp. This flag demanding an unconditional surrender, if I remember right was carried by Jim Cunningham, of Captain Sheetz's old company. There were two or three Cunninghams of the same name; the one I have reference to was called "Devil Jim" by his comrades, although I don't suppose he was really any relation to the old gentleman of that name.

Be that as it may, we watched the proceedings with hope and fear, hoping they would surrender and fearful that they would not, we had rode down toward the ford and made ourselves as conspicuous as possible and exhibited the captured picket by having them to sit on top of a high fence in full view of their camp giving their comrades to understand that there was danger, too, from that direction.

A horseman approaching in so bold a manner bearing a flag that could mean to them only one thing and coming from a direction in which, they had not anticipated danger, was, no doubt a surprise. It seemed to stir them up about the same as throwing a stone through a hornet's nest, minus the fight. In a few moments we saw the bearer of the white flag turn back, but after having gone a short distance checked his horse, faced about and rode back again, in perhaps ten minutes time he was seen riding toward the Confederate line of battle again, it would be more appropriate to say time of bluff, for that was all there was in it. If those Yankees had shown fight and taken a position behind the high river bank they would have seen no more of the Johnnies at that time, at least. But Cunningham, perhaps had not been very conscientious in representing numbers.

They no doubt were lead to believe that they were face to face with ten times their numbers. Be that as it may, we soon had the satisfaction of seeing the Yankees fall in line and march out perhaps 150 paces, stack their arms, break ranks and rush back to their tents. In a short time a line of Confederate cavalry came from the timber and advanced toward the Yankee camp, placed themselves between the stacked arms and the camp. When we saw the Confederates emerge from the woods we rode on to and across the ford. As I rode out of the river, I was met by a Yankee lieutenant, who held in his open hand a pocket knife which I recognized as one taken from me when searched the morning I was captured at Romney.

He said, "do you recognize this knife?"

I said, "yes and you too."

It was Lieutenant Cole, the man who had discovered my hiding place in the garret loft of father's house the morning of my capture. He said things seem to have changed since we last met, the boot seems to be on the other foot now.

After hearty hand shake he said, "where did you Johnnies come from anyhow?"

"Oh," said I, "we just dropped down."

The lieutenant seemed glad to see me. He was an Englishman and a gentleman.

The Yankees numbering from three to four hundred, were marched to Moorefield and paroled not to take up arms again until regularly exchanged. Whilst the paroling was going on their camp equipage, commissary, arms, ammunition &c., were being loaded in wagons and moved to town.

A picket composed of fifteen or twenty men was sent toward Petersburg to prevent a surprise in case the Yankees should get wind of what was going on and come down before the job at Moorefield had been completed. On approaching, what I think was called Bassard's ford, between Moorefield and Petersburg we discovered several four horse and mule teams coming toward us from the direction of Petersburg. The foremost was then in the river, a second one just entering the stream. There were about 25 cavalry guarding the train, part of them rode in front and part in rear of the train, about a dozen infantry were riding on the wagons. Soon as the Yankees discovered us they began turning back.

Our squad was commanded by Lieutenant Isaac Kuykendall, after captain. He ordered a charge, we received a volley as we reached the river, the ford being a shallow one we dashed through. The cavalry took to their heels, perhaps a dozen of us were close after them, the remainder of our squad had halted to take care of the teams and the infantry guard. We soon picked up a half dozen or so, who were not well mounted, which we disarmed and sent to the rear, escorted by two of our squad. We were detained for a moment, but were soon in hot pursuit again. They had gained on us considerably. When we came in sight of them again, they had halted and formed a line across the road, seemed ready to receive us. We were now within a hundred paces of them; I was better mounted than my companions or seemed to be and was a few lengths in advance of my companions.

The road was very dusty, they could not tell how many were following them. We were too close to turn back without danger of being ourselves captured. I shouted come on boys, we have them now, and with drawn sabers we dashed at them, although they were two to one, it seemed the only thing to do. When in about fifty paces of them they gave us a volley from their revolvers and took to their heels. Their aim had been bad no one was struck.

After pursuing them a mile or more, we reached the Petersburg Gap. I had heard of Petersburg Gap, but had never been over the road before and did not know how far I was from the town, and concluded that perhaps we had gone far enough. I halted thinking my comrades would be up in a moment, but no one came in view. I began to feel a little lonesome and spurred my horse to a trot; he was well nigh played out.

I was in great fear of Yankees following me back, thinking that I had been almost in sight of the village and felt sure that as soon the alarm was given a regiment of cavalry would be down to see what was up.

My horse didn't seem to care about moving faster than a slow walk, I began to fear that he would not go at all. However, I urged him on as fast as possible, keeping a sharp lookout to the rear until I reached a house near the road on my right. I don't know who lived there, an old gentleman saw me coming and walked to the gate that led to his house and said when I rode up, "young man are you drunk or crazy?"

I said, "neither I hope, have you a fresh horse that you would exchange with me, mine is a good one, but in his present plight I fear being overtaken if followed."

He said, "no, I have all my horses hid in the mountains, but if I had a dozen you should have one or all if necessary. But how come you to be following twenty Yankees all alone? To what command do you belong?"

I said, "McDonald company, Ashby cavalry, who are now at Moorefield. We captured all the Yankees down there this morning. Those Yankees you just saw go up the road were guarding a train which we captured down here at the river."

He said his name was Welton, if I am not mistaken. I gave him my name and rode on. At parting he said young man if you live through this trouble be more prudent.

After I had ridden some distance and began to feel better, believing I was safe from pursuit, when I was almost paralyzed at hearing the command halt from the bushes on the left of the road. I was thinking only of Yankees and expected to see a lot of blue coats step from the brush. No use trying to escape better I thought to settle the matter with my face to the foe than to be shot in the back. I always had a horror of being shot in the back. I felt like another being when Lieutenant Kuykendall and several of his men rode from the brush laughing at my evident surprise. The lieutenant said that after getting the teams and prisoners on the way to Moorefield under guard, with the few men he had left, had ridden up the road until he met the men who had been with me on their return, when they had taken the position in which I found them in order to relieve me if I returned as they expected I would with a pack of Yankees at my heels.

I was very glad to be among my friends again, having made up my mind not to act the fool again, we rode back to Moorefield, where the captured prisoners and teams had already arrived.

The teams were loaded, if I remember right, with commissary stores for the camp at the ford below town, which camp equipage had also been moved to town. The captured train was soon on the road leading up the South Fork, well guarded.

Captain Harness and Captain McDonald, who had been busily engaged in paroling the prisoners completed the job late in the evening. The paroled prisoners going toward New Creek Station and the Johnnies following their wagon train up South Fork.

Charlie Johnson, brother of Geo. H., and I got leave of absence for a few days, and after dark started for home. We parted on top of Middle Ridge, at what was then known as Salt Blocks. After having agreed to meet at the same place at a certain hour on the second day from that time, I reached home about daylight.

There were no Yankees at Romney, but there was a regiment of cavalry at Springfield, who scouted as far as Romney every few days. My horse got sick with what was called lung fever, caused from overheating and inhaling dust. I was compelled to leave him and take one of father's horses.

I met Johnson at the place and time appointed and on the second day, joined our respective companies at Harrisonburg, with out any mishap. About this time two companies, one commanded by Capt. Dangerfield the other by Capt. McChesney, were added to our battalion, each of these companies numbered about one hundred men. Our battalion now made quite a respectable appearance.

About the 15th of July our cavalry brigade marched to Gordonsville. On the march some of the boys winded a still house where persimmon lightning was manufactured. Three or four men from each company quietly gathered all the canteens in their company and quietly dropped out of ranks and did not reach camp until perhaps ten o'clock that night.

Next morning at roll call about one half of our company failed to answer to their names. While this kind of lightning was not as fatal as the genuine, it was for a time just as effective, as far as locomotion was concerned. Quite a number of the boys were very much demoralized, but we succeeded in getting all into camp that night at Gordonsville. It had rained continually all day. We reached Gordonsville about dark and went into camp.

The rain continued to fall, we had no tents and spent a disagreeable night. The day before General Jackson had reached Gordonsville with his corps. Next day news reached camp that a regiment of Yankees were camped at Raccoon Ford on the Rapidan River on the South side and could not go back on account of the sudden rising of that stream. Our brigade was sent to capture them, but they heard of our approach and swam their horses across and escaped to the other side.

We camped that night near Orange Co. Ct. House, found corn and hay for our horses, but nothing for ourselves. Rain had been falling all day and continued throughout the night. Next morning we returned to Gordonsville. By the time we reached camp the rain had ceased and the sun was shining for the first time in three days. It was here that Wm. E. Jones took command of the 7th Virginia cavalry and almost created a mutiny.

The 7th was Ashby's old regiment. The regiment felt that it was disgraced by having a colonel of infantry to command them. There was great dissatisfaction in the 7th. A few days after Col. Jones took command, several grindstones came into camp and orders were issued for the men to grind the sabres.

110

Col. Jones said to the men, "if you want to cut, have something you can cut with; if you want to bruise, better get a club."

The men said, "we will not have much need for either sabre or club. We'll never get close enough to the Yankees to use either while commanded by this old infantry colonel.

CHAPTER IX

Action in the Valley

A few days later the 7th went on a scout to Orange Court House; I got permission to go with them, being acquainted with most of company F., Captain Sheetz's old company. The road from Gordonsville to Orange Court House ran nearly parallel with the Orange and Alexandria railroad, which passed through the village in a northeast direction. The plank road leading from Fredericksburg to Liberty Mills passed through the main street of town in a southwest direction, passing through the town at right angles with the railroad.

The railroad station was on the outskirts of the town, on the south. Col. Jones approached from this direction. On reaching a knoll or spur at the end of the northwest mountain, some two or three hundred paces from the station, a Yankee was seen to ride behind the depot.

Col. Jones halted his command and said, "boys that Yankee is not alone, there may be a troop down there."

The main streets could not be seen from where the regiment was halted. Some of the men said in a low tone, "he is getting ready to run from one Yankee, we will not get a chance to dull our sabres to-day."

After a few moments the colonel said, "we will go down and see what is there. Forward," and the column moved toward the depot in an oblique direction, the colonel riding a few paces in front of his command. The moment he passed the south end of the depot turning to the left of command—"draw sabre, charge" rang out clear and distinct, in an instant every sabre flashed from its scabbard and every man pressed toward after the leader.

I had gone along with the command merely to get away from camp and to take a look at the country, didn't expect to see any Yankees and was not looking for a job. I had not been carrying a sabre very long and didn't know much about handling the thing of those who had had experience of that kind of work and being near the rear of the column I dropped back and trotted along in the rear urging the boys to close up. When the rear of the column reached the depot and wheeled to the left, the head of the column had reached the main street and turned to the right toward Fredericksburg, yelling like demons.

This was the first full grown Rebel yell I had ever heard. Although it was a bright warm day it made me feel a little chilly. Then the pistols began to crack at a very lively rate. I have heard men say they would as soon go into a fight as to eat turkey. I never was built that way. Just then I would have preferred turkey, even with the buzzard added.

The Yankees had fallen back to the end of the street and made a stand and seemed to be doing a good deal of business down that way, judging from the crowd and noise. The rear of the column had now turned down main street and after going a short distance halted, could go no further, the street being packed from one side to other.

The yelling and cracking of pistols had almost ceased, but the rapid flash and clash of the sabre could be distinctly seen and heard. The crowd seemed to surge first one way, then the other. I began to feel better believing it impossible for the Yankees to reach me through all that crowd, and if we had to retreat the rear I would be in front. I began to feel right brave, felt as though I would like to get in reach of the blue coats.

Next moment a column of Yankees wheeled into main street from the direction of Madison Mill's and without halting charged right at the rear of one column. Well, I don't know how others felt, but I believe I was pretty badly frightened for a moment. Some officer near the rear of the column shouted to top of his voice, "rear battalion wheel and charge, wheel and charge." There were several of us in the rear who had already wheeled several times, but hadn't charged. The time had come that something must be done.

The Yankees were bearing down on us not fifty yards away at a fast trot, firing their revolvers as they came, a few men and a few horses were struck. Most of their shots were passing over our heads. Then arose that terrible Rebel yell and with drawn sabre at a tierce point and rowels buried deep in our horses flanks, at them we went at full speed, when we met the blue and the gray was considerably mixed for a few moments. At the onset we had them at a disadvantage, they having charged with the revolver, whilst we used our sabre, their revolvers were now nearly all empty and for a few seconds they were almost defenceless, until they could replace the revolver and draw the sabre. This was our opportunity and we made use of it for a few moments. But it soon became evident that the weight of numbers was forcing us back. We were over matched in the mix. I found myself crowded against the houses on the left hand side of the street with several others on the opposite side of the street. Our men had given back faster and the Yankees on that side were forging past us. It looked for a few moments as though we must either surrender or be cut to pieces.

We kept backing and defending ourselves the best we knew how, until we had the luck to reach a narrow alley between two houses through which but one horse could pass at a time. Several of us made our escape through this alley. The truth is we were hemmed in by a whole brigade. Out numbered at least five to one. Over powered and very much demoralized. This was the way I felt, at least, each man got out the best way and any way he could. We made our way back to the knoll from

114

which we had started. Perhaps a hundred or more Johnnies had reached that point ahead of us.

In a short time Col. Jones, accompanied by forty or fifty of his men came up. The colonel sent a courier brigade to headquarters for reinforcements. The knoll on which we had rallied was about two hundred yards southwest of the town and had on it a nice grove of oak timber. The space between the grove and the town was through an open field. Here Col. Jones formed his men and awaited an expected attack.

The Johnnies continued to come a few at a time until perhaps two thirds of the original number had gotten back.

The Yankees seemed to be satisfied and did not attempt to drive us from our position. In about two or three hours General Robertson arrived with the remainder of the brigade and advanced at once, but the Yankees seemed to have had enough and had slipped away carrying their dead and wounded with them, going in the direction of Rapidan Station. Gen. Robertson pushed after them, but they had crossed the river before we came up with them. We turned back and reached Gordonsville about sundown. If I remember right, the 7th lost 75 men in killed, wounded and made prisoners. Some of the men did not get back to camp for a day or two. Col. Jones was at one time separated from his men and entirely surrounded by Yankees, but being an expert swordsman, he carved his way back to his men and escaped with a slight cut across his hand.

This was my first lesson in practical sabre exercises. I never heard any one after that day, doubt the old infantry colonel's fighting qualities. He was soon liked by his regiment and was afterwards the idol of the brigade, which he commanded. I never after went on pleasure trips of that kind. This affair occurred on the 2nd day of August. A few days after our company was ordered to picket at Barnett's Ford, a few miles north of Orange Court House, on the Rapidan River. Here was the old homestead of President Madison, situated on an elevation on north bank of the river. The house was a one story structure and resembled an old time barn, shedded all around on the south side of the river, the bluff a few hundred yards back, was much higher than on the north side, which was mostly level.

Our picket post was on top of the bluff or ride, on the south side of the river, our reserve a short distance in the rear. The Yankees posted their picket some four or five hundred yards back from the river near an old house which stood in a field about one hundred yards in front of a heavy body of timber in which the Yankees kept their reserve. One of our men carried a Belgium musket of large calibre, using a two ounce ball.

After we had been on picket a day or two, I shouldered the Belgium musket one morning before day went down to the river and secreted myself behind a pile of drift wood for the purpose of picking off the picket as soon as it was light enough to see. I calculated the distance to be about 600 yards and elevated the sight accordingly.

It was soon light enough for me to see my target sitting like a statue on his horse, only a short distance from the end of a negro cabin and in a direct line with it. As soon as it was light enough I took careful aim and fired, then watched the result, he dodged low on his horse and rode away a short distance behind a clump of trees, but by the time I had reloaded he rode back to his post and seemed to be looking up for something in the gable end of the house. I felt sure now that my aim had been too high and that the ball had struck the gable of the house. I ran the slide on the hindsight down one hundred yards, aimed as near the saddle seat as I could and fired, an instant later he fell forward appeared to clamp his horse around the neck; the horse ran back and disappeared in the woods, at the top of his speed, and I returned to our picket.

From our elevated position we had a fine view of the country for at least a mile in our front, with the exception of a considerable scope of timber, several hundred yards back from the river, in which the Yankees kept their reserve.

We had no idea what number of Yankees that body of timber hid from our view. However the picket in our front was left vacant from that time on.

That evening Capt. McDonald gave a half dozen or so of us permission to go over to the old house and see if we could discover where the two balls struck. We could only find where one had struck the gable of the house about 15 feet from the ground. We had only been at the cabin a few moments when a company of cavalry dashed from the woods, in a manner that did not appear to be friendly, and we scampered back toward the ford as fast as possible, when we reached the road which we had to follow something like a quarter of a mile to reach the ford. The road ran along the river bank which was high and steep. The only hope of crossing was at the ford. There was a high fence which compelled us to reach the river road at a right angle. A squad of Yankees on the opposite side of the fence by taking a straight course toward the river, came near cutting us off from the ford and came into the road only a short distance in our rear, but Capt. McDonald, who had held the remainder of the company in readiness took in the situation, dashed down to the river bank, on which grew a heavy growth of timber, and gave the Yankees a volley which checked them and saved us. We reached the ford and crossed without loss.

When we reached the top of the hill, on our side of the river, we discovered that there was at least a good sized brigade of Yankees about the cluster of buildings at the crossing. Madison Mills was located here.

The Yankees did not seem inclined to cross the river, but did not fail to fire at a Johnnie whenever he showed himself over the brow of the hill.

Toward evening Capt. McDonald dismounted a squad of his men and lead them by a circuitous route, followed a brushy ridge which reached down to the river a short distance above the ford and was covered with thick brush. On reaching this point they were within good rifle range of the Yankees.

The captain and his men crawled to the brow of the ridge and gave them a surprise in the shape of a volley that sent them to cover behind the houses on double quick, then for a few moments volley after volley was fired by the Yankees in quick succession, but the Johnnies had slid back over the top of the ridge out of danger and as soon as the firing ceased beat a hasty retreat and reached their horses in time to mount and prepare to receive the advance of the Yankee's column, which had now crossed the river and was advancing as though they meant business. Capt. McDonald sent a courier to brigade headquarters, then forming his company behind some timber about one hundred yards in rear of the summit of the ridge on which we had been picketing.

As soon as the head of the Yankee column appeared in view we took deliberate aim and should have emptied several saddles, but can't say that we did. They recoiled for a moment and came on at a trot, and we got away at a much faster gait. They soon checked up and followed at a more cautious gait.

Capt. McDonald continued to fall back taking advantage of every position of any strength to molest and retard their progress. It was now near sundown the Yankees gave up the chase, after pursuing us two or three miles, and turned back.

Capt. McDonald placed a picket and then retired a few hundred yards and held his men in readiness for an advance of the Yankees in the early morning, but they failed to appear. Capt. McDonald then felt his way back very carefully until we reached our original picket post without discovering any Yankees. The next day our company was relieved and returned to camp near Gordonsville.

The Yankees now in our front were commanded by Major General John Pope and was supposed to number about sixty thousand men, with headquarters at Culpepper Court House.

On the 7th of August, General Jackson moved his command from Gordonsville to Orange Court House. Next day Gen. Ewell's division crossed the Rapidan at Liberty Mills, several miles above Orange Court House. Gen. Jackson's division and the division of Gen. A. P. Hill, crossed at Barnett's Ford below the Court House.

A courier had been called for from our battalion and I was detailed and ordered to report at brigade headquarters, which I did. On the morning of the 9th I was ordered to report at Gen. Jackson's quarters. I found him near the middle of the day, sitting on his old sorrel horse, surrounded by his staff and was looking through his field glass toward Culpepper Court House, where a heavy body of Yankee cavalry was visible, to the naked eye, drawn up in line of battle, on an open ridge on the right of the road, about one mile distant from Gen. Jackson's point of observation, which was on an elevation in a field on the right of the road between it and Slaughter's Mountain.

When I rode up, the general lowered his glass, I saluted and reported having been ordered to report at headquarters by Gen. Robertson.

"Very well," said the general, "remain here, I may want you." And raised his glass again fixing it apparently on the Yankee cavalry in his front.

I now had a good opportunity of viewing what was shortly to be one of the hardest fought battles of the war, considering number and length of time they were engaged.

I will try to describe, as I saw it, the battlefield of Cedar Run, or Slaughter's Mountain, from General Jackson's post of observation, looking northeast, in the direction of Culpepper Court House. On the right of the road where Jackson and his staff were gathered, was a pasturefield on a ridge, which arose, perhaps two hundred yards in our front. The road crossed Cedar Run almost at right angle, leading in the direction of Culpepper, as far as the eye could see, in almost a straight course. After crossing Cedar Run, on the right of the road and immediately in our front lay a large cornfield, which extended for several hundred yards a gradual ascent until it reached a stone fence which ran at right angle with the road. On the opposite side of this fence was a pasturefield, which extended to what appeared to be a heavy body of timber. Still farther to our right lay Slaughter's Mountain, on the opposite side or left of the road and on the left of Jackson and his staff, was woods reaching down to where the road crossed Cedar Run. Next came a field of ten or fifteen acres of wheat, laying almost in a square and reaching to the road, immediately in rear of this wheat field, on looking almost due north, I could see what looked to be an old field grown up with brush and still back of this seemed to be an original growth of timber, which extended from the left of the road, near Jackson's post of observation in an unbroken body until it again reached the road in our front bounding the brush and wheat field on three sides. The southeast side of the wheat field reached the road, leading to Culpepper Court House, opposite the field of corn, beyond where the belt of timber reached the road.

On looking northeast I could see a large number of cavalry in line in a field on the southeast side of the ridge. Slaughter's Mountain was situated on Jackson's right less than a mile distant and terminated abruptly on a flat meadow or pasture land laying between its base and Jackson's post of observation on the hill near the road.

I have now given a discription, as it appeared to me, of the ground on which the battle of Cedar Run was fought, on the 9th day of August 1862, between the Confederates, under Gen. Jackson, and Federals, under Gen. Pope.

From Gen. Jackson's point of observation a view of the full extent of the battlefield could be had with the naked eye, although but little could be seen of the movements of the troops on either side, because of the timber which shielded them from view, except in front. When I reached General Jackson no troops were visible neither blue or gray, except Yankee cavalry of which I have already spoken of.

I soon learned that there was artillery on Slaughter's Mountain, also a line of infantry to our right, between Jackson's position and Slaughter's Mountain along Cedar Run, at the base of the hill on which we stood. About two o'clock a score or more guns were seen to belch forth fire and smoke from the edge of the woods in front of our right.

The Confederate guns on Slaughter's Mountain replied at once from their elevated position. They had a wide range and were themselves safe, the elevation being at too great an angle. The Yankee guns could not be brought to bear on them. It was Gen. Early in our front commanding a part of Gen. Ewell's division.

Soon several guns opened fire from an elevation to our right, near the base of Slaughter's Mountain, which Gen. Early had ordered up and places in position.

The Yankees now had several batteries in full blast. In a short time Gen. Winder arrived with his division and opened with his artillery firing obliquely from Early's left, from the left of the road. The artillery practice was now getting to be a little too interesting for one of our party, at least it was evident that some of the Yankee gunners had selected our party for a target and was getting the range most too well for comfort. At first their aim was too high, but very soon one of our party came near losing his head, another his horse, every few seconds the sod was being plowed up around us.

Up to this time General Jackson had been sitting with his right leg thrown across the pommel of his saddle as immovable apparently as a statue, with, his field glasses watching, seemingly, with great interest, the artillery duel then going on, apparently ignorant that we were being made a target of and in danger of having a shell burst in our midst at any moment. At length one of his staff said, "general had we not better change our position, we are being made a target." The general seemed not to have heard for a moment or two, then lowered his glass and straightened up in his saddle, and with a smile remarked that our boys were making it pretty warm for those people down there, at the same instant a shell exploded only a few paces in front of us killing one horse and crippling two others.

The general then remarked that we appeared to be in range and had better move a little farther to the right. He rode in that direction a short distance and halted and said, "I will stop here, you all ride back a little way where you will be hid from view, they will hardly aim at a single horseman." We didn't wait for a second invitation but were soon over the ridge out of sight of the Yankees.

The cannonading lasted, I would say, about two hours, when all at once it nearly ceased. We then rode up to the general. He was busily writing on a slip of paper which he handed to a courier and said, take this to Gen. Early, you will find him in that direction. In a few moments we saw a line of skirmishers coming through the standing corn, directly in our front closely followed by a line of battle which reached out at a right angle with the road toward Slaughter's Mountain on our left.

We had a fine view from our position. I was about to witness, for the first time, a regular battle, and looking on with great interest, watching every movement. It was now well on the after part of the day. Our position being a little back from the brow of the hill, the line of skirmishers had passed from our sight beneath the bluff, at the base of which the field of corn terminated at Cedar Run. The rows of corn lay parallel with the road and in a line with our position on the hill.

The Yankees line came on at a quick step and in what appeared to be a perfect line, without crook or curve, the skirmish line only a short distance in their front. They had almost passed from view beneath the bluff when the sound of the scattering volley of musketry fell on my ear, and a second later the most terrific roar of musketry that I had ever heard arose from the base of the hill on which we sat. My horse squatted and pricked up his ears in amazement.

I had been watching General Jackson very closely and wondering how much longer he intended sitting there, knowing that as soon as the Yankees appeared over the bluff that we would be in close range. I did not know that the 13th Virginia lay between us and danger. I began to get a little shaky. The general sat like a statue, apparently unconscious that anything unusual was taking place, or about to take place within forty miles. A moment or two before the roar of battle reached us he had replaced his field glasses in its case. His usual position when on horseback was a rather cramped one when not in motion, and not a graceful rider at any time. He now reined up his horse, straightened up in his saddle, all the while gazing steadily to the front.

I thought, at the first sight he gets of the Yankees as they raise over the bluff he will get away from there. I was not aware of there being any Confederates in our front until the firing commenced. They had taken their position before I reached Jackson. After the first volley the rattle of musketry was continuous along the whole line, which extended for

120

perhaps a half mile to our right, toward Slaughter's Mountain. The smoke of battle soon had everything in front from view.

Jackson now seemed to be a different person altogether. I will not try to describe him as he appeared to me. It seemed to be with the greatest exertion that he restrained himself from charging headlong down the hill into the midst of the fray. Both sides seemed to be standing their ground with a stern determination never to yield.

General Jackson now wrote a few lines on a leaf of a blank book handed it to courier and said, "carry this to General Hill, you will find him in that direction, (pointing to his right and rear), be as expeditious as possible."

The heaviest firing now seemed to be on our right where the Yankees seemed to have concentrated for the purpose of turning General Early's right, but Early was there himself and was holding his ground, although it was easy to tell from the firing on the other side that the Confederates were greatly out numbered. General Jackson wheeled his horse and galloped along the top of the ridge in that direction. We followed. When nearly opposite the extreme left of Early's line, Gen. Jackson halted. Here Early's artillery was posted and seemed to be in great danger of being captured. The contending lines seemed to be only a few rods apart, the musket balls were flying over and around us pretty thick, filling the air with that sizzing, hissing sound peculiar to the Minnie ball, a music which any old soldier will tell you is not pleasant at any time, more especially when compelled to sit quietly and listen to their singing with nothing to do except almost break ones neck by jerking his head from one side to the other whenever one of these little messengers fanned his cheek or brushed his nose, but a person must experience these things to understand them thoroughly.

The Confederate line seemed to waver, fall back a few paces, then press forward again. Gen. Jackson was looking steadily and I thought anxiously to the rear, as though expecting an attack from that direction. All at once his countenance seemed to brighten up as though he had been relieved of some great agony. He turned to one of his staff and said, "ride over to Gen. Early, say to him, stand firm Gen. Hill will be with him in a few moments."

A line of gray now broke from the woods to our right and rear, came at a double quick across the pasture field. I said line, but it was more like a drove or flock, for there was no regularity about it. Jackson rode toward them with his cap in his hand. They soon recognized him and yelled as only Johnnies could yell at sight of their beloved leader. Jackson rode at their head a short distance then drew his horse to one side and set barehead until the brigade had passed.

It was the 1st brigade of A. P. Hill's division, commanded by Gen. Thomas. Two batteries accompanied this brigade. The whole formed on the right of Gen. Early's line and overlapping the Yankee line and

121

swinging around their left flank, doubled it back toward their rear.

In a short time the remainder of Hill's division came up. The Yankees on this end of the line had now begun to fall back and were being closely followed by the Johnnies. Jackson now rode back toward his old position on the hill in rear of the 13th Virginia, on the right hand of the road.

The battle seemed to be in favor of the Confederates, the Yankees giving way except in front of the 13th Virginia, where the crack regiment, known as the "Pennsylvania Bucktails" continued to hold their ground with a stubbornness seldom equalled.

On the left of the road from what first appeared to be only a skirmish line, amusing themselves, but soon the rattle of musketry increased to a constant roar. The general was quietly looking toward Culpepper Court House, where in the distance a cloud of dust arose above the tree tops, which indicated Yankee troops hastening to the front. Occasionally Jackson would lower his glass and turn his head to the left, and appeared to listen very intently for a moment.

I was watching the general very closely. He seemed to be getting a little nervous. At length he said, "there is some hard work being done over there," at the same time drew a blank note book from a little satchel which he carried, wrote a few lines, tore out the leaf, handed it to a courier, gave him some instructions and away the courier dashed at the top of his speed.

One of his staff then called his attention to a line of Yankee infantry just entering the wheat field on the left of the road and moving in the direction of the firing, which had now become a continuous roar with very little intermission. The general wrote another dispatch, handed it to a courier, gave him some directions and said, "lose no time," as the courier rode away. Then listening a moment said, "that firing is very heavy."

The roar of battle seemed to be getting nearer. I felt sure that the Confederates were being driven back. A courier dashed up, saluted the general and said that he came from Colonel _____ and that Gen. Winder had been mortally wounded and could live only a short time. That they were being hard pressed and could not hold their ground much longer, unless they were reinforced very soon.

The general was sitting with his right leg thrown over the pommel of his saddle, without a word he dropped his leg, pressed his cap on his head, tightened the strap under his chin. This was all done in almost a second of time and would not have been noticed if it had been another than General Jackson. Without a word he wheeled his horse toward the road, pressed the rowells to his flanks and started at a rate of speed which threatened to leave us far in the rear. His staff was soon close at this heels with a half dozen couriers bringing up the rear.

The general leaped his horse over the fence at the road, which had been partly thrown down. Here he halted a second and ordered some artillery to the rear, which General Winder had ordered placed in position, but which was now in great danger of being captured. Jackson then leaped his horse over the fence on the opposite side of the road into the woods, and had not gone fifty yards when he met his men falling back in considerable disorder. It was here that it has been said that Jackson drew his sword for the first time during the war and called on his men to rally and follow him, that Jackson would lead them.

This may all be true, but how he could have been heard is a mystery to me. The rattle of musketry, the shouting, cheering and yelling was deafening. The smoke of battle and the thick foliage on the timber over head made it impossible to see but a short distance. The leaves and small limbs were falling thick and the bark from the body of timber flying in every direction, often striking a person in the face leading him to believe that he had run against a load of buck shot or something worse.

It appeared for a few moments as though we had struck a fullgrown tornado, loaded with thunder and lightning. This was the most hair-raising fix I had ever struck. When I began to realize the condition of affairs I found that I had lost the general or the general had lost one of his couriers. The confusion and noise at the time was terrible and this to me frightful, for a few moments I was almost paralyzed.

The Yankees seemed to be on three sides. The left of General Winder's line had been turned and doubled back and was now hard pressed in front, rear and flank, as near as I can describe the position of the Confederate line on the left it appeared to be somewhat in the shape of a fish hook, doubled back until the extreme left of the line was within a hundred yards of and in rear of the center of the line, inside of the hook about where the barb should be found General Jackson, surrounded by his men who were now facing the enemy and were slow forcing them back, at the point of the bayonet.

Then came a more deafening roar from the left of the original Confederate line, followed by a Rebel yell that arose above din of battle. Jackson heard this and recognized the war whoop of his old brigade. He rode among his men and urged them on. The Yankees were giving ground. The Stonewall Brigade which had been held in reserve had come up in the nick of time, delivered their fire and without halting rushed at the surprised Yankees with the bayonet, broke their already shattered line and captured about two hundred men.

Gen. Jackson now rode back to the road where the brigade commanded by Taliafero, were being driven back; also a part of Early's. Jackson's presence seemed to be all that was needed to rally them. They turned back and formed on the left of 13th Virginia. The Yankees now began to give way. Jackson rode back and took a position on top of the hill near that which he had occupied at the opening of the battle.

The Stonewall brigade had swept around the Yankees' right, were driving them into the stubble field, which now seemed jammed with blue coats. Next on the program, Branch's brigade of A. P. Hill's division, passed on our left, dashed down the hill in the direction of the wheat field. Then the whole Rebel line moved forward and the Yankee line moved back until the corn field and wheat field were about cleared of blue coats.

Then came the closing scene. A brigade of cavalry charged in column down the road as though they would break through the Confederate center. Vain attempt; fatal mistake. General Branch's brigade closed in on their right and the 13th Virginia on their left, rushed up to the fence and the Yankee column was nearly exterminated, a small remnant only being fortunate enough to get away. It almost seemed a miracle how any of them escaped with their lives.

The Yankees on the left of the road after being driven from the wheat field into the woods attempted to make a stand, but soon gave way, and the retreat became general along the whole line. General Jackson asked if there was a courier present from General Robertson's cavalry brigade, I rode forward, he handed me a dispatch and directed me to carry it to General Robertson, said that I would find him somewhere on General Ewell's right by following the downward course of Cedar Run. The general and his staff now rode toward the front, I turned to the right passing over the ground where the "Pennsylvania Bucktails" had met the 13th Virginia.

The "Bucktails" were a crack Zouave regiment. Their pants were red, the legs being made large and loose with a tight band at the ankle. Each wore the tail of a deer in his cap. This was said to be one of the best, if not the best regiment on the Yankee army, but when they met Col. J. A. Walker and the 13th Virginia they were over matched and left not less than two hundred dead and wounded "Bucktails" on that hard contested field of strife. Most of them must have fallen the first fire. They lay almost in a line. Many of the wounded had, no doubt, been carried off the field during the fight, but the "Bucktails" were not alone. The victory had been dearly bought.

On the other side of that narrow valley, within twenty paces of their late foe, lay a number who wore the gray asleep in death to hear of war no more.

I hurried on, glad to get away from the heart rendering scene. I found our brigade about dark, delivered my dispatch and started back to find Jackson.

The roar of artillery with an occasional volley of musketry in the direction of Culpepper Court House, made it plain to me that Jackson was still at work, and that I would find him somewhere near that firing. I rode in that direction.

The Eleventh Indiana Zouaves. Notice soldier's uniform in right foreground. *(DAVIS HISTORY HOUSE, ROMNEY, WV)*

The night was not dark, but moonless, nearly so, the stars shown from a clear sky, although dimmed by the smoke, which seemed to cover, like a shroud, the field of battle. I rode on until I reached the road leading to Culpepper Court House, which I followed for some direction, but soon found it a dangerous road to travel.

The Yankee batteries had the range and were making it a very unpleasant place to be. I was at a loss to know what to do. I rode back out of range and halted. The artillery firing had nearly ceased. I had halted perhaps twenty minutes when the 12th cavalry passed, I learned from them that the whole command was falling back. I rode with them until we reached Cedar Run, I had learned that they had passed General Jackson and his staff on the road. I concluded to wait until he came along.

I rode into the wheat field to give my horse a chance to get a bite of a shock of wheat. He had eaten nothing since before day that morning. I had not slept for two nights, having been in the saddle nearly all the time. Human nature would stand no more. I looped the bridle rein around my wrist, leaned back against the shock, stuck a finger in each ear to drown the moans, prayers and cries of the wounded and dying, which lay almost as thick as sheaves in a harvest field.

It was terrible, one poor fellow who lay within ten feet, kept begging for water. It was but a short distance to the run. I left my horse at the shock, went to him, got his canteen and filled it at the run; by moon light the water looked red as blood, no doubt it was colored. I was thirsty myself, but could not quench my thirst with that water. I hurried back and raised the poor fellow to a sitting position, then held the canteen to his lips. He seemed to be very weak and could take only a swallow or two at a time; when he had taken all he wanted he thanked me in a very weak voice. I then got a sheaf of wheat and placed it under his head. He thanked me again said something about his poor wife and child, I asked him his name, he said "raise me up."

I knelt down placed my arm around him and raised him a little. He seemed to sleep. I spoke to him but he did not answer. I eased him back as gently as possible, then got my blanket which was strapped to my saddle, folded and placed it under his head after removing the sheaf of wheat.

He seemed to be resting easy, although his breathing did not seem altogether natural, some way. I thought I would question him when he awoke as to his home and to what regiment he belonged, if there was any message he would like to send to his family, which I might possibly be able to get to them, (through some one of the prisoners captured that day) in case his wound proved fatal. I sat down beside him to wait and watch for General Jackson to pass by, when I would join him, at the same time watching my companion expecting him to awake any moment, and

Death on the battlefield. (HAMPSHIRE COUNTY LIBRARY)

listening to the suffering wounded, strewn all over that blood stained field, an hour or two before I was ready and willing to help butcher them.

Now while I sat and listened to their cries I felt that I would be willing to do anything in my power to relieve their suffering I felt that before the rising and setting of another sun that I, too, might lay cold in death. Then I thought of home and of those I had left behind. I felt, to tell the truth, more like a baby than a soldier. Soon I began to nod and lay down. I knew no more until next morning.

When I awoke the sun was up and shining bright from a cloudless sky. I sprang to my feet, my horse was eating at a shock about twenty yards from me, my patient was lying with his back to me in the same position. I placed my hand on his forehead, it felt cold and damp. I tried to feel his pulse, there was none. He was sleeping his last long sleep. His suffering was over.

I shall always remember that face. I left him as he lay. He was not alone, his comrades lay thick around him, many of them still crying for help. I could stand it no more. Mounting I rode as fast as possible. I had gone far before I found that General Jackson had withdrawn his men in the night and had passed through the corn field some distance below and to the left of the road, which was so blocked up with dead men and horses that it was impossible to follow it. I had now reached the ground occupied by General Early's brigade, during the heat of the battle. Many of his men were still there, having given their lives for the cause they believed to be right.

The wounded had all been carried off the field. I was getting alarmed, did not know but what I might meet the Yankees at any time. I rode to the top of the hill from which Jackson had viewed the battle the day before, and looking toward the south I discovered a large yellow flag which I knew to be floating over a field hospital. A large wall tent surrounded by a half dozen smaller ones, over which a yellow flag floated, its color indicating the kind of business carried on at that point. Also as a guide to the Ambulance corps engaged in hauling the wounded from the field during the fight to have necessary repairs done.

The school boy of today perhaps will not understand how the wounded were removed from the field of battle, whilst the battle was in progress. Infantry was generally followed by a detail from each regiment carrying stretchers. When a man was too badly wounded to walk he was placed on a stretcher and carried to the rear, then placed in an Ambulance and taken to field hospital for treatment. When a man was wounded and by the assistance of a comrade or two is able to walk he is taken to the rear in that way. There is never any trouble in getting some one to help a wounded man to the rear, but often trouble in getting the man that ain't wounded to the front again.

In the cavalry it's different. A cavalry charge is generally short and sharp, no time to care for the wounded, the cavalryman though wounded had better stick to his horse as long as the horse will stick to him. They use no stretcher, no Ambulance corps, they often fight when they least expect to and often don't fight when they most expect to.

Sometimes a cavalry fight reached for a distance of several miles. I call to mind one running fight of about fifteen miles in which I participated of which I may have something to say of later.

I soon reached the hospital where the surgeons seemed to be doing a slashing business, judging from the heap of limbs piled near by. The sight was too much for an empty stomach. I inquired where Jackson could be found, no one could tell me. I turned and rode back to where the dead were being buried. A line of Yankee Cavalry could be seen a mile or more distant in a hill field, toward the Culpepper Court House, which was the only Yankees visible. Everything quiet. What a contrast between the sitting of the sun on August the 9th and the rising of the sun on the morning of 10th.

On the evening of the 9th when he disappeared from the view behind the western hills, his brightness dimmed by the smoke of battle, the gray and blue were grasping as it were, each others throats in a death struggle for the mastery of the gory field, midst the deafening roar of artillery, the sharp piercing rattle of musketry and quick thrust of the flashing sword and bayonet all spoke in a language of its own, which the trained ear and eye of the soldier well understood to be a struggle of the most determined and desperate kind. This was something of what the sun looked down on at his sitting on August 9th 1862. But when he arose on the 10th how changed was the aspect. No roaring cannon, no rattling musket, no flashing sabre greeted him, no battle smoke to dim the splendor of his glory. Now scarcely a sound greeted the ear except low tones of the men at work burying from sight our fallen comrades in their shallow graves where they await the last roll call.

This was the first time I had ever witnessed a wholesale burial on the field of battle. The most favored mode was placing the dead in a ditch, made by heavy rains, if there be any in reach. Where several were buried together their burial were generally shallow, unless the work was done by a special friend. This was a sad and solemn duty. I soon tired of looking on and turned to ride away in search of General Jackson. I had reached the main road, turned toward Orange Court House, which I met an officer whom I saluted and inquired if he could direct me where I could find General Jackson.

He said he had left him only a few moments ago a short distance back. After questioning me as to where I had been and to what command I belonged, he finally said, "I am Gen. Archer and am going to take a look

129

at the battle field, come ride with me. The general will hardly have use for you today. I don't think there will be any more fighting here."

I turned and rode back with the general. We looked the field all over, in the woods on the left of the road where Jackson had met and rallied his men. There were saplings from four to six inches cut entirely off by musket balls, why every one in the woods were not killed is a mystery to me, although the timber indicated that about four out of five balls had been aimed too high. Many of them being twenty feet from the ground.

The Confederates' dead had all been buried on this end of the line. A good many blue coats lay scattered around. We next rode across a narrow hollow into the wheat field where the Yankees had been driven and slaughtered. It appeared to me that there was a Yankee on every ten square feet of that field. Gen. Archer remarked that he had never seen such slaughter.

A Confederate surgeon and his assistant were going over the field examining the Yankees' wounded, who had been left for dead by their comrades, when he found one that had a possible chance to live even a short time, he was sent to the hospital. We passed by where my companion of the night before lay just as I had left him, apparently in a natural sleep. We rode down to the road where the Yankee cavalry had made their gallant but foolish charge. The lane for two hundred yards was a sight. It was jammed by dead men and horses. This was the work principally of the 13th Virginia, commanded by Col. J. A. Walker, company I, of this regiment was raised in Hampshire county by Captain, afterward Col. Robert White, Company K, of this regiment was also from this county and many if its members are still living. We then rode through the cornfield, along the Yankee line of battle, or rather what had been. The Confederates' dead had all been buried.

The Yankees were strewn all through the corn field. The Pennsylvania "Bucktails" being easily distinguished by their dress, it was plain to be seen by the number of their dead left in the bloody field how they had suffered. They had met Col. Walker and the bloody 13th. After Gen. Archer had finished his examination of the battle field we returned to Gen. Jackson's quarters about half mile to the rear. Generals Jackson, Ewell, Hill and Steward were sitting on a log a little distance from the road holding consultation. Gen. Archer said best not interrupt the General now.

A little further on I recognized some of his staff and couriers. I reported to Jackson's chief of staff and was told where I could get something for myself and horse to eat. It then being after the middle of the day. I got a piece of raw bacon and two hard tacks, which was the first mouthful I had eaten for thirty-six hours. We remained here over night, and all next day, which was spent by the Yanks in burying their dead, under a flag of truce, which was granted them. That night Jackson fell back to or near Gordonsville. This ended my first experience as a courier.

I again reported to Capt. McDonald for duty, well satisfied, having determined in my own mind that the next time a courier was called for I would not be a candidate.

We remained in camp near Orange Court House a few days. Our company was then ordered down the plank road toward Fredericksburg and halted near a little village by the name (if I am not mistaken) of Verdierville. Here we picketed for several days, when we were relieved and returned to camp near Orange Court House. Roasting ear season was at hand, consequently we fared sumptuously every day whilst on picket. The favorite mode of cooking green corn was to bury the ears in a bed of live coals with the shuck on. In this way they soon roasted nicely. We often had to eat them with out salt. An over feed often caused great inconvenience to the imprudent, but we learned from experience that ordinarily from ten to fifteen ears were as many as the average man could eat with safety at one time. For my part about ten good sized ones were all that I could store conveniently.

Next day after returning to camp our cook was ordered to prepare three days rations for the men, and have them ready by daylight next morning. This was about the 20th of August. It was reported in camp that Gen. Longstreet's corps had arrived from Richmond and that "Uncle Bob" was with them. We began to suspect that something was about to take place but had no idea what it was.

Next morning by daylight we were in the saddle and were soon on the march. Crossing the Rapidan at Somerville ford, followed by General Jackson's corps. Our brigade accompanied by Gen. Steward in person moved in the direction of Culpepper Court House, where Gen. Pope had his headquarters, but that general had come to the conclusion to move to the north side of the Rappahannock.

Near Brandy Station we came upon a large body of Yankee cavalry, drawn up in line ready apparently to receive us, though not in a very friendly manner. In a very few moments we were ready for the reception and in a short time the gray and the blue were much mixed up, facing every point of compass, every man issuing and executing his own commands as he thought to the best advantage. The contending forces were to all appearances about equal and for a time fought with equal obstinacy. The Confederates usually relied on the sabre, while the Yankees depended more on the revolver. When the revolver was emptied, whilst returning it to the holster and drawing the sabre, if hard pressed, left him for a moment in a defenseless condition, which often proved fatal, or sent him to the rear either with a carved scalp or a punctured carcass. The sabre two out of three will decide the question in the affirmation. We finally persuaded the Yankee cavalry to cross to the North side of the Rappahannock, they did unmolested protected by their guns, which lined the heights on the opposite side, apparently frowning on the Johnnies in such a disagreeable way that our general prudently and to the satisfaction of the whole command concluded to keep out of range. General Robertson fell back a few miles having a company on picket and camped for the night.

Next morning, at an early hour we were again on the march, taking a direction parallel to the Rappahannock until we had reached a ford several miles above Beverly Ford, at which place the roar of cannon could be easily heard. We crossed the river and after going a few miles our advance reported a heavy body of cavalry moving on our right toward Beverly Ford. I had been ordered to report to General Robertson and was sent with a dispatch to Gen. Steward on the north side of the river, having a little artillery practice with the Yankees. I delivered my dispatch and asked for orders and was told to wait.

Soon the Yankees began to be reinforced when Steward fell back across the river and having been reinforced by the brigade of Gen. Taliafero, kept up an irregular firing all that evening. That night Gen. Steward with part of Fitz Lee's brigade joined Gen. Robertson where I had left him that day. Early next morning, with part of Gen. Robertson's brigade in addition to that of Lee's. He started, no one except himself, knew where.

We crossed the Rappahannock several miles above Warrenton Springs, passed through the town of Warrenton late that evening, and reached Catlett's Station on the Orange and Alexandria Railroad. We were now in rear of Gen. Pope's army and between him and Washington. When we reached Catlett's Station night had set in, a storm had been gathering since about sundown, in the west along the top of the Blue Ridge Mountain.

We were halted a short distance from the station. A large encampment was plainly visible by the continuous flashes of lightning. General Steward soon had his men in position to storm the camp. The storm which had been gathering, now struck us in all its fury.

The driving wind and rain leveled many of the tents from which the men were struggling to free themselves, when amidst the lightning's blinding flash, and the thunder's deafening roar, they saw and heard, (what well might have made men of sterner stuff quake with fear.) They saw the lightning flash on the blade of the drawn sabre and heard the demonic yell, which rose above the thunder's peel and the charging squadron bearing down on them from all quarters. The not over superstitious even might have imagined for a moment that the imps of darkness had been turned loose for a season.

If they were not frightened they at least showed no inclination to fight. We captured about three hundred prisoners, who had been left to guard the camp, the division having marched the day before to meet General Lee on the banks of the Rappahannock to oppose his crossing.

In addition to the camp equipage, (which was captured and burned) was General Pope's official papers, among which were copies of Pope's correspondence with his government. General Pope's headquarters were at this point. His wardrobe, including a new and very attractive uniform, belonging to the general, was among the trophies. For months after a robust negro could be seen, occasionally marching about General Steward's quarters in the same uniform, with chest thrown out and the step of a blind horse, to the great amusement of all who witnessed the ridiculous exhibition.

The rain continued to fall in torrents. After spending several hours in a fruitless attempt to burn a railroad bridge, which spanned a creek nearby, General Steward returned the same way he came, crossing the Rappahannock at Warrenton Springs, as far as I know without the loss of a man.

Maj. Gen. A.P. Hill
(POTOMAC EDISON'S VALLEY ECHO)

Col. Wm. E. Jones
(POTOMAC EDISON'S VALLEY ECHO)

CHAPTER X

The Second Battle of Manassas

T he rain continued to fall all night and next day, which caused the streams to rise rapidly. For the next two days we were in camp near a place, I think called Amisville. Almost a continuous artillery firing had been going on at the different fords below for several days. We privates did not know what it all meant, but imagined that as soon as the waters had fallen. "Uncle Bob" was going to cross with or without Pope's consent. General Longstreet had taken Jackson's place in front of the Yankees at Beverly Ford. Jackson had gone, we didn't know where. The river now being fordable. General Robertson started early in the morning and keeping well back from the river until he reached a little village called Waterloo. Here we were joined by General Steward with Fitzhugh Lee's brigade and crossing the river continued our march until evening when we discovered a large body of troops in our front at a place called Gainsville, on the Manassas Gap Railroad. They were moving toward Bristoe Station, on the Orange and Alexandria Railroad. We soon learned that it was Jackson's corps, which we privates had lost, not having seen or heard of them for the last three days. We learned that Jackson on being relieved at the Beverly ford, had fallen back a short distance from the river so as not to be seen by the Yankee signal stations and then moved his command parallel with the river until he reached a crossing some four or five miles above, where we had crossed that morning, and had followed the west side of a range of hills which hid effectually his movements from observation. He camped the night before at Salem, a station on the Manassas Gap Railroad, after having marched twenty five miles.

That day had we had passed through Thoroughfare Gap and was now heading for the Bristoe Station, where they would be between General Pope and Washington and which place was reached about sunset. A few moments later a train of cars was heard approaching in the direction of Brandy Station. Preparation was at once made to capture it but before sufficient obstructions could be placed on the track it dashed through and escaped. Two other trains that shortly followed were captured, but proved to be empty.

General Jackson had learned of the immense quantities of commissary and quartermaster stores at Manassas Junction, some four or five miles distant and determined to get possession of them that night, rather than wait until next day, when they might be destroyed. His quartermaster and commissary train had been left behind, and although a soldier may start on a march with three day's rations in his haversack he generally eats

Damage inflicted after Second Manassas. *(NATIONAL ARCHIVES)*

them the first day. This being the case with Jackson's command, who had been living for the last two days on green corn, had marched over fifty miles, were tired and foot sore, yet when they learned of the feast that awaited them only a few miles away, they were apparently as fresh as ever. I would have taken something more than human to hold them until they had secured all these ricks of bread and bacon.

General Steward, with part of his cavalry, accompanied by Brigadier Gen. Trimble with a brigade of infantry, started to capture the much needed rations. I had been sent to General Steward to act as courier. It was near midnight when we reached the Junction. General Steward halted the command when within a short distance of the station, and some part of his cavalry to the rear of the garrison, after giving them a little time to get in position. General Trimble divided his brigade and advanced on each side of the railroad. A regiment of cavalry advanced in front of the fortifications at Manassas. General Trimble now pushed his men forward as fast as the darkness of the night would admit.

The Yankees opened with grape and canister at close range, but did not have time to reload before the bayonet of the Johnnies had taken possession of their guns and very soon captured the whole entrenchments. The cavalry had followed close on the heels of the infantry, had closed in around the garrison and picked up a number of prisoners. The Confederates captured two batteries of field pieces, I don't know but I would say not less than three hundred prisoners, and several hundred horses, several large store houses, were packed with flour, bacon and pickled beef, barrels and boxes of crackers, sugar, coffee, cheese, potatoes, in short almost any and everything a man could eat or wear, and in addition to what these buildings contained were perhaps a hundred cars loaded and standing on a long switch, loaded with quartermaster and commissary stores and ammunition.

I was sent back as soon as the place was captured, with a dispatch to General Jackson. Early next morning, Jackson started for the Junction, followed by A. P. Hill's and Taliafero's division. General Ewell remained at Bristoe Station with his division to watch out for Pope and hold him in check as long as possible and then fall back to Manassas.

I rode along with Jackson and his staff and reported to General Steward at the Junction. The two divisions which had just arrived had scarcely had time to satisfy their hunger when the report of a cannon was heard on the left, which gave notice of the approach of a Yankee force from the direction of Alexandria. Soon they came in sight along the railroad, marching as though confident of being able to drive off any force that might oppose them. They were soon convinced of their mistake. They had marched into the very jaws of death, unaware, never dreaming that it was more than a few regiments of cavalry with which they had to contend. Generals Steward and Trimble had brought the captured guns to bear on them, ready to hurl death and destruction amidst their ranks at short range, the fortifications being manned with nearly ten times their number. It was said that Jackson, seeing their pitiable condition, rode toward them waving a white hankerchief as a signal of truce, but was fired on. Returning he ordered his men to destroy them. I don't say it was true, I did not see the General with a white hankerchief but inside of ten minutes all that could was doing their best to get away, scattering in almost every direction, with Stewart's cavalry at their heels. But few of them escaped, nearly all being either killed, wounded or captured. These troops were commanded by Brigadier Gen. Taylor, who was mortally wounded. General Jackson having no means of removing the immense amount of captured stores to a place of safety, allowed his men to help themselves to all the shoes, boots and clothing they needed. The Suttler's stores was first looked after, where many things outside of the regular army rations were to be found. Toward the middle of the day General Stewart started back along the railroad in the direction of Bristoe Station, with most of his cavalry, each man carrying with about ten days rations in their haversacks and saddle pockets being filled with coffee, sugar and hard tack, a ham of bacon strapped to the saddle, on one side and a pair or two of boots on the other. In short Stewart's cavalry was a sight to see that evening. Almost every man had provided himself with a new hat, decked out with fancy bands. Many of them had succeeded in filling their canteens with "firewater" and were just as happy as a lamb with two mammies. We reached Bristoe Station shortly after the middle of the day. Here Stewart divided his men, part following the railroad in the direction of Warrenton Junction, the remainder going toward the town of Warrenton. The Yankees were soon discovered advancing by the way of Warrenton, a courier was at once dispatched to Gen. Ewell.

General Stewart skirmished with the Yankee advance in front and flank without being able to check them to any extent. In falling back we passed through an old worn out field densely covered with pines. Here we passed Ewell's line of battle lying flat on the ground, patiently awaiting the advancing foe. Several batteries were also in position, hid from view by pine brush stuck in front. When in good range the ball opened. One volley was sufficient to send the Yanks to the rear on double quick aided in the maneuver by a few rounds of grape and cannister. They were soon reinforced by fresh columns. It was now evident that Pope had become alarmed for the safety of his supplies and ammunition and was now in front of Gen. Ewell with his whole army close at hand.

When General Ewell learned this fact he fell back and joined General Jackson at Manassas Junction. The bridge across Broad Run was now burned. The Yankees halted for the night near Bristoe Station. After Gen.

Ewell's division had supplied themselves, as the other division of Jackson's corps had already done, with a week's rations and many other necessary as well as unnecessary articles, the remainder was burned, which looked like a great pity, but there was no help for it. It was now plain to be seen that something was about to happen. Staff officers and couriers were hurrying here and there, regiments and brigades were formed in line. Gen. Steward started with Fitz Lee's cavalry brigade in the direction of Fairfax Court House. General Jackson commenced moving his men from Manassas the night of the 27th of August and by noon next day had his whole corps in line of battle near stone bridge. Robertson's cavalry being on the extreme right. On the afternoon of the 28th a cavalry scout reported the Yankee advancing in force on the Warrenton turnpike. Jackson could not stand still and let Pope slip by without making an attempt to stop him until Longstreet could come up, he being hourly expected.

It was nearly sunset when the storm burst with all its fury, and raged without intermission until about nine o'clock at night, when the Yankees gave up the struggle and fell back. The Confederates remained master of the field. Our brigade of cavalry took no part in the contest other than to watch and see that Jackson's right flank was not attacked by flanking column. The left flank was guarded by Fitz Lee's cavalry brigade. We learned that night that General Ewell and General Taliafero had both been dangerously wounded. Ewell had struck in the knee by a rifle ball and the joint shattered, so that amputation was necessary to save his live.

On the morning of the 29th General Longstreet forced his way through Thoroughfare Gap. Early in the morning clouds of dust could be seen rising from Thoroughfare Gap. We all hoped it was Longstreet, but were disappointed. It proved to be a column of Yankees who had been guarding the gap, but were now falling back on their main force at and near Bristoe Station. General Steward with part of Robertson's and part of Fitz Lee's brigade rode toward Gainsville, near where he met and routed a regiment of cavalry, then turned in the direction of Thoroughfare Gap. We soon discovered a cloud of dust rising in our front. Not knowing whether we were about to meet friend or foe. General Steward led his men from the main road to our right, behind a low ridge and placed them in line, ready to fight or run as circumstances might require.

It was now near the middle of the day. The roar of battle was gaining, increasing every moment in Jackson's front. It was evident that Pope's whole strength was massed in Jackson's front, determined to crush him before Longstreet's corps could reach him.

General Steward, with a few of his staff, who had been closely watching through his glass from a knoll in our front, the approaching column, called out that it was Longstreet's corps, ordered his men forward to the top of the ridge, halted them, then rode forward to meet

139

Generals Lee and Longstreet, who were riding at the head of the column a little way in the rear of the advance. I suppose General Steward reported as he rode along about condition of affairs, but I imagine that General Lee's practiced ear had already caught the sound of battle and read without erring therein the effort now being made to crush his favorite lieutenant. Gen. Longstreet corps was pressing forward at a quick step. General Steward had sent a courier to General Jackson, with news of Longstreet's near approach.

General Longstreet formed his line across the Warrenton turnpike, facing the east, almost at a right angle with the pike and with the right of Jackson's line of battle which occupied a line of unfinished railroad, which lay nearly parallel with the Warrenton, Gainsville and Centerville turnpikes, leading to Alexandria. When Longstreet's corps had passed Steward followed for a short distance, then bore off to the right in the direction of Bristoe Station. Longstreet was soon engaged in a lively artillery duel near Groveton.

About the middle of the evening Pope seemed to have turned loose on Jackson his whole strength with the determination of destroying him without more ado, at least that is the way it appeared to us, two miles away, as we sat on our horses, listening to the fearful roar of strife in progress along that unfinished railroad. Six times, we afterward learned, the Yankees charged and were each time repulsed. Many of Jackson's men are said to have fought with the bayonet, clubbed muskets and with stones after their ammunition had been exhausted. At one place the Yankees broke through the Confederate line. Immense numbers crowded the breach and was about to surround the regiments on the extreme left, when two regiments of reserves rushed forward and when within ten steps delivered their fire into the crowded mass, then charged with the bayonet, when every man that could get, got.

About this time General Steward received information from scouts that a large force of Yankees were advancing from the direction of Bristoe, to the right and rear Longstreet's line. A courier was dispatched to Gen. Longstreet, at the same time a cloud of dust was raised by General Steward having a part of his men drag brush along the road near Gainsville in the direction of Thoroughfare Gap. This continuous cloud of dust lead the advancing column of Yankees to believe no doubt that General Longstreet's right was being heavily reinforced by way of Thoroughfare Gap. The advancing Yankee column proved to be a corps of McClelland's arms, which he had landed somewhere below Washington and had marched across the country to reinforce General Pope.

General Longstreet strengthened his right by a brigade from his left. General Lee was on hand and kept an eye over the whole job. General Steward ordered the sharp shooters of our brigade to dismount and

140

skirmish with the Yankees, which they did, but the Yankees didn't seem to take much account of them, but moved forward without halting, our skirmishers falling back a little faster than the Yanks advanced, anxious to be mounted again.

A dismounted cavalryman was a good deal like a fish out of water. Longstreet's infantry skirmish line soon relieved us. Then the thing began to get interesting, the Yankees checked up and in a short time moved forward in line of battle. In a few moments the firing was getting pretty brisk, but it soon died out altogether. General Stewart had moved our brigade around toward the left and rear of the Yankee line. I suppose he was watching an opportunity to strike them a blow.

The Yankee column soon began moving toward their right and rear apparently with the intention of reinforcing Pope's right, now warmly engaged with Jackson's corps.

General Longstreet now advanced his line and forced the Yankees in his front back until dark. Stewart with Robertson's brigade of cavalry still covering his right flank. Longstreet's men fell back a short distance and lay on their arms without rations ready for the fray, the day. The battle had ceased to rage on General Lee's left, in front of General Jackson's corps. A line of cavalry pickets was thrown around the right and well to the rear our of right wing. General Longstreet's corps had captured several hundred Yankees that night by the cavalry. This was the night of the 29th. We had but little sleep or rest since the 22nd.

For seven days and nights our saddles had only been off our horses backs a few times and then only for a few hours. It was impossible to keep from dozing a little while on picket, although within musket range of the Yankee lines.

I don't think any punishment greater than having to stay awake when one can't do it. After the longest night of the century, seemingly so at least to the weary guards, who had watched with longing eyes for the first streaks of day in the east, at last the night had passed and another day had come, with it could be distinctly heard the dull heavy rumble of artillery wheel as they pass over rough places while taking their positions to be in readiness to take part in the final struggle about to take place between the gray and the blue. The tread of the battalions and regiments could also be heard taking their places in line, many of them having answered to roll call for the last time until the last trumpet call shall awaken the sleeping dead, to answer to their names at the judgement seat.

Our brigade was early in line on General Longstreet's right; Fitzhugh Lee's brigade was on General Jackson's left; our brigade reached out in the direction of Manassas Junction and terminated on a slight elevation from which we could see clouds of dust in our front, some two or three miles away, from which we inferred that both sides were maneuvering for the last act in the drama.

As we sat on our horses patiently waiting and expecting each moment to hear the first shock of battle, which we knew full well would soon reach us. The morning was bright and clear. I glanced up and down the line, the men's faces wore kind of a do or die look. Serious but determined, but few smiles and but little jesting was heard. No doubt nine tenths of them were thinking of their homes and of the dear ones who were anxiously hoping and praying for their safe return, and many were at that moment offering up a silent prayer for protection through the day on their own behalf. Soon we heard skirmishing in front of General Longstreet, then the report of artillery for a few moments, then all seemed quiet. Then again skirmishing could be heard at a greater distance in another direction then all would be quiet again. Thus it continued at intervals until the sun had reached the middle of the western sky. We could not imagine why the battle did not commence. Many of us began to think the day would pass without more fighting, others even ventured the assertion that the Yankees would fall back that night to the fortifications around Centreville and await reinforcements from McClelland's army. These surmises all proved erroneous. About three or four o'clock the whole earth seemed to tremble, as though shook by an earthquake. In a short time our line was moved forward a short distance and halted, then moved forward again. In less than an hour after the battle commenced the noise of the contending thousands began to weaken. The Rebel yell could now be distinctly heard. Then Gen. Stewart and his staff rode down the line, said the Federals were being driven back, now is our time forward and we started on a trot, and was soon close on the retreating mass of the beaten Yankees.

The artillery was pushed forward at a gallop from one position to another, pouring grape and canister into the herd of beaten and demoralized Federals, whenever opportunity offered itself, without endangering our own infantry, the whole line of both Jackson's and Longstreet's were yelling at their heels as they delivered volley after volley at close range into their retreating ranks. They were given no time to rally or make a stand. The cavalry kept close on their flanks, cutting down or capturing those who straggled from the main retreat. This running fight was continued until between nine and ten o'clock when the noise of strife ceased.

The victorious, but warm and weary men, when the excitement of the pursuit was over, sank down and slept on the hard contested field, which nothing but determined bull dog courage had won.

The Federals continued their fight until they had reached the fortifications on the heights of Centreville, which had been erected by Joseph E. Johnson during the winter of '61.

142

Late in the evening General Robertson's brigade met a brigade of Yankee cavalry and after a short but sharp contest routed them, capturing over three hundred prisoners. We fell back a little ways and camped in a piece of timber a short distance from Bull Run, without rations for our horses, although we still had for ourselves a part of the rations issued us from the Yankee commissary at Manassas Junction three days before. After placing a strong guard around our prisoners, those not detailed as guards, lay down to get a few hours sleep.

Toward day rain began to fall, not withstanding we did not suffer inconvenience, most of us having supplied ourselves with gum blankets and gum coats, since we had been in active business. Next morning our prisoners were turned over to the infantry, who already had several thousand, which they had captured the day before. Our wagon train arrived early in the day, rations were then issued for man and beast. We were soon in the saddle again heading toward Centreville.

The rain was now falling almost in torrents. It seemed that always after a battle of any consequence there was sure to be heavy rains in a short time. Gen. Stewart soon learned on reaching the neighborhood of Centreville that the remnant of General Pope's army had been heavily reinforced by McClellan's army and had made a stand at Centreville. We halted in a piece of timber near by. A courier was sent back to General Lee.

We soon learned that General Jackson was again making a flank move for the purpose of getting between the Federals and their capital. General Longstreet's corps remained behind to bury the dead and care for the wounded.

Next day the Yankees on learning of Jackson's flank movement commenced a hurried retreat toward Fairfax Court House. General Stewart having on their flank and rear ready to strike whenever opportunity offered.

General Jackson reached Fairfax in the evening and found the Yankees ready to receive him in a strong position, on what was known as Ox Hill. Jackson formed his lines and advanced at once. The combat was a fierce one the Yankees knowing that the salvation of their army depended on holding their position. Night came on and put a stop to the conflict. That night General Longstreet's corps arrived ready to take a hand next day, but when morning came the Yankees were gone, having slipped away under darkness of night and were now in reach of their strong fortifications around Washington. And further pursuit was abandoned.

On the 3rd of September General Lee put his army in motion, with General Stewart's cavalry in front heading northward. Our battalion was now composed of several companies and was commanded by Col. Lomax, Capt. Harness' company and Capt. McDonald's formed the 1st squadron and was left behind under the command of Capt. E. H. Mc-

Fairfax Court House during the Civil War. *(NATIONAL ARCHIVES)*

Donald, Capt. Harness being absent his company was commanded by Lieutenant Alexander.

The Yankees had asked, under flag of truce, permission to bury their dead and care for their wounded, which had been granted them. Capt. McDonald had been left behind to keep an eye on them while they performed this sad but necessary duty, and to await further orders. Capt. McDonald selected a place to camp, then for several days we rode over the battle field and talked with the northern people. Old men and their wives and daughters who had come out from Washington and from many of the northern States in search of fathers, husbands, sons and brothers, who were reported missing and supposed to be either dead, wounded or prisoners.

It was a sad, a sickening sight to see those old fathers and mothers turning the dead, who had fallen on their faces, to see if it was the loved ones for whom they were in search. The object of their search was often found cold in death. Then the scene was sometimes one calculated to melt a heart of stone, to see an old gray haired mother and father kneeling and kissing the lips of their idol, it may have been their only child. Then again a young girl, yet in her teens could have been sitting by the side of, it may have been an only brother, sobbing as though her heart would break.

I saw hundreds, I might say thousands of wounded men who had lain on that field of carnage for three days in a scorching August sun, or drenching rains, many with swollen discolored tongues protruding between their parched lips showed how terrible was their thirst. Many of them could move a hand or make a sign, yet their tongue and throat was so dry and swollen that they could not speak, though it was easy to understand that they were begging for water to quench their intolerable thirst. Many of their wounds were filled after three days with vermine. There were numbers of wounded still lying on the gory field, although an ambulance train which at a distance, might have been taken for a great serpent, had been slowly winding its way up on one side and down the other of the narrow valley. After riding over the battle field and examining it closely for three or four days. The positions of the Confederates on the 29th and 30th were so well fixed in my mind that I will here give a short description of it, from memory, although it has been over thirty six years since I looked upon that scene of human slaughter.

Imagine two lines starting at the same point running, one almost north and the other something like thirty degrees east of north, and you will have a figure something in the shape of a flat iron; now follow each line from the angle, until they have separated about a half mile, then draw a line from one to the other and you will have two angles. On the north west angle of this last figure rested, Jackson's right. General Taliafero's division, now commanded by General Stark. In the centre was General

145

Ewell's division commanded by General Lawson, General A. P. Hill's division on the left. General Jackson had placed his men along an unfinished railroad, which crossed the foot hills of the Bull Run Mountains, with here a cut and there a fill which made the position a very strong one. On higher ground covered with timber in rear of this line was stationed his artillery, which could be discharged over the heads of his own lines into the ranks of the advancing foe. General Jackson's line of battle was almost parallel to the turn pike leading from Warrenton to Centreville and not over one and a half or two miles distance on the north west. The following information in regard to their movements, I got from a Yankee Captain, who was detailed to assist in superintending the removal of the wounded and burial of the dead. This Captain claimed to belong to General McDowell's staff, he was a New Yorker and was a real jolly kind of fellow. I met him several times as we rambled over the battle field. The water was very unwholesome and could only be had from pools along a small stream which had been dry until the showers, which had fallen in the last few days, but the bed of the stream being filled with the dead and water being well covered with vermin, we did not partake of it unnecessarily. This Yankee Captain carried a canteen that appeared to be a living fountain, at least it seemed never to go dry. I took several drinks with him. He recommended the contents of the canteen as an antidote for the possible bad effects of the water, which we were compelled to use (advised liberal doses.) The second or third day after we lay under the shade of a tree, talking of the war more particularly of what he termed their late disastrous defeat. We had taken several drinks, I thought from the first that he wanted to get me in a talkative mood and then get what information he could in regard to our forces, or of their intended movements if I could give him any, but if he had known how little I really knew, he would have realized how his time and the contents of his canteen had been wasted. I suspicioned his object and while I appeared to be taking long drinks I was in reality swallowing very little. I soon found that he had been caught in his own trap and was ready to tell all he knew in regard to the movements of their army. Of the future of course he knew nothing, but of the past he seemed to be pretty well posted especially in reference to the movements of General Pope within the last few days.

He said that when General Pope first heard of Confederates being on the railroad in his rear he supposed it to be only a cavalry scout, but he learned that Jackson with his whole corps was in the rear and that his base of supplies was in great danger of being captured at Manassas Junction. General Pope determined to capture Jackson and his whole corps (before he could be reinforced) by pushing forward his whole force and placing them between Jackson and Thoroughfare Gap, through which General Longstreet's corps must pass in order to unite with Jackson. Pope ordered

General McDowell to march his own and Seigel's corps, and a division (I think Reynold's). They were to follow the turnpike leading from Warrenton to Gainsville on the Manassas Gap railroad, placing forty thousand men or something near that number between Jackson and the main body of Lee's army. Two other divisions were ordered to support this force, Pope, with Hooker's Division, followed the Orange and Alexandria railroad toward Manassas Junction. Porter's corps was also ordered to Gainsville. General Banks remained at Warrenton, McDowell reached Gainsville on the night of the 27th. Pope with Hooker's division reached Bristol station in the latter part of the day, and found General Ewell ready to receive him, as has already been stated. My informant said they were uncertain as to where they would find Jackson up to this time, but was now sure that he was at or near Manassas Junction and were rejoiced to think that they had him trapped where he had no possible chance of escape being cut off from any possible succor, surrounded or would be next day, with at least five to one.

Pope dispatched McDowell the night of the 27th to move rapidly at dawn of day, to Manassas Junction. In his dispatch he had said, "if you move promptly and rapidly we will bag the whole batch."

Hooker, Kerney, and Porter were ordered to advance from Bristol Station along the railroad upon the same place, but said the captain, "when we were ready to demand an unconditional surrender, to our surprise, there was nothing to surrender; Jackson had given us the slip and where he was at the time we had no idea. Some of the time we had no idea. Some of the boys said they really believed that he had gone to Washington and when next heard from would have captured the capital."

When Pope reached Manassas with Hooker's, Kerney's and another division, I can't now call to mind whose, about noon of the 28th and found nothing but the ashes of his burnt stores, of which men and horses were now very much in need, from the best information to be had it was the general impression that Jackson, finding himself cut off from the main army, without possible hope of succor, had determined to make a stand within the fortifications around Centreville. Pope dispatched McDowell, who had not yet arrived to direct his march on Centreville instead of Manassas Junction. The troops already at Manassas were also ordered to Centreville.

General McDowell was compelled to retrace his steps until he regained the Warrenton turnpike in order to reach Centreville.

"It was getting late in the evening of the 28th," said the Yankee captain, "when we regained the Warrenton pike and turned toward Centreville, where we were confident of having Jackson treed, and were pressing forward in order to witness the surrender of the command, which had done more harm, and was more dreaded than all others combined. But we found Jackson sooner than we had expected, and he showed no signs of surrendering, either. As we were marching along near Groveton, we were fired on from our left and was soon hotly engaged with, we knew not who, night was at hand when the conflict ceased, it had been short but furious. We soon learned that the command, which had attacked us, was the command whose surrender we were hastening to witness. We had found Jackson and didn't seem much inclined to surrender, either."

Pope did not find Jackson at Centreville and did not learn until the morning of the 29th where he really was then, although he had been heavily reinforced by McClellan, his army was so scattered that he could not get them in shape to crush Jackson before Longstreet, who had forced his way through Thoroughfare Gap, was at hand. Porter had been ordered to flank Jackson's position on the right and get between him and Thoroughfare Gap, but when he attempted to do this he found Longstreet in the way and Pope's opportunity for crushing Jackson's corps alone, was past.

Now we will return to the position of the Confederates which I was trying to describe, held by them on the 29th and 30th. Longstreet formed his line with the left resting on the angle opposite to Jackson's left and something like a half mile distance from it, crossing the Warrenton turnpike and reaching in the direction of Manassas Junction, the two lines facing each other. Jackson's left resting on Bull Run. The two lines were formed at an angle of about thirty degrees. Between Jackson's right and Longstreet's left, which was separated by a distance of half mile, about midway between the two lines was a considerable ridge. On this was placed some thirty or forty pieces of artillery, which from their position could be made to make a column, attacking either Jackson or Longstreet.

About four o'clock Pope had massed the bulk of his army in front of Jackson's left, Pope unaware of Longstreet's arrival, ordered Porter to attack Jackson's right; at the same time Hooker was ordered to move against Jackson's left, but Longstreet was in Porter's way, so he did not move. Jackson's right being protected by Longstreet, enabled Jackson to reinforce his left from his right, and Pope's assault proved a failure.

"To tell the truth," said the Yankee staff officer, "we had the men but did not have the officers to lead them properly; if we could have had a Lee or Jackson your army would have been defeated. When General McDowell was at Gainsville with forty thousand men, instead of marching on Manassas Junction fifteen miles distant, he should have marched to Thoroughfare Gap, five miles distant, which with his forty thousand, he could have held against Lee's whole army, making it impossible for Longstreet to get Jackson or for Jackson to fall back and join Lee. Then General Pope with the reinforcement being hourly received from McClellan could easily have destroyed Jackson's command, and then with near two hundred thousand men crushed or captured the remainder of the Confederate army and gone straight to Richmond without hindrance and this war would have been over in a month. This is what your Lee would have done."

But Pope had left the way clear for Longstreet to advance or for Jackson to retreat and had maneuvered his men until he had them between the two Confederate lines and from fifteen to twenty thousand stayed there, and said he, "after having been over the field and seeing the commanding positions of Confederate artillery I wonder that any of our men escaped."

I have here given his ideas in his own language as near as I can remember. We mounted and rode down the little valley for a mile or so, along the unfinished railroad in front of where Jackson had held his ground for two days against overwhelming numbers, for one mile and with one hundred yards of that unfinished railroad men lay within touch of each other. It was a difficult undertaking to ride among them. Here I parted with my Yankee friend, after taking a full dose of the healing fluid. The boys who had not been as fortunate as I, were many of them sick.

The weather was very warm, the stench was something that would have to be experienced to be fully understood. The only way we could use the water was by first straining, to free it of vermin, then make a strong coffee. We had plenty of coffee captured from the Yankees at Manassas, also from the haversacks of the Yankees, who had no further use of it. Although Capt. McDonald had been ordered to remain where we were and await further orders, he determined under the circumstances, to move to a more congenial atmosphere. We had heard nothing of General Lee since the 3rd, when he had marched his army in the direction of Leesburg.

Capt. McDonald followed in the same direction until we reached Leesburg. He there learned that General Lee had crossed into Maryland, but could learn nothing further of his movements. Capt. McDonald then concluded to cross the Blue Ridge at Snicker's Gap, in order to reach Winchester, where a few companies of cavalry were stationed, under the command of Col. Angus McDonald, father of Captain E. H. McDonald. We reached Winchester in the afternoon of the second day after leaving Bull Run, in rather bad condition, short of both commissary and quartermaster stores. However Col. McDonald soon supplied our wants, and when we had gotten rid of the dirt and dust which had been accumulating for the last two weeks, we felt somewhat better.

At Harper's Ferry there were several thousand Yankees, also at Martinsburg, guarding the B & O railroad.

Col. McDonald was picketing the roads leading in the direction of those points.

The Yankee cavalry had been in the habit of chasing our pickets from their post a mile or two below Bunker's Hill. Col. McDonald concluded to set a trap and see if a few of them could not be captured. That night or as soon as dark set in four companies under the command of Major Massie, started down the Martinsburg Grade. Capt. McDonald with his own and Capt. Harness' company, commanded by Lieut. Alexander, accompanied them. Major Massie reached the advance picket post and placed his men in a piece of woods a short distance in rear of the picket and on the right of the pike leading in the direction of Martinsburg. Major Massie's plan was to attack them from the rear as soon as they had passed in pursuit of our pickets.

We sat quietly on our horses until about eight o'clock in the morning, more asleep than awake, when we were suddenly aroused by firing in our rear. A company of Yankees had attempted to capture our picket by getting between them and Winchester and had waked up the left of our line by firing a few shots among them, but they soon found that they had awakened the wrong passenger and "skedaddled" from whence they came. A few of our men followed them for a short distance, but soon returned. Major Massie thought perhaps they would reinforce and return. We remained where we were until near the middle of the day when we gave the expedition up as a failure and started back toward Winchester. Major Massie's command in front, Capt. Harness' company next with Capt. McDonald in the rear. Just before entering the village of Bunker Hill, we crossed a small stream, where the men halted to water their horses, causing those in the rear to halt also. The head of the column continued to move forward, the men further back following as fast as their horses could quench their thirst, and were scattered for perhaps the distance of a mile. Our company was not yet through watering our horses, when the report of a pistol in our rear caused every man to look in that direction, where we saw our pickets coming over a rise in the pike at the top of their speed not over two hundred yards away. A short distance in their rear arose a cloud of dust which plainly showed they were being closely pursued. Some of our horses failed to get water at that time. We moved on quick time, closing up on Harness' company. On reaching a road or street near the center of the village, Lieut. Alexander wheeled his company and short to the left; Capt. McDonald led his through the town and turned through a pair of bars on the left into a grove of trees and formed a line facing the advancing Yankees and not over one hundred yards from the end of main street of the town. When the Yankees reached the village they halted and began firing at us from behind the houses. We had no idea of their number.

The captain said boys it will not do to sit here for a target, let us charge them. The motion was seconded and we moved out into the road, filed to the right and charged in column of "fours". The Yankees gave until they reached the middle of the village, when they moved forward pushing us from their front, killing Mathias Brill and capturing George Hott, Ab. Shingleton and Frank Myers. The dust was so dense that it was difficult to distinguish friend from foe. W. N. McDonald and I found ourselves pressed back on to the sidewalk on the right of the passing column where they seemed not to notice us for a moment or two. At length an overgrown Dutchman pulled out of the column and with revolver leveled at McDonald demanded our unconditional surrender. McDonald carried a revolver of an English pattern, a self-cocker, a few of which had lately gotten into the company and were very unreliable, some of them failing to fire nine out of ten times. This was now the case with McDonald. It refused to fire, although he was using every effort to get it to do so. The Yankee seemed to be in same fix his pistol refused to fire, though I doubt very much if he had a chamber loaded. I looked on hoping that McDonald pistol would fire first, he kept saying to me, "shoot him, shoot him." I believed my revolver to be empty, but on glancing at it discovered one chamber had not been fired. I raised it quickly and fired, at the same instance McDonald's pistol fired. The Yankee dismounted head foremost.

McDonald's horse had backed against a small gate which gave way, and we passed through into a small yard, rode around the end of the house or rather between two houses and through another small gate into a garden from which we kicked off a panel of dilapidated pallings and was soon in the timber only a rode distant. We made our way back to the mountain and reached Winchester about dark. We found that nearly all the boys had made their escape, although the Yankees had pursued them for two or three miles. We rode to Col. McDonald's quarters, Will knew that his father would be uneasy on his account until he heard from him. We found the old gentleman a good deal excited, fearful that his son, William, had been killed or wounded, for he would never surrender alive, but said he, "Blue, when I learned that when last seen you and my son were together, I had some hope that you both might come off all right, for I felt confident that if there was any way out you would find it."

The colonel seemed to think I was due all the credit for his son's safety, with which I had nothing in the world to do.

At parting the old gentleman said, "Blue, I feel very grateful to you and any favor that I can do you I will do cheerfully."

I thanked him and we rode to our quarters, glad to be with our company again. The whole command had lost less than a dozen men killed, wounded, and missing. We had gone to surprise the Yankees, but they had surprised us, and we had but little say. My horse was about played out, so I concluded to ask for a ten day furlough and go home and get another horse. I had no trouble to get a furlough and started at once for Hampshire, provided the way was clear. I reached Capon Bridge and stopped there overnight. I learned at the Bridge that Gen. Imboden was in the neighborhood and that there were no Yankees nearer than Green Spring run, so I went on and reached home in the after part of the day, when I learned that there was a company of cavalry and a company of artillery at Green Spring and that the cavalry scouted as far as Romney every few days. I did a little scouting around, visited a few neighbors and slept in the woods. I then heard that Gen. Imboden had come down the river and was then camped at Mr. Stump's.

Gen. Fitzhugh Lee
(POTOMAC EDISON'S VALLEY ECHO)

James Longstreet
(POTOMAC EDISON'S VALLEY ECHO)

CHAPTER XI

Second Capture

N ext day I went up to see the boys, a good many of them being from Hampshire county. I was surprised to find Ike Parsons at home. He had gotten a furlough for a few days. General Imboden was on his way to destroy the bridge across the South Branch on the B. & O. railroad to prevent the Yankees from being reinforced from the west, while Lee was in Maryland. I had learned by some means that a couple of young ladies from Patterson's Creek were visiting Dumpling Hollow and that they accompanied by a Miss Fox and a Miss Herriott, would visit Mrs. Susan Parsons next day. Confederates soldiers having been a little scarce in this section for sometime was considered to a certain extent privileged characters, so I made it convenient to call at Mrs. Parsons' next day to see her son, Ike, on business, and expressed great surprise as well as pleasure at meeting so unexpectedly so many friends; some of whom I had not seen for quite a while. I was on my way to General Imboden's camp, but allowed myself, after considerable persuasion, to spend the day at Mrs. Parsons, which proved to be a very pleasant one to me. But it came to an end too soon. The ladies returned late in the evening to Mrs. Fox's. Ike and I gave them to understand that they might have a call that night from a couple of Confeds. We were a little cautious about traveling on the public highway, for fear of meeting a Yankee scout.

After dark, we started. Ike told his mother that we would go out to the Cheshire place and camp that night. The Cheshire place had on it vacant house and was perhaps two miles from the public road. I suggested to Ike that the safest route for us would be to cross the river at the ford just below his mother's house and follow the mountain around, but Captain George Stump having passed down the road with his company late that evening and not having yet returned. Ike thought it would be safe for us to go down at least as far as what was known as the Kercheval Ford and then cross to the other side of the river. We rode on something like a half mile until we came to what was known as Old House Hollow. The moon was about full though its light was dimmed by a hazy sky. When within fifty yards of the hollow, upon making a curve in the road we discovered a dozen or more horsemen. It was too dark to tell the color of their clothes. I remarked Captain Stump is just getting back. We turned down the hill and when within about thirty paces of them one of them said, "halt," I said at once, "Ike those are Yankees. Now unless we can out run them we are gone up."

We wheeled our horses and started back at their best speed, with the

Yankees at our heels tiring as they came. Ike was well mounted and could have easily distanced them, but I was riding father's old riding horse, having left my own at home to rest up a little. He could run a fair gate for two or three hundred yards and then he was done. At Mrs. Parsons' they heard the firing and the clatter of the horses hoof coming up the road. The young ladies, Miss Sallie, Miss Jennie and Susie, ran out across the road and opened the gate and let Ike and I pass through and closed it again before the Yankees could pass through, though they soon had it open and were close after us. I found my horse was played out. There was a narrow wagon road which wound up the side of the steep hill on the left of the hollow. I said to Ike I will dodge off and follow this road and the Yankees may not notice me. You keep on up the hollow, you can get away, my horse is given out. I turned up the hill but did not go fifty yards when my horse could go no further and stopped. The Yankees was close enough to notice me when I switched off. A few of them followed Ike, but most of them were now within a few feet of me. I wheeled my horse across the road and slid off the opposite side from the Yankees, at the same time resting my revolver across the seat of my saddle. The foremost Yankees were now within twenty feet of where I stood. I roared out as bold as a lion, "halt!" They obeyed the command at once, though I suspect the moon beams on the barrel of that revolver had more to do with their sudden halt than the command. They appeared to be very much excited or had taken an extra charge of fire water, I didn't know which. They all seemed to be shouting surrender, surrender, I yell out on what condition?

This demand caused a lull in their gabble. A Yankee in front, I suppose he was an officer of some kind, said with an oath, that was calculated to make a scared Confed submit to any terms, "the only conditions you will get is that your life may be spared, provided you drop that revolver and raise your hands above your head, otherwise we chop you to pieces.

I said, "I don't accept your conditions. Now listen to what I say, I have not thrown my ammunition away, every chamber of this revolver is loaded with certain death for every one of your number. Now if you think your dead body of one Confed would be equal to six Yankees, pitch in and you will find when you get through with the job that what I tell you will be true."

I was ready to surrender but was sure that most of these fellows were under the influence of liquor and would not spare my life, so I determined to empty my revolver among them and then take to my heels if the craft was still in sailing condition.

At this moment Capt. Sommers who was in command rode up and said, "Lieutenant, I know who you are, it's folly for you to throw your life away by resisting longer, you cannot escape, and in a few days, will no doubt be exchanged and with your friends again, then why not surrender when the odds are so much against you."

I said, all right, I have been wanting to surrender for some time, but your men seem to be very much excited or very much drunk, and I don't care about being carved after I have surrendered."

He said, "mount your horse and come along, I am Captain Sommers and I am in command. You will be safe from harm." At the same time ordered his men back to the pike.

I rode back alongside of the captain. After riding some little distance he asked for my arms. I told him I had no arms, having tossed my revolver down the hill when I surrendered. I had dropped it by my side in the road. Ike got it next day. We rode back to the pike and was sitting on our horses, the captain making a detail to escort their prisoner to Green Spring. Just then a single horseman rode down from the direction of town and rode up within thirty paces of the Yankees before he discovered his mistake. The horseman was I. T. Brady. He had just came from Imboden's camp and knew that Capt. Geo. Stump had gone down the rode that evening, had been deceived, supposing that he was meeting Captain Stump.

A dozen or so Yankees pursued Brady, but he being well mounted soon distanced his pursuers. Six men accompanied me to Green Spring Run, where we arrived about one o'clock in the morning. I had flattered myself that I would be able to make my escape somewhere on the road but no opportunity was given me. I was too well guarded by six men, two of which rode in front, one on either side and two in the rear. The Yankees had a kind of blockhouse built of cross ties, in which I was closely guarded under the immediate supervision of one Captain Dike, a man whom I did not admire. An hour or so after my escort and I arrived at Green Spring, Captain Sommers returned with his company. The captain said he had gone as far as Romney. Said that he heard in Romney that Captain Stump was with his company camped about two miles above town; said that he was very near going on and surprising him that night, but was afraid most of them would make their escape, in the dark, so he had concluded to leave them alone until next day, when he intended to pay them his respects. He then asked me some questions about Captain Stump, if I belonged to his company or if I had seen him.

I told him that I did not belong to Captain Stump's company, but that I had seen him pass through town last evening and supposed that he had gone to Winchester. In reply to the question as to the number of men he had, I said I did not know for certain, but from appearances did not think there were over forty men with him when I saw them.

Well, said he if Captain Dike will hold you here until tomorrow evening, you will have the pleasure of being accompanied to Camp Chase by Captain Stump and most of his men. Said that he must get a little sleep and went out.

157

Next day from a port hole in my prison, about 8 o'clock in the morning I saw Capt. Sommers start toward Springfield with, I thought, about one hundred men. I thought to myself if you knew what backing Capt. Stump has you would be very clear of going on this expedition.

About the middle of the day a train came up from Martinsburg and I was put aboard for Cumberland. To my surprise I found three men belonging to the same company that I did, Capt. McDonald's. They were Frank Myers, Geo. Hott and Ab. Shingleton. They had been captured a few days before in our surprise party at Bunker Hill when we went down to surprise the other fellow and the other fellow surprised us. When we arrived at Cumberland and were marched to the provost martial office, but one was admitted at a time. I was last to enter. Col. Porter was provost martial. He questioned me as to what command I belonged, where the command was then and how I came to be in the neighborhood of Romney when captured.

To most of his questions, I am ashamed to say, I did a good deal of lying; it was war times and was a military necessity sometimes, and this was one of the times, at least I thought so.

It seems a little strange how quick the father of lies will prompt a person some times. I had told the colonel that the regiment to which I belonged was with General Lee and I did not know where he was; that the last I had heard of him he was in Maryland. He then asked how it come that I was not with them. I said I had got tired of soldiering, didn't feel sure that I was doing right to fight against the Union; didn't have any negroes to lose and had about made up my mind to stay at home, if I could, by taking the oath of allegiance to the United States; said that I was now absent from the command without leave and was afraid to go back, and didn't want to be exchanged for fear of being shot as a deserter and would like to get a parole, until I could have a talk with my father as to what he thought about my taking the oath.

The colonel said it seems to me that our boys captured a Rebel spy over near Romney a few months ago by the name of Blue, John Blue, I think was his name.

I said yes, John Monroe Blue belongs to General Imboden's command. He was a son of John Blue, who lives a few miles below Springfield. John always was a wild, reckless kind of boy.

Well, said the colonel we can not parole any prisoners now, but I will hold you here until General Kelley, who is now at New Creek, returns; although I have a squad of Rebels to go to Camp Chase in the morning. He said that he did not know just when the general would be down from New York, and said that the guard house was not a very desirable place to be in at the best. And said that if I would give him my word of honor that I would not attempt to leave town and would report at his office at nine o'clock in the morning, I was at liberty to go where I pleased within the city limits. I thanked him in a very feeling manner for his kindness, but said colonel, I can't accept a parole of the city, for the reason that I have no friends or acquaintances here, have no place to stop over night and have not a cent with which to buy a meal. Without saying a word he took from his vest pocket a roll of bills and handed me a ten dollar greenback and said to go to a hotel and when that is gone call on me for more. I again thanked him almost with tears in my eyes, for I really felt thankful and I believe that if, through the fortune of war I had ever met Col. Porter and had him in my power, I would have let him gone free, or if necessary would have protected him with my life.

As I turned to leave the office, who should I meet at the door, but Lieut. Cole, who, the reader will remember, I had met on former occasions. We shook hands in a very hearty manner and expressed our delight at having met again so unexpectedly. The colonel remarked you men seem to have met before. I said yes, I happened to be along with a few Rebs a few months ago who had the good fortune to capture a bunch of Union soldiers at Moorefield and became acquainted with the lieutenant on that occasion. I saluted and bowed myself out in the most approved style I knew how, and asked the lieutenant to walk with me to the hotel as I was not acquainted with the town which the colonel had been kind enough to give me a parole of.

I was very anxious to get Lieut. Cole away from the colonel for fear he might give me away. As we walked up Baltimore street he informed me that he was there under arrest and said that he was staying with his brother-in-law, a Mr. Golden. Said that he had a room and bed and that I should board with him, it would not cost me a cent. I much preferred a private boarding place, so went with him. I found Mr. Golden and lady to be very kind and sociable people. They had no family. After retiring to his room that night I gave Cole a short history (at his request) of my adventures since we had parted at Moorefield. He then informed me that after being paroled they had gone to New Creek and that the authorities at Washington would not recognize their parole and had ordered them to report to their command for duty. This he had refused to do, claiming that he was in honor bound not to take up arms again until exchanged. He was then placed under arrest and ordered not to go out side of the city limits without leave of the department commander, unless he concluded to report to his company for duty which he was at liberty to do at any time, which he said he would not do until regularly exchanged.

I found Lieutenant Cole to be a gentleman in every respect. He was an Englishman, said that he had a position in coal mining up George's Creek when the war broke out, that mining all stopped and he was out of a job, the miners had raised a volunteer company and offered him the first

159

lieutenant, which paid, if I am not mistaken, ninety dollars per month, and having nothing to do, accepted, thinking it would only be a little frolic anyhow at good pay, but said that it then looked to him like the frolic would last much longer than any of them had thought it would at the start.

I then explained to him, why I had not been sent to the guard house with the other prisoners and that in addition to the kindness he had already shown me I had a request to make and felt sure before asking that it would be granted, which was that I did not want Col. Porter or General Kelley or any one else to know that I was the Blue who had made his escape at Romney, a few months before, as I felt sure his knowledge of my identity would send me to Camp Chase or some other prison, and my hopes of getting a parole would be in vain. I said you are the only man in Cumberland that could give me away, now the favor I ask is that whenever you have occasion to speak of me, to anyone, let our first acquaintance date back to that Sabbath day at Moorefield when you accepted the parole, for which you are now, in a military sense, being disgraced because you had manhood and honor enough to keep your solemn promise. Let our first meeting be on that day instead of the night when you pulled me from my hiding place in my father's garret.

He said, "I see the point, am glad you spoke of it I came near giving you away at the Provost's office."

"Yes," I said, "that was what I feared and why I was in such haste to get you away. I was aware of appearing rude, but I was very anxious to get you away."

He said "that at the time he thought I acted a little strange, but it was all plain to him now, and that I had nothing to fear from him."

We talked until late at night and did not awake next morning until called for breakfast, at 9 o'clock.

Lieut. Cole accompanied me to the Provost Martial's office where I reported to Col. Porter, who said that the general had not returned yet and that I might still consider myself on parole, and continue to report at nine each morning until further orders. Lieutenant Cole said that he would be responsible for my appearance at the hour named. We then loafed around town until about the middle of the day then went to dinner, then took a short nap, then strolled around until night.

Next morning again reported at the appointed hour, and then spent the day killing time the best way we could. I met a good many southern men whom I knew and who would have done anything in reason for me, but they were watched and were afraid to recognize me and not wishing to get them in any trouble I passed them by as total strangers.

On Saturday morning my friend Cole being somewhat indisposed did not accompany me to the Provost's office where I met General Kelley, he having come down from New Creek that morning. Colonel Porter introduced me to the general, who said the colonel has just been telling me about you. I know your father and like him very much, meet him frequently whilst in Romney. Said that colonel tells me you had come home with the intention of taking an oath of allegiance to the United States when our boys picked you up."

I said "yes, I had nothing to fight for and did not see why I should risk my life in a cause that could do me no good if successful of which I could see no prospect. But I had always been in the habit of asking advice of my father in all matters of any consequence, and in order to so do now would be very glad to get a parole if only for a few days."

He said, "I will give you a parole feeling sure that your father will advise you as I would do and that you will be back in a few days and take the oath and stay at home and care for your father and mother as a dutiful son should do."

Then after lecturing on the "blind folly" as he termed it, of the southern leaders and the certain disaster to which they were destined, he handed me a regular parole with his signature, and gave me a pass, at the same time cautioned me not to attempt to carry with me anything contraband of war, such as gun caps, powder cartridges or ammunition of any kind or gray goods of any kind, which would subject me to arrest and might give me untold trouble. I said no danger of my doing anything of that kind. I don't expect to have use for such things soon. The general and colonel each gave me their hand at parting with a good deal of advice, which to the best of my recollection I did not follow very close. I then went back to Mr. Golden's and offered to pay for my accommodation, but they refused to take any pay. Lieut. Cole had gone out and I never met him again. After thanking Mr. and Mrs. Golden for their great kindness, I started for home.

As I passed up Baltimore street I dropped in to speak a word with a man that I was well acquainted with, who was a merchant tailor. I told him that I had gotten a parole and was going home.

He said, "let me sell you a piece of gray goods to make you a nice uniform when you get back to Dixie."

I said, "no, in the first place I have been positively forbidden to take gray goods of any kind with me and again you would not like to trust me until this war is over."

"Oh," said he, "you come through all right, if you don't your fadder, he pay me, I know him, he is all right."

So he cut enough gray cloth from a bolt of nice cloth to make me a nice suit.

"Now," said he, "you go down the tow path along the canal; when you come to culvert go under him and across over to other side of the river and you meet no picket. Gen. Shackson he catch all them fellows mit, Harper's

Ferry and Martinsburg and the soldiers all gone from here to some place down below Antietam, or something like that way, where Stonewall Shackson make more musick. Soldiers mighty scarse here now, news came last night Stonewall, he shoot South Branch bridge in the river, no railroad, no telegraph, no news, no nothing. Soldiers all gone away last night. You go like I tell you meet no soldier."

The truth was that the battle of Sharpsburg was going on. The troops stationed at Cumberland had been ordered to that place with the exception of one regiment, which had marched sometime during the night, down the tow path toward Green Spring Run, on account of having received news of General Imboden being at the railroad bridge at the mouth of the South Branch. At that time no reliable news from the seat of war could be had in Cumberland, but the excitement was intense.

I bade the old Jew good bye. At parting he said, "when this fight gets done you come back, I make the wedden clothes, (which he did). With my roll under my arm I started following the old Jew's directions. I reached Mr. William Taylor's house about noon in time for dinner. Mr. Taylor lived on what was then known as the Swanpond farm. I was not feeling altogether at ease about gray goods which I carried with me contrary to positive orders, and for which I had paid with the ten dollar greenback given to me by Col. Porter. I felt a little mean about the way I had acted, felt like I should have given the money back not having used it. But I kind of eased my conscience by the thought that I had offered to use it for the purpose it was given me, by paying old Mr. Golden, for value received. He refused to take it. If I had gone as directed to a hotel the money would have been received, so decided the case in about this way. I had received what the money was intended to buy and the money really belonged to Mr. Golden but he gave it to me by refusing to take it and I had a right to use it which I did.

As I said before I was not feeling safe so close to Cumberland with that gray goods in my possession. Although Mr. Taylor gave me a kind invitation to remain over Sunday, I determined to get rid of my gray goods as quick as possible by getting it home and determined to reach home that night if possible. Mr. Taylor then kindly offered to loan me a horse to ride home if I could get him back again. The old gentleman's daughter, Miss Miranda, now Mrs. Wilson, came to the rescue, said that she had been thinking of visiting her sister Mrs. Michael Blue, soon and would accompany and take a colored boy, on the horse behind her to ride the horse back which I would ride over. This arrangement being sanctioned by the old gentleman, we were soon mounted and on our way. We had gone but a few miles when we met Mrs. Michael Blue accompanied by an old man by the name of Mr. Merritt, on her way to visit her father. They turned back and we reached Mr. Michael Blue's house early in the evening. After supper Mr. Merritt went with me home and returned with the horse I rode. I soon had my gray goods in a secure place and felt very much relieved in my mind.

It was now between the 15th and 20th of September, 1862. When I informed my father how I had managed to get a parole, he proceeded to lecture me more severely for lieing, said it would have been far more honorable to have gone to prison than to get a parole by lieing. I claimed that in time of war sometimes a person would be justifiable in telling a lie. He said no person is never right in telling a falsehood, you have not been taught to lie. I said no, but it was easily learned in this case. If I had been an ordinary prisoner I would not have asked for a parole, but I had been a prisoner before, charged with being a spy, had assaulted the guard and made my escape, a reward had been offered for my body dead or alive, the same charges might be brought against me again. I had settled the matter in my own mind that if I could not get a parole, I would make a desperate effort to escape, before reaching Camp Chase, for fear of being identified. If I had not been captured so near home I could have easily changed my name, for these reasons I had not stuck strickly to the truth. Father said, "you are liable to be arrested again at any time."

I thought that I would be safe for a time, at least, as the Yankees had all they could attend to just now, their thought being otherwise engaged. General Lee was in Maryland and had to have attention. For these reasons I felt reasonable safe for a time.

I remained at home for nearly three months, but never felt, during the time, altogether safe, and but seldom slept in the house, until the weather got cold. I spent much of my time in the woods, when the night was favorable I could generally be found watching a deer lick. Deer were right plentiful, I killed several during the time I was home. I succeeded in killing three one night, at a single shot, with a smooth bore musket, which I had hid in a hollow tree at the commencement of the war. I had also a home rifle hid in the same place, with which I hunted during the day, when the day was favorable.

After the battle of Antietam, Yankees were very scarce in Hampshire. For several months occasionally a scouting party passed from New Creek to Cumberland or from Cumberland to New Creek, generally halted for a short time in Romney.

General Jackson remained in the lower valley, between Winchester and the Potomac, after the battle of Sharpsburg, until about the 20 of November. The B. & O. Railroad had been rendered useless from Harper's Ferry to Cumberland. There was therefore no necessity for guarding it, which relieved the people of Hampshire of having soldiers stationed among them for several months. I don't remember to have met Federal soldiers more than three times face to face in the three months that

I was on parole.

About the 1st of October the young folks had a gathering at Abraham Parker's one evening to which I was invited and of course went. The party did not break up until next morning, when it become known that two horses had been stolen from the pasture field where they had been turned during the night. One belonging to Mr. Parker the other to Mrs. Fox, which had been ridden there by her daughter, and would be a great loss to the family, horses being very scarce at this time could hardly be replaced. It was generally believed by those present, the horses had been stolen by Yankees and had gone to New Creek, as their tracks showed that they had gone in that direction, but I felt sure that no Yankee would venture that far from New Creek to steal horses, when their horses were furnished them by their government. A Confederate cavalryman must furnish his own horse or be sent to the infantry. I knew that Imboden's command was somewhere on the South Fork and was of the opinion that the stolen horses had gone there and determined to investigate a little in that direction. Mr. Parker's son, Mose, volunteered to go with me. We followed the river road without making any discoveries until we reached a ford about twelve miles above Romney, where we discovered that two horses had crossed the river, either late in the night or early that morning. We now felt sure that we were on the right trail and pushed on reaching Mr. David Vanmeter's house about dark and inquired of him whether he had seen any one or two persons pass that day, riding a gray horse and roan mare.

He said yes, two men stopped here riding horses of that description, had their horses fed and got dinner. We told him that those horses were stolen, one from Abraham Parker, the other from Mrs. Rebecca Fox.

"Is it possible," the old gentleman said in a very excited way, "that one of them horses was stolen from Cousin Rebecca Fox? If I had only known they would have gone no further.

We asked to get feed for our horses as they had eaten nothing since morning, and also something for ourselves. The old gentleman then asked our names. I said "Parker and Blue."

"What Blue."

I told him a son of Garret I. Blue.

He said, "I know your father, have been at his house, bought a lot of cattle from him once and I have heard of his son. Sit down."

Our horses were soon cared for and we seated at Mr. Vanmeter's table enjoying a substantial meal. Mr. Vanmeter said that the men who had stopped at his house; said the command to which they belonged was then in the Valley near Harrisonburg and that they expected to stop over at Imboden's camp on the South Fork and would go on next day by way of Howard's Lick and Brock's Gap. We then asked to stop with him until say two o'clock next morning as we would like to reach Imboden's camp by daylight next morning.

He said, "if you start from here at three in the morning you can reach the camp by daylight and now you boys come with me and take the saddles off your horses and give them hay and then I will show you where to sleep and I will call you in time."

We said we would sleep in the barn so that we would not disturb the family next morning.

"No," said he, "you go to bed, and I will get you off in time. I am anxious for you to catch the scoundrel who stole Cousin Rebecca's horse and that she may get her horse again."

We were soon in bed and asleep. About half past two the old gentleman called us. We arose at once and went down stairs and to our surprise found a warm breakfast awaiting us. I don't think the old gentleman had laid down for fear he would not awake at the right time.

Our horses had been fed and by three o'clock we were on the road. When we got within a mile of the camp, Parker refused to go any further, he was as much afraid of the Confederates as he was of the Yankees, for good reasons. He said he would stop in a thicket until I returned. I did not urge him to go farther, and went on alone. I reached the picket about daylight, the picket was just being relieved and I rode with them to camp. Nearly the first man I met was Capt. Stump, who asked in a very emphathic way what I was doing there. I dismounted and went with him to his tent, where I explained to him the cause of my visit.

He said, "them rascals are here. I somehow thought I knew them horses. You stay here until I come back, don't show yourself, I am going to see the colonel."

In a few moments the captain returned accompanied by Colonel George Imboden. The colonel questioned me as to what I knew in regard to the horses. In a short time the parties who had stolen the horses rode past showing them off to best advantage for the purpose of selling them. The colonel and captain walked down to the road and seemed to be examining the horses at the same time questioned the men as to where and how they came with the horses.

They claimed to have captured them on New Creek from a pasture field, where the Yankees had quite a lot of horses in pasture. Captain Stump was well acquainted with the young men who were brothers and who lived a few miles from his home. I will not give their names. The captain said, "boys I know these horses, you stole them from Abraham Parker's pasture on Mill Creek, night before last; one of them belongs to Widow Fox, the other to Abraham Parker, and there is a man in my tent now that came for these horses."

The captain then called to me I walked down, the colonel asked if I knew those men. I said I did. Then asked if I knew the horses. I said I did and stated the facts.

I felt sorry for the boys, they felt bad, judging from their looks. The colonel talked very plain to them, and he did not allow horse stealing about him. Ordered the boys taken to the guard house and turned the horses over to me to be returned to their owners. I was riding a nice mare which I had purchased a few days before, which Capt. Stump took a fancy to and sold her to him, then saddled and mounted one of the stolen horses led the other and started on the back track. I found Parker where I had left him. He was getting very impatient and was about to start back without me. We reached Mr. Vanmeter's house again shortly after noon, fed our horses and got our dinner. The old gentleman was greatly rejoiced at our recovery of "Cousin Beck's" horse.

I turned over to Mrs. Fox, shortly after dark that evening, her mare safe and sound, to the great relief of the family.

I had learned that General Jackson was in the valley somewhere below Winchester, and had a great desire to pay the boys a visit, but knew it would be a dangerous thing to do. No doubt I was being watched and would be reported if I returned and it was known that I had been to the valley. But I could not resist the desire to go and started one night shortly after dark and rode all night, reaching Winchester about daylight next morning. I learned that Gen. Robertson's brigade of cavalry was camped near the Opequon on the pike leading from Winchester to Berryville. I rode on and reached the camp to which I belonged was on picket near Charles Town and would not be relieved for several days. I concluded, after taking dinner with Company F of the 7th regiment, to go in search of the 11th, which I found at a place called Ripon. I remained with this company a few days and started on my return, Saturday evening. On my way down I found David Fox, a member of Captain Kuykendall's company, very much complaining and had directed him to a George Calmes, who lived some four miles from camp and promised to meet him there Saturday evening. Calmes had at one time lived in the farm where J. G. Monroe now lives, near Springfield. I knew him, having seen him several times at my father's house.

I arrived at Mr. Calmes' house late in the evening, found David had arrived and was not in the best possible humor, the old gentleman was not at home, the old lady and daughter hesitated about taking him in. He told them who he was and where from, but they seemed to know nothing of the family. David was a pretty sick boy and felt a little ruffled at the treatment and told the ladies that I was to meet him there that evening and that he would remain until I came and dismounted.

The old gentleman arrived at home about the same time I got to his house. He was well acquainted with Colonel Fox, David's father. We remained with Mr. Calmes over Sunday and were kindly treated, in fact I thought the daughter parted with David rather reluctantly.

On Monday morning we offered to pay for our accommodation, but the old gentleman refused to take anything. After thanking them for their kindness, bade them for adieu and started, David for camp and I for home. I stopped with company F of the 7th, Capt. Kuykendall's camp, until in the afternoon and reached the Five Mile House on the Northwestern Grade and stopped for the night. I here found an old acquaintance from Romney, Mr. Jonathan Harmison. He was doing a little private huckstering for the benefit of himself and the southern boys, generally. One of his horses was taken sick and died. The old gentleman was in a bad fix. He claimed to be dealing principally in butter and eggs, but I noticed that most of his load seemed to be put up in five and ten gallon kegs, well secured with iron hoops. If those kegs all contained the same kind of butter and eggs that I sampled, I should not wonder if friend Jonathan's horse didn't die of manuapotua, caused from inhaling the fumes of the contents of those kegs. I was riding a fairly good horse. Friend Jonathan was compelled to have one and offered me one hundred dollars for him. (Confederate money was then worth almost as much as gold in the South.) Mr. Harmison was very uneasy for fear a troop of cavalry might chance to pass that way, and possibly confiscate the contents of those kegs as being contraband of war. I had proposed selling the horse when I left home if I could find a buyer. I said something to Capt. McDonald about selling him but did not like the idea of footing it home. The captain said his old horse was in pasture about five miles from Winchester, in care of a man called Pingly. Said if I should sell my horse I could ride him home. Here then was my opportunity; my conscience would not allow me to ask friend Harmison two prices for the horse, but came very near it, by letting him have the horse for two hundred and fifty dollars, which Mr. Harmison, said in very emphatic language, was worse than robbery. He paid me the cash. I took my saddle on my back and started to get Capt. McDonald's horse, about a mile away. I soon had the horse and was on my way.

I reached Romney near sundown and concluded to flank the town, by passing in rear of the Academy, then occupied by a Mr. Nelson, who claimed to be a subject of the English crown. There being no fences to hinder I was making my way down town run, when spied by Mr. Nelson. He hailed me and called me over and insisted on my getting down and taking a drink of Irish whiskey with him. He suspicioned me with having been in the valley. He was a true Southern at heart, a Presbyterian preacher and a man who could be trusted.

Mr. Nelson was very anxious to hear the news from the Confederate army in the valley. I gave him what news I could and started on again. When I had nearly reached the toll gate where Mr. Cherry then lived, I heard hollowing behind me, on looking behind me I saw coming down town hill, a company of Yankees almost at the top of their horses' speed, yelling like Indians. I thought at first that they were after me for sure.

I rode on at a slow pace not seeing any way to escape them, they soon began passing me without halting. The captain was riding in the rear when he came up, he spoke very politely and rode with me for a short distance, said they had come over from New Creek and were on their way to Cumberland, said the boys were feeling their whiskey and that he would have to ride on and check them up or no telling where they would stop. He bade me good evening and rode on at a brisk gate, and I certainly was not sorry at being left alone and reached home about dark.

I now kept very close and was not often seen away from home by daylight, did most of scouting after night. About the middle of December I got hold of the Baltimore American where I saw that all prisoners captured before a certain date had been exchanged and those on parole were ordered to report forthwith to their commands for duty. I knew now that I would have to get away or I would be arrested.

One object in going to the valley had been to see a Mr. Marker, who was quartermaster of our company. Mr. Marker had a very fine horse which I wanted, but could not buy him from Mrs. Marker unless I could get an order from Mr. Marker, to get an order for the horse was the chief cause of my trip to the valley.

Next day after seeing the notice of exchange I was in the blacksmith shop making a pair of spurs when a squad of Yankees rode up and inquired if my name was Blue and if I was not a paroled prisoner. I answered affirmative, I was then handed a note from General Kelley, in which he said that I must come to Cumberland and take an oath of allegiance to the United States otherwise he would have to have me arrested and sent to prison. That night I went to Frankfort, presented my order for the horse, paid the price named in the order and got the horse and got back home before daylight. John Linn, of Cumberland, Md., had been at father's house for a few days waiting until I was ready to accompany him back to Dixie, where he proposed offering his services to the south, as two of his brothers had already done.

Brig. Gen. Benjamin F. Kelley
(NATIONAL ARCHIVES)

Gen. J.D. Imboden
(NATIONAL ARCHIVES)

CHAPTER XII

Back into the Fray

T he night following we started for the valley and reached Capon Springs early next morning, where we fed and had breakfast then pushed on. When we reached what was the back road in the valley, we were held up by a picket, belonging to Captain McNeil's command, who refused to let us proceed farther and sent a man to Captain McNeil's quarters, a short distance in the rear.

The captain's headquarters were in a fence corner of which was a fire built of old stumps of trees. I handed the captain my parole and said that I was on my way to report to my company on duty.

After asking me a few questions in regard to the Yankees in Hampshire and Hardy counties, he informed me that I would find the 11th Virginia a short distance above Winchester and allowed me to proceed on my way. Linn had met some of his friends from Cumberland who belonged to Captain McNeil's command. He concluded to remain with them and afterward joined Captain McNeil's command. I reached the regiment to which I belonged that evening, but found only a few of company D in camp. Captain McDonald with nearly all his company, a part of Captain Harness' and part of Captain Kuykendall's had gone to Moorefield on a scout. The Yankees got information of their movements and surprised them in town of Moorefield while they were engaged in biding adieu to fair ones who they might never see again. It was a mean trick, but no doubt the Yankees enjoyed it, whilst most of the boys made their escape. Captain McDonald rallied a few of his men and attempted to make a stand, but they returned to camp a few months later by way of Camp Chase, Ohio. Capt. McDonald made his escape on the way down the Ohio River and made his way across the Confederacy to Richmond. In his absence, Lieutenant Taylor commanded the company. We had a quiet time for several weeks, doing a little picketing. At length the Yankees advanced to Winchester. The infantry had all left the valley in care of William E. Jones, formerly colonel of the 7th regiment, now a brigadier.

General Jones fell back to Edinburg. The 11th Virginia regiment was camped just back of the village, the 7th, 6th and 12th regiments were camped a mile or two up Sandy Creek. If I remember right, General Imboden's brigade was also camped no great distance up Stony Creek. Captain McDonald and the boys who had been captured had reported for duty again.

The Yankees were not supposed to be nearer than Winchester, our picket post was about two or three miles below Edinburg where a cross road connected, what was called the back road, with the valley pike.

We had been camped here perhaps two weeks, half of our men away on furloughs, having gone home to get fresh horses. A large majority of the brigade were raised in the valley and could visit their homes without danger, and had taken this opportunity to do so.

One morning the latter part of February, General Jones, who made his headquarters with the 7th regiment. About nine o'clock a courier dashed into camp with the news that the Yankees were coming and would be up in a few moments. General Jones ordered Colonel Funsten to call out his regiment, the bugle call to saddle up. We were in the saddle in a very short time. We knew from the sound of the bugle that we were required to be as expeditious as possible, but did not know what was to pay. When we got into the line there were about two hundred of us. General Jones remarked, "Colonel, is this all the men you can muster?"

The colonel said, "it seems to be all that are present this morning."

The general said, well, come on, we will go down and see what's wrong, I expect a scouting party had frightened our picket."

The general sent a courier to the 7th ordering them to follow as speedily as possible.

We started down the valley pike, Gen. Jones and Col. Funsten rode a short distance in advance of the column. A few days before several inches of snow had fallen, but had melted rapidly, the pike was covered with a thin batter of mud. After marching something like two miles, we met our reserve picket. The officer in command informed the general that a column of Yankee cavalry had attempted to get in the rear by moving up the valley on the back road and then crossing over and reaching the valley pike in the rear. An old citizen who lived on the back road had given them information in time for them to fall back behind the point on which the Yankees aimed to reach the pike. That on receiving information of the advance on the back road, a courier had been sent to camp. At this moment one of the two pickets, which had been left a little way down the pike rode up and reported a column of Yankees having just reached the pike coming down a narrow valley on our left at right angles with the pike and was supposed to be about two hundred strong.

From where we had halted the pike wound with a gradual descent around the point of a ridge, bearing to the left until it reached the valley, by which the Yankees had reached the pike. It then curved to the right, crossed a small stream near where an old stone mill had stood, crossed the narrow valley and again turned to the left and ascended the opposite ridge, forming almost a perfect S.

The Yankee column, which had come down this narrow valley, on reaching the pike had halted with the head of the column in the direction of Winchester. This column was a part of the 13th Pennsylvania cavalry,

172

the bulk of which had followed the valley pike. The two columns had met and had halted, being lapped one column going up and the other down the pike. This was the position the Yankees were in when the command from General Jones of "draw sabre, charge" fell clear and distinct on their ears. When the pickets departed the Yankees near by in our front, General Jones ordered us to move forward as quietly as possibly.

The pike passed through a body of timber with a thick undergrowth and was not discovered by the Yankees until the head of our column, on making a rather short curve in the road, came out in full view and not a hundred yards distant. It was at this moment that the order to charge was given and at them we went. There was nothing else to do. A single glance sufficed to satisfy us that we were out numbered three or four to one. It was well for us that we had them at a disadvantage. They were whirling around like drift wood in an eddy, some trying to face the music, but the greater part started toward Winchester at railroad speed. Before those who stood their ground could get in shape to receive us we were on them, and for a few moments things were very lively, but they could not stand the sabre and we soon had them on the run. Something like a hundred surrendered. We were close on the heels of the fleeing foe, who covered us with mud, often having to claw the mud from our eyes to enable us to see. We pressed them hard, every little while picking them off from the rear of the column, as their horses gave out and dropped behind, We followed them through Woodstock and on through Strasburg. Our boys had gone back with prisoners. Many of their horses had failed until not more than a dozen Confeds were in sight, as we neared Middletown.

Captain McDonald, who was mounted on a fine blooded mare raised by the Sloans of Patterson's Creek, led the chase. After a running fight of fifteen or more miles, nearly all our horses had played out some four or five hundred Yankees had been over hauled, disarmed and sent to the rear, often one man guarding several Yankees. For the last few miles we had no men to spare and on overhauling a Yankee disarmed him and sent him to the rear without a guard; if they were not soon met by straggling Confeds, who were glad of an excuse to turn back, no doubt they made a flank movement at the first opportunity, and reported that night or next day, not at Edinburg, but at Winchester. When a prisoner was disarmed and sent to the rear without a guard, his arms were carried a short distance and dropped by the side of the road, some of which were picked up in our return or by those who had followed on. As I said before, when only a short distance above Middletown, on making a short turn in the road we found ourselves face to face with a line of Yankees, drawn up apparently ready to receive us. Captain McDonald halted his men, numbering, if I remember right, five were Hampshire boys, Captain Ed McDonald, Samuel Bane, Conrad Umstot, Isaac Parsons and myself.

173

The Yankees were not over a hundred yards distant. He said, as we formed fours, "boys what's to be done? These fellows look as though they meant business, they are too many for us, but it may be that we can bluff them with the belief that we are well backed. Suppose we charge them and if they don't run when they see us coming we will fall back the best we can."

We turned in the saddle, looking to the rear and beckoning as to some one in the rear to hasten up. We trotted toward the Yanks, which was the fastest gate we could get up yelling at the same time in a way that should have started anything living on the run. But these Yankees seemed determined to stand their ground. When we were within fifty yard of them we halted, they showed no sign of advancing. We returned and rode slowly back. They did not attempt to follow. We soon rounded a curve in the road and was hid from their view. We then moved as fast as our tired horses could take us.

After going a mile or two we met the 7th regiment which followed on after the Yankees and overtook them at Middletown, where they had halted, to allow the stragglers, who had not been captured, to come up, believing that the race was over, and that the Confeds had gone back. When the 7th returned that night they brought with them one hundred prisoners.

We reached camp about ten o'clock at night the tiredest, dirtiest, muddiest lot of men ever seen. It would have been difficult to tell the color of our skin or of our clothes, so completely were we plastered with mud.

Next morning I went to where the prisoners were surrounded by a guard. If I remember right there were about six hundred of them. Among them I recognized a big Dutchman for whom I had been compelled to do a little carving, the day before, in a manner that didn't improve his appearance that I could see. But when one had a revolver stuck in his face he does not always take time to think, and often does things in an unbecoming manner, but accidents of this kind often happened during the unpleasantness of the sixties.

The prisoners were sent to Staunton and shipped south. The regiment, which we had come nigh annihilating the day before was the 13 Pennsylvania regiment, which had been mustered into service a short time before. Their equipments were all new, arms, saddles, bridles, halters, gum coats, gum blankets, &c. Almost every man in our regiment supplied himself with these very necessary conveniences, in short the equipments of the 13th Pennsylvania had been transferred in a great measure to the 11th Virginia, I believe from that time on it was the best equipped regiment in the service. Many of the men had carried to camp extra arms which were concealed for their friends, who were absent.

The bloody 13th, as it was called, had left Winchester, so some of the prisoners said, with between nine hundred and a thousand men. They had never been in a fight and many of them had never seen a Reb; that they had left Winchester, determined to cross sabres with them if they had an opportunity to do so and said a Yankee captain, "here is where the opportunity has landed us."

We heard afterwards, from some of the same regiment whom we captured on the Rappahannock, several months after, that instead of being called the bloody 13th, they had, since their experience in the valley, been called the muddy 13th.

Our brigade, soon after our chase down the valley, moved to Krotzer Springs, a few miles north of Harrisonburg. While here our company, and having but one lieutenant was ordered to elect two more, a second and a third. I was elected second without opposition and Isaac Parsons was elected third lieutenant. Whilst camped here I took the opportunity to have a uniform made by a tailor in Harrisonburg, from the gray cloth which I had secured in Cumberland. The Confederate Government now required all commissioned officers to uniform according to regulations of the Confederate army.

CHAPTER XIII

West Virginia Campaign

T he latter part of April General Jones left his camp at Krotzer Springs, and led his brigade by way of Brock's Gap to the South Fork of the South Branch of the Potomac, where he halted his command for a day or two, on account of high water, then crossed the North Fork some distance above Moorefield and, although many of the men swam their horses, only one man was drowned. We crossed the mountain to Patterson's Creek, and reached Greenland Gap shortly after dark. It was known that a body of Yankees occupied a large log church, which stood on a raise near the road. When the column reached within a short distance of the church it was halted. Major White's Maryland battalion was in front. The garrison was called on to surrender. The call was answered by a volley of musketry from the church. The battalion was then dismounted and ordered to take the garrison by storm. The gallant Marylanders rushed up the ascent in the dark, but were repulsed with heavy loss, considering the number engaged. The Yankees felt that they could hold their position and meant business. The Marylanders were very much incensed at their loss of a dozen or more men killed and wounded. They soon, under cover of darkness had the church on fire, which left but one of two things for the Yankees to do either to come out and surrender or perish in the flames. They chose the former, threw down their arms and marched out. I can't call to mind the captain's name, who commanded the company which numbered about ninety men.

When they discovered the odds against which they had been contending and heard the revengeful threats of the Marylanders, although they were no doubt brave men, yet many of them turned pale and quaked with fear, expecting, no doubt, to be massacred at any moment. It really looked for a few moments as though those Marylanders could not be restrained, but General Jones was on the ground and said, "boys these men have thrown down their arms and must be protected and treated as prisoners. It would be cowardly to do otherwise, these men have done their duty as brave men and what I hope you would do. These men must be cared for."

The Yankee captain said he was sorry that they had fired on us and if they had known anything of our number would not have done so. They supposed that they were attacked by Capt. McNeil's company, as they had expected to be at any time. They were sent under guard to Moorefield, from there I suppose they went to Staunton and thence to a southern prison.

Our column was again put in motion and reached the Northwestern grade in the latter part if the night at Mount Storm. The command halted for a few hours, fed our horses and slept an hour or two then started again. Capt. McDonald was ordered back to Hartmansville, thence by way of Elk Garden to Altamont and join the regiment at Oakland. As we were descending the mountain near Altamont a station on the B. & O. Railroad, we heard a train approaching from the direction of New Creek. Captain McDonald halted us in the woods a short distance below the station. The train stopped at the station and all hands went to the grog shop near by, I suppose to take something. We rode briskly forward and captured the train before it got away. There were eight or ten cars, all empty except two which were loaded with oats. It was now about middle of the day. We fed our horses all they would eat, each man carried a two bushel sack and put into what oats he could conveniently carry, then the captain asked if there was any one in the company who knew enough about an engine to back a train a short distance down the road then open the valve and let her run over a bank in a little way above the station, at the same time sending men to tear up the rails, so as to run the train off. Dr. John Dailey, a member of our company, said that he could back the train. He mounted the engine and proceeded to back the train, but he got the wrong motion the train moved forward instead of backward. The doctor jerked the valve open and jumped off; the railing had not yet been removed and the train rushed on at a rate of speed I will venture to say never equaled before or since. We could see the train for a long distance, as it rushed onward toward Oakland, through a comparatively level grade. The farther it got the faster it seemed to run until at length it appeared to just sail through the air.

The 12th regiment had reached Oakland and had been ordered to await us at that place, but when they heard a train approaching at such a high rate of speed they hastily withdrew supposing that the coming train had troops aboard, being sent up from New Creek.

When we reached Oakland about sundown, we found the train standing at the end of the bridge, which had been burned, the steam having been exhausted in an up grade. The engine on reaching the abutment, dropping its front wheels over and the train stopped.

The 12th regiment had crossed the Youghiogheny and followed the road leading to Kingwood. We pushed on following the same road; we did not halt until late in the night, hoping to overtake the 12th, about 10 o'clock we halted in a meadow by the side of the road, where we found two or three hay stacks. We gave our horses hay and lay down for a few hours sleep. We were up early next morning, found the ground frozen and covered by a white frost. We were a good deal chilled, but being in an enemy's country, feared to make fires. After feeding our horses, ate our ration of hard tack and a slice of raw bacon and was on the march by the break of day, hoping to overtake our friends before they broke camp. Soon after sun rise the bushwackers commenced to fire on us with the home rifle from the top of knobs near which the road passed, but the distance was generally too great to do much execution. We escaped with having a few horses struck; the men escaped not having suffered, only from fright. On reaching Cheat river at General Fairfax's home, who was an uncle by marriage of J. D. and Lieutenant Ike Parsons, of our company.

The general was not at home at least was not visible. He had several good looking horses in his stable. We had two or three horses bushwacked and unable to go further. One of the horses wounded that morning belonged to J. Don Parsons. If I remember right we exchanged three horses with the general, although he was not present, he was well represented by his wife who began to show blood in her eye as she marched among the men with a good-sized hoop pole about ten feet long in her hand. The old lady expressed herself very emphatically, in a style peculiar to her family in which they generally said what they meant and meant what they said. The old lady came near demoralizing the whole troop.

The bridge had been burned, the 12th regiment had crossed the night before, the river was rather deep to ford; General Fairfax, had a small ferryboat, in which three or four horses could be carried over at a time. The work of ferrying had commenced, perhaps a dozen men had been landed on the other side when a volley was fired at us from a high knob near by, by perhaps as many as twenty or more bushwackers. The men, most of whom a few moments before had opposed fording the stream, suddenly changed their minds and took to water as freely as a flock of ducks. Those mounted on tall horses, many of them at least, got over dry, but those were wet to their necks. At least one half of our pistols and carbines were useless until the loads could be drawn.

The bushwackers continued to fire at us from the mountain side on the opposite side of the river, but the distance was too great for them to do serious harm. However we were soon in pursuit of the 12th regiment again. On nearing Kingwood we met a man who said that there was a regiment of Yankees cavalry at Kingwood.

I supposed the fellow, who did not seem to be very bright, had seen the 12th Confederate and took it to be a Yankee regiment. Anyway we felt that we were in a strange place and not among friends, and were not feeling altogether safe. We soon came in sight of the town and halted for a moment or two to hold a council and decided that there was but one thing to do which was to press on Yankees or no Yankees. We had heard of Kingwood and there not being over fifty of us we feared being attacked by the citizens, even if there were no Yankees in the place. Our column kept well closed up, there was no straggling now and if it had been necessary to fight I don't think there would have been no place to run for safety. We rode straight through the town without seeing more than a half dozen persons on the streets. All were old gray haired men who looked at us in a sullen way but said nothing. We felt relieved when we had left the town some distance in our rear. Occasionally we met an old man or boy of whom we inquired if they had seen any soldiers pass that way during the day, if so how far ahead. One would say about a mile, another five miles, another probably would say just around the turn.

We halted about the middle of the day and fed our horses and ate a slice of raw bacon and pushed forward again, reaching Morgantown about sundown. We learned that the Confederates had left the town about an hour before and gone up the river. We followed on and about ten o'clock we were halted by the Confederates picket and soon with our regiment again, after being separated from it for nearly two days and nights. We took our saddles from our horses' backs for the first time since they left Moorefield, fed them, finished our rations of crackers and bacon, then lay down for a nap. We learned that a good deal of uneasiness had been felt for our safety when the 12th regiment reached the brigade without having heard anything of our company.

Next morning two hours before day, we were in the saddle again heading for Morgantown. The brigade was now altogether again. The evening before the citizens of the town had notice of the approach of the 12th regiment and had run their horses to a place for safety, but when the Confederates left town they supposed they were gone and brought their horses in again. On entering the town about break of day—a good many fine horses were secured. We came near capturing Senator Willey, who escaped to the woods near his house in his night clothes. The brigade crossed over the wire bridge to the other side of the river and placing a guard on the bridge allowed no one to pass either way without a pass from headquarters. The brigade went into camp in a field on a hill a short distance from the bridge. The quartermasters and commissaries of the different regiments soon pressed teams and had forage for the horses and rations of meat and crackers and bread for men, also coffee and sugar. We remained here all day, watered and fed our horses in evening and made preparations to stay all night by building up our fires, by piling on more rails and then lying down, was soon asleep.

Near midnight we were quickly awakened and ordered to saddle up as quietly as possible and take our place in ranks without further orders. We were in the saddle in a very short time not knowing what was going to happen. Our regiment was first to move out into the road, followed by the remainder of the brigade. About twenty men from our company rode a little distance in front, as advance guard to the command, piloted by a man acquainted with the country. We rode in silence until day began to break, when we were halted. General Jones rode forward and instructed the advance, (which I had the honor to command) that if we were halted, (which we were likely to be within the next half mile) that we should dash forward and capture the picket if possible. A dense fog made it impossible to see only a few paces. The road lead us up a narrow hollow; on either side was a steep hill, immediately along each side of the road was a high fence staked and ridered. We moved forward slowly and cautiously, peering through the fog to discover if possible the expected picket.

We had in this manner proceeded not over a half mile when the command to halt reached us, only a short distance in our front. We dashed forward, met a few scattering shots, which passed harmless over our heads. The picket was stationed at a log school house, which stood close to the road-side. The pickets escaped by scaling the fence and climbing the steep hill on the right of the road. The fog hiding them from view. We had gone but a short distance farther when we were fired on from a high hill to our right and front by a whole regiment. They could not see us and no doubt fired in the direction of the sound made by our horses' feet. The balls mostly passed in our front, though many struck the fence above us. I was struck in the right shoulder by a spent ball which passed through a heavy leather strap, (which passed diagonally across the body and supported the sabre belt) through my overcoat, dress coat, waist coat and under clothes. My sabre dropped from my grasp, the shock came near unhorsing me.

We halted, turned and rode back a short distance, when we met General Jones at the head of his column, coming up at a lively gate, asked where the firing came from and pressed forward. Lieut. Ike Parsons came up where I was sitting on my horse by the side of the road and said, "What's the matter have you been wounded?"

I said, "yes," in rather a weak tone. I really felt sick and faint.

He said, "where are you struck."

I said, "shot through the shoulder," at the same time point to the hole in my overcoat.

Ike said, "get down and lets examine it, may not be as bad as you think."

I said I would soon bleed to death. My boot felt as though it was full of blood. I got down and sat on a stump, while Ike removed my belt and unbuttoned my coats and vest and opened my shirt bosom, when an Enfield musket ball dropped out. Ike roared with laughter, said I come near bleeding to death without having lost a drop of blood. The skin was scarcely broken, but the jar had turned the shoulder a dark purple color. I had little use of the arm on the side for several days.

After discovering that musket ball, I felt better at once, and mounting our horses, overtook the command as they entered the town of Fairmont. I had discovered that my horse had received a more serious wound than I, a ball had passed between his neck and the shoulderblade, how far it had penetrated I could not tell. It was evident that I must trade horses or soon be on foot. I rode to a large stable belonging to, I believe, the only hotel in the place at that time. There were several horses in the stable; I made a selection and asked the hostler how he would trade that sorrel horse, with white legs, for my horse. The old fellow said the horse belonged to a citizen and he could not trade him. I said that I had always heard that it took two to make a bargain, but this time I would have to make a trade alone. The hostler said that he did not like to let the horse go as he knew the man the horse belonged to would not like to part with his horse. Oh well if he is not satisfied with the trade, tell him to bring my horse over to Harrisonburg and I will trade back to pay him the difference. I directed Isaac Wolf, who was with me, to change the saddles and I was soon mounted again well pleased with my trade.

A regiment of Yankees were camped on a hill near town over on the side next to the river. The road which we followed on leaving town led us through a piece of woods along the top of a ridge, then through a lane. The Yankees were camped in a field on our left, not over one hundred yards from the road, along which we had to pass, where we were exposed to the fire of the Yankees for a distance of seventy five or a hundred yards. Our men ran their horses through the lane at the top of their speed, a few at a time, lying as close to the opposite side of the horses as possible, being somewhat protected from the Yankee fire by the high fence between us and the Yankees. When my turn came to run the gauntlet, I started and as soon as I passed from the timber I gave old Mulligan a severe dig with my spurs; (Mulligan was the name given my new horse.) The moment the spurs touched him he commenced to kick up and turn around on his front feet. Finally I got him started to the rear in the direction we came. On reaching the shelter of the woods I had me a good sized cane, and rode to edge of the timber. I had my right arm in a sling and had to use my cudgel in my left hand. Taking the rein in my teeth I fired him pretty freely with my cane, he went through all right. On my way through the lane about half way I noticed a dead horse and in the corner of the fence lay David Ream, of Romney, flat on the ground firing at the Yankees with his carbine over the ground log of the fence and I have no doubt he did execution. He was a very cool and brave man. As we passed over the hill we turned to the right and formed in line on the opposite side of the hill from the Yankees, then some men were up on foot to throw the fence down on each side of the road, so that we could charge the Yankee camp.

When the Yankees saw that we were about to make a charge they hoisted a white flag, in token of surrender. We rode over to their camp.

They had already stacked their arms, and marched out a short distance from their camp, when a train was heard approaching, it brought reinforcements for the Yankees, but came too late. They fired a few shots from a piece of artillery, which they brought with them, but did no harm and seeing they were too late to aid their friends, soon left again.

The prisoners about seven hundred, were paroled, the railroad bridge was destroyed and we left that evening. I can't remember what route we followed on leaving Fairmont. I remember crossing a railroad at a place called Bridgeport. I think it was on the Parkersburg road. We had a brush with some Yankees at this place. The next place I remember was Weston, then West Union where we arrived late in the evening.

The town from a distance seemed to be well garrisoned, judging from lines of infantry visible on the hills, around the town. They appeared to be ready and waiting to receive us. Gen. Jones halted his men just out of range, then exhibited them to the best advantage, by marching them across a hill, fields on either side of the road, and counter marching in the hollows and again passing across the high ground in full view of the Yankees, this kind of maneuvering was kept up until the shades of evening hid the opposite lines from view, when Gen. Jones, quietly left the Yankees in possession of the town and move in another direction.

The Yankees no doubt had lain on their arms all night expecting to be attacked at daylight next morning, but next morning we were perhaps twenty miles away having marched all night, or nearly so. We passed through Ritchie and Wirt counties, and reached Burning Springs, on the little Kanawha river. At or near this point were several oil wells in full blast. The oil being floated down the river in large flat boats built with square tanks in them oil tight. These tanks were, if I remember right, as much as fifteen feet square, being the full width of the boat, and looked to be four or five feet in depth. These tanks were filled with oil and floated down to, I suppose somewhere on the Ohio river. There was one of these boats tied up to the warf, loaded down to within a few inches of the water. When we reached the village, and I think as much as five hundred barrels of oil piled on the warf; there was also tied up to the warf a large flat boat divided into two rooms, the front one was used for dry goods, the rear one for a ware room. With a good stock of goods on hand, the proprietor had locked up and departed just where no one knew.

The whole village seemed to be deserted. A company of Yankee infantry had been stationed here, but had received news of our approach and gone down the river to a place called Elizabeth, if I am not mistaken. Our company was the advance of the command, and not finding any one at home proceeded to unlock the store and having been a little short of rations for several days proceeded to help ourselves to whatever we saw of which we were in need, such as sugar-cured hams of which we found a nice lot on board, almost every man had something for his mess; one a ham, another a bushel or so of crackers, another a half bushel or more of sugar, another coffee or tea, hats, boots, in short our company supplied itself with many needed articles before the brigade arrived.

The store was soon empty. General Jones now ordered the oil in the boat set on fire and shoved out into the river, the sides of the boat soon burned and the oil spread over the water, the river soon appeared to be on fire, the barrels piled on the warf had been fired and began to burst like cannon. The oil wells had been set on fire, and the forked flames were darting a hundred feet skyward. We had secured feed for our horses and gone back several hundred yards on the side of the mountain and halted for the purpose of feeding our horses and making a cup of coffee, but the heat became so oppressive from the burning oil, that we were compelled to move farther away. I can't remember now what route we followed after leaving the oil wells, I was wholly unacquainted with the country, and nothing of an exciting nature occurred to fix the route in my mind. The next place I remember was a place called Sutton, no, I think, the Gauley river, in Braxton county; here an old wooden bridge spanned the river but was not safe.

At Sutton our regiment separated from the brigade and followed the Gauley river to its source; the other regiments of the brigade followed what was called the Western and Gauley Bridge turnpike, in the direction of Lewisburg in Greenbrier county.

Our regiment commanded by Col. Lomax, followed the Gauley river until it was only a small stream, scarcely large enough to run a small mill. We were in the wilderness for three days and nights. A pilot on foot led us over the mountains by what was called an old Indian trail. We followed our guide in single file. When the front files had reached the summit of a mountain and looked back the rear files could be seen winding their way down the steep mountain side, a mile in the rear, of the timber was of oak. The buds had not begun to swell on the mountains, but in many places the mountains were covered with heavy pine timber, which stood so thick that there was scarcely room to ride between them. Then again in many places the laurel grew to the height of twenty or thirty feet. It would have been impossible for a man to find his way out of these thickets only by the trail, which was so overgrown that in the middle of the day it seemed as though night was at hand.

In passing through these thickets, several times the scream of a panther, or catamount near by, caused the boys to seize up their carbines and close up their ranks, while the cold chills chased up their backs, expecting at any moment to be attacked by one of those fierce animals. We had nothing for our horses and only a little corn meal for ourselves to eat. We camped at night on some small streams, which were numerous. As soon as the command would halt for the night two or three from each mess would go in search of crickets and bugs to use as bait for catching trout, of which the mountain streams seemed to be alive. These we broiled on coals. We mixed our corn meal into a stiff dough, then baked on a smooth rock which had been made hot in the fire to which the dough would soon stick and was then set up in front of a bed of coals and was soon dried through. Both bread and trout might have been more palatable if we could have had a little salt, but we enjoyed our meals all the same.

The last night in the wilderness we camped on top of a mountain, where it was said a man by the name of Hinkle, if I remember right, Dr. Hinkle had undertaken to clear a large tract of land, by deadening the timber. A great deal of timber had fallen and afforded abundance of wood for camp fires. Here we halted for the night without any food of any kind for man or beast. There was a double log cabin on the clearing, in which a man, his wife and an old colored woman lived. The man was not at home, although was somewhere near by in the brush. The old lady had a pet lamb for which our mess offered to pay fifty dollars in Confederate green backs, but the old lady positively refused to sell her lamb, at any price, and locked him in the end of the cabin called the kitchen. Now this kitchen had a chimney built of logs for six or eight feet lined on the inside with rock, then carried up above the roof with split lath and mud. This kind of chimney was generally of large size. Although it was the 1st of May the nights on the mountains were cold and frosty.

I was laying rolled in my blanket near the middle of the night when Lieut. Parsons awoke me and said get up and get something to eat. In a case of this kind I very seldom asked questions, but wondered how or where the eating came from. However, I did not wait for a second invitation but arose and followed Ike a little distance to where a bright fire was burning. Close by all the members of our mess was gathered, including a few invited guests. A wash kettle sat on the fire, from which an odor arose that reminded me very much of lamb cooking. I asked no questions but felt sure that the old lady would never see her lamb again. Our cook kept probing into the kettle with a sharp stick, and soon pronounced the contents done. The kettle was removed from the fire and all were invited to pitch in. The meat had been cut in about four pieces, each man had prepared a sharp stick and proceeded to fish from the kettle a chunk of fresh, tender, juicy meat. Although it had been cooked and ate without salt or bread, I thought it the best and sweetest meat I ever tasted. I afterward learned the history of that meat, which was about this: After the boys had laid down hungry kept them awake. They could not sleep. If they happened to doze they dreamed of starving with a nice roasted lamb almost in reach. So three or four of the boys held a council and decided unanimously that it was a military necessity and that lamb must

185

die, but how to get at him was the question. Finally the problem was solved in this way; a member of the company by the name of Dailey was let down the chimney by tieing halters together and the lamb hoisted by those on the top, then a wash kettle was secured in the same manner. The lamb was dressed and cooked.

The old lady made a thorough search next morning for her lamb. She said it was a great mystery what had become of her lamb. As far as she was concerned the mystery was never solved.

Next day we reached Warm Springs, in Bath county, if I remember right, where we found an abundance of grass for our horses and ourselves. We had been here two days when we were joined by the other regiments of the brigade. The brigade was now united and remained in the neighborhood a few days to give our horses time to rest, then moved on through Bath and Augusta counties and reached Harrisonburg in Rockingham county. It was here that we first learned the death of Stonewall Jackson, who had fallen seriously wounded at Chancellorsville, on the night of May the 2nd 1863, and on the sabbath day of May the 10th about 3 o'clock in the afternoon his spirit passed over the river of time to rest under the shade of the trees. His mortal remains had been laid to rest at Lexington.

General Jackson's death was sad news to us. For several days a sadness seemed to settle over our camp, brave men spoke to each other of the idol of the army, as though they had lost a near relative, men who had followed Jackson through his valley campaigns had faced the storm of grape and cannister without quaking, who had witnessed many scenes of death with indifference, now strove in vain to restrain the unbidden tear which dimmed the eye that never quailed and damped the cheek that had never blanched, when following to victory or to death, their loved but lost leader. No more would we hear his encouraging words, "Press forward men, press forward these people are giving away." But in war the bravest and best often fall first.

Many of the horses were unfit for service when we reached Harrisonburg. If I remember right some twelve or fifteen men of our company were in company on foot. Nearly all were from Hampshire county and could get fresh horses if permitted to go home, but there was grave doubts as to whether all would return if given a furlough.

After a few days Captain McDonald succeeded in getting his dismounted men furloughed for fifteen days to procure horses. I was put in charge of the squad and held responsible for their return. We left Harrisonburg on foot early in the morning and camped well up in Brock's Gap the first night. Next day we reached Mr. Joseph Inskeep's, on Lost River, next night about nine o'clock we reached Judge Allen's house, above Moorefield.

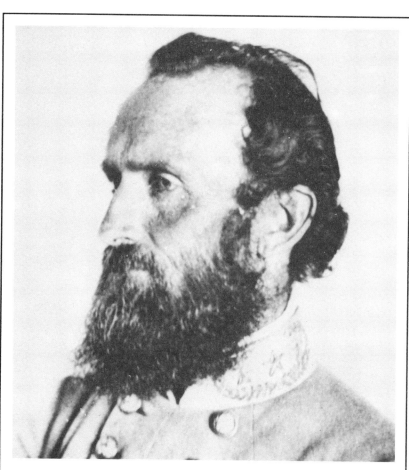
Gen. Thomas J. "Stonewall" Jackson
(NATIONAL ARCHIVES)

CHAPTER XIV

Returning Home Again

W e learned from the judge that a company of Yankees had open camped on the fair ground near Moorefield for a day or two and was there late that evening. The judge said there was about forty Yankees in the company. The judge gave us supper and we started again having determined on a night attack, although out numbered four to one. We had determined to try to stampede the Yankees undercover of darkness, by yelling and firing our revolvers making them believe, if possible, they were attacked by at least a thousand Confeds. We reached the top of a ridge east or southeast of the fair ground about midnight. We could see below us the dim light from burned down camp fires and were only a short distance from the camp. Dr. John Dailey and I stole down as quietly as possible to reconnoiter and find where they had their horses and locate the Yankees. The boys were to remain where they were until our return. The night intensely dark and our progress necessarily slow. With the stealthy tread of Indians we approached the camp, halting at almost every step with ear and eye strained to catch, if possible, a sound however faint or an object though dim, which would aid us in locating the object of our search, but no sound reached our ear except the plaintive wail of the whippoorwill; no object reached our vision except imaginary ones. At length we discovered that the camp was deserted, no Yankees there. We returned to our comrades, held a whispered council and concluded to fall back a short distance in the brush and take a nap and await daylight for further developments.

Daylight soon came, but no blue coats were to be seen. We concluded not to enter the town not caring to have it known that Confederates were in the neighborhood. We pushed on in the direction of Romney, but kept away from the public highway until we reached the Glebe, then kept by a man by the name of Patterson. It was now near the middle of the day. We halted in the woods near by. Dr. John Dailey was well acquainted with Mr. Patterson and went to the house to get some rations and learn if there were any Yankees at Romney. In short time Dailey returned accompanied by Mr. Patterson, both being well loaded with commissary stores of which we were in much need.

Mr. Patterson informed us that a company of Yankee cavalry had passed down toward Romney, that evening before, just after dark.

These were no doubt the Yankees who had been camped on the fair ground at Moorefield. He also said there was a regiment of the Yankee infantry camped at Romney and he had heard that there was a company of cavalry quartered at Springfield and had also learned that an infantry picket was quartered in the old log school house near the lower end of Hanging Rock gap and that my father's house was being watched both day and night. This was important news to me, as I expected to visit home, before we returned to our command.

After satisfying the inner man, we thanked Mr. Patterson for his hospitality, also for his information and again started in the direction of Romney. On reaching Mill Run, some three or four miles above town, we halted, to hold a council. Nearly all of our squad lived south and east of Romney. Amos Roberson, Ike Wolf, Ab. Shingleton, George Hott and Charlie Watkins, I remember to have been of the number. These could all reach their homes without much risk of being captured. After arranging to meet in ten days from that time at the North River Church, now Rio, we parted. Dr. John Dailey, Herman Seniff and myself continued our course down the river in the direction of town. It was between ten and eleven o'clock at night when we reached the point of a ridge, just south of the grade where it winds down town hill and opposite the cemetery. The night was clear and the moon shone bright. From where we stood could be seen the form of a sentinel near the entrance of the cemetery and another marched back and forth in the pike at the north point of Fort hill. The night was so bright that we hesitated for sometime, considering as to whether we would attempt to cross the pike between the sentinels and make our way along the steep bluff between the cemetery and river or flank town on the other extreme, which would give us something like three miles over steep ridges and through thick brush. We were tired and determined on the former route. We made our way as quietly as possible across the hollow and lay down in a thicket of pines, where the colored people now have their cemetery, to await the relief guard, which we knew would be along in a short time. In about half hour they passed down, relieved the guard below and returned again. As soon as they had passed from sight around the turn we crawled across the pike in almost full view of the sentinel in the road below, who could not have failed to see us if he had looked in our direction. Luck favored us and we crossed the Green Spring pike a half mile below town without being discovered, and proceeded as rapid as possible until we again reached the Green Spring pike at the Washington farm, five miles below or north of Romney. Here we parted, Dailey and Seniff going to Mr. George Washington's house, I to my father's house. The two houses were little over a mile apart, I promised to meet Dailey and Seniff on the second night at the line fence between Mr. Washington's and father's farm, at a point where stood several large oak trees.

I had not forgotten what Mr. Patterson had said about my father's house being watched. I approached the house with great caution lying

190

flat on the ground. I at length discovered persons on the front porch and was satisfied they were Yankees and crawled away again without being noticed. I went to a log stable about one hundred and fifty yards from the house. The stable was built on a knoll and was a strong position if well garrisoned. Here I determined to make a stand and take a short nap, although I knew that it could not be more than an hour until daylight. Father kept his favorite horse in this stable and always fed him early in the morning. I knew that he would be over, so climbed into the hay loft and was asleep in five minutes time.

I awoke about daylight and looking through an opening between the logs saw father coming with corn for his horse, when he had entered the stable I stuck my head through the mow hole and said "good morning."

The old gentleman was very much frightened and said "my God boy, what possessed you to come here? The Yankees are watching the house day and night, under pretence of guarding our property, but the truth is they are watching for you and will shoot you on sight. One of them told me so, now get away from here as quick as possible. The Yankees lay on the porch at night but through the day stay over across the road, on the hill, under the big white oak, where they can see in every direction. No one can approach the house without being seen." He continued, "go at once or it will be too late, they always go over on the hill as soon as daylight."

I looked through a crack between the logs and saw the Yankees already at their post. I said, "father it's too late now for me to get away without being seen."

He said, "you will have to stay here until night then, the Yankees do not come over here often and may not come over today, but you had better get back in the loft and I will cover you with hay and when I come to water Tom I will bring you something to eat."

I said "no, I have got out of worse plans than this, I have a Colts rifle, which will shoot six times and an extra cylinder that I can put in a few seconds and have six more shots. I then have my revolver to fall back on in close quarters.

"But", said he, "you are not going to do anything of that kind here and have us burnt up."

I said "not if I can help it, but I am not going to be captured."

The old gentleman was very much distressed and said, although he would be very glad to see me whenever he could do without danger, yet he hoped that if I got away this time I would not venture home again until the war was over.

I said, "father, do you always wear that red wampus and straw hat when you come out in the morning to feed?"

"No," said he, "I often come without either, barehead."

191

Colt's rifle. Notice revolving cylinder. *(RALPH HAINES)*

I then asked what time the Yankees relieved their pickets. He said shortly after sunrise. I then said leave your blouse and hat and go back to the house and don't show yourself again until I come to the house.

I watched patiently through a crack between the logs of the stable until the picket, which had been on duty during the night had been relieved and had passed around the hill from sight.

Father was as straight as an Indian and walked with a quick springy step, but at this time was suffering from a recent attack of rheumatism, which caused quite a limp in his gait.

I was soon ready for exhibition to those Yankees over on the hill, who, no doubt, would have given a month's pay at that moment to have known that the object of their vigilance by day and night, now stood in full view, but little over two hundred yards away within deadly range of their Enfield muskets, with no protection save the covering of an old red wampus, so called at an early date, which reached nearly to the knee and an old broad-brimmed straw hat, which flopped down over the shoulder in rather a slovenly manner. Thus attired I had a moment before I stepped from the stable door and now stood facing those who were ready to rob me of any liberty or my life; for a moment I realized my situation, but to turn back now might prove fatal; to carry out my plan of action determined on was the only thing to be done. I walked with a limping gate, imitating my father as much as possible, to a lot near by where the cows were penned at night, righted up and replaced some rails which had been thrown down; then limped toward the house, which stood nearly mid-way between the stable and where the Yankees stood on the opposite side of the hollow. When I reached the woodyard I was but little over one hundred yards from the picket, I halted at the wood pile and picked up an arm full of wood, as father often did, and carried it to the kitchen. As quick as the change could be made, father was himself decked in his red blouse and straw hat, went out at once, carried in another turn or two of wood, then knocked around as usual.

The family was very nervous over what they thought and believed to be my great danger, except mother who never got nervous, although she is now over ninety years old. I doubt if she was ever excited in her life. Mother now took command and said I was safe in the house as anywhere else and unless some of you children show it by your actions the Yankees will never know that John is in a thousand miles of the place. Anyhow said she what is to be will be. This was generally the closing argument.

I was directed to go up stairs and keep as still as a mouse, for said mother, the Yankees, are liable to come in at any time. I soon had breakfast and was stretched on the floor sleeping as sound as though I had been far away from every danger. In the midst of my snooze one of my sisters awoke me, said there were two Yankees coming to the house and I must stop snoring or they would hear me. The snoring stopped at once. I was never more awake in my life as I lay stretched on the floor a few moments later listening to the conversation going on below between the Yankees and my sisters. I was satisfied from their conversation that they had no suspicion whatever of being, at that moment beneath the same roof with the person of all others, whom they most desired to see. They talked for a half hour or more and went away no wiser than when they came. I gathered from their conversation that they were New Yorkers and seemed to be, judging from their conversation, gentlemen.

No more visited the house that day. I had early supper. Between sundown and dark the Yankees left their post and started to the house. Now their picket post was not really over one hundred yards from the house on an air line; yet by having to cross a hollow they would have to travel double that distance to reach the house. When the Yankees had reached the hollow I passed from the rear part of the house into the garden beneath a grape arbor, which extended to the opposite side of the garden and screened me securely from observation as I passed through the garden. At the farther end of the arbor was a wilderness of hop vines; here I concealed myself until dark, then crept to the stable, changed my apparel and went calling, saw a few friends and returned before morning, and went through the same program as before with some slight variation. I lay up stairs during the day, most of the time asleep, but on the Yankees approaching the house I was awakened for fear my snoring might frighten the Yanks and cause an investigation which might not be pleasant. I continued to visit a few special friends at night and slept at home during the day. A special lady friend or two called on me for an hour or so but feared to remain long.

During the week quite a lot of Dixie mail reached the house on its way south; at night it was hidden away in the mow of hay. The second night I went to meet Dailey and Seniff, but in their stead I met the general himself. He informed me that he had been down to Springfield that day and made arrangements with Dailey's brother to meet he and Seniff at a certain place near town that night and they had gone down that way.

I saw no way of capturing a horse so bargained with Mr. Washington for a nice young blooded horse, which he loathed to part with, but feared he would lose him if he tried to keep him. I then went back to my castle and went to bed on the mow of hay, but did not sleep very sound from some cause.

After the Yankees had guarded me several days, they had an alarm, it was Sunday morning about ten o'clock in the day two of the pickets were at the house, I was as usual stretched on the floor above listening to the conversation going on below, gathering what information I could as to the movements of the Yankees who were being questioned for my benefit.

About ten o'clock a cavalryman dashed down the road and called to the pickets to come at once the Rebs were coming. They didn't wait for a second call but started on a double quick. The two at the house left at a fast trot; when they had reached the top of a knoll about hundred yards from the house, father and I walked out into the yard, I called to them not to be in a hurry the Rebs would not hurt them.. They halted and turned as though they would come back. I was about to break for my castle, when they again turned and started up the road. I then went to the stable, secured my arms and Dixie mail and took a position on a high hill in rear of the house where I had a good view of the pike leading from Romney to Green Spring on the B. & O. railroad, also a good view of the surrounding country; not caring in case of an accident to be caught with a Dixie mail on my person, I hid my package of letters in a secure place and seated myself to await developments.

Soon I discovered a cloud of dust rising from the pike in the direction of Romney. In a short time a company of cavalry came in view followed by a train of wagons; a column of infantry brought up the rear. They seemed to be in a great hurry.

After they had passed, I remained where I was, anxiously looking for and expecting the Confederates every moment in hot pursuit, but I looked in vain; no gray jacket was visible in any directions. I soon became impatient and determined to wade the river and take a look at Romney from the mountain, on the opposite side and try to learn the cause of the hasty retreat of the Yankees.

I reached the top of the mountain in the afternoon and to my joy and surprise I discovered a body of Confederate cavalry, infantry and artillery camped along the river a mile or two above Romney. I had no idea of what command it was or where it came from or how many there were. After securing a favorable position I sat down and tried to figure out what command it could be. Finally I came to the conclusion that it must be Gen. Imboden. His brigade had been with Gen. Jones in West Virginia, but I had lost sight of him and did not really have an idea where he then was. Night was approaching and an unpleasant sensation in my stomach was not misunderstood having eaten nothing since morning. I went down to Capt. Herriott's house and got all a heart could wish for in the eating line, even to drink of extract of peach which the captain said was thirty years old. Its age surprised me. It was so mild, but its effect surprised me more.

I learned from the captain, who had seen some one that day, that it was Gen. Imboden's company that I had seen. Night was at hand and I started for home, but stopped at the next house and remained over night.

Next morning I learned that Gen. Imboden had gone to Cumberland. C. B. Withers, a young man from Cumberland, who was refugeeing at Mrs. Fox's and I concluded to follow the command it being opportunity for him to visit home. We were soon mounted and in pursuit, but did not overtake the command before it reached Cumberland, and left in a short time.

Here I again met Dailey and Seneff, both of whom had mounted themselves in very fine horses at the expense of the United States government. They had succeeded in mounting themselves in this way as well as can remember. There was at that time camped in Springfield a company of cavalry, who kept their horses in what was then Shouse's stable. Gen. George Washington rode down to Springfield and made arrangements with young Dailey to meet his brother and Seneff at a certain place at a certain time that night. At this meeting Dailey learned where the horses were kept and how guarded. The stable was entered from the street, but had a door in the rear which opened in a lot and was fastened on the inside. A guard walked on the street in front of the stable and was relieved every two hours. Dr. John Dailey, being a rather small man, determined to enter the stable from a small opening, I think where a trough protruded, bridle and saddle a horse for each then open the door and lead them out one at a time, turning them over to Seneff, who was in waiting near by, having previously opened the fences near town on their purposed line of retreat. If I remembered right Dailey led three horses from the rear of the stable, saddled ready to mount.

The night being somewhat cloudy and windy, with no moon light favored their enterprise, which was an entire success, although pursuit was commenced early next morning and pressed with vigor, but Dr. John Dailey was raised in Springfield, knew every path within five miles of the place and with an hour start a bloodhound would have found it no easy matter to overtake him. This I think is about the way those horses changed hands, however, if I am wrong Dr. John Dailey still lives and can make the corrections necessary if any are required.

From Cumberland General Imboden moved toward Hancock destroying bridges and railroad as he went. He was on his way to Gettysburg, but his destination was not known at that time unless to a very few.

CHAPTER XV

Road to Gettysburg

O ur furlough had about expired and the time for us to return to our company had arrived. I purchased a horse from Mr. W. V. Herriott for one of the men who had not succeeded in mounting himself. The men were all on hand at the time and place appointed. My neighbor and schoolmate, Ephraim accompanied us, having determined to enlist in the Southern cause. When we reached Harrisonburg we called on the Provost for information in regard to our regiment and learned to our surprise, that a few days after we had started for Hampshire the brigade had been ordered west of the Blue Ridge and had taken part in the greatest cavalry engagement of the war at, or near Brandy Station, on the 9th of June 1863.

We were informed that Gen. Ewell had driven Milroy from Winchester, captured most of his men and that there was now no Yankees in the Shenandoah valley, and all soldiers, who had been away from the command on leave of absence or otherwise were ordered to report at Winchester. Had we known that the Confederates were at Winchester before we left Hampshire it would have saved us a ride of perhaps a hundred and twenty-five miles. But there was nothing to do but face the music, so we turned our faces toward the Potomac and started down the valley for Winchester, where we arrived the evening of the second day after leaving Harrisonburg. Here we found our regiment under Col. Lomax, camped near town. The brigade had arrived the day before from east of the ridge, where they had been left by Gen. Lee to guard the passes in the Blue Ridge, for the purpose of keeping the Yankees ignorant of General Lee's movement in the Shenandoah valley, where his whole army was now gathered, ready to cross the Potomac. Our brigade halted for a day or two at Winchester. We were glad to be with our comrades again, though sorry to learn that three of our company with whom we parted a few weeks before in health and vigorous manhood, now lay rolled in their blankets beneath the sod of the gory field, which their valor helped to win, and on which they had given all that a soldier could give for his country's cause. At roll call their names were passed over in silence. Their furlough will last until time shall end. They sleep in death and will hear of war no more.

That night as we lay on our blankets in the open field, the heavens above our only covering, one of my comrades gave me a short sketch of where they had been and what doing. After leaving Harrisonburg, the main features of which sketch I wrote in my diary next day and give here that part which may be of some interest, as I have never seen in history of the war an account of the greatest cavalry engagement ever fought on American continent.

My informant stated that they only remained at Harrisonburg a few days, (after our detail started for Hampshire) and started, they knew not where, but finally halted near Culpepper Court House, when they learned that nearly the whole cavalry force belonging to the army of northern Virginia were nearby under the immediate command of Gen. Stewart. On the 8th of June 1863 the advance of Gen. Lee's column reached Culpepper. On that day a short distance east of the Court House, Gen. Lee sat on his horse, on a little knoll, eight thousand cavalry were drawn up in line, afterward passed in front of General Lee at a gallop, with Gen. Stewart and staff at their head, with sabres at tierce-point. Then a sham battle took place.

General Jones, who commanded our brigade, from some cause did not like General Stewart, was heard to remark after the review was over that Stewart has had his horse show and sham fight, but that tomorrow, he would have a fight without the sham. "No doubt," said he, "the Yankees who have two divisions of cavalry on the other side of the river, have witnessed from their signal stations, this show in which Stewart has exposed to view his strength and aroused their curiosity. They will want to know what is going on and if I am not mistaken, will be over early in the morning to investigate," and General Jones' prediction proved true.

Before it was light enough to see the ears of the picket, at the river, commanded by Capt. Gibson, detected the approach of the enemy. The captain at once sent a courier to headquarters, then prepared to check as long as possible the advancing column, and thus give the Confederates time to get ready to meet them.

Captain Gibson, who was a brave and prudent officer, had already blockaded the road as best he could with the material at hand, and waited patiently to receive them. When at close range the captain gave the word and a sheet of fire flashed in their faces and the shower of lead poured into their ranks, emptied many saddles and caused the advance to recoil, but the head of the main advancing rapidly to the support of their advance. Capt. Gibson was compelled to fall back, the Yankees pressing close on his rear. It proved to be General Beeford's division. It crossed at what was known as Beverly's fords, at break of day.

Some of the Johnnies were up and preparing their breakfast, but a majority of them were rolled in their blankets. They had no breakfast or dinner that day; the men aroused from their slumber scarcely had time to mount when the Yankees were upon them, so fierce was the assault that the Confederates were driven back on General Stewart's headquarters on what was called Fleetwood Hill, but were checked by several pieces of artillery which was quickly got into position. The Confederates had now formed in line and charged in turn. At the same time Gen. Gregg's division crossed at Kelley's ford below and attacked Gen. Stewart's rear, but they were met and repulsed as they ascended the hill and charged in turn.

Then said my comrade a person might have stood on Fleetwood Hill all day long and looking on one direction and see the Yankees chasing a brigade of Confederates and in another direction the Confederates could have been seen chasing the Yankees. On a commanding rise on the battle field the Yankees had placed a battery which from its commanding position could allow the other to use these guns. Around these guns the battle raged in all its fury. The horses had been killed, the battery had been taken and retaken several times during the day. At length it was captured by the 11th Virginia and held against every assault. Near sundown the Yankees began to give way and by sundown all who could do so had recrossed the river.

The Yankees had been supported by two brigades of infantry, although they took little or no part in the engagement, but did good service in covering the retreat. This fight, my comrade said, had been with the sabre. When the carbine and revolver had been once emptied there was no time to reload. Our company lost three men killed and several wounded, several others lost their horses nearly all of whom succeeded in mounting loose horses caught on the field of battle. The number of cavalry engaged on both sides were thought to be twenty thousand. General Jones' and Robertson's brigades had been left to guard the passes of the Blue Ridge and had found plenty do to keep the Yankees back in order to protect General Lee's rear and keep his line of communication open.

On the afternoon of the second day our brigade left Winchester and started down the Martinsburg grade. I was left behind in command of the rear guard with orders to gather all the stragglers and bring them along, some of the boys had taken too much fire water and declared they would not leave town that night. I had several under guard in the old market house where I was trying to keep them together. When we were ready to start I had persuaded all by threats or otherwise to mount their horses, several of whom had to be helped and held after they were on. All had been mounted except George Duval, a member of our company with whom I was well acquainted; he was raised in Winchester but had lived in Romney some years before the war. I did not want to use any harsh means with George. He was not a bad boy when sober, but no persuasion would induce George to mount. Swore he would not leave town that night. Dan Seymour, a member of our company from Baltimore, a big stout young man, undertook to put George on his horse; George resisted, both got mad and a regular fight ensued, Seymour being much the stoutest man soon had George underneath,; I dismounted and caught Seymour by the collar of his jacket and pulled him to his feet. He swore he would shoot George and attempted to draw his revolver; I jerked his arms behind him and held them. Duval rose to his feet with a brickbat in his hand, which he threw at Seymour's head with all his strength, Seymour dodged, the brick passed over his shoulder and struck me square in the forehead and sufficient to have dropped a beef and would have dropped me had I not had a good grip of Seymour. As it was I did not know but what the market house had fallen. For a moment the brim of my {hat} had been doubled back and a gash cut through both brim and crown and laid bare the bone. I suppose the sharp edge severed a blood vessel. It seemed as though the cut would never stop bleeding. I again ordered George to mount. He refused, I then had him put on his horse and his feet tied together. One of the men took the rein and we started, overtook the regiment at Bunker Hill where it had gone into camp.

My head was paining me so that I could scarcely sit on my horse. When we reached camp I went at once to our surgeon, Dr. Suttle, and had him dress my wound. He said that if my skull had not been as thick as a bear's that blow would have caved it in. As it was he thought possibly it was cracked, advised me to get leave of absence for a day or two and go to a private house. I got a leave of absence for a week upon the recommendation of Dr. Suttle and went to a private house a mile or so from the main road, where I was kindly treated. The pain in my head was so severe that I got no sleep that night. I did not like the idea of being left behind, not knowing where the command was bound for. The house at which I was stopping was occupied by an old widow lady and one daughter, who looked to be on the western slope of life. An old colored man and his wife completed the household. The old lady said her son was in the army. She was very kind and kept clothes wet in cold water, to my head through the day. That night I got some sleep. Next morning my head felt better and I determined, although the old lady insisted that I remain another day but I had made up my mind to follow the command and started soon after the sun was up. I followed on the trail by way of Martinsburg, Williamsport, Green Castle and Chambersburg, which place I reached after dark and found the command camped near town. This had been a miserable day to me; I had ridden perhaps fifty miles or more through a broiling sun, at times was compelled to halt in the shade of a tree for a short time, then push on again. Toward evening I overtook two cavalrymen whose horses were about played out and was glad to have their company for the remainder of the evening. I found Dr. Suttle, he removed the bandage which had become dry and hard, dressed the cut and my head soon felt better.

Next morning early we were on our way to Gettysburg and took a position on the right of General Lee's side about the time the most wonderful artillery fire that ever was heard on this planet, (it was more like musketry firing when the rapidity was considered) began. Two hundred pieces of artillery were fired as fast as they could be loaded.

The roar was deafening, the very earth quaked and tremble. Our horses seemed to quiver from fright. After two or three hours of frightful cannonading, the firing on the Yank side on Cemetery Hill seemed to be growing weaker and finally almost ceased. For some time the Confederate batteries continued fire then ceased, when from our position on Cemetery Ridge, perhaps two miles away, by aid of a small field glass, which I had gotten in Cumberland, I saw a line of Confeds crossing the valley between Cemetery Ridge and Cemetery Hill. The valley may have been a mile wide, the line I saw was General Pickett's Division. They appeared to be marching in perfect order elbow to elbow and knee to knee. On the left of this double line marched what seemed to be a brigade in column of battalion. The right of the line was hid from view by a low ridge. It was only for a short time this advancing line was visible. The artillery had ceased firing on each side and for a few moments the line of gray was plainly visible to the naked eye, but very soon the Yankees again opened a terrific fire of grape and cannister on the advancing Confederates, which were soon hid from view by a dense smoke out of which could be seen what appeared to be an almost constant flash of lightning. Very soon the rattle of musketry could be heard mingled with the roar of artillery. One might have easily imagined Cemetery Hill, at the moment, to have been a full-grown volcano, doing business on full time. Nothing could be seen now on the hill except a dense cloud of smoke from which dim flashes were continuous roar and rattle. The roar of artillery soon ceased, when the rattle of musketry alone could be heard which told but too plainly of the terrible strife then being enacted on the smoke screened summit of Cemetery Hill. For a moment or two the firing seemed to cease. Pickett's division had driven the Yankees from their breastworks, but they rallied on a second line. Seeing that the Confederates were not supported they charged in turn and drove them from the ground which had cost Pickett more than one half his division to win.

The rattle of musketry now increased in volume every moment. Soon the repulsed line of Confederates could be dimly seen through the smoke when they had nearly reached the valley again, followed by their victorious enemy numbering to all appearance ten to one. The Confederate artillery opened again, when the Yankees gave up the pursuit and hastened back to cover behind their breastworks.

General Pickett's division numbered about five thousand men all Virginians, every man a hero and the very flower of the army of the Potomac. Of Pickett's three brigade commanders, Gen. Garnett was

Battle of Gettysburg — charge of the Confederate army. (HAMPSHIRE COUNTY PUBLIC LIBRARY)

killed, Gen. Armstead was left dying and Gen. Kemper fearfully wounded. Of fourteen field officers, who were in the advance only one came back. Of the five thousand who made the assault thirty-five hundred were left behind. Pickett's charge on Cemetery Hill will be read on History's pages with wonder and admiration by coming generations, while time shall last. It was said that Gen. Pickett shed tears when he looked on the remnant of his division.

Heaps on heaps the deathless Virginians lie;
Brave Pickett beheld them with a tearful eye.
They had fought their last fight, their duty o'er.
They sleep in death and will hear of war no more.

A general advance was expected, but the Yankees seemed to be satisfied with having repulsed the assault on Cemetery Hill.

Shortly after Pickett's repulse General Jones moved his brigade out on the Fairfield road. Many were the conjectures as to where we were going, but when nearing Fairfield the 7th regiment, which was in front, met a column of cavalry and began exchange of compliments at once. Our regiment, the 11th, formed on the left of the 7th, with a large apple orchard immediately in our front, where the Yankees awaited our attack. We were soon formed and ordered to advance. The carbine and revolvers of the 7th were already making music on quick time. As we neared the orchard we became convinced that something more than apples were to be found in that orchard.

Col. Lomax ordered his men not to fire until they were face to face with the enemy. We charged up a considerable ascent lying close to our horses, (I was at least). The Yankees firing rapidly from the orchard, wasting ammunition, and emptying their arms, most of their shots passed over our heads. In a very short time we were contending with what proved to be the ninth Michigan, (United States regulars). They were stubborn fighters, rather inclined to be mulish and hard to drive. But we had the advantage, our revolvers were loaded whilst most of theirs were empty. We finally persuaded them to follow the left of their line, which had already been driven back some distance by the 7th regiment on our right. When they left the orchard their line was badly broken and we gave them no time to reform and soon had them on the run on the road leading in the direction of Fairfield. Their running qualities were fully equal to their fighting. The chase was soon given up, General Jones no doubt feared being lead into a trap. We had quite a number of prisoners. In his official report of the affair, General Jones mentioned Capt. Kuykendall's Co. F of the 7th regiment Virginia Cavalry for conspicuous bravery on that occasion.

We left a strong picket, fell back a short distance and went into camp. The next day July 4th, there was no fighting except a little cavalry skirmishing, the enemy trying to find out what the Confederates were doing and they trying to keep the Yankees in the dark. In the afternoon the ambulances and wagons in which such of the wounded as could be moved, were moved toward Chambersburg, followed by the empty supply train of the army, escorted by Imboden's cavalry. In the evening rain began to fall as usual. It seldom failed to rain after a big fight, it rained steadily all night. Our company had been on picket all night, was called in at daylight and directed to follow after the brigade, which had taken the Fairfield road.

I don't remember how long we had been without eating, but I for one was feeling pretty thin. As we plodded along wet, weary and hungry we discovered a large farm house and barn in a grove some half mile from the road. Some of the boys asked permission of Capt. McDonald to go to the house and see if they could get something to relieve an empty stomach. At first he refused, but finally gave the desired permission, but charged them to be cautious and lose no time, as we might be followed and overtaken any time. Three or four of the boys started across a large field; Dr. John Dailey in command, if I remember right. If Dailey with John Erten and Bob Morehead for assistants, could not find something eatable when they went foraging, then eatables were very scarce in that neighborhood. We halted to await their return in hope and fear. We soon saw them coming back each carrying some thing in front of them, which to our joy proved to be bread, meat, a basket of pies, a crock of butter, and another of honey. They had enough for the whole company and to spare. The boys reported having ridden up to the barn when an old Dutchman came out. They asked to get something to eat. The old farmer declared that they did not have anything for themselves. The soldiers he claimed had left them nothing.

One of the boys took a match from his pocket and began scratching it against the side of the barn. The old Dutchman had evidently heard of barns being burned and asked in great alarm what he was going to do with that fire. The reply was if we can't get bread we will burn this barn. The old man said, "come to the house I will see the vimins."

He went into the house but soon returned followed by an old lady who said maybe she could find a loaf of bread which they had saved for themselves and proceeded to unlock the cellar door and entered. The old man took his stand on the outside of the door; one of the boys dismounted and attempted to enter the cellar. The old man objected, said the old woman would get the bread in a little time.

"I must see that no poison is put in the bread," said the Johnnie, and shoved the old man aside and entered. An instant later he appeared in the doorway, called to the boys for one to take charge of the horses the others to bring their sacks and come quick. He had discovered what they were in search of. A long table loaded down with bread, meat and pies; they also found several rolls of butter and jars of honey. Each cavalryman carried a sack which was used to carry grain for their horse when necessary. These were filled with bread and meat which they threw across their horses, then with a basket of pies, a crock of butter and a bucket of honey they reached their hungry comrades who certainly enjoyed the feast, although it had no doubt been prepared for the boys in blue. The rain had ceased, roads were in a fearful condition, the heavy rain followed by the wagon trains and artillery of the whole army had made the road almost impassable.

We came up with the rear of our brigade before the middle of day. Near Fairfield quite a force of Yankees made their appearance and threatened an attack on the rear of the retreating army. General Early, who commanded the rear guard, soon had his men in line across their front ready to receive them, but they concluded not to attack and soon disappeared, when Gen. Early resumed his march disgusted and disappointed at not having had an opportunity (as he expressed it) of sending some of them to a warmer climate.

Our brigade continued to move on the flanks and in the rear of the retiring column, throughout the day. Night set in with a drizzly rain falling. How the night could have been darker would be hard to imagine. Toward midnight (if I remember right) it was reported that the Yankees had attacked our train and we were ordered forward but our progress was very slow on account of the difficulty in passing in the darkness the artillery and wagon train which blocked the way. After an hour or two we found some wagons that had been cut down and soon found that we were mixed up with some other cavalry. We could not see the color of their clothes but was soon satisfied that they were blue. The other fellows, I feel sure were satisfied that there was a streak of gray got mixed up with them. They passed by the wagons without disturbing them for fear, no doubt, that the man at his elbow might quietly run him through if he should be imprudent enough to show by his actions where he belonged. Not a word was spoken. After we had passed the wagons I dropped out of ranks as most of the command who had been mixed up with the blue coats had already done. I found myself in a body of timber and succeeded in getting a few rods from the road and waited with all the patience I could until day began to break when I moved a further from the road. I soon discovered a column of cavalry moving on the highway. It was soon light enough to see that they were dressed gray. I soon joined them and learned that we had politely escorted the Yankees until they had passed our train, then let them go without hindrance. But our general was missing. No one had seen him since daylight. We did not know what had become of him. Train now moved forward with our brigade in front. About nine o'clock we

205

heard cheering in front which we could not account for, but soon learned that it was caused by the return of Gen. Jones. He had been mixed up with the Yankees the night before and did not succeed in getting away until near daylight. He had followed a by road and not being acquainted with the country had found himself several miles from the line of march. We had about come to the conclusion that somehow the Yankees had discovered that he was a Confederate and had captured him, as he was at the head of the column and had no doubt been among them, in the darkness. No doubt he was as glad to get back as we were to have him with us again. The rain had ceased the sun had broken through the clouds. We were moving along at rather a slow gate our horses were jaded and hungry. We were wet to the hide, tired and hungry as hounds and sleepy as owls. Many of the boys were sleeping soundly as they rode along. All at once the boys in front began cheering, which we could not account for, a little way in front stood an old stone mill. A few feet further a dwelling house with a porch in front. Several ladies stood on the porch, among them was a young girl, I would think about fourteen or fifteen years of age. She wore a white apron which she had fashioned into a Confederate flag. It was the light of this little flag that caused the cheering. The one ray in the land of the foe, which lighted up the gloom which reigned supreme within the breast of many despondent Confederates as in sadness and sorrow at having to leave so many of their comrades behind they retraced their steps toward their children's homes. Captain McDonald halted in front of the young lady and politely asked her to present him with the apron flag. I had halted by the captain's side and remember as though it was only yesterday, instead of thirty six years ago on the sixth day of June eighteen hundred and ninety nine. With out a word she reached with her right hand to her left side. With a single jerk tore the apron flag from its moorings and threw it over the railing. The captain caught it, expressed his thanks and with a lordly bow passed on amid deafening cheers from hundred of Confederates throats.

The History of Hampshire County by Maxwell and Swisher errs in saying that Charles Watkins carried the apron flag. H. Madison Watkins was the youth who asked the captain to let him carry the apron flag, whose folds that same evening were stained with his life's blood. Watkins was but a youth yet in his teens. He and another youth, John Saville, enlisted at Winchester on our way to Gettysburg. Our regiment had marched on a different road from that followed by the other regiments of the brigade, did not reach Hagerstown until well in the afternoon of the 6th. We passed the town a short distance and halted; the greater part of the brigade had arrived earlier in the day and judging from the noise in the direction of Williamsport was having trouble of some sort. We were halted in a field on the left of the pike leading from Hagerstown to Williamsport. Because of a body of timber in our front we could see only a short distance in that direction, but could hear very distinctly what was going on. The trouble was this, General Pleasonton had been looking after General Lee's wagon train but when about to fall upon General Imboden's cavalry escort he found a body of cavalry in his rear, rather close for safety and must be rid of before attacking Imboden in his front. General Pleasonton had halted and formed his line across the pike at right angles, behind a stone fence, through which their artillery was being worked. Their cavalry were dismounted and lay behind the stone fence. To reach them the Confederates had to pass through open fields for several hundred yards.

We had been halted only a few moments when a courier dashed up to Col. Lomax and the next moment the order "forward" rang down the line. We reached the pike and turned to our left in the direction of Williamsport. We had to ascend a considerable rise then for perhaps a half or three quarters of a mile to the Yankee position. The road was straight and nearly level with pasture fields on either side. The pike had been macadamized and was solid as a rock.

The Yankees had the range and were making a kind of a bowling alley of the pike. Judging from the horses and men strewn along it did not seem to be a healthy place for Johnnies.

We soon reached a gap in the fence on our left through which the colonel lead us into a field. We soon reached a low place in rear of a low ridge or elevation, here we were halted and formed in line of battle. No doubt everyman in that line offered up a short prayer for protection from the great danger that we well knew awaited us and to which we would in a very moments be exposed. We were ordered to draw and examine our revolvers and see that the chambers were all charged and were ordered not to fire a shot until we reached the fence behind which the Yankees lay, then empty our revolvers in their faces. We walked our horses to the top of the rise then came the command to charge at a gallop, and away we went straight at the stone fence not over two hundred yards away. Not a man could be seen, not a gun fired, all was silent as the grave. We well knew what this silence meant and what to expect at any moment.

It appeared to me that I was riding on a line with and was looking straight into the mouth of a twelve-pounder which protruded through the stone fence. I don't know how the other boys felt but about this time I felt like I was a fit subject for the hospital. It is surprising how rapid thoughts will follow each other when a person expects the next breath he draws may be his last. But the suspense was soon over for the time being. When we were within a hundred paces of the fence the muzzle of that gun, from which I had not for an instant taken my eye, belched forth fire and smoke. At the same instant I felt a sharp pain in my right foot. My first thought was that my foot or leg had been shot away. A shell had burst not ten feet in our front. My horse lunged forward and rolled on his side to rise no more. My wounded leg was beneath my horse and every effort to release myself proved futile. Our line was shattered and broken in many places by the storm of shot and shell, which was poured upon it from behind that fence. Our line fell back behind the low ridge from whence they started. Colonel Chew's battery had followed us as we advanced and had in-timbered on a little elevation on our left and commenced a brisk fire at short range on the stone fence, which caused the dismounted cavalry to back to the timber for shelter. While this artillery duel was going on I lay beside my horse between the contending batteries. The screech and hiss of shot and shell as they passed over or burst in the air, tearing up the ground around me; I just got as close to the ground as it was possible to get, closed my eyes and with my fingers stuck in my ears to shut out the hideous sound which raged around, expecting every moment to be the last. On the short space of a moment every mean thing that I had done through life seemed to pass through my mind. I asked forgiveness, protection and deliverance and believe that my prayer was heard. The ground seemed to tremble. I ventured to raise my head a few inches and to my joy saw the charging squadrons of the Eleventh rapidly advancing. Capt. Chew's battery had ceased firing (to have continued longer would have endangered our own men). I raised to a sitting posture and waved my sword over my head, to attract notice, fearful of being crushed beneath the horses feet. The boys saw me, the line opened a little and dashed on until they reached the fence, where the Yankees were making a desperate effort to get away with their artillery. When they had driven the Yankees from the fence and captured several of their guns, two or three of the boys came back and released me from my confinement.

I certainly felt relieved when I found that I still had two legs and could stand on my feet, although one of them appeared to be in a bad shape, the boot had been torn from my foot and a pretty good slice of the foot had disappeared. I asked the boys to get me a horse, of which there were plenty riderless ones around. Simon D. Taylor, a member of our company, soon had a good looking U. S. horse by my side, I mounted. Scarcely ten minutes had elapsed from the time the line had charged by until I was mounted again. The boys thought I had better go back and have my foot dressed.

The Confederates had torn several gaps in the fence, passed through and now seemed to be hotly engaged with the enemy in the woods beyond. Although my foot was right painful and bleeding freely, I determined to go on with the boys and was soon up the line trying to get some satisfaction for the way I had been treated.

The Yankees fought with a good deal of stubbornness. After perhaps a half hour determined work, when it began to look as though we would not be able to drive them further, at this moment rapid firing accompanied by the Confederate war whoops, while our regiment attacked in front, the greater part of the brigade had under cover of the wood, made a wide circuit and reached the rear and left of the Yankee line.

The blue coats concluded to give up the contest and get, but quite a number had been caught between the Confederate lines and failed to get away. They pursued some distance, a number of prisoners and several pieces of artillery were captured. Night was at hand and the pursuit was abandoned.

I had several times during the combat struck my lame foot against a tree or caught it in a bush which kept it bleeding and now that the excitement was over seemed more painful. The command, or the 11th regiment, at last fell back near Hagerstown and camped. S. D. Taylor and I went to a small house near by and asked to get a basin of water and some old rags to tie up my foot. There were two old ladies in the house who were Southern sympathizers. We dismounted, one of the ladies brought me a chair, the other a basin of water and Taylor washed and bound up my wound the best he could. It was a painful though not dangerous wound. A piece of shell had peeled the flesh from the top of my foot, the nails on four toes were gone. We asked for a piece of bread and permission to sleep in a small shed near by. They said they would give us something to eat and we could sleep in the house, which we gladly accepted. There was a good sized yard around the house. Taylor removed the saddles and let our horses graze in the yard. By this time the old ladies had prepared some bread, butter, and milk for us, which we ate heartily, not having eaten anything for thirty-six hours. The old ladies offered us a bed but we declined. They went upstairs and left us in possession of the lower part of the house. Dudley soon had our blankets spread with our saddles for pillows. Then by the light of a tallow candle we examined and recapped our revolvers, then with naked sabre and pistols by our side we lay down, hoping to get some sleep, as we had not slept any the night before and but little for the last week. In five minutes Dudley was sleeping as sound as though he was in a feather and no Yankees nearer than the moon. Neither army produced a braver man or better soldier during the war than was Simon Dudley Taylor. I was glad that he could get much needed rest, not knowing what the morrow would bring forth, surrounded as we were by enemies in enemies' country, our future was a little uncertain. But for me there was no sleep, the pain of my foot was much too great to admit of sleep; morning came at last. Dudley saddled our horses and before the old ladies made their appearance we left the premises in search of the command, which we found near Hagerstown. I then learned that H. M. Watkins, the boy who had carried the apron flag the day before and christened it with his blood, was then lying in a hospital tent near by in a dying condition. He was struck by a piece of shell in the thigh. It was found necessary to amputate the limb, but this could not save his life. His career as a soldier was short but H. M. Watkins and that little apron flag will live on history's page, when men who wore the stars and bars will be forgotten.

I had our surgeon examine my wound. After dressing it he said he would give me a pass, that I had better go to Winchester. I objected to going to a hospital, did not think it was necessary and thought I could stay with the command and would be all right in a short time. The surgeon said that wound is not necessarily dangerous, yet it might cause you great pain and loss of limb. Said he, my advice to you is to go at once to Winchester. Said he would give me a pass for two and I could take with me who I pleased. The doctor said no telling what we will have to endure before we reach Virginia soil again, yet I could not make up my mind to go.

I knew that the hospital at Winchester would be crowded as soon as the wounded could reach there. I saw Capt. McDonald, he advised me to take the doctor's advice and said he, take Charlie Riley with you. His home is in Winchester and he can get you in a private family, where you will be well cared for. I was suffering considerable, the regiment remained in camp awaiting the arrival of General Ewell's division. I had a talk with Riley. He was very anxious to go, said he had, if remember right, a cousin who was a fine doctor, who lived on the Pughtown road a few miles from the Martinsburg grade. I concluded to go and procured the necessary pass.

In the afternoon we started and reached Williamsport late in the evening. An attack was momentarily expected. The lines of the blue could be plainly seen on the high grounds not far away. General Imboden's command, reinforced by several hundred teamsters, seemed to be patiently awaiting the attack. I recognized Col. A. Monroe and Col. Ed Beall as we passed, or would not have known that it was Imboden's command. It was near sundown. The pontoons had partly washed away, the wounded being ferried over in boats. We could see no prospects of getting across the Potomac that night. We rode up the river a distance and ran across an old darkey who had a small canoe with which he was doing a little private ferrying for his own benefit. We gave him a five dollar Confederate bill to ferry us over, which he agreed to do. We took the saddles from our horses and placed all our traps in the canoe. I led my horse on the lower side of the canoe, or attempted to, but had to let him go. The old darkey could not keep up with him. When we had gone a few rods Riley started his horse after us. The horses and I were soon landed on the Virginia shore. The old darkey then went back for Riley and soon landed him also. It was now getting dark. Where we landed was a narrow bottom well covered with grass. We let our horses range at will, spread our blankets on the ground with our saddles for pillows, (as usual), we lay down. Riley had captured a large gum blanket used for covering artillery. This we spread over us and after planning for the next day's march, tried to sleep. Although I was far from comfortable, I was worn out for sleep and got several short naps during the night. Rain had fallen continuously throughout the night.

Daylight came at last, our horses were feeding a short distance away. Riley soon had them saddled and having nothing for breakfast we started toward Martinsburg, trusting to luck for something to eat. Having had no supper we were beginning to feel a little wolfish. Our horses had filled themselves during the night and now made good time in the direction of Martinsburg, which place we at length reached. Finding it well filled with wounded soldiers, we pushed on toward Winchester. When we reached Pughtown road Riley proposed that we take this road and go to a cousin's of his some four or five miles distant, who, he represented as being a very fine doctor, where I could get my foot dressed which was now giving me great pain.

We reached Doctor Houston's house in the evening, found the doctor at home. Riley explained to him the situation. We were invited to dismount, I took a seat on a bench in the yard, when the doctor proceeded to remove the bandage from my foot, which had become dry and hard and was the chief cause of my suffering. Although a quantity of creepers had found a lodgment in the wound, when these had been cleaned out and the wound dressed with a milk and bread poultice, I felt much more comfortable. Doctor Houston was a bachelor, perhaps fifty years of age, had no family. An old colored woman kept house for him. A colored boy twelve or fourteen years of age made up the family. The doctor had inquired, when we first arrived, how our rations were holding out. Riley informed him that the commissary department had not been replenished for the last twenty-four hours and that a contribution in that direction would be very acceptable. Our horses were stripped and turned loose in a large yard that surrounded the house. In a short time we were invited in to supper which was abundant, considering the times. The doctor was a real jolly old gentleman. He had heard but little news from the seat of war. We enlightened him the best we could, but soon retired for the night. I slept fairly well until near day. The poultice on my foot had become dry and gave me considerable uneasiness.

At daylight all were astir. The doctor removed the bandage from my foot as soon as he learned that it was not comfortable, dressed and bound it up, directing me to keep the bandage wet with cold water from the pump at the end of the porch. We remained with the doctor three or four days. We had been getting all kind of news from the front. Perhaps in the

211

morning we would hear that General Mead had attacked General Lee at Williamsport, had been repulsed and was being driven back on Washington with great slaughter. In the evening of the same day we heard that General Lee had been driven across the Potomac, losing all his artillery and most of his train. We did not rest well that night. Riley thought we had better get a little farther from the main road; I did not object, was really as anxious to get away from the Martinsburg grade as he was, if not more so.

Early in the morning we saddled up, offered to compensate the doctor for his kindness, which he declined. We fell back to Pughtown and stopped with an aunt of Riley's, a real nice old lady by the name of McCool. We remained with her for two or three days, but could get nothing reliable from the army and having learned that there were no Yankees in Romney and could hear none nearer than Cumberland in that direction, I determined to visit Hampshire county again. I left Riley at his aunt's and started early in the morning and reached home before sundown, without any mishap. A few days after I got home, Ephraim Herriott, John J. Inskeep and several other Hampshire county boys being nearer home than they would likely be again for a long time perhaps, availed themselves of the opportunity while General Lee remained in the Shenandoah Valley, to visit their homes once more and it might be to some of them for the last time. I kept pretty close and did my own picketing for about two weeks. Several times I heard of Yankee scouts being in Romney, or passing on the pike a quarter of mile from my father's house. Although it was well known that I was about home I was not molested. The Yankees treated me in this respect with great consideration. I was told by a Union man who lived near Romney, after the war, that Capt. Jarboe came into town one day on a scout and that he had said to him that it was reported I was at home wounded, that it would be a good time to take him in.

Capt. Jarboe replied, "yes it would be a good time to go down there and leave one corpse dressed in gray and bring back a half dozen dressed in blue. I know the man," said he, "better leave him alone while he is doing no harm."

So I was not disturbed. About the first of August we learned that the Confederate army had left the Shenandoah Valley and again gone east of the ridge. Further that there were then no Confederate troops below Harrisonburg. The Yankees were reported advancing from the direction of Winchester. Herriott, Inskeep and I held a council of war and considering the situation concluded that we were rather far from our base of operations and determined that we had better make a force march, by way of North River Church, Lost River, Brock's Gap, to Harrisonburg, where we would be likely to learn where we would probably find our brigade.

CHAPTER XVI

McNeill's Rangers to the Rescue

W e agreed to meet at John J. Inskeep's home next morning, at an early hour. That night I called on a few friends, bade them adieu, and before the sun was up next morning had buckled my sword, bade farewell to my childhood's home, and turned my back on all that was dear to me, with but little thought of what danger, suffering and privation I must endure before I would again be permitted to look on those cherished scenes. Again I joined Inskeep ready to move, but Herriott had not reported yet. A troop of Yankees had reached town that night. We were rather near the public highway for safety, and not being sure that we could capture the town we concluded to flank it, and started up Buffalo Hollow, expecting Herriott would overtake us soon. After we had gone some distance up the hollow we halted to wait for Herriott, expecting him ever moment. After a stop of perhaps an hour, we concluded that something must have happened to him and concluded to proceed on our way.

Our intended route lay through Grassy Lick country. We soon found our way blocked by squads of Yankee infantry moving in the direction of Romney. We afterward learned that it was Gen. Blinker's Dutch, who straggling along the pike in squads, carrying their camp kettles on tent poles. We moved farther toward Frenchburg and took a position on the ridge near the pike, opposite the lane crossing the North Fork of Little Capon, between where Mr. Haines and Mr. Vandergrift now live. From our elevated position we could see the pike for quite a distance in the direction of Frenchburg and watched it closely until near sundown before we saw a chance to cross the pike without being discovered. We reached Mr. Benjamin Pugh's house about dark and halted for the night.

At Mr. Pugh's house a Confederate soldier was always sure of a cordial reception and hospitable entertainment. Not only Mr. Pugh himself, but his most excellent wife and accomplished daughter were ever found ready to minister to the necessities of the Confederate soldier. Next morning we bade the family adieu, and I saw them no more until the war had ended. I then learned that the fair daughter had been captured by a dashing Confederate major, and plans for the future had to be abandoned. As we rode out from Mr. Pugh's our comrade, for whom we had felt no little uneasiness, rode up. He too had experienced no little difficulty in running the blockade. The Yankees had given him quite a chase through the mountains; but they had as well as chased a red fox as to chase Ephe after he once struck the brush. After a good deal of doubling and dodging, he succeeded in eluding his pursuers and joined Inskeep and me, having sustained no injury, except the loss of his hat, which had been struck from his head by the limb of a tree, and being so closely pressed by the Yankees, had not time to recover it. After his pursuers gave up the chase he stopped, if I remember right, at "Big" Sam Buckman's, who administered to his necessities the best he could for the night, and kindly supplied him with head gear. Although several sizes too large, the color of his clothing could easily be distinguished. Glad to be together again we pursued our way with caution, keeping an eye to the rear as well as front and flank.

It appeared that since Lee had left the lower valley the Yankees were scattered broad-cast over the country, hence the necessity of prudence in our movements. Near sundown we reached John Shull's house (Old Keg's) who had got afraid to remain at Shull's Gap and had moved well up into the Lost River valley. Mr. Shull insisted on our stopping with him over night, which Ephe and I did. J. J. Inskeep went a few miles farther up the valley and stopped with a cousin of his, Mr. Angus Wood, where he would await our coming next morning. We now felt that we were beyond the radius of Yankee scouts and felt comparatively safe. There at least was a narrow strip of Virginia soil never yet pressed by the foot of the invader. Feeling thus secure we retired early and slept the night through without awakening until called next morning to breakfast, after which Mrs. Shull supplied our haversacks with rations sufficient to last us for a siege of ordinary duration. We well knew that to offer to pay for our entertainment would be to offer an insult. We bade Mr. Shull and family goodbye, and started to find Inskeep, expecting to reach the valley that day. But how uncertain are oftimes our best laid plans in time of peace, but far more so in time of war.

Little did we think when we mounted our horses fresh and vigorous, armed to the teeth and full of fight (if necessary), that before the sun had reached the meridian we would be prisoners without arms, from whom we felt perfectly safe for the time being at least. Nevertheless such were the facts. Had John Shull said to us that morning, boys you will be prisoners before night, we would have given no more heed to his words than if he had said, boys the sun will not set today. So entirely secure did we feel that we could scarcely believe our own eyes, that blue was really blue, and not gray. When surrounded by a company of Yankee Cavalry, without having a chance to either run or fight was compelled to surrender ourselves prisoners in the hands of our enemies. The change of base was very unexpected to us, and happened this way. We reached Mr. Woods' house early in the day, expecting to find Inskeep ready to join us, expecting to reach the neighborhood of Harrisonburg that day.

When we arrived at Mr. Woods' we learned that Inskeep had joined several Confederates who had been camping a few days in a vacant house of Mr. Woods, some distance from the road, and had gone up the river a few miles to have a deer chase and only expected to be gone a few hours. We waited until near the middle of the day. Mr. Wood said there was a small lot of good grass back of the barn where we could turn our horses. That we should go no farther until after dinner. We agreed to this proposition. A short time before dinner was announced Mr. George Turley rode up to the house having left Moorefield that morning. He said the Yankees were reported at the river below town where he left. A company of Yankee Cavalry had left the North Western grade at Hanging Rock passing up North River until they reached Rio, then crossed over to Lost River, following that stream until they reached the Howard Lick road by which they expected to cross over to the South Fork and thence to Moorefield picking up any Confederate soldier or citizen, who on the approach of the Yankees (by the way of Romney) not wishing to be captured, on leaving Moorefield and vicinity would follow the Howard Lick road, it being the most direct one to the Lost River Valley and on to the Valley of Virginia. The Yankees had been informed as to what would probably occur, and had sent this company out to intercept any one fleeing from the Moorefield Valley on what they considered a safe road to retreat and would, in all probability, have as much expected to meet an elephant as a Yankee. Turley's horse stood hitched at the gate, our arms were stacked in one corner of the room. We had taken our seats at the dinner table and had eaten but a few mouthfuls when a door immediately behind me, leading into another room, opened and a young lady who lived with Mr. Wood put her head through the opening and uttered one word, "Yankees," at the same time slipped through the door snatched up our swords and pistols and carried them into the other room (we afterward learned hid them between the ticks of a bed in the room). When she said Yankee I turned my head and glanced from the window. Sure enough, there sat a full grown Yankee on his horse, with his carbine leveled on the table through the open window. I glanced through the opposite window, there sat a half dozen more. We had been surprised, surrounded, disarmed and prisoners at the mercy of our Captors.

Capt. Kurr, who commanded the company, walked into the room and asked whose horse that was hitched at the gate. Turley replied, after hesitating a moment. Said that it was a borrowed horse, and he had rode it there. I take you to be a Rebel soldier, said the captain. No said Turley, I am a citizen, do not belong to either army. Where did you get that cavalry saddle said the captain? I borrowed it from the same party I got the horse from, said Turley. I guess we will take you with us, said the captain. The day was very warm. I had removed my coat of many colors, made from the gray goods I had got in Cumberland. With all the army regulation requirements tacked on, that coat was quite an ornament and very

215

attractive, so much so that I didn't care to have it shot to pieces by the enemy, believing they were firing at General Lee or one of the division commanders. In a fight if the weather was not cold enough to wear an over coat. It now seemed to attract the notice of Captain Kurr. He walked across the room and took it from the window where it lay, held it up, examined it closely as I thought, and then asked to whom it belonged. No one answered. He asked a second time. I said it was mine. "A colonel," said he, "better luck than I expected." No said I, not quite a colonel. Said he, "this is a colonel's uniform, no officer below a colonel wears two rows of buttons." I said no more. He then asked Herriott who he was. Herriott replied that he was a citizen. Well said the captain I guess I will take you three with me. Get ready, I asked to be allowed to finish our dinner. He said you will have to be in a hurry then. Mr. Wood invited the captain to have some dinner, which he declined, but walked back and forth across the floor a few times and said that he could not wait longer, we would have to be going. As we filed out through the yard an old lady by the name of Inskeep, I think a sister of Mr. Wood, walked by my side and said in a low tone, if you have any letters or papers about you give them to me. I slipped two letters and my pocketbook into her hand, when I thought I was not being watched, but one of the Yankees saw the transfer and demanded the pocketbook. There was nothing to be done but give it up, but the old lady, not knowing but what I had given her something that might be of importance to the Yankees, gave up her own pocketbook instead of mine. The Yankee put it in his pocket without examining it. We were soon mounted, Turley on his own horse, Herriott on a horse which the Yankees had picked up somewhere on the road and I on a mare belonging to Lieut. Alexander, of Captain Harness' company.

I had taken the opportunity at home to have an old shoemaker by the name of Nelson, who lived at the Wire Bridge, make me a pair of cavalry boots. My lame foot was not yet in a condition to wear a boot. I wore one and tied the other to my saddle. It had already been captured. When I had mounted a big six footer came around and said, "Colonel, where is your other boot?" I said I had a sore foot and could not wear it. "Now that's too bad," said he, "that fellow shall be punished. Let me have the boot you have on and I will find the mate to it and return them to you." At the same time he laid hold of the boot and tried to pull it off. I knew my boots were gone and made no resistance. We were ordered to take our place in ranks, with a Yankee by our side. The columns moved up Lost River until we reached a Mr. Garrett's, where the Confederates who had been having a deer hunt were congregated. The Yankees were not discovered until near at hand, when the Confederates broke for the brush, under fire from the Yankees, scattered in different directions. B. F. Maloney, brother of James and Justice Maloney, ran across a narrow bottom toward the river. Two or three of the Yankees sprang from their horses laid their guns on the fence, took deliberate aim and fired. I felt almost sure that Ben was a dead duck. Each carbine fired at the same instant. Ben sprang about three feet in the air and appeared to get on an extra pound or two of steam, and leaped the fence at the river, clear as a buck, without showing any sign of having been severely wounded. The brush was thick along the river bank. Ben had only gone a few rods from the fence and laid down. Two of the Yankees ran across the bottom to the fence where Ben had cleared it at a single bound. They found blood on the fence and was in the act of following the trail when three or four shots were fired from the brush on the other side of the road, which caused them to change their minds. They came back on the double quick, mounted their horses and the column moved on for some distance at a quick pace.

The deer hunters all made their escape. The Yankees left the Lost River road and followed the road leading to Moorefield, by the way of Howards Lick. The Yankees advanced, a dozen or so kept well in front and were dressed in gray. In crossing the mountain refugees were picked up, being deceived by the gray dress worn by the Yankees. Among the number were two Confederate soldiers, Joseph V. Williams, Company F of the 7th, and Criss Hoffman Company B of the 11th. They were deceived by the gray dress, and rode up to the Yankees before they discovered their mistake. They were disarmed and sent to the rear. If I remember right, Mr. Ed Williams and old Mr. Alexander, of Moorefield, were among the captured. After crossing the top of the mountain and going a short distance we came to a path which leads off to the left, down what was Shooks Hollow, or Shooks Run. When we reached the foot of the mountain, when an order was sent a file or two in front of me, turned his little sorrel into this blind path gave her the rein and the spur at the same time, dashed into the brush, and down the mountain side, leaping ledges and logs with a recklessness, only equaled by that of General Putnam down the stone steps, followed by a shower of bullets from Yankee carbines. He was pursued only a short distance, when the column moved on. We had gone no great distance when Hoffman wheeled his horse to the right into the woods and was gone like a flash. The Yankees seemed to be getting nervous, and moved with great caution. About sunset we met three little boys, ranged in a row along a path on the upper side of the road, who seemed to be watching the column with childish interest. At length one of the little boys said, who are you fellows anyhow? Oh, said one of the Yankees, we are Rebels. No you are not, said the boy, you are Yankees; you better look out, Mr. McNeill's horse company is down at Mr. Randolph's. From that time on the Yankees were very much demoralized. As night set in they would halt every few rods and consult, then move a little farther and halt again.

217

I now felt sure that if Williams or Hoffman succeeded in reaching McNeill in time there would be no trouble for those Yankees before they reached Moorefield. We had reached the foot of the mountain, when an order was sent back to the guards that if they were fired on to shoot the prisoners, to not let one of them escape. I said to my guard that would be rather hard on us prisoners, since we would have nothing to do with your being fired on and would be in as much danger as you. Yes, he said, but we must obey orders. I said no more, but made up my mind that he would not shoot me if it could be helped.

We had now reached a heavy piece of oak timber and were moving at a very slow gait. It was almost dark to see the guard who rode by my side. If I remember right the other prisoners were farther to the rear. The column was well closed up and moving more like a funeral procession, than Yankee raiders. I thought surely if Captain McNeill received the notice in time that he would attack them before they had reached the open country on the South Fork, and of all others this would be the place. I had begun to despair of our rescue, when a pistol shot rang out on the stillness of the night, instantly followed by a blinding flash, and rattle of near a hundred carbines and double barrel shot guns not ten feet away.

The firing came from the right of the road, the side I was riding on. I was expecting or rather hoping for something of this kind, but had begun to fear that those boys were mistaken about Capt. McNeill, or that he was not aware of the approach of the Yankees. I had determined to slip from my horse and make a break for liberty. A moment later and I would have been on the ground, but that pistol shot and what followed caused me to change my mind. For an instant the night was lighted up by the flashing of arms, as by flashes of lightning. I saw my guard raise his pistol. I grabbed for it, caught him by the arm, his pistol fired at the same time, I think in the air. I gathered my feet in the saddle under me, threw all my weight against my guard, pushing him from his saddle, and with one foot on his empty saddle I made the longest leap of my life, more to escape the deadly fire of Capt. McNeill's men (from which the Gray and Blue fared alike) than to escape from the Yankees. I have no idea how far I leaped. It may have been twenty feet, it may have been more, but I rather expect it was less (I am satisfied it would be much less now). Anyway the last link was strained in that effort to escape the fire of my friends, and don't think I was ever in more danger from my enemies. To my surprise I landed on a bank nearly as high as a horse's back, and started on a run. Had taken but a few steps when I came in contact with an old log, took a header and measured my length on the opposite side. An instant later I was stretched close by the side of that log, and while my heart was making about two hundred revolutions per minute, I was trying to pull myself together enough to determine with some degree of certainty, whether it had been an earthquake or a cyclone through which I had just passed.

The firing had now ceased. I cautiously peered over the log, but the curtain of darkness hid from view the first act of the tragedy. A great deal of loud talking was going on, well striped with profanity. After listening to the conversation for a moment or two I concluded that our Yankee captors no longer bossed the circus, and that we were free again. I arose to my feet and cautiously approached the road, fearful that some excited Confederate might take me for a blue coat and punch a hole in my hide. I slid down the bank into the road to find the cold muzzle of a revolver stuck in my face. Who are you and why are you here? was asked. I said, I am a Confederate soldier and came here a prisoner. To what command do you belong? was the next question. I replied Company D, 11th Va. Cavalry. Your name? Blue, I answered. His pistol dropped by his side as he grasped my hand and exclaimed, "My God, Blue, I am glad we were in time to release you fellows; hope you have not been hurt." I said no unless the scare should have some bad effect. It was John Lyn, of Cumberland, Md., who held me up this time. We had not met since parting nine months before on the back road between Winchester and Strasburg, he to join Capt. McNeill and I to join my regiment near Winchester.

Capt. McNeill and his men were hastily gathering together the spoils of war, such as horses and arms, of the captured, wounded and killed. If I remember right they had about thirty prisoners; something like the same number killed and wounded. By the light of burning leaves the wounded were made as comfortable as possible, under the circumstances. One of the prisoners was then enrolled and sent to Moorefield to acquaint their friends with the situation, and request them to look after their friends; that they would not be molested while carrying for their wounded and dead.

Capt. McNeill did not lose any time in getting away with his prisoners, as few of the Yankee advance had made their escape and gone as fast as they could in the direction of Moorefield, and might, in a short time, have a regiment of Yankees in his heels. The Captain moved his command up the South Fork and did not halt until late in the night, We prisoners all escaped injury except young Branson, whom the Yankees had pressed into service as a pilot. He was seriously wounded. Eph Herriott was also struck in the hip by a pistol ball, but the wound was slight. I rode several miles with Capt. McNeill that night. He seemed very much gratified at the result of the engagement and at having been able to release from captivity his relatives and friends at so light a cost, but said it was by a mere accident that we were released and was brought about as well as I can remember in this way. The Captain said he had been with his company in the neighborhood of Moorefield for several days, resting his men and horses; was in camp near Mr. Randolph's on the South Fork; that one of his men had come to camp that morning with news that the Yankees were advancing on Moorefield by the way of Romney, with several thousand men; that he sent out a scout to ascertain the facts, but before the return of his scouting party he received a dispatch from Lost River saying, that the Yankees were then at Mr. Wood's. Capt. Harness Co. B of the 11th informs me that it was he who sent the dispatch to Capt. McNeill, having rode among them, being deceived by their gray clothes. After emptying his revolver among them he succeeded in making his escape only by the superior speed of his thoroughbred charger.

Capt. McNeill had determined on the approach of the Yankees to fall back to Lost River by way of Howard Lick road, but being in the dark as to the number and destination of the Yankee raiders and for fear of being caught between two fires concluded to move his command up the South Fork and reach the head waters of the North Fork of the Shenandoah in Brock's Gap, where the road would likely be clear of Yankees in the Valley.

On the return of his scout, who reported the Yankee cavalry at Moorefield, he had started up the fork and gone several miles when met by a dispatch from Joseph V. Williams, informing him of about the number of Yankees, in the company, of their advance, being dressed in gray, and the number and names of their prisoners. Also the road they were following. The Captain determined on receiving William's dispatch, to await the coming of the Yankees and if possible release the prisoners, some of whom I believe he said were relatives of his. He accordingly selected a favorable position a little way out on the Howard Lick road, in a flat heavily timbered. The road here seemed to have been worn or washed out until there was but little more room than necessary for a team to drive along. The banks on either side seemed to be three or more feet in height. Capt. McNeill had dismounted his men and placed them on the right of the road leading from Howards Lick to Moorefield. Night had set in, there being no moon the darkness beneath the heavy timber the Captain said, was so great that it was impossible for him to discriminate between friend and foe. Having placed himself on the right of his men and ordered them not to fire until he fired his double barrel shot gun, which would be the signal for them to proceed to business. The Captain said that he had let several Yankees pass him and had about made up his mind to let them all pass rather than endanger the lives of his friends. As he stood behind a tree only a few feet from the road, straining his eyes, trying if possible to discover whether the prisoners were in the front or rear of the column, in peering from behind the tree he had made some noise or been seen by a Yankee, who fired his pistol at him.

His men supposed it to be the expected signal and let loose on friend and foe alike. The Captain said that on account of his friends who were prisoners he did not fire a shot.

The Captain always carried a double barreled shotgun well filled with buckshot. Whenever the Captain brought that gun to his shoulder in a business way, one or more blue coats were very apt to be taken with their last sickness.

I saw J. V. Williams a few days ago and got from him a short sketch of his experience that day. I was well back in the column and not often in sight of the advance, who, I suppose, had picked up all their prisoners or rather had met them on the road, as had not seen them until we passed Howard Lick. Williams says that a few gentle men from the South Branch with a colored cook had determined to camp for a short time at Howard Lick, a point where, up to that time, no Yankee had reached. Joe says that he was absent from his regiment on sick leave. I am inclined to think it was heart trouble, and that a certain young lady in the vicinity of Moorefield was to blame. He says that he came on this camp unexpectedly, and needing rest concluded to accept their invitations to stop with them a few days, and on that evening Mr. Alexander, Mr. Ed Williams and himself had taken their horses up the mountain to a pasture field directly in the road to Moorefield. He said they saw the owner of the pasture in his field not far off, and called to him to come to the road, but before he reached them three or four cavalrymen dressed in gray, which they took to be McNeill's men, but when within ten steps of them the head of the column appeared dressed in blue. It was then too late to run. The Yankees closed in on them and began to exchange horses; said one fellow ordered him to dismount, when he informed him in a very confidential way that his mare was crippled and advised him to stick to his own, she would do him no good and would give out in a short time. The Yankee believed the story. Joe's mare was one among the best in the service. Said he at once took courage when his mare was not taken from him and determined to leave them at the first opportunity, which came when we had gone but little over a mile, when we reached a blind path where he knew, into which he wheeled the little sorrel and let her go, and although the path was steep and crossed in many places by fallen timber, she carried him through all right. Joe said that although he had ten miles farther to go to reach the fork and McNeill than the Yankees had, yet he succeeded in getting word to Captain McNeill in time. When he reached the South Fork several miles above McNeill he met one Havener, a Confederate soldier, if I remember right, a member of Captain McNeill's Company. Being mounted on a fresh horse Williams sent him on to McNeill, while having no arms, stopped at Dr. Parrin's to let his mare get her wind for a few moments, then armed with the Doctor's double-barreled gun, pushed on and joined McNeill.

The next morning I made a thorough search among the prisoners for my boots, but failed to find them. Captain McNeill was soon on the march heading toward the Valley, for the purpose of turning over his prisoners to the provost at Harrisonburg. When we reached Fish Water's in Brock's Gap, E. Herriott and I turned back and reached Mr. Wood's before night, found Inskeep and several other Confederates camped in the old vacant house belonging to Mr. Wood. They did not know what had become of us, but supposed that we were on our way to prison. I turned over to Mr. Wood, Lieutenant Alexander's mare, which I rode away the day before. Herriott stuck to the horse on which the Yankees had mounted him, and as no one could show a better title we took him with us over the Blue Ridge and sold him for, if I remember right, three hundred dollars, which Herriott divided with me. So it will be seen that our misfortune was rather fortunate financially, having cleared one hundred and fifty dollars each in twenty four hours, less one pair of boots. We found our horses and equipment all right, also my pocketbook, which was rather a surprise to me, as I was not aware that the kind old lady had given up her own and kept mine, thinking that perhaps it might contain something that would give me trouble if it came to the Yankees. I was very sorry that the old lady had made the exchange, thus losing some valuable notes and papers, which I am not aware that she ever recovered; although she may have done so.

CHAPTER XVII

Back to the Shenandoah Valley

N ext morning we started for the Shenandoah Valley, fully satisfied with our experienc e in the Lost River Valley. We crossed the mountain by the way of Arkney Springs, thence to Harrisonburg, where we learned that when last heard from our Brigade was in the vicinity of Orange C. H. I had concluded, as I was getting a little tender, that I had been barefooted about long enough, and had better try and have some shoeing done before crossing the Blue Ridge if I could find a shop in blast. After considerable search and enquiry I found a small concern run by a real nice old christian gentleman. I am not sure, but think he was some kind of a preacher. His name was Hoffman. The only thing that came near filling the bill was a pair of boots which the old gentleman said he had footed for an old farmer several months before, but had not seen him since he left the boots. I tried to persuade him to sell me the boots, but he shook his head, said, no that would not be right. I knew how hard it was to get either boots or shoes, and pleaded with all the eloquence of a Demos-thenese. I told how ridiculous I felt wearing the uniform of a Confederate officer, that would at that time have cost at least two hundred and fifty dollars, and barefooted. Still he shook his head. I said perhaps the owner of these boots is not living or has left the country, yet he would not consent for me to have the boots. I said what could you make me a pair of boots like these for? He said if I could get the leather I could not make them for less than forty dollars. Finally I said, Mr. Hoffman, the owner of these boots can not need then as bad as I do, otherwise he would have been after them. I am going to leave with you, forty dollars, the amount you priced them at, and take the boots without your consent, and when he comes for his boots tell him all the circumstances and give him the forty dollars, and if he is not satisfied with the sale to bring me the forty dollars and get his boots. Where shall I direct him to look for you? I told him that really I could not tell him, but if living I could be found by enquiring for Co. D 11th regt. Va. Cavalry, C. S. A. Giving my name I sat down on a bench and hauled on the boots, which were about two sizes too large, but it was the best I could do, and lots better than being barefooted. Next morning we started for Orange C. H., by way of Swift Run Gap, Stannardsville, Burtonsville and on to Orange. We had to forage for substance, but while corn was getting a little hard, sweet potatoes were all right.

We found General Lee's army in the vicinity of Culpepper Court House. Our regiment was picketing on his left, on Hazel River, in the direction of the Blue Ridge at a place called Rixyville. General Mead's army lay facing General Lee along the North Branch of the Rappahannock; so near to each other that the band's of either army could be plainly heard by each other, each taking their turn, the other listening. They would generally start up about dusk of the evening, the Yankees playing Yankee Doodle, the Confederates replied by playing Dixie. It seemed strange how men could lay on their blankets or sit and enjoy the sweetest music I ever heard, and a few hours later were ready to slaughter each other, but so it was.

A few days after we arrived at camp our company was ordered to take our turn at the advance picket post, at a ford of the river some four or five miles in advance of our regiment. On either side of the river was a narrow strip of bottom land; a little further back the bluff arose rather abruptly to the height of two or three hundred feet. On this bluff some distance from the ford our advance picket was posted, the company in reserve something like a half mile in the rear. The Yankee picket occupied a like position on the opposite side of the river with their reserve about a mile down the river in the direction of Rappahannock Station. Our orders were not to fire on the picket post unless there were an advance of the enemy in force. At the ford about midway of the stream there was a small island. This island was considered neutral ground. An understanding, brought about in some way between the Johnnies and the Yankees, and although positively forbidden at head quarters, the pickets met on this island every day to trade tobacco for coffee, and some times saddles and arms or exchange newspapers; generally a few games of cards closed the meeting for that day. But little was said at these meetings in regard to the war. One company generally remained on the outpost twenty-four hours and were then relieved by another company. About fifteen of our company had become dismounted, their horses having been killed or broken down. In the Confederate service the cavalry furnished their own horses. When a cavalryman lost his horse and could not procure another, he was sent to the infantry. Capt. McDonald concluded to make an effort to mount his dismounted men by a requisition on the United States government. The Captain, Corporal James Ream and myself made a reconnaissance for the purpose of locating the position of the reserve picket post, and determine what the chances for a surprise of the Yankees might be. Also the risk to be taken and the probability of success in the undertaking. We located their camp about a mile down, and not over three or four hundred yards from the river, situated on a low bluff in a piece of timber near the county road. At the foot of this bluff and across the strip of bottom land that lay between the camp and the river ran a small stream of water, the banks on each side being covered by thick brush. We thought by wading the river at the mouth of this run, and following it under cover of the brush, a surprise party might succeed in getting within a few yards of the Yankees without being detected. The surprise to be attempted under cover of darkness. When our turn came to go picket again the dismounted men of our company followed us and reached our reserve a little before night. Captain McDonald's plan was this: Corporal Ream was to take him the dismounted men (if I remember right) fifteen men in number, and when darkness had set in they were to wade the river at the place determined on, and proceed cautiously up the stream until opposite the camp, which was on a steep rise above them and not over thirty yards away. When they reached this position they were to lay quiet if not discovered, until the moon (which arose about an hour after dark) appeared over the mountain and lighted up the surroundings, when they were to rush up the bank firing and yelling like furies. Captain McDonald was to have his company mounted and move down as near the ford as possible without alarming the picket on the opposite side, ready to dash through the river the moment Ream and his squad made their attempt. About nine o'clock p. m. Oct. 1, 1863, just as the moon began to show herself from a cloudless sky over the top of Bull Run mountain, making the night almost as light as day, we sat mounted in nervous suspense awaiting the signal to go to the aid of our comrades. The moon had scarcely cleared the mountain top when the rattle of firearms reached our ears. Forward, gallop, was the command and away we went. The picket at the crossing fired as we dashed through the river. We had scarcely covered half the distance to the reserved Yankee picket, when we met the boys coming on a force march, each mounted on a good charger.

The requisition on Uncle Sam had been filled satisfactorily. Ream had managed the attack with consummate skill and followed instruction to the letter. The boys had waded the river at the place fixed upon, although the water was pretty cool, and struck a few of the boys, who were of short growth, considerably above the girth, yet, all landed safe on the opposite side, then cautiously followed the small stream under cover of the brush until they reached, without discovery, a position immediately opposite the camp, which was located on a bluff above them not more than twenty yards distant. To reach the camp they had to charge up a steep bank. They reached the point desired a short time in advance of the moon and had to wait, although shivering from cold in their wet clothes, until she had turned darkness into light sufficient to locate a man or horse a short distance. In the mean time Captain Griffith and his men were entertaining the boys in gray unaware with amusing stories and joking with each other. On the out post the reserve picket never removed the bit from his horse's mouth only long enough for him to eat, he is always saddled, ready to be mounted at a moments notice. The Yankees had retired for the night rolled in their blankets. Many of them were no doubt fast asleep and may have been having pleasant dreams of their distant homes and of the

225

dear ones left behind, when they were rudely awakened by the unearthly and unwelcome yelling and firing of Ream and his fifteen men as they charged in among five times their numbers. The surprise was complete. The Yankees so unceremoniously and rudely awakened made no resistance, outside of a few pistol shots, but broke for the brush scattering in all directions, some running on all fours, with all their blankets wound about them, leaving their arms behind. Ream and his men were not after Yankees and did not pursue them. Horses was the object, each man without halting or loss of time ran to a horse, loosened him, mounted and started for the ford, and was coming at a rattling gate when we met them. The boys had one prisoner with them, an Irishman, mounted on a big gray horse. He said he had been disturbed in his sleep and was half waked up when he discovered the boys climbing on their horses in a hurry like; he did the same and came along with the boys, not caring to be left behind, when he did not know just which end was in most danger. When he had gone a little way and got wide awake he discovered he was on the wrong train and had not been able to get off again. We rode back to our side of the river without being molested by the demoralized Yankees. When we reached the high ground a few hundred yards back from the river we heard the Bugal call to saddle up at the Brick church, some three miles below, where a Brigade of cavalry was camped.

In a short time the sound of the approaching column could be distinctly heard; then soon we discovered by the light of the moon a dim line (scarcely more in appearance than a pencil mark) moving through the fields opposite side of the river, with frequent challenges, a flash followed by the report of a pistol. A stump or bunch of briars having been mistaken for rebel, and pierced with many balls, no doubt. Whilst these evolutions were being enacted we sat secure from present danger on the opposite heights enjoying ourselves hugely. After maneuvering and hopping around for an hour or two they gave up the search for Rebs, and returned from whence they came.

Next morning we found that we had sixteen cavalry chargers, the same number of saddles with gum coats and gum blankets strapped on, also several sabres and revolvers which had been left on the ground by the Yankees in their fright or scrabble to get away to shelter, and one very much demoralized Irishman, who said, "be jases" if his General would follow him he would see Richmond a dale sooner. The only casualty or loss on our side was one man shot through the wrist, the ball passing between the bones without breaking either. The wound soon healed.

The Yankees left a whole company at their picket post. The boys mounted their captured horses and rode slowly along the top of a ridge in an old field, in full view of the Yankees, and got a complete cursing, with threats to get even in the near future, for their trouble.

When our turn came again to go on picket, we found that the Yankees had spotted us. Some one of the other companies had given us away, for fear of a surprise themselves. After dark the Captain moved his reserve picket a half mile, or nearly so, farther back and placed his men facing a road which led off at right angle from the one we were picketing on. This road led toward the Yankee camp at the church. We felt sure that if the Yankees attempted to surprise us they would aim to get in our rear by following this road. The Captain had arranged to give them a warm reception, if they should attempt to capture our post. Our horses had been sent to the rear, and we lay in line waiting and expecting the Yankees. A little two-year old bull had been bellowing and pawing up and down along the road all evening, late at night he had managed to get between the men and their horses, when some of the men in charge of the horses gave him a fright and he came charging through the brush into our line; the boys more asleep than awake thought sure it was Yankees, opened fire on the bull and soon brought him to a stop; but he came near creating a panic. It was hardly daylight when a single shot was heard at the out post. We had scarcely mounted when our picket came in view, closely pursued by a squad of Yankees, which we quickly brought to a halt, and in turn drove back on the head of their column which proved to be a brigade. Captain McDonald sent a dispatch to regimental headquarters, giving notice of the cavalry advance in force. We continued to fall back checking the advance whenever a favorable position could be had, although but little could be done against such great odds. The regiment reached us about ten o'clock, when every foot of the ground was stubbornly disputed, fighting as we fell back until we met the brigade coming to our relief still we were not able to drive the enemy, but were ourselves forced back in the direction of Culpepper C. H. It proved to be General Kirkpatrick's division, who had been driving us back since early in the morning. In the after part of the day we were joined by Fitz Lee's command; about the same time General Kirkpatrick was reinforced for the direction of Brandy Station. General Stuart was now on the ground, and I suppose directed the movements on the Confederate side. A great deal of work was done on the skirmish line by the dismounted men, but no general engagement. Late in the evening the dismounted men in front of the eleventh, seemed to have more on their hands than they could manage. Our sharp shooters were sent to their relief, commanded by Captain Ware, who was brave but rash. The racket was going on in a piece of timber with thick undergrowth; the Captain led us in on a double quick with the same old yell, but it was no go; the Yankees would neither scare or run, so we fell back after loosing about one half of our number. Night was now at hand, and both sides seemed to be satisfied with the days work and willing to drop the matter for that day. The Yankees fell back to the Rappahannock and the

227

Confederates in the direction of Rapidann.

The day had been a day of skirmishing; principally there being no regular engagement that I heard of, although we had lost a good many men during the day. It seemed to have been the object of the Yankees to locate the Confederate forces and find out, if they could, just where they were. We at length went into camp tired and hungry. We or our horses having had nothing to eat for twenty-four hours, and got nothing until the next morning.

Our company a day or two later was sent out to picket on a road leading from Madison C. H. to, if I remember right, what was called Williams Gap in the Blue Ridge mountain. We reached our destination late in the afternoon, stationed our picket perhaps a half mile in advance of our reserve or company and proceeded to make ourselves as comfortable as possible. The nights were getting cool, and we soon had camp fires built from the abundance of material close at hand. We were in a wooded country near the base of the mountain. We had passed a large patch of sweet potatoes a mile or so back and three or four of the boys had gone back as soon as dark came on to see how they would turn out. They came in toward the middle of the night each with a sack of potatoes.

We were up early next morning and had about two bushels roasted for breakfast. By the time we fed our horses, readjusted our saddle blankets, strapped on our over coats and blankets to our saddles and bridled our horses ready to mount at the first note of alarm from our picket up the mountain gorge. By the time we had completed our preparation to either fight or run, whichever circumstances might demand, we found that our breakfast of sweet potatoes were ready and were squatted around the heap of ashes, scratching them from the heap of embers, our minds intent on the expected feast. But the old saying of "many a slip between the cup and the lip" often cause disappointment. A noise on the side of the ridge on our right like some one stepping on a dry stick, caused some of the boys to rise to their feet in some alarm. Some soldiers are always a little nervous when on the outpost. I was always a little that way. An old sow and some shoats had been around on the side of the ridge the evening before. The Captain said after listening a moment, its that old sow gathering chinkapins, and all hands except myself resumed their work of removing the potatoes from the fire. I was not satisfied that a hog had caused the stick to break and was still standing erect looking in the direction from which the sound had come, and thought I heard the click of a gun lock. Almost instantly a whistling bullet, a cloud of ashes, followed by a sharp crack of a carbine, were signs not to be misunderstood. "Yankees, boys!" came from the Captain. "Mount your horses." We did not wait for a second order to mount, although it was right hard to give up the sweet potatoes on a empty stomach, but to do so seemed to be a military necessity at this time and we did it. I grabbed up a handfull and started for my horse but it was no go, they were too hot, I had to drop them. Our horses were tied near by in a thicket of pines. The bullets were now zipping and spatting around pretty thick, coming from the side of the ridge above us. We were quickly mounted and making tracks toward Madison C. H., closely pursued by a column of Yankees.

The Yankees had cut our pickets off and attempted to capture the reserve by sending dismounted men down the ridge, under cover of the timber, for the purpose of getting in our rear. When the main column would press forward and take us in, but in anticipation of the sweet potato feast we had risen early and fortunately were not caught napping, as the Yankees had no doubt expected to find us. As it was we got away without the loss of a single man. Our picket, when they found they were cut off, took to the woods and escaped, reaching camp next day. Captain McDonald dispatched a courier to brigade headquarters with news of the Yankees advance, with what appeared to be a large body of cavalry.

After the first mile or so the Yankees advanced with a great deal of caution. We continued to fire on their advance from turns in the road, causing then to deploy skirmishers on each side of the road. But when we reached the open country they found but a small force in their front and pushed us back steadily without halting until within a few miles of Madison C. H., when they halted to await two other columns which were advancing on different roads, as it afterwards appeared. Our pickets had been driven in that morning in the different roads between the Blue Ridge and the Rapidan river, along the south bank of which stream General Lee's whole army, both infantry and cavalry, were now gathered. Our company was relieved and another took our place. We reached the Rapidan a short distance above Madison Mills after the middle of the day fed our horses and got some rations, an hour or two later was on a force march with the regiment in the direction of Jack's shop on the road between Madison C. H. and Liberty Mills. At Jack's shop General Stewart had met the Yankees about 4 o'clock, and the meeting seemed to be getting very interesting, when our regiment came on the ground. We crossed the pike in the rear of Stewart's lines and took position on the Confederate's left. Our regiment was halted in a deep, narrow hollow with a timber ridge and a cleared ridge on our left; here we dismounted; the regiment formed in line on the extreme left of the Confederate line of battle and moved forward up the ridge through the timber. I was left in charge of the horses with orders to move them a little ways up the side of the ridge and await orders. Each man had the care of four horses. We moved up the ridge until well sheltered by the timber. The roar of battle which seemed to be mostly on our right, could be distinctly heard. The Confederate yell and the Yankee cheer told to the practiced ear of the varying success of the contending parties in their death struggles for mastery. After perhaps an hour of what, judging from the sound, seemed to be a fierce conflict. The Yankees had gradually extended their line of battle until they were immediately in our front and appeared to draw near. Still we received no orders to move. The firing appeared to be passing to our left on the opposite side of the ridge. We began to be a little skittish for fear of being surrounded. We could not tell why the boys did not come for their horses, or why we did not get orders to move them to a safe place; but the first duty of a soldier is to obey orders and we remained where we were expecting the boys every moment to get their horses. Although I felt sure the Confederates were giving ground and that we were in great danger of being surrounded and captured.

The firing immediately in our front entirely ceased, but continued farther to our left. It now struck me that the boys might have missed the place where they had left their horses. I said to the boys, turn the horses heads to the rear and be ready to go straight up through the field on the opposite ridge. The ascent was not long but steep. On top of this ridge was a high rail fence staked and ridered, which I sent two men to open in several places in case an emergency, which I felt sure was close at hand. Although it was dangerous ground to retreat over with an enemy at close range in our rear. It was, I well knew, the only avenue open by which escape was possible, as the firing had now passed both on our right and left. I still hoped our boys would come for their horses. Solid shot and shell had begun to pass over our heads. We were all getting very nervous, I said to the boys that I would go to the top of the ridge and see if I could learn anything of the boys before we moved the horses, which I felt justifiable in doing. I rode to the top of the ridge or near the top, when I discovered a man through an opening in the timber, perhaps a hundred yards away, and supposing it to be one of our boys, but thought the clothing was rather dark.

I slipped from my horse and dropped to one knee that I might get a better view beneath the limbs of the timber; a second later a bullet fanned my cheek, followed by the report of a carbine. I hastened back as fast as I could and shouted forward to the boys who had heard the shot and understood its meaning and were already on the move. The Yankees had ceased shelling the woods, and their skirmish line had no doubt heard the command (forward) and had halted on the brow of the ridge expecting an attack. They did not know that in this case forward meant to retreat instead of an advance. The trouble was our boys had to fall back and had passed to our left leaving us in a trap that was about sprung. As we were making the best speed possible encumbered with the horses we were leading; the Yankees had discovered that our forward movement was to the rear and began to make it very unpleasant for us. Two gaps had been opened in the fence through which the horses were being crowded under a lively fire from the Yankees on the opposite ridge in our rear. I was some little distance in the rear below the boys and did not feel in much danger. The bullets were passing over my head. I urged the boys to scatter and open the fence farther to the right and left, but they continued to crowd through, and why the Yankees did not kill one half at least I cannot understand, but not a man was touched until we were passing over the summit of the ridge. Corporal Ream, John W. Poland and myself were bringing up the rear and were riding almost in a line perhaps ten paces apart. I heard a ball strike Ream and heard him hollow. I looked in his direction and saw him jump from his horse and run by his side a short distance and then mount again. By this time I was at his side and asked if he had been struck, and he said yes. I asked where, but he made no reply. I saw that he was very pale and began to reel in his saddle. I caught him by the arm to steady him and called to Poland who was now a little in advance he turned and rode back. We were yet in view of the Yankees who knew that we were the only target in sight seemed to concentrate their fire on us, and were making it very unpleasant. In fact we were expecting one or all to be struck at any time. We could not stop if we did it would be but a few moments at most, when we would be either killed or captured. We moved on at a slow gait Poland leading Ream's horse while I steadied him in his saddle. He soon became so limber that he could not sit upright. Poland said he was dying. I lifted him in front of me and carried him for near a mile in my arms. When we reached the pike over which our boys were being rapidly driven back toward Liberty Mill's short distance in the rear or in the direction of Jack's Shop, from where we came on the pike. A squad of Confederates had made a stand, and were holding the Yankees in check. We turned toward Liberty Mills and had gone a few hundred yards when Ream came to and asked to put down, said that we would be captured, and begged us to leave him and save ourselves. We turned off the pike a few yards, Poland lifted him down after spreading our blankets and placing his own for a pillow, we laid him gently down. I had noticed a hole in the back of his jacket which I now hastily opened and found that the bullet had passed entirely through his body. He took from his finger a plain gold ring and asked that I give it to a young lady, whose name I will not mention. I could not wear the ring and turned it over to Poland, who slipped it on and supposed delivered it as requested. All this had only taken a moment of time. The squad of Confederates who had check the Yankees for a few moments now dashed by closely pursued by the Yankees. Ream urged us to go as we could do him no good by staying, and held out his hand to bid us good-bye. Said he knew he must die but was not afraid. We mounted our horses and dashed across the road into the pines on the opposite side.

231

The Yankees were nearly on us when we cleared the road. A moment later and we would have been too late. We pushed our way through a pine thicket and timber for at least a half mile, when we reached the top of a considerable ridge with cleared fields in our front, looking toward the Rapidann river, perhaps half a mile away, we discovered a bunch of what appeared to be a cavalry near an old barn. At first we were uncertain as to whether it was friends or foe, but knew that we were being pursued and concluded to go forward. We soon discovered that they wore the gray and hastened to join them. We found the men to be Col. O'Farrel about twenty men who had gotten separated from the command. We were glad to be with friends again, and of being with an officer capable of leading us.

When we reached the party at the old barn a body of Yankee cavalry had made their appearance on top of the ridge, which we had left a few minutes before. Col. O'Farrel, or some of his men found a joint or two of old stove pipe in the barn and had mounted it on the hind carriage of an old wagon, which stood on the opposite side of the barn from the Yankees. This harmless piece of ordinance the Colonel had run around the end of the barn by hand the men then fell back a few paces while the Colonel busied himself getting the range. The Yankees were evidently fooled and fell back over the top of the ridge from view, and we saw no more of them.

It was now in the dusk of the evening The Colonel led us back toward the Rapidann, between Madison Mills and Liberty Mills, where we arrived shortly after dark. Nearly all the boys came into camp that night.

In falling back the dismounted men had gone to far to the left and in this way had missed their horses. General Stuart had rallied his men near Liberty Mills, and in turn driven the Yankees until dark closed the combat.

We were on the move early next morning expecting the exhibition to again commence where it had left off the evening before. But the Yankees had gone back from whence they came. Poland, myself and several of the company went to the spot where we had left Ream but his body was not there. Strips of old cotton rags lay around where we had left him, and we could learn nothing farther.

We concluded that his wound had been dressed, and that he had been carried away by the Yankees. We never heard of him afterwards. Thus fell as true and faithful a soldier as ever shouldered a musket or drew a sabre. In his early youth he gave himself to Christ, and when yet but a youth enlisted in defense of his home and of those he loved, and on that bright Sabbath morning of May 18th, 1861, bade adieu to his aged mother and sisters, took his place in the ranks of the Hampshire Guards and with them and Frontier Rifleman obeyed Virginia's call and went to Harper's Ferry. And with his company followed Stonewall Jackson to his fall on the 2nd of May 1863, at Chancellorsville. The Hampshire Guards had now become reduced to a corporal guard. James W. Ream came to our company (D. of the Eleventh Va. Cav.) We called him the boy preacher. His deep piety when in camp, and daring bravery when in the battles front where charging squadrons met and crossed sabres in the death struggle ever show a conscientious desire to do his duty faithfully both as a soldier of the cross, and of his country, now in an unknown grave moulders the remains of the soldier of the Confederacy. But in paradise will ever live the immortal spirit of James W. Ream, a soldier of the cross. In sorrow and sadness, we returned to our camp on the southern banks of the Rapidann. Master Robert gave us but little time to brood over our loss of brave and loved comrade. Early next morning a column of infantry dressed in gray began passing our camp moving in the direction of Madison Court House. There was a great deal of surmising as to where Gen. Lee was going many of us believed and hoped that he was going to the valley. The bugle call to saddle up was soon heard, and in a short we were mounted and in column. In a few moments Gen. Stuart and Gen. Hampton, accompanied by their staff, rode to the head of the column. The column then moved forward, taking a course or direction nearing parallel with that taken by Gen. Lee, on his right flank, and between him and Robison river on which stream the Yankee Cavalry were picketing.

On the 10th of Oct., if I remember right, Gen. Stuart came up with Kilpatrick's cavalry near James City. After a sharp engagement, in which Stuart held the field, the Yankees fell during the night. Next morning we were early in the saddle and moving in the direction of Culpepper Court House, where we found some Yankee cavalry, but the infantry had all disappeared. The Yankee cavalry fell back with a great deal of stubbornness and quite a lot of heavy skirmishing had to be done late in the afternoon. Kilpatrick was joined by Buford and Pleasants and Stuart by Fitz Lee. Business now became very brisk until night put an end to the contest; neither party had much to brag on in this affair. Our regiment lost some good men, among others were Capt. Wilson and Lieu. Pendleton. This engagement took place on the ground where the greatest cavalry engagement of the war was fought on the 9th of June previous. That night the Yankees crossed the Rappahannock and blew the railroad bridge in their rear as they fell back. The next day, the 12th of Oct., 1863, (I have good reasons for remembering this date.) We passed through the town of Warrenton in the afternoon where on corps, if I remember right, Ewell's of Gen. Lee's army had halted. Gen. Stuart with two brigades of cavalry after passing Warrenton moved in the direction of the Orange and Alexandria railroad, which runs nearly parallel with the Warrenton pike, leading to Centreville. After passing a small village, if I am not mistaken by the name of Auburn, and going a short distance toward Catletts Station, when we discovered a large wagon train parked in the open field not far away. Gen. Stuart immediately made preparations to capture it; but before the attempt was made discovered that it was guarded by a strong body of infantry, which rendered the enterprise dangerous as well as doubtful. The attack was not made. Gen. Stuart had halted his two brigades under cover of a piece of timber. On the left of the road, which we had been following, the country was mostly timbered. On the right the land was mostly cleared. On Gen. Stuart's right lay several large pasture-fields, through which a narrow valley lay crossed by several rail fences.

Several hundred yards down this valley could be seen an old house and an old stone mill, partly down, near by. General Stuart handed me his field glass and said, Lieut., take with you a squad of men and go down to that house and keep a sharp lookout, and report any movements of troops if you should discover any. I took with me a half dozen or so men mostly from Co. D. I remember E. Herriott was in the squad. We passed through two or three high rail fences, which we were careful to open well so as to have no trouble in getting over them if we should have to do so in a hurry. We followed an old race, filled with mud, weeds and water, until we reached the old house, which was empty, and from appearance had not been occupied for years. From the upper part of the old building we had a fair view of the wagon train not over a half mile away. Also had a fair view in the direction of Warrenton Station. When the sun was not over an hour from setting, by aid of the field glass, we discovered what appeared to be a column of infantry moving on a road which we had crossed at right angles about two mile back toward Warrenton. We reported this discovery to Gen. Stuart at once. Just as the sun touched the tree tops in the West the wagon train began to move off down the railroad toward Catletts Station. We reported this fact also. The column of infantry continued to move on the road named, until it became too dark to see at so great a distance. Night was now near at hand; we could no longer discern objects only a few hundred yards away, and concluded to go back to the command, and started up along the old millrace; and had gone perhaps two hundred yards and reached the first fence, when one of the boys looked back and discovered some one was coming down the bluff to the old mill from the direction of the wagon train. I said to the boys, hold on here and I will ride back and see where that fellow came from. I galloped back, and as I came near, saw that he was dressed in blue, but did not appear to be armed, although I drew my revolver, being a believer in precaution when in the presence of the blue. We reached the old mill at the same time. I said, hello stranger where do you come from, and who are you? His reply was, and who are you? I was within less than ten feet of where he stood; he had stepped up on a large rock. I pointed my pistol at his breast and said, answer my questions. He then said he was a Union soldier and had taken a stroll a little way from the camp. Now said he, who are you? to which I made no reply, but moved my horse near the rock on which he was standing and said, you are my prisoner, jump on behind me. He said I guess not. I said, if I leave you here I leave you a corpse. The click of the revolver I think helped him to make up his mind; he jumped on and we started back at a brisk trot. At the moment of starting back I heard some of the boys hollow, but could not understand what it meant, or what was said. It was now getting quite dusky. We had gone but a short distance when I thought I heard the jingle of sabres; on looking to my right about seventy five yards distance I saw a body of cavalry who had just emerged from a skirt of timber and was charging down the bluff at a headlong speed along the fence and I saw at a glance that unless I got rid of my prisoner they would reach the gap in the fence before I would. We were approaching the gap at right angles to each other. I said to my Yankee, jump off; he said, I guess not, and clamped me around the waist. There was no time to argue the question. I stuck the revolver over my shoulder; when the Yankee's holt loosened and he went off over the crooper. Relieved of encumbrance and being now satisfied that I was cut off from the gap in the fence, and from my companions, who were out numbered five to one and could give no help. My only safety for hope of escape was in getting on the other side of the old mill race filled with mud and water and not less than fifteen; and may have been twenty feet wide. I was riding the same horse on which I had been mounted when wounded on the retreat from Gettysburg. He was a good one; I called him Kilpatrick. I pulled him off to the right, made a short circle and brought him square at the ditch, gave him the rein and the spur at the same time. He caught the opposite bank with his front feet, but his hind ones sank deep in the mire; for a moment I feared that he would go back. I leaped to the bank, my horse soon struggled out and was not long in carrying me out of reach of my would be captors who had halted when they reached the race.

I soon joined my comrades again none the worse off from the little fright. Gen. Stuart had commenced to fall back toward Warrenton by the same road he had come. We were deployed and ordered to fall back in line a little in the rear of the command, but to be careful and not become separated. The moon was about full and gave a great deal of light, the night being clear though very smoky. The Yankee skirmish line followed on our heels, often so close that either party feared to speak for fear that he might address an enemy instead of a friend. After having continued to fall back for some time, in this manner General Stuart found that his way was blocked by a column of Yankees across his path, and came to a halt, or rather left the main road and turned to his left, passed up a hollow into a piece of woods behind a low ridge; here our line of deployed troopers were directed to follow. When all the command was well hid

235

under cover of the timber and by darkness. We were halted and ordered to keep as quiet as possible. The Yankees who had followed us had evidently lost the trail and our whereabouts was not discovered during the night. Along the road on the opposite side of the ridge the Yankee column which we had observed moving on this road late in the evening had evidently halted and gone into camp apparently not more than two hundred yards away. Their voices could be easily heard; also the rattle of their cooking utensils as they prepared their evening meal. General Stuart had a guard placed at short intervals along the brow of the ridge. During the night two Yankee officers took a stroll in our directions and were taken in by General Stuart's camp guard.

I imagine every man in the command realized the fact that we were hemmed in between two heavy columns of infantry; in a trap from which, to the ordinary soldier, there seemed no avenue of escape. This trap we well knew would be sprung on us at early dawn, as further concealment would then be impossible. Colonel Chew's battery, which was with us, was pushed and pulled in to the brow of the ridge by hand. Imagine the surprise of the Yankees, when at early dawn without any warning whatever, like a thunder clap a battery of artillery scarcely a stone's throw away, poured grape and cannister into their midst, carrying death and carnage among the sleeping soldiers.

In a very short time several batteries were replying to Colonel Chew in very much of a business way; and the Confederates began leaving the brow of the ridge and crowd the hollow below, it being a much safer place just at that time, although the shot and shell were making a great deal of unhealthy music over our heads.

General Stuart had, no doubt, realized the fact that his position was not a good one in which to maneuver with cavalry, and had commenced a retrograde movement. As we moved down the hollow I spied General Stuart and two or three other officers sitting on their horses a little to the left. I had not yet had an opportunity to return his field glass, and thought this would be a good opportunity to do so, I rode over, saluted and returned the glass.

The General said, Lieutenant ride up the hollow a short distance you will find Colonel (I can't recall the name) of the 1st North Carolina, direct him to make a feint in his front and then fall back and follow the command. I soon found the Colonel and delivered the order. The Colonel at once ordered one squadron of his regiment down through an old field grown up with low pines. I rode along with the Colonel and Adgt. Lieut. Armstead. We went down the hill on a charge firing in the air and yelling like savages not expecting to run on to Yankees, as least I was not. We had gone but a short distance when the boys in blue seemed to spring up as thick as Mullen stalks in an old pasture field, and closed around us. The morning was a very foggy one. When the smoke of battle became mixed with the fog, objects could be seen but a short distance. The Colonel, no doubt, concluded that he had carried out his orders to the letter and that his feint was a success. He turned back after having thrown his revolver in the face of the enemy, of course I could not fight Mead's whole army, and followed the Colonel. Not over a half dozen mounted men who wore the gray were gathered around the Colonel which was all that could be seen and appeared to be all that was left of the squadron, which it always seemed to me was offered a sacrifice to save the command from capture.

Our revolvers were empty and useless. With the sabre we were making a desperate, though vain effort to extricate ourselves from the living raging sea of blue that surrounded us. It was cut, thrust and parry; parry, thrust and cut. We were slowly carving our way back to the top of the ridge; the horde that surrounded us was much thinner. I now began to hope that some of us would be left to tell the tale. The Colonel and his Adjutant had gone down, three of us were left together. We had nearly reached the brow of the hill when a regiment or brigade only a short distance to our right, which owing to the fog and smoke, had not been seen, gave us a volley, and I was alone, my two comrades went down. My horse blundered and fell on his knees, but rose again and I urged him on, though I felt from his weak, feeble gait that he was badly hurt and could not carry me much farther. Unfortunately when I reached the top of the ridge I was in range of the Yankee guns which had been opened on Chew's battery; either a shell or solid shot nearly severed my horse's neck. We both came to a halt, my horse was dead and for some time I was almost as bad off as my horse. Only after a time I came to life again, though memory seemed to have departed. I could not tell where I was, how I came there of what had happened. Right here my experience as a soldier in the field closed, and my experience as a soldier in prison commenced.

CHAPTER XVIII

Old Capitol Prison

J ust what had happened, how I had come there or how long I had been there I could not tell. My first recollection when consciousness began to return was of two strangers who were kneeling by my side. While one supported me in a sitting posture the other held to my lips a canteen, from which he was striving in vain to have me swallow some of the contents, (which was whiskey). My refusing to do so had always been proof, satisfactory to my mind, that I was not conscious of what I was doing. But it was not long until my new found friends were satisfied that I was not a prohibitionist. At length my mind began to clear a little and by degrees I remembered what had happened and also realize my condition as well as situation. I required no further evidence to satisfy me that I was a prisoner, and my feelings told me that I was pretty well used up. One of my Yankee friends said, "your name is Blue, is it not?" I could not for a moment remember my own name. I at length said I believe you are right, though I cannot say certainly. I believe I have forgotten my own name, my head was hurting me so badly. He said his name was Margret, and his home was in Bedford county, Pa.; that he had met me about four years before at a Baptist Association held near Rainsburg, Pa., and that he had afterward been at my father's house and stayed for two days, trying to purchase a brown, bald, faced horse which I owned at that time, a fine saddle horse. I remembered having accompanied Rev. George Loy to attend an Association near Rainsburg a few years prior, but had no recollection of the man, although afterward I remembered all about the circumstance. At this time a Yankee surgeon rode up, dismounted and proceeded to make an examination to see what damage had been done.

He first felt of my head very carefully. My hair and whiskers were so clotted with blood and dirt that he said he could not tell much about it but that it was in a bad fix and might give some trouble. He then asked if I had been hurt otherwise. I said that I had a bad pain in my back or side. He ordered my Yankee friends to strip me. When my coat had been removed the surgeon looked it over carefully and remarked that if my body had been as well ventilated as my coat I ought not suffer for want of fresh air. He said there was at least a dozen holes in that coat that were not tailor made. After making a hurried examination the surgeon said, "Colonel, you have received pretty bad treatment; you have at least three ribs loose from your back bone; have a bullet in your left knee and have been three times punctured with the bayonet, but your head is by far your most serious hurt." He directed my captors to assist me to an ambulance near

239

by, where he dressed my hurts as best he could, for the time. He had to do it in the ambulance. The train had been ordered to move. I was helped aboard and was soon going at a gait that added nothing to the comfort of the passengers, of whom there were three, a Yankee sergeant with a sabre cut on the side of his head, a lately imported Irishman shot in the shoulder, whose groans and lamentations were pitiful to listen to. Although I was unable to understand a word he said. On parting with my captors Margret proposed a drink from his canteen, said that we might never have another opportunity to drink together, but the Surgeon, who seemed to be a kind hearted man, objected, said that he would not advise me to drink any spirits of any kind for a few days, or until by head was in a better shape, so with some reluctance I returned the canteen without having tasted the contents, bade my Yankee friends adieu, with my heart felt thanks for their kindness, and have never heard of either of them since. I hope they all pulled through and are all enjoying life.

As our ambulance jostled over the highway many groans of pain escaped the lips of the occupants. A short distance to our right and rear, rapid volleys of musketry could be distinctly heard. After we had gone two or three miles as well as I could judge, we passed over a considerable rise or knoll on top of which was gathered a dozen or more officers, several of whom had their field glasses to their eyes looking in the direction of Warrenton. As we passed this group of officers the sergeant pointed out to me, Gen. Mead and Gen. Hancock. This was the only time I ever had the opportunity of seeing two of the best Generals the North put in the field during the war. As our ambulance passed in it became mixed up with the wagon train moving over the same route that we were following. The wagons were drawn mostly by mules, four generally but some times six. As the train was passing down a narrow valley, perhaps fifty yards in width, where several routes had been made through the timber in a wet time by artillery and wagon trains. The ambulance train had wound its way through the wagon train until near the front, when a report was heard from the left and rear, followed in a quick succession by several others, the shells bursting over our heads among the tree tops. It was evident the train had been sighted and was being shelled. The teamsters were nearly all negroes. In a very few moments the train was stampeded, each teamster trying his best to pass the one in front of him. With eyes almost ready to burst from their sockets, many of them lay as close to their saddle mule as possible, whipping right and left allowing their lead mules to go where they pleased. For a short time I would have rather been in the battle's front, than been mixed up with that demoralized train, but our driver seceded by hard work and skillful engineering in reaching a place of comparative safety on one side of the valley, and halted, said he would rather take his chances for the Rebel shells than among them crazy negroes. We now felt that we were safe from being crushed and I, for one, rather enjoyed the circus. Often when a shell burst near a team the driver left his team and got away as fast as his legs would take him. Another would run against a tree and tear off a wheel, near where our ambulance had halted, because of the high bank of a stream which, from some cause had changed its course from one side of the valley to the other, thus causing the different routes down the valley by which the teams were racing to converge into a single route, with several teams reaching this narrow passage at the same moment with brakes up and a full head of steam, the result can easily be imagined. The way was blocked, many of the wagons rolled down the bank into the stream. Many, if not all, of teamsters who had escaped the wreck, mounted a mule and leaving the others behind to the tender mercies of the destroying angel, which he evidently believed to be close at hand, as with ashy cheek and wild rolling eyes he dashed down the valley. But to understand what a stampeded train, with an occasional shell dropping in their midst is like, must be seen, it can not be described. The blockade was complete for some time at least, so our driver backed his team into the road and moved on. I don't know what became of that train.

In the afternoon near Bristol Station I noticed a large body of infantry lying in the South side of the railroad behind a fill, some fifteen or twenty feet, in height. On the opposite side of the fill or bank, was a field extending back with a gradual rise something like 200 yards to the woods. Although I was suffering great pain I could but notice this heavy body of infantry and their surroundings. It seemed evident that they were expecting something. I afterward learned that it was Gen. Warren's Corps, which a few hours later repulsed an attack made on his position by Gen. Hill. Late in the evening we went into camp near Fairfax Station. I was ordered out of the ambulance and marched a little distance where I joined 5 other Confederate prisoners. I was suffering much and walked with much difficulty. This was the 13th day of October, 1863. I had had nothing to eat for 30 hours. Without fire or blanket we lay down on the wet ground having had a heavy shower about dark. I did not sleep a wink that night, two guards walked near us through the night, and next morning we were given about half a pint of coffee and a few hard tack. Shortly after daylight we were ordered to board a train of cars that stood on the track near by. I felt so sore and stiff that it was almost out of the question for me to move. The Col. and Adgt. Lieut. Armstead of the 1st North Carolina, the regiment with which I had made my last charge, were on the train. On reaching Alexandria, where the Colonel died, we made a short stop of perhaps an hour and proceeded to Washington, where we arrived about the middle of the day, and were escorted to the old capitol prison and placed in the hospital. There were 11 prisoners in the squad, all Carolinans, except myself. I was not in a very presentable condition, especially for a person visiting the capitol of the Nation for the first time. I had had no opportunity to wash, with hair, face and whiskers caked with dried blood and dirt. I imagine my appearance was more that of a Choactaw or Shawnee, or some other tribe, in his war paint, then of a Virginia gentleman. To tell the truth I felt very much used up and felt very much like crossing the River. But my furlough had not yet expired. I was taken to the bath room stripped, scrubbed and head shaved. Was then given a pair of cotton drawers and shirt; my clothes were all rolled together, tied with a cord, labeled and thrown into a small room kept for the purpose. I was then taken, more dead than alive, to a room in which there were three surgeons, a ward master and two other assistants. I was told to sit in a large chair while my head was being put through an examination for which much more time was consumed than was necessary, least ways I thought so. The probing, squeezing and bandaging was completed. Then I was told to lie down on an iron cot when my back and side was put through the same process, and resulted in the verdict: "head busted, three ribs broken, bullet taken from left knee, three slight wounds from bayonet thrusts." I was sent to one of the hospital wards and ordered to lie on my left side, but I soon found that I could not lie at all, because of a severe pain in my head, which throbbed as though the whole top might burst off, when lying down. For several days and nights I sat in a chair. At the end of three weeks my clothes were returned to me and I was sent to a front room on the third floor of the building, which was already occupied by two Captains and two Lieutenants. A Captain C. G. Fitzhugh, who, if I remember right, hailed from Hagerstown, Md., Capt. Shearer, of Winchester, Va. The Lieutenants were Carolinans, one by the name of Allison. The name of the other I have forgotten. Capt. Fitzhugh at the breaking out of the war was manager of iron works for his uncle; was finely educated and a gentleman in every sense of the word and I would say about thirty years of age. Capt. Shearer was a young man, not over 25 years of age, about six feet high, rather stoop shouldered and would have weighed 175 pounds and carried no unnecessary flesh. Shearer was charged with having been captured whilst recruiting inside the Yankee lines, a serious charge, which meant if not death, a ball and chain or a dungeon. In my opinion Shearer was rough and daring. He was very uneasy in regard to his situation. A man by the name of Woods was Chief of Police, or seemed to boss the prison, at least 5 feet 9, I would say in height, a good deal stooped in the shoulders and about 165 in weight. I imagine a good slugger. The devil has not yet got his own; I am told that Woods still lives.

Miss Belle Boyd, notorious during the war as a Confederate scout and spy, was at this time a prisoner at the Old Capitol. She seemed to be very intimate with Woods, and often accompanied him when inspecting the prison. She was rather tall, slender and pale faced with no expression, very talkative and very impudent and unladylike in her manner. In fact, I sized her up as capable of taking a hand at almost anything.

A man by the name of White was second in command of the prison and seemed to take a great delight in tantalizing Shearer in regard to the fix he was in. Shearer would laugh and tell White that he would show him a Yankee trick one of these days, that he had better keep his eye on him, that he would be absent at roll call some morning without leave. White would say to him, "I am sorry for you Shearer, your case is a very aggravating one. An example must be made of someone. The Government feels that recruiting inside our lines must be stopped. I fear it will be hard on you, but you had as well submit there's no possible chance for you to escape, you are too well watched." Shearer would reply by saying something like this, "White you can't scare me. Your charges are all false. You can't prove them, you only want to frighten me into taking the Oath of Allegiance to the United States." Conversation some thing like this would pass between White or Woods and Shearer almost everyday. Shearer was no fool and no coward. And in Fitzhugh he had a level headed advisor. We were kindly treated, each had an iron cot, good mattress and plenty of covering, sheets were changed twice a week, a wash bowl and plenty of water in the room, a grate with plenty of hard coal to heat the room, a regular old Virginia darkey to wait on us who brought our meals regularly three times a day and would bring anything in reason what we asked for cooked any way we wished it. I did not really see how we could be made more comfortable. I began to think it was not so bad after all to be a prisoner of war. There was a small back yard perhaps a hundred feet square, where we were allowed to exercise ourselves.

I learned from my comrades that one reason Capt. Shearer was so closely watched whenever he left his room, was because of an attempt he had made a few weeks before to escape through the cook house by way of a small window which opened on a narrow alley. Shearer had on several occasions bribed the sentinel who stood near the cook room door to allow the cook who slept in the cooking department to crawl through the window and get a bottle of whiskey for him. It seemed Capt. Shearer had been very intimate with this particular sentinel offered him a bribe to let him enter the cook room when the cook was asleep and escape through the window, and no one but the sentinel would ever know how he had made his escape; this guard or sentinel came on duty about 12 o'clock at night.

When Capt. Shearer informed Capt. Fitzhugh of the plot, Fitzhugh tried to persuade him not to make the attempt for, said he, "that Yankee has a face that can't be trusted. I have watched him closely when you and he were talkin' together. Don't make the attempt you will get in trouble. A squad of Yankees will be on the outside ready to receive, and may be shoot you without a challenge. Neither Woods or White have any kind of feeling for you, and would be glad to be of you." But Shearer would not be persuaded. At the appointed time he bade his room mate good bye and went in to the yard. The guard refused to take the bribe of ten dollars agreed on, but said the cook was snoring and the way was clear and for him to be in a hurry as the officer of the guard might come in at any time. Shearer said whenever a Yankee refused money something must weigh heavy on his mind, and he began to think that after all Fitzhugh may be right, but he entered the cook room and went over to where the cook lay and found him awake, spoke to him calling him by name, said, Capt. Fitzhugh has cramp colic, here is ten dollars get him a bottle of whiskey, quick! If you are back in ten minutes the balance of the ten is yours. Get through that window, the Sentinel said it will be all right; I will wait and perhaps he would fall asleep in a short time. The Sentinel seemed to be very nervous and said the cook knows all, he will give no alarm, go at once or you will be too late. At this moment what appeared to be the discharge of at least a half dozen muskets was heard on the outside. Capt. Fitzhugh remarked, just as I expected Shearer has been shot. A few seconds later Shearer burst into the room as pale as a sheet and exclaimed with an oath that he had a narrow escape. Neither that cook nor guard was seen about the prison afterward. Shearer thought it was a trap set for him but caught the cook. I give this story as it was related to me as near as I can, and believe it to be true.

Capt. Shearer was very uneasy. The charges against him he admitted were true and if proven would be bad for him. Some plan by which he might have a shadow of a chance to escape was discussed everyday in a low tone, while one of our number sat near the door and read the Daily News from the front in a loud tone. Finally a way was suggested by Capt. Shearer himself which, though desperate, seemed to be the only one that allured of a single hope of success. To understand Captain Shearer's plan of escape I will have first to describe as well as I can for the benefit of those who have never visited what was called the Old Capitol Prison during the sixties. I never visited the city of Washington, before or since my visit as a prisoner of war, but unless there has been changes made I think that I would recognize the location of over 37 years. Our room was on the third floor facing the street; to the left hand only a short distance was a corner. On the opposite side of the street stood a row of trees. A person on crossing the street and turning to the left would reach a corner in going forty or fifty yards. Two guards paced on the pavement and met immediately beneath our window then faced about and marched a distance of fifty paces or such a matter in opposite directions. The

Old Capitol Prison as it appeared during the Civil War. *(NATIONAL ARCHIVES)*

window was crossed perpendicular by iron rods several inches apart entering the window frame at each end. Capt. Shearer's plan of escape was, to cut with his pocket knife a groove through the window sill by which he could remove a rod, and then by tearing our sheets in strips make a rope of sufficient length to lower him to the ground and then take his chances to escape. He and Woods had some words that morning when Woods informed him he expected a room in Fort McHenry with a ball and chain for a companion in a very few days.

That night as soon as dark came Shearer commenced work, with one of us all the time at the door with ear to the key hole to detect any approach from the outside. Before midnight he had succeeded in removing the rod. In another half hour a rope was ready. It was the night of the 21st day of November, 1863. The night was cold and windy, more clear than cloudy; the moon was near its last quarter and the dark wind clouds which sailed beneath and cast their shadows on the earth made it impossible at times to see a man walking beneath and the shade of the trees on the opposite side of the street, although a lamp was lighted on the corner not far away. Without a moments warning the cloud would pass, and the moon break forth in all her midnight splendor, so much so that objects moving on the opposite side of the street could be seen almost as plain as by the light of day; then again a cloud would sail between and all was changed. Capt. Shearer was ready to descend, to he knew not what, dressed in a gray shirt and pants with a smoking cap on his head. When the Sentinels with the caps of their greatcoats turned over their ears, had met beneath our window and faced about with measured step and fixed bayonet at shoulder arms, had separated perhaps 40 pace. A man could have been seen emerge from a window in the third floor of the Old Capitol prison with no covering on his feet except a pair of socks and a do or die expression on his face. We lowered him as rapidly as possible. Our rope proved to be too short, but Shearer dropped to the pavement. We hauled in our rope and a moment later saw a man walking leisurely along on the other side of the street, whom we recognized as Shearer. The iron rod was soon in place again. The groove through which the end had been slipped out of place was filled with bread mixed into a paste. When the job was completed it would not have been noticed only by close inspection. Some books and papers were then placed in the window and things looked natural again. While I was engaged in the repairs of the windows, Captain Fitzhugh and one the Carolinians were busy getting away with the rope by cutting it in pieces and placing them beneath our pillows. All the while a sentinel had been kept on duty with ear to the keyhole. We had no light in the room except that made by the coal in the grate. We were soon stretched on our cots snoring, having been warned by our sentinel of the approaching foot steps in the hall. Capt. Shearer's cot stood behind the door and had been arranged to appear though it was occupied. The door opened a little distance, a head protruded for a moment, was then drawn; the door softly closed and all was quiet, except the heavy breathing of the sleepers within. Before day each one had disposed of his share of the rope, by turns. All that remained of our sheets was a few ashes when daylight appeared. We all slept unusually late that morning. White came in as usual about sunrise to call the roll. Capt. Shearer's cot had been slept on that night. White asked at once for Shearer. Capt. Fitzhugh said that he had gone down to the yard, he supposed, as he was not in the room when he awoke; I had not awakened yet. The Carolinans said he had gone down before they were awake. White said no more but went through the other rooms on that floor and came back, asked if Shearer had come up yet, and was answered to the negative. He went out, and came back and again asked for Capt. Shearer and was informed that Capt. Shearer had not yet made his appearance.

While White was yet in the room Woods entered and said, "you boys are playing a joke in us, you have Shearer hid under one of those cots," and proceeded to make a search, but all in vain; no trace of Shearer could be found. We professed to believe that he had been sent to some other prison and that their pretended search was a sham. Since we were satisfied that there was no possible way for him to escape. No further search was made in our room. I am unable to say whether the authorities ever learned the manner in which he escaped or not. A few days later about 100 officers who had been collected at the Old Capitol were sent to Johnson's Island, situated in Lake Erie near Sandusky, Ohio, where we arrived early in December. On leaving the Old Capitol we marched in front of the present capitol. President Lincoln and several others were standing on the steps. When opposite the front entrance some ill mannered Confed yelled out, "three cheers for Jeff Davis." Every man swung his cap in the air and cheered lustily for the Southern President. The line of guards on either side commanded us to double quick, and threatened to use the bayonet. As we struck a trot some one sang out three groans for Abe Lincoln. Our guards strove to prevent this last outrage, but no use, the groans were given with a will, long and loud.

On reaching Sandusky City, we were marched on board a steam boat and carried over to Johnson's Island, (if I remember right) about 3 miles from the mainland. The selection of this island for a prison was a good one; only a fish or fowl could hope to reach the mainland without help. The island seemed of an oval shape with a gradual descent to the water's edge, although from our prison pen we only had a view of the western side looking toward Sandusky City. If my memory serves me right there were about 5 or 6 acres enclosed within the prison bounds, by plank fifteen feet long placed in an upright position as close together as they

247

View of Johnson's Island, near Sandusky City, Ohio. *(NATIONAL ARCHIVES)*

could be placed. About three feet from the top of the out side of this fence was a platform or rather a box in which the guards walked day and night. On top of the fence at a distance of, I would say, about seventy-five yards apart lamps burned the night through; between these lamps a guard walked his beat, being relieved every two hours. The prison grounds were in the shape of a parallelogram, and lengthwise of this enclosure was built two rows of barracks with a street about 100 feet wide between them. Each building or division as they were called, was built two stories high with four rooms in each, sufficient in size to accommodate 50 men in each room. The barracks on the north were built within seventy-five feet of the fence; on the south side of the street the distance to the fence, I should think was seventy-five yards, with a gradual descent to the lake shore. Near where the fence stood, on the side were pumps, where prisoners procured water for drinking, cooking and washing. The head quarters of the post were near the north west end of the enclosure and the wharf or landing was near the same place. The enclosure was entered through a gate at the north-west end of the street near headquarters; through this gate our rations of beef, flour and wood were delivered. It was delivered to one of the prisoners or chief commissary, as he was called. The chief of each division then drew their share according to the number of men each had on his roll, which was called every morning by a Yankee Corporal, each division being called and counted at the same time by as many different Corporals. There was a large cooking and eating department where each division detailed its own cook, who boiled our beef and potatoes, baked our bread, divided our rations according to number and arranged them on the table, when dinner was announced the chief of each division marched his men to the dining room door in single file; when the doors were thrown open the files separated and marched down on each side of the table until all were in position when they halted faced to the right and left and charged the rations set before them with a will that showed they meant business. In a very short time the tables were cleared and the men were on their way back to their quarters. Our bread was made by mixing flour and water to the proper consistency and baked on the stove; our beef and beans were boiled in large kettles. We often had black eyed peas which might be a cooked all day without any great change.

Now having gotten rather ahead of my experience I will go back a little way. On entering the gate the usual warning was given and the echo ran from division to division. "Fresh fish, fresh fish!" this cry brought forth from the door of each room a stream of prisoners anxious to see for themselves if a friend or acquaintance were in the last batch of fresh fish (as every fresh lot was called). I found several acquaintances here whom I did not know were prisoners. The first man I recognized was Monroe

249

Blue, a cousin and a Lieutenant in the 18th Va. Cav. Soon Capt. Ginevan of the same regiment came forward; also Aaron Welton, of Hardy County, and David Lynn, of Cumberland, Md. A few days later Captain Jacob Warden of the 18th Va. paid Johnson's Island a visit. The division in which Monroe Blue was quartered was full, but in the next division a vacant bunk was found of which I was told I could occupy, and my name was placed on the roll of division No. 8. The bunks, as they were called, were built in tiers of three, one above the other; the first about a foot from the floor, the second at a distance from the first sufficient for a man to sit upright, and the third about the same distance from the ceiling, They were built all around the room with one end to the wall and the other extending in to the room; each tier being made fast to two upright posts. The bunks were about three by six, with about the same distance between each one. Each prisoner was given a blanket at the gate as he entered. A large egg stove stood in the centre of the room around which the prisoners gathered when the weather was cold and either froze or roasted according to location. Those on the inside of the ring being pressed from the outside in a hot stove were very soon willing to exchange places with those on the outside, where they had a good chance to shake and shiver from cold for several hours before getting another chance to get near to the stove. Each division had a certain quantity of wood hauled and thrown in front of the division each morning, which was at once divided by the chief of each room. In very cold weather we had to economize with our wood to such an extent, in order to make it last from one day till the next, that the temperature of the room was often down to zero. I shall not forget while memory lasts New Year's Day of 1864. Prior to this time the weather had not been cold—had been rather mild for the time of year. The day before New Years of 1864, was clear, calm and unusually warm. Some of the prisoners had provided themselves with washing implements and ran a kind of laundry through the prison, usually did their own washing, many of whom did not have a change and did but little washing. I was in this class. I had, when captured, a very good silver watch, which was not taken from me. Before leaving the Old Capitol my shirt gave out, I concluded to go down to the Sutler and trade my watch for some clothing, and a satchel to carry them.

I had figured out about what my watch was worth and what wearing apparel I needed most. I concluded to get a pair of pants, a change of underwear, a change of woolen socks and a satchel: including some stationary. When I had made out my list of dry goods I went down to the window of the Sutler shop, and informed the old jew that I was in need of some clothing; that I had no money but had a good silver watch that I would like to trade him. He said, let me see him. I handed him the watch. After a close examination he handed it back and said I trade you what you

250

want. I asked to look at a woolen over shirt. He threw two shirts on the counter, fairly good shirts. I supposed the shirts were worth $1.50 each. I asked the price—he said, I give you one of them shirts for dat vatch. This offer nearly took my breath. I said you must be joking. He said, I not shoke some; I give you dat shirt for dat vatch. I put the watch in my pocket and went up to my quarters. For the next three or four days the old Jew came to our room each day to trade for my watch. On the day we left the Old Capitol I traded him my watch for a shirt and a pair of socks.

Now I will go back to where I left off, I had but one shirt and did not like to wash it too often for fear of wearing it out before I could get another; but the day was so bright and warm that I concluded to wash my shirt and have it cleaned for New Year's Day. I did as many others, went down to the pump where there was a large trough; we had neither soap nor warm water, but gave them a good sousing in cold water. I hung mine against the sunny side of the house to dry. Many of the prisoners could have been seen with their shirts off examining them very closely as though they were looking for something that they were finding, but in prison those searches were very necessary and the more frequent they were made the more satisfactory the result, by turning first one side and then the other to the sun. I had my shirt dryed and closely inspected before night. We lay down that night without covering of any kind, and before midnight we were shivering with cold. During the few mild days we had saved a part of our allowance of wood, and soon had our stove red hot, but it didn't seem to warm the room. Capt. Warden and I occupied the same bunk. We had been lucky enough to get possession of two blankets left in our care by our next neighbor, who had been sent to the Hospital a few days before. At 6 o'clock each morning a small steam boat came over from Sandusky and brought rations for one day, of beef and flour, then returned and made a second trip about 8 o'clock with wood, but before reaching the wharf on her return trip that morning ice had formed so rapidly that she could not reach the wharf, and the greater part of the prisoners were without fire all the day through. Our rations which had been cooked the day before was frozen so hard that we could not eat them. About sunrise or shortly after when the Yankee corporals came in to call the roll they reported the thermometer 30 degrees below zero. The guards had all been taken off duty. A strong gale was blowing from the South carrying with it a thick snow, almost as fine as coarse meal dry and hard as granulated ice; and carried with it a very unpleasant sensation when it came in contact with the naked skin. By this time our reserved wood was exhausted and it was evident that the only way left to keep the blood in our views from freezing was exercise and plenty of it. Our sleeping apartment was too much crowded to admit of the necessary exertions. A part of each division repaired to the cook or feed room as it was mostly called. By a double quick step around the tables, we succeeded in keeping up a circulation above the freezing point until late in the evening when several sled loads of wood came to our relief, over the ice, drawn by two mules to each sled. The reader can form some idea of the intensity of the cold when ice had formed in less than ten hours of sufficient strength, for a distance of not less than three miles to bear a sled, two good sized mules and a cord of wood. The snow had drifted so that the teams could not enter the gate; the wood was thrown off at the wharf. The gate was thrown open and we were told to make a detail from each division of ten men and send them to the wharf for wood if we wanted any. This was quickly done. I was on the detail and went out with it, but wished before I got back that I had not gone. Many had their ears and fingers frozen, and were not out ten minutes. The culinary department was soon in full blast boiling beef and baking bread for supper, and breakfast next morning. By 12 o'clock at night our cook announced supper, a rush was made for the cook house, and the storm continued to rage. Our half cooked rations were soon devoured, and the double quick was again taken up. Before daylight our wood was all gone. Many of the prisoners who had been on the island for a length of time had succeeded in getting warm clothing for winter from their homes, when their homes were near enough to the border to get them through the lines; others had relatives and friends in the north who gladly supplied their wants so far as the powers would allow them to do so. There were many, however, whose homes were in the far south, and they beyond the reach of those who would have so gladly helped them in this time of their sore need, in a freezing conditions on Lake Erie's ice bound Island. Some of those boys had never before been where the thermometer dropped below the freezing point, I really pitied them, but was powerless, could give no aid. My own wardrobe was not what I would have liked it to be. My boots were about gone, my socks were only kind of frames repaired, my only pair of drawers had failed to answer roll call for some time and had been laid to rest, or rather used as a covering for a block of soft wood which I used for a pillow. But now my socks needed repairing, and timber being scarce on the island, I was compelled to use the covering of my pillow, with which I lined and weather-broaded my socks, and made them really uncomfortable, although they were not much for looks. It had become necessary for some repairs to be done to that part of my pants mostly used when sitting around with nothing to do. Material was very scarce for repairs of this kind. Finally the necessity of something being done become so urgent that I concluded to cut about six inches from the bottom of each leg of my pants, and still leave them long enough to reach well down into my boots. In this way I procured material, but little the worse for wear, having been worn all the while in my boots, but I was a little trumped as to how the repairs were to be made. I had but one pair of pants and the weather was cool, I had no needle or thread. Each division, or rather each man in each room, had to take his turn sawing wood into stove lengths; he being called in his turn by the chief of the mess at roll call each morning. That morning Lieutenant Beaty's name was called. Beaty said, "I will give a ten-cent sutler check to any one who will take my place." Here was a chance to get a spool of thread and a needle. I was quick to take the job, although to saw, split and carry it in, required nearly half the day. When I had completed the contract and received my check I started to the Sutler store, which was built on the outside of the pen, a window having been cut for the convenience of the prisoners. I asked the price of a spool of thread, ten cents was the reply; a needle, five cents. I explained to him how bad I was in need of a needle and thread, and how I had worked hard for half a day for ten cents, which was all I had, and that the thread would do me no good without a needle.

At length he said, I will loan you a needle. I promised to return the needle or pay for it (I returned it, but he said he would make me a present of it for my honesty). I hurried back to my quarters, stitched two edges of a blanket together and soon had a shirt, which I made fast around the waist with a piece of wire taken from an old, worn out broom with an old knife taken from the cook house. I got my work in shape and soon had a fair job of quilting completed. It was a good deal drawn, and puckered but comfortable for all that. My next job was to repair the socks spoken of. All this had been completed only a few days before the blizzard struck the Island.

Now having given the reader some idea of the condition of my wardrobe, which was better than that of many others, I will return to that ever memorable night we loped, racked, trotted and went around those tables at every imaginable gait. Apparently, after an age, daylight came again. By sunrise several sled loads of wood had reached the island and our stoves were in full blast again. At roll call that morning the corporal reported the thermometer at 40 degrees below zero, and remarked that it would be a good chance for you Johnnies to visit Canada, not over twenty miles away. Some one remarked that it would be a risky business without a compass. The Corporal said keep the wind on your cheek and you will be all right. Two buildings were blown down that day on the Island, one Yankee reported killed and two or three others hurt. If I remember right about 20 from our room determined to make an effort to reach Canada that night if the way was clear and no guards in the way. I went in to Monroe Blue's quarters to see what he thought of the enterprise. Be ready to make the attempt. I was not very enthusiastic over the proposed expedition and tried to persuade Monroe, that there would be 99 chances to freeze to death where there would be one to reach Canada; but he was determined. We concluded to see Capt. Mat Ginnevan, and whatever he thought about it we would do. He agreed with Monroe and I agreed, but under protest. I insisted that we would all freeze to death, and would never see the light of day again. Monroe argued that we had as well freeze attempting to escape as to freeze shut up in that pen; but I argued that it would be better to wait until the weather had moderated. Then said they the guards will be on again and there will be no show of getting out. Finally, they said, we believe that we can go through all right, and are going to make an effort; if you are afraid to go, that settles the matter. I said I would go. The day was mostly spent in making preparations. We prepared a ladder by nailing pieces of boards across a long bench, with which each room was furnished with several. This bench was placed against the fence on the inside. When the time for action came a stick of wood with a snag on one end was made into a hook with which to reach the top of the fence; in this way a person could draw himself up until he could reach the top with his hand, when it would be easy for him to scale the fence. A patrol passed around on the outside of the fence carrying a lantern, every half hour. About 10 o'clock p.m. all was in readiness, each carried two blankets and wearing all the clothing he possessed. The patrol had paraded on their round. Monroe shouldered our bench and in a very short time about 20 of us were on the outside of the pen, and were making a bee line of Canada. Several other squads from other divisions had gone over the fence in the same manner. Those left behind had removed the benches. The snow had ceased but the wind continued to blow at a lively rate; the moon could occasionally be seen dimly through the clouds. I had noticed when we started that the moon was on our backs. When we had gone perhaps a mile we came to a crack or opening in the ice, which looked to be twenty or thirty feet wide. We had to change course. The ice had been swept clear of snow by the wind. We had taken the precaution by tearing blanket strips and wrapping them about our feet to protect them from the cold as well as to prevent slipping on the ice. Soon a driving snow squall swept over the lake and for a few moments five of us were squatted together on the ice holding to each other for fear of being separated, surrounded by almost Egyptian darkness. But in a few moments the cyclone had swept on, but the wind now seemed to blow from every point of the compass. Capt. Thompson said, boys our fate is sealed unless we can find our way back to the Island. We were all of the same opinion, but no two could agree as to the course we should go to reach the Island again. We had lost our bearing the wind was no longer a safe guide to follow. In a few moments we agreed on the course to be taken by vote, which stood, if I remember right, 3 to 2. We pressed forward as fast as we could for perhaps a half a mile as near as I could guess; the clouds began to break away, the moon shown through for an instant and then hid again; but I had caught a glimpse of our shadow immediately in our front and exclaimed at once, boys we are going in the wrong direction, the moon should be in our face instead of our back. All seemed to think I was wrong. I was getting numb with cold, and well knew that if I reached the Island alive there was no time to lose. I said, boys, if we keep the moon in our face and push forward we may reach the Island, but if we continue the course we are now going we are lost; I for one am going to take the back track, and started as fast as I could move. They all turned back and in less than an hour we came in sight of the light from a large lamp stationed on top of the headquarters building. When we reached the fence around the pen we were too numb from cold to scale the fence, but the patrol was near and we were glad to surrender, and were turned in at the gate after being laughed at for not having more sense. I was soon thawing by the stove thankful that I was back in prison again fully determined never to attempt to go to Canada on ice again. Next day several were brought in alive, but so badly frozen that amputation of feet and hands was necessary to save life in some cases. I can't remember how many of the Yankees reported found dead. I never heard that a man reached Canada who started that foolish expedition. Just as well started for the North Pole; would have had about the same chance of getting there, which was none on earth. When I got thawed out the machine appeared to be in fair condition, with the exception of the ears and feet, they were a good deal out of plumb; my nasal organ was considerably bulged, also; but not seriously damaged; unless it was from an expansion idea which seems to continue to grow. At roll call 17, I think, were absent without leave and not accounted for. The Corporal said the General, who had command of the prison, (Ferry I think was his name) said he would not care if more of you fellows would fail to answer roll call from the same cause. The weather now began to moderate and for several days the thermometer stood at zero through the day, though 10 or 15 below at night. The next morning after our raid to Canada, when the wood sleds brought in our wood, a Corporal had us carry all our benches out and load on the sleds and hauled out side of the pen and thrown on a pile. When the Corporal was asked why this was done, replied that the General did not think it safe to leave them as more of us might be tempted to freeze ourselves to death, and for our own good thought it best to remove them. From that time on we sat on our bunks, on the floor or stood upon our feet.

A few days after our sitting conveniences had been taken from us a young man made his escape from the Island. His name was Triplett, Lieutenant Triplett, from Mt. Jackson, Va. He was a young man, I would think, at that time, not over 25 years of age, a nephew of Dr. Triplett of that village. He made his escape in this way; he managed to get hold of a Yankee overcoat and cap and had repaired a bench that had been broken down and overlooked by the Yankees. When the sleds came in with wood it was about breakfast time for the Yankees and not more than one, or perhaps two were in the pen at that time. As one of the drivers passed up toward the gate, after having delivered his wood, Triplett stepped from the door of one of the rooms with the bench on his shoulder, halted the driver, and with some remark, not very flattering to the Johnnies threw the bench on the sled, took a seat on it, told the teamster to drive on. The gate was opened by the guard on the approach of the sled which passed out and on about 30 yards and halted where the benches had been piled by the side of a building. Triplett stepped off took up his bench, carried it a few steps and threw it on the pile with the others. The sled was driven on toward Sandusky. Triplett appeared to be arranging the pile of benches for a few moments and then started over the ice toward the city. He met several persons on his way over. Monroe and I watched him from a second story window until he had nearly reached Sandusky City and mixed with the crowd. This was the last time I ever saw Lieut. Triplett, but I afterward heard of him through a friend of his, who gave me a history of his proceedings, which I will give to the best of my recollections. On reaching Sandusky he ascertained at what time a train left for Columbus, Ohio, to which place he procured a ticket. On entering the car he discovered, as he thought, a detective, who seemed to have his eye on him. Triplett concluded that the closer he got to him the better and walked back and took a seat by his side. The supposed detective asked him a great many questions as to where he hailed from and where bound too. Triplett was sharp as a tack. He had fixed up a furlough with leaf of absence for 30 days, approved by Gen. Handcock, whose corps he claimed to belong, and so informed his companion, who said he also belonged to the same command and that they would be company. At Columbus a friend of the detective joined them. Triplett was now satisfied that he would be arrested as soon as they reached Washington. He determined to quit the train the first opportunity after leaving Cumberland. He was so closely watched that escape seemed almost impossible. On reaching Martinsburg late in the evening, for some reason the train was detained for several hours, Triplett feigned illness, and concluded to stop over night in Martinsburg, and join his company the next day in Washington; but they said as they had several days yet before their furlough expired they would stay with him that night and take care of him in case he should need help, and insisted on occupying the same room. Triplett, to all appearances, was in a short time very much intoxicated, and after having one of his companions have his flask filled and placed in his pocket, declared his purpose of going to bed. His comrade assisted him to his room and removed his boots. He asked the boys to take a drink with him, which they declined to do. He had them move a stand near his bed on which to set his flask. His comrades tumbled him in bed without removing his clothes, said they would be back in a short time and went out. Soon as their foot fall died away in the hall, Triplett arose, removed the key from the lock of the door and dropped it in one of his boots, then raised a window and emptied his flask, lay it on the stand and lay down again, but not to sleep. Toward midnight his companions returned to the room and went to the bed and gave Triplett, (who was lying on his face) a shake and asked how he felt, but there was no answer. One of them picked up the flask and remarked, the d—m brute has emptied his flask; I doubt if he ever awakes again if he is not already dead he will be before morning. He has whiskey enough in him to kill two men; we need not have any fear of loosing him tonight. In a very few moments they were in bed and appeared from their deep breathing to be in a sound sleep. When Triplett became satisfied that this was the case, he quietly arose, took his boots in his hand, hat and overcoat (belonging to one of his room mates) under his arm noiselessly left the room locking the door after him, then draw on his boots and overcoat and was soon moving at a 2:40 gait in the direction of Winchester. He was now among friends and with a fair knowledge of the country succeeded in making his way through the Yankee lines in the lower valley and reached the Confederate lines in safety.

Another prisoner a few days later escaped from the island as follows; all the gates in the pen were froze up so that they would not work. A gate on the South side of the pen was thrown up, morning and evening, and the prisoners allowed to pass out to the Lake between two lines of soldiers extending from the gate out on to the ice, for the purpose of filling their buckets and tubs with water. A sightseeing crowd was usually present on these occasions. Many of whom came over from Sandusky City on their skates, composed of men, women and children. I was not personally acquainted with the prisoner, who made his escape on this occasion and cannot now call to mind his name. But like Triplett, he had managed in some way to provide himself with a blue coat and cap and went out with the water detail, perhaps as many as 50 in number. When they reached the hole cut in the ice for the purpose of dipping the water there was generally a jam. That morning a stiff breeze was blowing from the North east, the soldiers had the capes of the great coats gathered about their heads and faces, while the skaters were shrouded in furs. The attention of the crowd, both soldier and skater, seemed to be fixed on several objects approaching at a rapid rate before the wind, which could have easily been mistook for almost anything except what they really were. Men, who said they had come from some place in Canada since daylight, and claimed to have made 25 to 30 miles an hour. Each one had what appeared to be a blanket secured about the neck and stretched on two sticks across their backs something like a sail,

257

at least that is the way the rig looked to me. These men said they had sailed over cracks in the ice as much as 25 feet wide by springing in to the air on reaching the opening, when the high rate of speed at which they were running would land them on the other side (that is what they said). This was the prisoner's opportunity, which he took advantage of by slipping through the guards and mixing with the crowd, which soon began to disperse and make their way back toward the city, he going with them. I never heard what became of him. In the meantime another party had planned to escape from beneath their division or barracks (which was raised some two feet from the ground) until they passed beneath the fence near the Lake shore. The ground was frozen to a depth of two or three feet making a secure arch over head. The dirt was removed by the use of an iron poker and shovel (used about the stove), and carried from the tunnel in an old bucket and piled under the building; one man working at a time, by lying flat on his stomach.

When the job had been completed and the frozen earth nearly burrowed through on the outside of the fence. On a dark, windy night the five or six who were in the secret started on their underground expedition in quest of their freedom. But alas, their hopes were soon blasted the leader was too large to pass through the opening and hung in the frozen crust, on attempting to quit the tunnel, and could neither go forward nor backward and before the man following could release him the patrol came along, discovered him, got a pick and dug him out. Those who were worming their way after him reversed steam, crawled out and abandoned the enterprise as a complete failure. A few days later a wind storm swept over the Lake, and the waves broke the ice in huge cakes and in a few hours the channel between the island and the mainland was clear of ice, and the overland route to freedom by the help of ice was closed for the present.

Our prison was now visited by a fatal type of erysipelas, which appeared to be contagious. A great many of the prisoners succumbed to its fatal stroke. It was worse than smallpox. Our hospital was inside the prison and our own surgeons attended the sick; all the medicine they needed was furnished them. A detail was made by turns from each division for nurses. Generally the sick had special friends who looked after them. Our cooking was so badly done that six of us concluded to go into a trust, get a small cooking stove and do our own cooking. Our mess answered to the names of Capt. Jacob Warden, Hardy county, Va; Lieut. Edward Beaty, Baltimore, Md.; Lieut. Hugh Brinkley, Portsmouth, Va; Lieut. Monroe Blue and Lieut. John Blue, Hampshire county, Va. We appointed a committee of one to see the sutler and ascertain what a small cooking stove would cost. The sutler agreed to deliver us what we wanted for $12.00. That evening the stove was set between our bunks ready for business. Next morning we drew from the commissary rations of beef, flour, beans and wood for six men and set up house keeping. Lieut. Beaty's father was well to do, so Ed got fat boxes of provisions from his home every week; also money when he needed it. About this time Monroe Blue received a box of good things from my aunt, Mrs. Isaac Long, of Md. These commissaries, it's useless to say, were enjoyed by our mess. Division No. 1 and 2 were divided into small rooms, which were occupied by Brigadiers, Colonels and Majors. Monroe and I had a contract to saw and carry wood to these rooms, and usually made from 75 cents to $1 a day in Sutler checks of which these men, or some of them at least, seemed to have plenty. We spent these checks with the Sutler, since we could not spend them elsewhere, for coffee, sugar, butter and molasses, for all of which we paid about three prices. Moore and Brinkley did the cooking. Capt. Warden was fairly successful in shuffling the pasteboard. We were getting along nicely until some of our room mates began to envy us; then our trouble commenced. Some of them contending that we had no right to take wood from the other stoves for our use. We contending that the wood burned in our stove went as far toward heating the room as it would do if all was burned in one stove. But we agreed to leave the dispute with the chief of the room to decide. Capt. Allen was our chief. He was a Captain of Cavalry, and hailed from Richmond. The Captain was an old school baptist preacher, about 50 years of age, over six feet in his stockings, straight as an Indian and weighed about 180 pounds and was said to be a dangerous man to meet in a charge. Our chief gave the case against us. There was no appeal so we submitted, and made a contract with the party who furnished wood to the prison to furnish us wood each morning, sufficient to run our stove for one day at a certain price. We were now all right on the wood; but we soon came to the conclusion that we were not getting an equal share of rations, and had some loud talk with the chief about the matter, but all for naught. The room was pretty equally divided, one half siding with our mess, the other half taking sides with the "Old Apostle", as the prisoners called him. Some of them didn't like his doctrine, others said he preached and prayed too long. They did not know that the old hard shell Baptists were all long winded. There were several chaplains in the prison who preached every Sabbath and often at night during the week. Capt. Allen always sang a hymn and had prayer before 9 o'clock each night at which hour all lights in the prison had to be extinguished. There were many Christians among the prisoners who took part in these exercises, while many others were often engaged in a game of cards, and to all appearances unconscious of the prayers for mercy then being offered up in their behalf. But in a crowd of several thousand men, almost every sort may be found. Two names were called each morning as their turns came to sweep the room. One morning my name was called for the purpose named, when I very emphatically declined to assist in doing the work, for the reason that our mess swept much more than our share of the room each day. The old Captain spoke rather harshly (as I thought) of the trouble our mess had already given him. I said in rather a rough way that his assertions were false. We were standing near the center of the room, the Captain reached for my collar; I threw his hand aside and stepped back between the bunks and threw off my coat, then confronted him and said, Captain, this thing has gone on long enough, I am ready to settle it for all time. The Captain raised his hand as I thought to strike. I stood on the defensive ready to repel the attack. The old Captain slowly removed his hat from his head and said let us pray. That was the longest prayer I thought that I had ever heard; although it really did not exceed 15 minutes in half that length of time I was the worst whipped boy any one ever saw, when I saw the tears run down the old man's cheeks as he so earnestly prayed for my guidance and protection amidst dangers both seen and unseen that surrounded me, and prayed that I might be spared to return (when this strife was over to) my home and friends again. I was almost too weak to stand alone. When he ceased speaking I stepped forward, offered him my hand and in a choked voice said, Captain, I was wrong and owe you an apology. As he grasped my hand and said, "Young man you owe me nothing, but you should ask earnestly of our Father in Heaven forgiveness for the ugly oaths you made use of a little while ago; promise him now that you will never again take His holy name in vain." I believe that promise has been faithfully kept to the present time. I turned away from the Captain, put on my coat and hat and went out, feeling, I imagine, very much as Judas did when he betrayed our Lord and Master. I roamed around all day feeling very much out of sorts some way. After dark I slipped in, but had little appetite for supper and crawled into my bunk early. I felt so ashamed of myself that I could scarcely look any of my room mates in the face. Next morning I was feeling so bad that I did not get up for roll call and was reported on the sick list. Capt. Allen came over to my bunk and enquired how I felt and now I was complaining with as much solicitude as though I had been his own son, but never hinted about our little trouble the day before, and never spoke of it afterward, but always met me in the most friendly manner possible. I was suffering with a severe pain in my head, but next day was much better.

CHAPTER XIX

Point Lookout, Maryland

A day or two later, one mess Ed Beaty, who had been complaining for several days from an old wound received at Greenland Gap, which at the time was thought to be fatal, but he pulled through; and although never stout afterwards had gone to his command again, been captured and sent to Johnson's Island. He was taken to the hospital. He seemed to want me with him all the time. He said I could lift him and turn him so much easier than the other members of our mess so I spent most of my time with him. At length we received notice that four hundred prisoners would be sent from Johnson's Island in exchange, and would be taken in alphabetical order. Monroe Blue and I felt sure that our names would be called. We began at once to concoct a plan of escape in case an opportunity offered. Monroe declared that he had no faith in the exchange business since Old Ben Butler had been made commissioner of exchange by the United States after having been outlawed by the Confederate Government. He contended that we were only going to be sent to another prison, and that he was determined to make his escape if possible. Many of the prisoners spent their time in making rings, chains and other trinkets from guttaperche buttons and rules, which we got from the Sutler; we also got files and small chisels to use in the business. I often spent many of my idle moments in this way. I had a small three sided file with which I had made a saw from an old table knife, which I used in sawing the guttaperche into pieces of a proper shape out of which to fashion the desired article. I now put my saw in good working order ready for use when the time came. Next morning at roll call four hundred names were called. Those answering to their names were ordered to be in readiness to pass out at the gate as their names were called at 1 p. m. sharp. From that time until the appointed hour for our departure for City Point, which we were told was our destination, there was a continuous hubbub. Those whose names had been called were busy packing their belongings; those left behind were engaged in writing to dear ones down in Dixie. I had nothing to pack except a change of underwear, which I put on, stuck my saw in my boot, bade my acquaintances good bye, then went to the hospital and spent my last moments with Lieut. Beaty, whose name had been called, but he could not answer, he was dangerously ill. A few moments before Monroe and I bade him good bye his mother and sister arrived with authority to take him home, but he was too ill to be moved. I learned from one of our mess mates who came on with a second lot of prisoners that he only lived a few days. The bugle now called us to the gate, through which we passed and took our place in line on the outside. As soon as all had been called whose names were on the list we were marched on the boat, which lay at the wharf in readiness to carry us over to Sandusky City, where, after some delay, we were put aboard a train and in a few moments were moving with fair speed toward Pittsburg. This was the 7th day of February, 1864. About 4 p. m. Monroe and I had succeeded in getting seats together. About sundown a Yankee passed through our car and handed each man four crackers. Night soon came on, when Monroe and I proceeded to make preparations to carry out our plan of escape, which was this, while one lay on the seat feigning sleep (but closely watching the approach of Yankees who occasionally passed through the car) the other lay on the floor between the seat with a sharp pointed knife cutting a hole though the floor through which to get our saw to work. Our plan was to saw a square through the floor of the car large enough for a man to drop through on the outside of the wheels of the car when the engine was taking water at some point east of the Alleghany mountains, where we calculated we would be some time that night. Monroe did the carpenter work while I kept guard. Whenever a Yankee officer entered the car I touched Monroe with my foot, when he would cease work and commence snoring in a frightful manner. When the danger had passed I reached down and gave him a pinch, then he would proceed to business again. In much less time than I had anticipated Monroe pronounced the job complete except about an inch or so at two of the corners, which had been left to hold the floor in place until the time came, when only a moment would be required to remove the square of flooring and the opening would be clear. All things were now ready for us to take our departure, when the time had come. We reached Pittsburg about midnight, as near as we could tell, where the train stopped until next morning, when we were transferred to another train and did not leave Pittsburg until sometime in the evening. We were very much disappointed at what we called bad luck, but determined to renew our efforts. When about to start as we thought another train backed up and we were ordered forward and found we were on an emigrant train or stock train; the seats were long benches set lengthways of the car, a few small windows in each side gave rather a dim light, in each end of the car two guards sat on a short bench behind the doors facing each end of the car; our hopes of sawing a way was now out of the question and had to be abandoned. The snow which had been falling rapidly for about twelve hours, now looked to be about twelve or fifteen inches deep; toward night the clouds seemed to break away. Our car was lighted by a few candles which made rather a dim light. By ten o'clock the clouds had dispersed and the moon, now making the night almost as light as day. Monroe and I talked the prospects for escape over in a whisper. He determined to attempt to escape by going to the water bucket which sat on the floor on the right hand side in the corner of the car by the door, a tin cup hung on a nail above the bucket, but no one was allowed to go to the bucket at the same time. I concluded since the heavy fall of snow not to attempt to escape, as I was nearly bare footed, but thinly clad and had no over coat, I thought the chances were too much against me. I tried to persuade Monroe not to make the attempt that we might possibly be exchanged as I could see no good reason why they would be taking us to Washington when it had been less than two months since many of us had been taken from there; but he would not be persuaded, but was determined to make the attempt. He had received a box from home a short time before containing, among other things, a good warm suit of clothes; also a heavy over coat and socks, all home made. When I found that I could not persuade him to abandon the attempt, I said to Monroe, if you will go you are in my opinion now at a point as near to Cumberland as you will be, we are east of the Alleghany mountains. I have been in that part of Pennsylvania in the fall of 1859, and calculated that we were then between 100 and 125 miles almost due north of Cumberland. Capt. Jones, who was a prisoner at Johnson's Island, had been a sailor pointed out to several of us (after our attempt to reach Canada over the ice) the north star and how to locate it by the help of a dipper; if the night was clear that the north star could be seen and a person knew the course he wanted to go there was no necessity of loosing his way. I asked Monroe if he thought he could locate the north star. I said, keep the star to your back by night and the Alleghany range of mountains on your right by day, and in less than 125 miles, if you have good luck you will strike the North Branch somewhere between Cumberland and Green Spring Run.

He said, "I don't believe in this exchange talk, and I don't see how I will make my condition much worse; take charge of my satchel; make use of any thing in it you need. I have a memorandum and a few little trinkets, which I would like mother to have if you can get them to her in any way." He said, "cut that bell rope if you can." He pressed my hand a last good bye, arose and walked to the bucket, took the cup from the nail and as he stooped to dip the water placed his left hand on the knob of the cardoor. As he arose to an upright position threw open the door, stepped to the platform and without an instants hesitation took a flying leap for liberty, not knowing where he would land. The Yankees were quickly on their feet, but the bird had flown. In an instant Monroe Blue had gone from my sight. We never met again. I had but little doubt that Monroe would get through all right if he did not kill or cripple himself when he jumped from the train. He reached home all right. I got a history of his experience from his brother, after the war, which I will relate as I remember it. He had received no injury when he leaped from the train, except a twist of one knee, which interfered somewhat with his locomotion, although the snow was deep. He was a good shaken up, but in a moment was on his feet and racing away at a speed scarcely exceeded by the train, which seemed to be on a down grade and was running very rapidly. A single shot was fired from the rear of the train. He heard the whistle of the bullet but received no injury from it. He at length reached a road leading in the direction he was going and followed it the remainder of the night. In some way he had managed to get hold of a pick, which he carried all next day to make the impression that he was a road or farm hand. The snow was deep and the road had been but little traveled, which rendered progress, especially on foot, slow and laborious. By night he was so weak from hunger and exertion that he could hardly travel, having eaten nothing for about 48 hours. After dark he concluded to mount himself, and entered a barnyard for the purpose when he discovered a chicken roost in the yard and feeling so raving or owlish, thought he could make a light meal off a raw chicken. He accordingly captured one, beheaded it, picked the feathers from one leg, took a bite or two, but it was no go. He succeeded in getting a horse which he rode nearly all night until he was played out. When daylight appeared Monroe had been thirty six hours with out food and felt that he must have something to eat before going much farther, otherwise would have to throw up the sponge. Soon after daylight he came to a house and asked for something to eat, representing himself as a railroad hand on his way home, near Cumberland, Md. He was kindly treated and got a good breakfast free of charge. That day he passed through Bedford without being questioned and in the evening succeeded in getting another square meal; that night slept an hour or so in a barnyard by the side of a straw rick, and before daylight crossed the North Branch of the Potomac near the mouth of Patterson's creek. He was now among friends who gladly administered to his wants and concealed him from the Yankees, who at that time held the South Branch Valley, where his father lived. He found safe quarters with a friend, and rested all that day. That night he reached home, but it was not a safe place to be, so he fell back to Jersey Mountain, a few miles from his home, where he made his head quarters until he could procure another horse and make other preparations for a campaign as soon as spring opened. There were several Confederates in the neighborhood at this time on furlough, whose horses had been either killed or broken down in the service. Their object being to make a requisition on Uncle Sam's quartermaster for what they wanted. Monroe joined these Johnnies and was soon mounted and armed, ready for the prey. In a short time he joined his command (then in the neighborhood of Harrisonburg) in time to take part in the battle of New Market where General Siegel was defeated by Generals Breckenridge and Imboden. Siegel fell back behind Cedar creek, Breckenridge was withdrawn from

264

the Valley to reinforce Gen. Lee. Gen. Siegel had been relieved by Gen. Hunter who had been instructed to move by way of Staunton and Charlottsville and thence if possible to Lynchburg. Before reaching the latter place he expected to be joined by Gen. Crook and Averell, who had already reached the Virginia and Tennessee railroad. Gen. W. E. Jones had joined Imboden with between 3000 and 4000 men, and was anxious to prevent a junction of these forces, determined to attack Hunter, which he did near a place called New Hope, about half way between Port Republic and Staunton. Gen. Jones was killed and the Confederates defeated. Here, too, Lieut. Monroe gave his life for the cause he believed to be right. I have this from an eye witness. Gen. Jones called for an officer to lead the dismounted men who had lost their horses by being either killed or wounded. Frail breast works had been hurriedly built of rails, behind which these dismounted men were stationed, but were flanked and driven from their position; the officer who commanded them had been killed. It was now that Gen. Jones called for an officer to lead theses men and recover the defences which were the key to his position. No one volunteered. A moment later Monroe leaped from his horse said, "General, I will lead them, boys, follow me and we will soon have then on the run." With his cap on the point of his sabre he dashed forward followed by the dismounted men. This was Monroe's last charge; before they reached the enemy he fell shot through the neck by a musket ball. Thus ended the career as gallant a man as ever leveled a musket or drew a sabre. He knew no fear, he never counted noses, it differed but little to him whether one or ten opposed him it was all the same. It was men of the ranks like him, who, with their life blood, won for Lee and Jackson the imperishable crowns of military glory which will continue to shine with increasing splendor on history's page as the years roll on.

I will now return to myself. After Monroe had gone I wished that I to had made an effort to go with him, although I could not see how two of us could have managed to get off at the same time, as only one was allowed to be on his feet at the same time. The car made no halt. The Yankees, after a few moments, came in, closed the door and remarked that another d—m fool had broke his neck. Another prisoner on a rear car as we afterward learned, complained of being sick and persuaded one of the guards to let him step out on the platform for a few moments that he might get a little fresh air, when he jumped off. The guard fired at him, result not known. Our train reached Baltimore at day break. Here a little fellow, a Capt. Allen, I think he hailed from Georgia, made his escape by jumping from a window and mixing with the crowd that at this early hour lined the pavement. We were marched from the train and put aboard the exchange boat for New York, where rations of crackers and beef were issued us about the middle of the day. Soon after the boat steamed out the bay. This was the 9th day of February, 1864. The day was calm, bright and warm; about 100 were allowed on deck at one time, while the other 300 remained below. Those on deck remained about an hour and were then sent below and another hundred was allowed to take an airing, and so by turns; I yankled around so that my turn came three out of four times.

There was among the prisoners Gen. Jeff Thompson, who had a reputation for doing gunboats along the Mississippi river. He and some of the other officers had conceived a plan to capture the boat after dark and run her to City Point under cover of darkness. I don't know just how the plot was to be executed, I was not in the secret. But before the time came to attempt the execution of the plot, the Yankees, consisting one company of infantry, found out in some way that something was in the wind. When the batch that was on deck was sent below, the hatchway was closed and no more were allowed on deck. Soon after the boat stopped for some cause, to us unknown, and lay quiet until the next morning, when the hatches were opened and we were invited to come to the surface and bring our baggage with us. To our surprise and disgust we found the New York anchored at the wharf at Point Lookout with a gun boat along side. About 150 yards distant a regiment of Zouaves were drawn up on the beach to receive us. We were marched to the Hospital and quartered in the empty wards. The commandant at that place was a man by the name of Patterson. There may be some old people and possibly some young ones who don't know where to locate Point Lookout. It is a narrow strip of land laying between the Chesapeake Bay and the Potomac river. On the extreme point of land between the two waters was situated a hotel, or what had been a summer resort, but occupied now by the officers in charge of the prison and their families. A little further on was a pen surrounded by a plank fence built on the same plan as the one already described at Johnson's Island. Several thousand prisoners of war were confined there living in tents. The Hospital was a very large building; in design or shape the building would remind one of a wagon wheel with spokes reaching out in all directions from the centre. The several wards of the Hospital extended in like manner from a common centre for a distance of, I would think, 300 feet or more; the office or medical department was in the centre. The wards were not less than 20 feet in width, on either side of each ward were windows about 5 feet apart beneath each window stood an iron cot with mattress, sheet, pillow and blankets. The wards were well heated with large coal stoves with a large drum attached. Here we were quartered for the time being. We were told by Major Patterson that some little misunderstanding had deferred our exchange for a few days.

Another attempt to escape was made while we were quartered in the Hospital at Point Lookout. A supposed Rebel, though a Yankee detective

266

disguised in gray, informed one of the prisoners that there was a good chance for escape, as follows: This wolf in sheep's clothing said that 1 1/2 miles up the Point was a row of pickets driven in the ground close as they could be gotten and about ten feet high extending across the peninsula and some distance into the waters of the Chesapeak on one side and of the Potomac river on the other; at this place the strip of land was narrow. Our information was that at low ebb of the tide a man could easily pass round the picket fence by wading in water not over three feet in depth. A short distance beyond the fence was stationed a company of cavalry, who did picket duty across the narrow neck of land. One dark, windy night 10 men quietly and silently gathered on the beach, on the Potomac side of the point, and cautiously moved along the shore until we came in sight of the lamps on the fence at intervals of perhaps fifty yards. We halted at a safe distance from the lights to consider the best thing to do. We had not expected to have our path lighted up at the point of danger. We lay flat on the pebbly shore and consulted in a low tone. Some were in favor of retreat at once, others believed that we could keep out far enough from shore that with only our heads above water we could not be discovered from the shore. We took a vote on the question as to whether we should advance or retreat. A majority of two favored an advance. We started at once for deep water and were surprised at the distance we had to go before reaching the desired depth it really seemed that we were in a fair way to reach the Virginia shore. We at length reached our depth at, I would guess, something over a hundred yards from the shore. With the rising tide rippling about our ears we moved with the tide, slowly and cautiously made our way up the Potomac, at times on the tips of our toes, at other times in a stooping position, so that too much of our scalp would not appear above water; yet the bottom of the river seemed almost as smooth and level as a house floor. We passed the picket fence and beyond the rays of the lamp without being discovered, and concluded that immediate danger had been passed and that we could shape our course toward land with safety. We according shape our course at an angle that soon brought us into shallow water. We learned in a very short time that it was far more comfortable when in water up to our necks than in water knee deep wearing wet clothing with a strong March breeze considerably below the freezing point. When within a rod or less of the shore the command halt! reached our ear. At the same moment a Bulls eye lantern was aimed on us, when to our surprise, and I may say, horror, we discovered at least a score of dismounted cavalry drawn up in a line not more than 25 paces away; of course, we obeyed orders and halted. The Lieutenant in command said, "come ashore boys you may take cold, it's rather early for bathing, is it not? We were glad to get ashore again, after having been in the water it seemed to be at least three hours. Our clothing

267

Point Lookout, Maryland. (NATIONAL ARCHIVES)

was frozen and we were nearly so. We were marched back to the reserve picket, where a fairly good fire was burning. We were allowed to warm and partly dried our clothing amid the taunt and jeers of the Yankees, which we bore the best we could; but one of the party at least was feeling very blue. We tried to laugh and joke but the attempt was a very lame one. Next morning, which was not long coming, we were marched back to camp and had a hearing before the provost Martial of the prison and were told that if a second attempt of this kind occurred he would have us strung up by the thumbs two hours each day for ten days. This threat was enough for one of our party at least to make an inward promise never again to attempt escape by the same route. Then the penalty was quite enough to deter almost anyone who had ever witnessed it executed. For the benefit of those who never witnessed the performance or enjoyed the pleasure of being suspended by the thumbs, I will explain. It was managed this way; a pole was arranged similar to that prepared by a farmer on which to hang hogs; a small cord of sufficient strength was looped over each thumb and made fast to the beam over head, which was then would up like a windless until the victim was compelled to rest the weight of his body either on his toes or on his thumbs; when the feet rather toes fail, the strain is all on the thumbs, when the pain often became unbearable and victim looses consciousness, the Sergeant who bosses the job would order him lowered, and when consciousness returned the prisoner was either sent to the pen, or to the guard house it might be, to nurse, as best he could, his lacerated thumbs until the next day at the same hour, when he was made to take another course of the same medicine. This punishment was considered the most severe, and, but little short of the death penalty.

The usual punishment for a rebellious Rebel was to march up and down in front of the guard house with a log on his shoulder, as long as he could stagger beneath the weight of his load. We were sent back to our quarters wiser, but in a very bad humor; although a sharp lookout was kept for the fellow that was the cause of our trouble. He was never seen afterwards, or at least, was not recognized by any of our party.

About the 1st of April we were moved from the hospital to the pen which had been prepared for our accommodation, adjoining one occupied by privates. Our pen contained, I would say, about three acres and reached down to high tide on the Cheasapeake Bay. We were quartered in a double row of large tents with a street thirty yards in width running east and west, between. The entrance being on the west or from the Potomac side of the point. About three hundred yards away, out in the Potomac river, lay a gunboat at anchor. From our quarters we could look into the mouths of its heavy guns and shudder at the thought of what might be the consequence were these dogs of war, turned loose on our imprisoned crowd, loaded to the muzzle with grape and canister. The thought was almost enough to chill the blood in a fellows veins; at least I always felt bad some way when ever I looked in their frowning mouths. Ten men were quartered in each tent. In our tent were Maj. Chinn, of Louisiana; Capt. Wheeler, Capt. Bullock, of Tennessee; Capt. Barrett, of North Carolina; Lieut. Luther Ashby, of Virginia; Capt. Chidester, Lieut. Fellow, Lieut. Brinkley, of Portsmouth, Virginia; Capt. Fitzhugh and myself. Capt. Chinn, if I remember right, was captured at Port Hudson. By the terms of capitulation the field officers were allowed to retain all their private baggage. The Major had two large trunks, one containing his wardrobe and bedding; the bedding consisted of a single hair mattress, pillow, sheets, blankets, &c. The Major was wealthy at the commencement of the war. He owned a fine sugar plantation, owned over five hundred slaves. He said that he had built a fine house two years before the war on a bluff near the Mississippi river, above Baton Rouge, that cost him $25,000. Major Chinn raised and equipped a battalion of 500 men at his own expense, and marched with them to Port Hudson, Louisiana. On the fall of Vicksburg, Port Hudson was surrendered, conditionally, the field officers being allowed the above named privileges of carrying with them their private baggage. These officers were sent to Johnson's Island, where I met Major Chinn for the first time. He seemed to take a great liking for me from our first meeting, and always called me Bryan Brew, after some bully of Irish outlaws of that name. When we moved into our new quarters the Major insisted that I must take up my abode in the same tent that he did. A few days after we had moved from the Hospital the Major received the unwelcome news through a prisoner and a neighbor of his, recently captured, that his elegant house had been burned, and that his wife and daughter, an only child, were living in a negro cabin on the farm and cared for by some of the aged Slaves, who refused to leave them. The Major was made up of American, French and Creole; the language used was of about the same complexion. When this unwelcome news reached the Major his language was by far more emphatic than elegant. The fumes of sulphur could almost have been imagined. The news was a heavy blow. It seemed that some raiders had gathered a lot of mules from the neighborhood around, and in loading them on a boat at the wharf near his house after night, some of them had fallen into the river and drowned. The officer in command had ordered the house set on fire to give them light to work by. For several days it seemed as though the Major would loose his mind. One morning he called me to where he lay, and handed me his pocketbook, said, "Bryan, this is sad news for me; I care nothing for my house and slaves, but the thought of what my wife and daughter may have to endure, is almost more than I can bear. They, who have from early infancy; had every known wish gratified, may now be in want of bread. But I have, or had, a few old and faithful servants, who nursed then and

270

me from our earliest infancy; I cannot believe these will leave or foresake them, but will care for them as best they can." This may not have been his exact language, but it us as near to it as I can remember. "I feel like eating something; go to the Sutler and get a sugar cured ham, some eggs, bread and butter and anything else the Sutler may have that you think we would enjoy; don't be afraid to spend those Sutler checks, I can get more." I was soon back with rations enough, as I thought, for a week. "Now," said the Major, "take this key and open that mess chest and lift the tray out, and in the bottom you will find a frying pan, some plates and mugs and what is called an Old Dominion coffee pot." I had never seen anything like it. It was a two story arrangement, the upper part held about one and a half pints. The bottom of this cup was covered with a fine wire screen. The desired quantity of ground coffee was placed in this mug; it was then filled with boiling water and left to filter through to the lower apartment, when it was almost as strong as lye. The Major usually drank about a half pint of this beverage. Strength enough was usually left in the grounds for a half dozen cups of ordinary strength, which was given to the other members of the mess. The tent in which our cooking was done was immediately in the rear of the one we occupied. I was permitted to fry our meat and eggs and anything else we had to cook. The Major said if I would attend to the culinary department he would foot the bills and we would call it even. This I willingly consented to do, and living like a fighting chicken for a time. This was very pleasant place for a summer resort; the nights were cool and a person was not comfortable when sleeping under two blankets, although from about six in the morning until twelve or one o'clock, for days, not a leaf stirred, the heat from the sun was almost unbearable, but after the middle of the day the tide began to come up the bay accompanied by a stiff cool breeze, which made this place a very pleasant summer resort. A light weight coat could be worn with comfort until next morning, when the calm and heat had to be endured again for several hours. We, who hailed from the mountain regions of our native States and had never seen anything that floated larger than a canoe or a ferryboat, enjoyed watching, for hours, a dim curl of smoke miles away down the bay which grew in density and volume until the hull of a steamer seemed to rise from beneath the water, and after hours plowed its way like some great monster, going either up or down the Chesapeake Bay or the Potomac river. We watched for hours, objects down the bay that seemed to be not larger than a duck, of almost dazzling whiteness. It was the top sail of a becalmed vessel waiting for breeze to fill her sails and send her on her journey. When the tide began to rise a breeze sprang up, her sails filled and in a few hours what had appeared to be only a gull or duck now glided past our prison pen, before a stiff breeze with every sail filled to its utter most. The sailors high up in the rigging looked to be about the size of a half grown monkey. When I looked for the first time at close range on one of those ocean vessels I almost felt that it was a thing of life and did not belong to earth. Each day was spent by the inmates of our prison pen about as the preceding one, until one morning a large gate near the Chesapeake shore was thrown open.

We were told that we could go for a bath in the bay for two hours, any who desire to do so. Very soon the pen was almost deserted, one man only being left to guard each tent. We passed out the gate by fours close order, between lines of blue coats until we reached the water, not over fifty yards from the gate. At this time in the morning the tide was at its lowest ebb and the distance from the gate to the water's edge was almost as smooth and solid as a house floor. At the water's edge we broke ranks and soon several hundred Confeds were enjoying a treat which many of us had never enjoyed before, which was bathing in salt water. The bottom of the bay seemed as smooth as the shore which had been washed for centuries by the rising and ebbing tide. At a distance of, I would say, two hundred yards, the water at low ebb was not over five feet in depth. There were many good swimmers among the bathers; some of whom swam out into the bay until their heads seemed to be no larger than puff balls floating on the surface. No doubt some of them would have made an effort to reach the other shore, which was visible to the naked eye, had there not been an obstruction in the way in the shape of a well manned gunboat. We enjoyed this privilege hugely for several days, until one morning there was a regular stampede, which happened this way: We had been out but a short time, many of the prisoners could not swim; these usually on entering the water waded out until they could no farther and then made their way toward the shore, being taught in the mode of swimming by those who had already mastered the art. The Yankees had said to us several times, "You Jonnies had better not venture out too far, you may run against a shark." We had, of our number, some few who had been sailors, who assured us that a shark had never been seen at this point. The morning of which I now speak was cloudy and threatened rain, a light mist or fog seemed to rise from the water. As we passed out the Sergeant at the gate said, "boys this is a good morning for sharks to visit shallow water, better not venture out too far." Some old Rebel sang out, "No danger boys a shark is as much afraid of a Confederate as is a Yankee." Those who could not swim had about reached their depth; many who could swim were much farther from the shore. "Sharks! sharks! to the shore, to the shore" came from the throats of at least a hundred men. I happened that morning, to be among the furthest from shore. We were in the habit, several at a time, of getting in line and diving in the direction of the gunboat to see who could cover the greatest distance before coming to the surface. Now, whilst I did not claim to be an expert swimmer, I did claim to be fairly long winded under water. It so happened that four of us were testing our endurance under water when the warning of danger was given and it failed to reach us. I rose to the surface a few seconds after, and perhaps one hundred feet in advance of my competitors; at the same instant a noise reached my ear, which sounded like several persons striking the water with paddles a short distance away. Hastily drawing my hand across my eyes to rid them, to some extent, of the salt water which hindered my vision. I looked down the bay in the direction of the sound and only a short distance away, discovered to my horror what I took to be several sharks. They appeared to be having a war dance, of some kind; were swimming around in a circle; or appeared to be. Their backs could be seen above the surface; every few seconds one or more sprang clear of the water and appeared to turn a summesalte, striking the water with their tails, which created the noise mentioned. These appeared to be several feet in length, of a dark gray or black color; at least this was about the way they appeared to me. For a moment I was almost paralyzed with fright. I turned to my companions, when, to my surprise and dismay, they were fifty yards away and making such time as they never made before. In the twinkling of an eye I was following in their wake with a full head of steam. Many had already reached the shore. Several would have surely drowned (being so much frightened that they were almost helpless) had they not received assistance. I soon began to come up with and had passed several whose strength had almost failed them. The knowledge that I was not the last file in the stampede was very consoling, believing that those in rear would first fall victim to those dreaded monsters of the deep; yet I continued to crowd on every pound of steam possible. It seemed like a second nature with me to want to be in front particularly on a retreat when the danger was at the other end. I was rapidly forging my way past the weaker crafts, when a familiar voice near said, "Bryan, don't leave me, I am played out." I recognized the voice of Major Chinn, not ten feet away, who was making a feeble effort to reach the shore. The Major was a large fleshy man; although there was great puffing there was very little progress. He was merely floating on the surface, which requires but little exertion in salt water. He said, "I will go to the bottom in another moment, write my wife," all the while gasping for breath. I said, Major, wade out, the water is not four feet deep. I saw that he was very much exhausted and might need help, although in a great hurry, I turned for the purpose of rendering what assistance I could, and when nearly in reach of him dropped to the bottom and found the depth of the water to be less than I had anticipated. I looked back almost expecting to see those unfortunate fellows in the rear already within grasping distance of these dreaded man eaters. "Are they coming," asked the Major, who was now on his feet and forcing his way through the water

273

in a way that bade fair to carry him beyond the reach of danger in a very short time without even a glance in the direction of the expected danger. "Bryan, don't stop, how near are they? have they come up with any of the poor fellows, yet?" I said no, drop anchor and take in your sails. They are at least a half mile down the bay and appear to be going the other way. The Major halted, straightened up, and shading his eyes with his hands, looked steadily at the supposed man eating Shark, which continued springing from the water every few seconds. "Those are not Shark," exclaimed the Major, "they're nothing but Porpoises and no more dangerous than tad poles," then he roared with laughter. The Yankees seemed to enjoy themselves hugely at the expense of the "Johnnies" as they called us.

About this time nearly one hundred of Gen. Morgan's officers arrived at Point Lookout and were turned in to our pen and tents were erected for their accommodation. Most of these men seemed to be gentlemen; although a few were imprudent, hot tempered and insulting in their remarks. The Yankee Sergeant, who had charge of our own and looked after the wants of the prisoners, was named Fox. He belonged to a New York regiment and was much liked by the prisoners. He was always willing and ready to do anything in his power for our comfort. He seemed to have been well raised and well educated, very quiet, not over bearing or insulting to the prisoners, which was not always the case with those in authority. One of Morgan's men seemed from some cause, to take a dislike to Fox and appeared to take a delight in saying mean things to him at every opportunity. Fox seemed to avoid him as much as possible; at length a negro regiment just organized, but had never seen any service, was sent to the Point to guard the prisoners.

The first morning they went on duty the Kentuckian (I can't remember his name) met Fox in front of our tent, which was nearest the gate; some words passed between them which I did not hear, but as I came from the tent I heard Fox say to the Kentuckian, "If you want to live don't repeat that remark." The Kentuckian said, "yes I will repeat that you are nothing but a d__n negro lover and too much of a coward to shoot and kill a sheep dog; at the same time pulling open his shirt bosom, stepped toward Fox and dared him to shoot. Fox quickly raised his revolver and fired. The Kentuckian fell without a groan, shot through the heart. Fox turned and walked rapidly to the gate and passed out before twenty men were aware of what had been done. There was great indignation among the prisoners, more especially Morgan's men who were furious. It really seemed for a time that they could not be restrained. The long roll was being beat on the out side; the gunboats on either side of the point seemed to be doing an unusual amount of blowing and tooting. While the volume of smoke which poured from their smoke stacks, showed very exclusively that the manufacturer of steam was in rapid progress. The Kentuckians appeared for a time to be determined to blow down the fence and go out and avenge the murder of their comrade, but the cooler heads prevailed. Many of the prisoners had noticed and did not approve of the course pursued by their fellow prisoners in seeking to insult and abuse the Sergeant at every opportunity, without any cause whatever. After perhaps an hour comparative quiet had been restored, and the dead man was washed, shaved and prepared for burial in the best manner possible, under the circumstances. Soon after the body had been cared for (a company of the New York Zouaves, who had been guarding us prior to the appearances of this dark cloud which now threatened us with trouble), the corpse were placed on a stretcher and carried out, and I suppose, buried. When the gate swung open the Zouaves and colored troops could be seen drawn up in line ready for action in case an attempt was made by the prisoners to escape.

Next morning, as usual, we marched down to the gate, for the purpose of taking our morning bath in the Bay, but found the gate locked and a big colored soldier on guard, who, when we were within fifty yards of him, sang out, " Halt dar, you fellars, don gon bout fur nuf since your mishaved yesterday; you done git no more frolikin in de Bay, so you can gest file round, march home and quick too, cause you see the bottom rail don got on top; now you all gest turn round by the rear flank and be in a hurry, fore dis gun fo loos in dat crowd and somebody fot hurt fore dey nows it." We faced to the rear and counter marched at a fairly quick step as the click of the musket lock was distinctly heard in our rear, expecting every moment to hear the report of a musket and each one expecting, no doubt, to feel the sharp sting of a Minnie ball. We reached our quarters in safety, but in a very bad humor. The well from which we got water was near the entrance to the pen; on our return to our quarters one of Morgan's men took a heavy wooden pail and went for a pail of water; but, to his surprise, found a negro guard marching between our quarters and the well, something new. The man walked in a direct line toward the well, but was halted when he reached the guard's line of march as he was refused access to the well, he asked, "How are we to get water?" "Go round de end o' this tromp," said the darkey. "What is that for?" said the Kentuckian. Dem am Corporal Dick's orders, "said the darkey. "Tell Corporal Dick to go to h__l", said the Confed, and started on. The negro made a lunge at him with the bayonet, which the prisoner caught in his hand, and swung the heavy pail against the guard's head with such force that the bucket went to staves and the negro measured his length on the ground, at a distance of about fifteen feet. The Confed went back to his quarters followed by the colored soldier, who had quickly regained his feet and was shouting at the top of his voice for Corporal Dick. When he had located the tent where the

275

Confed entered he trotted back to the gate, where he was met by Corporal Dick, followed by about twenty of his veterans, who had never met a Confed on the battle field, and no doubt felt brave as lions, charging down on an unarmed foe with a great deal of fire in de eye, as they expressed it, although it was a very white eye, to have fire in it. The tent where the prisoner had taken refuge was instantly surrounded and the man who struck Sam Jackson was called on to "come outen dat tent without stoppin," on penalty of having, the tent and every man in it blown sky high. A crowd was rapidly gathering and it began to look as though Corporal Dick and his men might get a furlough that would last them until Gabril sounded the last trump. With cocked and leveled muskets Corporal Dick demanded the unconditional surrender of "de man what dun busted de bucket against Sam Jackson's hed." We were expecting every moment that the highly excited negroes would fire into the tent, but the folds of the tent parted and a Kentucky captain stepped out and said, "Corporal, don't allow your men to fire in this crowd, I am the man you want and will go with you, lead the way." At this moment Sergeant Fox, who had not been in the pen since shooting the Kentuckian, hastily made his way through the crowd to the prisoners side and said, "What's the trouble men?" Corporal Dick explained, "dat man don busted Sam Jackson's hed wid de water bucket when he don had no business to do it, cause Sam was obeying orders." Fox said, "Corporal, take your men to their quarters, I will take charge of this man at the same time slipped his arm through that of the prisoner and started for the gate, closely followed by the rapidly gathering prisoners, some of whom favored making a dash and capturing the whole business, releasing the prisoner and disarming the guard; but a leader was wanting which was fortunate for all parties, as many lives would have been lost to no purpose, as several thousand privates were only separated from us by a plank fence, in an other enclosure, and would have quickly joined us. There were but two regiments guarding us, one a New York Zouave, the other a raw colored regiment, which now seemed to be destined to bring trouble. The Zouaves, or some of them, at least, had assured us that they would not interfere if we would manage to drown every negro on the Point.

The gunboats, which were kept with a full head of steam ready to move at any time, now began signaling each other; and the fresh clouds of smoke rising from their smokestacks showed plainly that the crew was not sleeping. By this time I believe every man in the pen had gathered at the gate, armed with anything they could get hold of from a pocket knife to a stick of stove wood. It now looked as though something was going to happen very soon, we didn't know just what. Col. Patterson, who was in command of Post, now appeared on the scene, accompanied with several other officers. On the outside of the fence had been erected a platform, on which the prison guards walked with head and shoulders above the top of the fence, here the commandant and his companions stood. Col. Patterson said something like this, so nearly as I can remember. He roared out almost at the top of his voice, "prisoners, why do I see this unusual and unwarranted gathering." Disperse at once and go to your quarters, otherwise it may be worse for you; in short he gave us quite a lecture as to our duties as prisoners and Rebels, fed and cared for by the best Government the world ever saw, and intimated that a hemp rope would be the proper ration for traitors. We had in our pen a Col. Begonia, a Frenchman, who had lived in or near New Orleans from childhood. He was an artillery Colonel and had command of a garrison, somewhere not far from New Orleans when captured. Col. Begonia stood, I would think, about six feet six in his shoes, at least a head above those around him. He now stepped forward and said something like this, although I cannot remember his exact words, "Colonel, in this game bluff will not win; only a little while ago one of our comrades, unarmed and in cold blood was shot down before our eyes; when the sun and wind have scarcely had time to dry up his life's blood, on the ground where he fell, and our hearts are still sad, another of our comrades had been torn from our midst and marched at the point of the bayonet in the hands of a half civilized mob to, we know not what. We feel that you have added insult to injury by placing our own slaves over us with arm in their hands to shoot us down with only a shadow of pretext." The Colonel spoke for several minutes in this strain, during which time a profound silence reigned. In concluding his remarks he said, Now, Col. Patterson, pay attention to what I am going to say and weigh well my words, because they are not idle or meaningless forbearance with us will no longer be considered. Send our comrade back to us unharmed within ten minutes; remove from our sight these negro guards and hereafter only soldiers of our own color be placed as guards. On these conditions we will quietly disperse, but on no others. It remains for you Colonel, to determine whether quiet shall be restored or within one short hour when the waters of the Chesapeake and Potomac mingle their waters together they will be colored alike with the blood of the blue and gray. I am done, choose which you will, for you have ten minutes to decide."

Col. Patterson and his companions, without a word in reply, disappeared from view, for a few moments all was as silent as the grave, not a whisper could be heard. The thoughts of many no doubt had traveled back to their childhood home, where dwelt to them all that made life worth living. A look at the face of those who stood near me showed no fear, but rather a determination to risk all to be free again; thus they looked to me, with one exception. There was a youngster in that crowd who came to the conclusion very quickly that he had seen the light of day about ten

277

years too soon, and would certainly have entered a noisy protest could he have looked into the future and seen what the next few years had in store for him. True he had been in close quarters, but nothing to compare with what the present seemed likely to be. We were about to attack Uncle Sam by sea and by land, in our front were both infantry and cavalry, how many we did not know. We knew that two regiments of infantry, one white, the other colored. On either bank lay a gunboat with steam up, portholes open through which the muzzle of their heavy guns could easily be seen in close range for grape and cannister; in our rear as far as the eye could reach lay a sheet of water. This surrounded, with no weapons of attack or defence, I felt that we were about to take a very rash and dangerous step. A little to one side had gathered, perhaps a dozen or more officers of high rank in the Confederate army. The central figure in this group seemed to be Gen. Jeff Thompson, he, it appeared was the man most relied on to lead the Israelites on this occasion. Gen. Jeff Thompson, as I remember him, stood about six feet in his stockings, rather slender, weighed about 140 pounds, dark complexioned, stoop shouldered, sharp features, long, thin nose, about 40 years of age and wore a rather scant mustache and goatee. He was a native of Jefferson county, Va., but for about seventeen years had been living in Missouri, most of the time at St. Joseph. In him the Yankee always found a foe ready for the fray. A few moments later the gate opened and our comrade entered the pen accompanied by a guard, who took the posts of the colored guards who had all left the pen. Gen. Thompson made a short talk to the prisoners. He advised them to quietly retire to their quarters, since Colonel Begonia's terms of peace had been accepted, to all appearances, at least. Gen. Jeff Thompson remarked that a game of bluff could sometimes be as successfully played on the battlefield as in the gambling den. I, for one, was well satisfied that the bluff had won; although I really believe that quite a number were disappointed in not having had an opportunity to die for their country.

CHAPTER XX

Fort Delaware

Q uiet having been again restored things seemed to drag along in about the same channel with a report almost every day that the exchange of prisoners was about to be resumed, and we might expect to be sent to City Point within a few days at furthest. Reports of this kind had become stale. When at roll call on the morning of June 25, 1864, we were ordered to hold ourselves in readiness to go on exchange at any hour during the day. This was joyful news to us. Our morning meal was a hurried one. Within an hour each man had his effects ready for shipment, done up in cotton hankerchiefs old worn old shirts, drawers or pants stuffed and thrown across the owners shoulder. Some few were lucky enough to own a carpet bag.

After waiting for several hours filled with hope and fear, the gate, was thrown open and we were ordered to form a column of fours and pass out and were marched between lines of infantry on board a boat, which lay on the wharf, not over a hundred yards away and packed in the cellar, or believe they call, it the hole of the vessel. Two rows of posts placed at short intervals throughout the entire length of the boat supported the floor over our heads, although we were beneath the surface of the water. The darkness was not so near great as a backwoodman would suppose. There was near the floor over our heads, on either side, a row of round holes about twelve inches in diameter, if I remember right, in which was secured heavy glass, and although these were beneath water the light from them was much more than a landsman would suppose. And although the large boilers and engines were located down here the heat was not as great as one would imagine. The boat was now aground but the tide was coming in and soon had her afloat, when she steamed down the bay at a rate of speed, which bade fair to land us at City Point before daylight next morning. Night soon came on when the prisoners generally retired for the night by stretching themselves on the floor of the boat with their wardrobes under their heads, and in a few moments many of them were, no doubt, dreaming of their childhood's happy hours. I, with several others who had elected to stake off our "claim" for sleeping room early, was compelled to reclaim sitting with our backs resting against the boiler room. We had snoozed for sometime in this position when I was awakened by my close companions who said, "I believe there is a fight on some where; I have heard cannon several times, but can't get the direction." After listening a few moments, I heard what appeared to be the boom of a heavy gun not far away. By this time several had heard the sound and were inquiring what it meant. Finally a Georgian stuck his head through a little window in the engine room and inquired of one of the fireman, where the shooting was? "In the clouds," replied he, "did you never hear it thunder where you came from?" Yes, but not in a darned hole like this," the Georgian said as he slid back into his former position. Soon the boat creaked and squeaked as though it might break into pieces; and appeared to bob around like a cork on a fishing line, when a breeze stirred the water. In a few moments a regular storm had struck us—an almost continuous roll of thunder. I will not attempt to describe further this one night of my experience, couldn't do it.

Next morning we were allowed to go on deck, perhaps a hundred at a time, to get a little fresh air which certainly was never more needed for the preservation of life than on this occasion. By good management or good luck I reached the deck with the first squad. I never saw a more beautiful sight. The sun just rising apparently from the water, which was all that could be seen as far as the eye could reach; nothing but one unending sheet of water in all directions; no land was visible. There were perhaps two hundred negroes on board the boat, who had been gathered up or had made their way into the Yankee lines in Virginia and were now being sent North. They were chiefly old men, women and children. Three or four of these had died during the night, I imagine from fright, which gave those of us who were in deck an opportunity of witnessing a burial at sea. They were rolled in some course material, very much like that now used for packing wool, and, without ceremony, they were slid overboard. Almost before the corpse reached the water a Shark seized it and darted away chased by an hundred or more others which had been leisurely following the boat.

They soon returned and took position is rear of the boat again. These were the only Sharks I ever saw; they are certainly hideous looking fish. I hope it may never be my lot to be buried at sea. We allowed to remain on deck for perhaps a half hour and were then sent below and another squad brought to the surface and aired for about the same length of time. By watching for an opportunity I succeeded in spending at least one half of my time above water. The day was clear and calm except a gentle breeze which blew steadily all the while soft and balmy; under other circumstances we would have enjoyed the ride far more. Before noon, land was visible to the naked eye on either side of the boat. It soon became known that instead of City Point our destination was Fort Delaware. This was very discouraging to many of us and dispelled every hope of an early exchange. As we were steaming up Delaware Bay we passed several large sailing vessels with canvass well filled, bending to the breeze. A sailor high up in the rigging appeared but little larger than a monkey. A large sailing vessel is worth seeing by a back woodsman, at least one who never saw anything of the kind. About 2 p.m. we were landed at Fort Delaware and ordered to take our place in line as our names were called. When the roll had been called, and each prisoner searched , the prison gate was thrown open and we filed into the enclosure containing, I would guess, about two acres enclosed on three sides by twenty-eight barracks, a cook house and eating apartment, on the fourth side a plank fence sixteen feet in height separated the officers and the privates. About three feet below the top of this fence, throughout its length, a platform had been erected on which the sentinels placed day and night with each pen in full view.

A short description of Fort Delaware, as I remember it, may not be out of place here. The fort was built on an island in the Delaware Bay, about forty miles below Philadelphia, a short distance below Wilmington and nearly opposite New Castle on the Delaware side of the bay. The island on which the fort was built was called Pea Patch island. A vessel loaded with peas was said to have sunk here many years before which caused the formation of the island. As this happened before my time, I cannot vouch for its correctness. But am sure that thirty-five years ago the island was there, and a fort was there, built principally of stone laid in cement. The stone seemed to have all been hewn in cubes and squares weighing several tons each. The walls were of great thickness, I would say not less than twenty five feet, perhaps fifty. I had but one opportunity to view the inside of the fort, and only a small portion of it. If I remember right, there was said to be one hundred and twenty pieces of ordinance in the fort and on top of the walls ready for action at very short notice. The ones I saw were said to throw a solid shot of several hundred pounds weight. At the breech these guns were five feet or more in diameter, mounted on tracks placed on a track similar to that of a railroad. The casemates through which the guns are fired are bomb proof, being closed with heavy iron doors. On top of the fort wall thirty heavy siege guns were trained on our pen. A few rounds of grape from these emptied into our midst, and a few remnants of gray clothing would have been all that would have been left of the Confederate prisoners. On entering the prison gate I felt more depressed and discouraged than at any time since I had been a prisoner. I almost felt in truth that "he who enters here leaves hope behind." On entering the enclosure our ears were greeted with the accustomed cry of "fresh fish!, fresh fish!" although many us had been salted down for several months; we were soon surrounded by nearly three thousand prisoners, each eager to learn if there were any relative, friend or ac-quaintance among the late arrivals. Soon to my surprise and joy I spied, making his way through the surrounding crowd the well-known face and figure of my kindsman and school-mate Capt. Isaac Kuykendall, Co. F 7th Reg. Va. Cav., followed by Lieut. J. T. Parker, another school mate, belonging to the same Company and Regiment; soon Lieut. Chas. P.

Johnson of the same squadron and regiment to which I belonged (Lieut. Johnson was a brother to Z. H. Johnson, sons of Okey Johnson of Patterson Creek, now Mineral county). I did not know up to this time that these boys were prisoners and had no thought of meeting them, but the satisfaction felt at seeing a well-known face among a sea of strange ones in a strange place unexpectedly must be experienced to be realized. Most of the crowd I think found friends and acquaintances here who took charge of and escorted them to the quarters assigned to each in the different divisions. On entering the gate each prisoner was handed a blanket, many of which had seen service and were worn yet, when folded several times and placed between the naked boards of our bunks and the sweenyed hip, great relief was experienced, but of a protection from cold those old blankets were of little service. Capt. Kuykendall not having a bunk mate at this time we concluded to set up housekeeping together on the lower bunks, Division No. 1. I found several acquaintances here other than those already named, among whom were Lieut. Cayoner, Capt. Mark Lovett, Lieut. David Ream and Lew Welch, besides several other Hampshire and Hardy county men; I also had the pleasure, if such it could be called, of shaking hands with several acquaintances among the privates by sticking a finger through a knot hole in the division fence which separated the two pens. Ordinarily we were not allowed to approach nearer than thirty feet of this fence, but occasionally a kind-hearted guard would allow a prisoner to talk with his brother for a few moments through a small opening between the boards. I soon learned that Hampshire county was well represented on the other side of the fence. Among those were J. J. Inskeep, David Fox, I. T. Brady, Thos. Goldsborough, W. M. Parsons, Samuel Fleming, Mich Poling, W. Montgomery, Peter and Abraham Barnes, Thomas White, Holland Taylor and H. C. Kuykendall. There were others whom I cannot now call to mind. Plank walls were laid in front of each Division; also through the center of the pen, otherwise it would have been impossible to have gotten about many times on account of the mud. We were allowed two meals each day; the first between eight and nine in the morning, the second some time before dark. Our rations were about 2 oz. of very ordinary old cow with frequent changes to mule, and occasionally about an inch square of bacon; we usually got two army crackers about four inches square or one-quarter of a small loaf of bread about the size of a butter plate. If this bread had been analyzed it might have been found to contain about equal quantities of rye and corn; this at least was the decision of many of those who had the opportunity to regrind it. For our afternoon meal, instead of meat, we got either a potato boiled with skin on or a cup of bean soup, minus the beans; such were our daily rations. Without variation, among the prisoners could often be heard the cry of "a tater and a hardtack for a chew of tobacco." The little meat we got was often unfit for use and was cast away, especially in the heat of summer. I really believe that many of the prisoners died from starvation. But, have never blamed the Yankee government altogether with this state of affairs, but rather to the cold-blooded murder of the man with whom the government contract to furnish a certain number of rations according to specifications, and, for which that contractor was paid but never delivered. The man who contracted to furnish rations for the prison at Fort Delaware was a brother in law to the commandant of the Fort.

No one landed or departed from the Island without General Schoeff's knowledge and consent. No mail of any description was allowed to leave the Island without first having been inspected by a Yankee officer. This being the case it can easily be seen how small was the chance of the outside world knowing what was being done on Pea Patch Island. Here, I think, lay the whole secret, as it appeared to me. It was a money making scheme. The man who contracted to furnish our rations had a Sutler store, convenient to the prison, and to which the prisoners had access through a small window. The Yankee government forbade the Sutler selling to the prisoners anything other than stationary and tobacco. Notwithstanding a prisoner who had the checks could get anything kept in stock. Many of the prisoners had relatives and friends in the North who supplied them with all the money they wanted. Also many more received money in many ways from friends in the South, where the Yankee had overrun the country. The prisoners were not allowed to receive money. Their mail was all opened before being delivered. When it was found to contain money the money was removed, and a receipt took its place for the amount the letter contained. The amount having been credited on the book kept for the purpose in lieu of the greenbacks the prisoners received Sutler's checks, or small squares of pasteboard on which was printed: 5c, 10c, 25c, 50c, $1.00. With these checks anything the Sutler's store contained could be bought by the prisoners, notwithstanding the order of the War Department to sell to the prisoners only writing material and tobacco. But these orders were disregarded; the Sutler accepted the amount printed thereon as readily from a Confederate prisoner as a greenback from a Yankee soldier. These Sutler checks were redeemed with the money credited to the prisoners, on the deposit or bank book, when presented for payment by the Sutler, but no other person could get one cent on those checks. Of the ten thousand prisoners at Fort Delaware, perhaps one-fourth of them received money from outside friends. In order that the Sutler get this money the prisoners must be pinched with hunger. This was done in a scientific manner. Those who had checks, spent them at the Sutler store to relieve a craving stomach. Those who were not so fortunate tightened their belts occasionally and bore the griping pangs of hunger as

283

best they could, until reduced to skeletons, when many fell an easy prey to disease, diarrhoea being the most fatal, aggravated to a great extent no doubt by the unwholesome water with which we were compelled to quench our thirst. Usually our drinking water was brought down a boat from Brandywine creek a small stream, which empties into the bay short distance above the Fort, and was forced through a leather hose into large tanks with a capacity sufficient to supply drinking water for several days. Occasionally for some cause, unknown to the prisoners, the tanks were filled from the bay. The water brought from the creek above was fresh, but about the temperature of 100 degrees after being in the tanks for a few hours. The water from the bay was always salty; to drink of it every hour in the day a person's thirst would not be quenched only for a few moments at best. We were allowed to use water from the tanks only for drinking and cooking purposes, for washing, either of clothing or person, had to be done in a ditch dug through the pen and filled with water from the bay by rising of the tide. We had no means of heating water with which to do our washing, so the laundry was not first class. Many of the prisoners did not have a change of underwear and did but little washing in cold water, but spent much of their time sitting in their bunks wrapped in their blankets waging a war of extermination against the prisoner's relentless enemy, the "gray back", whose attack could be expected at any time, either day or night, without fail. They were no respector of persons; the corps, commander and privates were alike their victims. Their number was innumerable. In summer it was oppressively warm in the prison pen where no breeze could reach us because of the barracks with which we were surrounded. In winter the cold was severe, but the raw, damp air caused the place to be chilly and disagreeable in the extreme. Each division had a good sized egg stove around which the inmates gathered in cold, damp weather, which was very unsatisfactory all round; while those on the inside of the circle were being roasted those on the outside were almost frozen. There was an air line mail route between the prison, pens carried on in this way: when the weather was not too rough at any hour of the day a good number of the prisoners were taking exercise by promenading up and down through the pen. Early in the morning the daily mail began to arrive in this way: a note was written wrapped around a rock or something with weight enough to carry it over the fence, then direct to the person for whom intended and the division to which he was quartered; then watch for an opportunity when the guard's back was turned in the right direction, toss it over; someone will pick it up and carry it to the division where directed and deliver to the proper person. This mode of exchange was usually successful but was sometimes captured by a guard, who saw and demanded the package, which had to be given up. Although the guards were under orders, but few of them were mean

Lt. John Blue - picture taken while prisoner at Fort Delaware
(POTOMAC EDISON'S VALLEY ECHO)

enough to carry out the order.

A few days after our arrival at Fort Delaware I met a Colonel Brewer who made his escape from this place about twelve months before by swimming to the Delaware shore on a board. When he hoisted anchor and the said the tide was coming in and carried him about twelve miles up the bay or river before he succeeded in landing. He was well-nigh exhausted, but after some narrow escapes from being captured reached the Confederate lines in safety, and took part in the battle of Gettysburg. He is not himself now, but, for what he considers good reasons, claims to be a cousin of himself, or rather of the fellow of the same name who was supposed to have been drowned in an attempt to escape from the Island, and so accounted for at roll call by the Yankee Corporal.

Capt. Ahl, Asst. Adg. General, seemed to have more control of the prison than Gen. Schoeff, the Commandant of the Fort. The prisoners were almost unanimous in considering Capt. Ahl the most contemptible, unfeeling scoundrel then living. There were but few of the prisoners who ever received a kind word from him. His second was Lieu. Wolf; this pair would certainly have been hard to best. If these men, or either of them, spent much of their time South of Mason and Dixon line and met with many of their old acquaintances of Fort Delaware and did not receive a warm reception then I am very much mistaken.

When we had been at the Fort about ten days everything seemed to be as quiet as usual. One night several officers attempted to make their escape by crawling through a ditch filled with mud and water passing beneath the floor of one of the divisions, its entire length, terminating on the outside of the pen. One would scarcely have believed that a human would ever attempt to escape by the route through which a Muskrat would not have ventured of his own free will. But few, who escaped from the pen, were ever heard from again. I have no doubt that a very large percent of the poor fellows anchored at the bottom of the bay, at least, but few of them were ever heard from again, so far as I ever heard. Since the weather had warmed up the prisoners had been disappearing, something the Yankees could not account for—their absence from roll call—after having taken every precaution to prevent their escape. The night of the 6th of July, 1864, Capt. Burk and Lieut. Patton attempted to make their escape but failed.

The patrol came on them when they took refuge under a bridge across the ditch but was too late in reaching cover and was discovered. The mysterious disappearance of the prisoners was now solved. The next morning at roll call the Yankees made a new roll and compelled every man to take his place in line. Until now the chief of divisions, had been reporting as sick, those who failed to appear and answer to their name. In this way those who made their escape from the pen were not often missed for several days. This morning the Yankees seemed to be very cross, no privilege or favors were granted the prisoners; it was seldom that a civil answer could be had to question asked of a Yankee during the day; the whole bluecoat family seemed to be riled. They had learned upon a recount if the roll of the prisoners that a far greater number were absent without lief than they had imagined. In the dusk of the evening the report of a musket rang out clear and distinct over the pen. Some of the prisoners had predicted that something unusual would happen before the day was over. Capt. K and I were on our bunk when the report reached our ear. A moment or two later the sad news that Col. Jones had been shot was known to almost every prisoner in the pen. On returning from the rear he had been shot by one of the guards and mortally wounded, from the effects of which he died next day. This was certainly one of the most cowardly, dastardly cold blooded murders known to a civilized people. Col. Jones was a cripple and compelled to use his crutches. He was shot down without a word of warning or provocation, so said those who witnessed the tragedy. Oh, God!, oh, God! what did you shoot me for?, he exclaimed, he fell to the ground. I was not personally acquainted with Colonel Jones, but whilst the murder was being discussed by those who knew him I learned that his home was Middlesex county; that his father was a New Englander and had died young when the Colonel was but a youth, leaving him quite a fortune. The Colonel had been educated at the North, had studied medicine but never practiced it. He was about thirty years of age when the band of the assassin cut him down. He was elected Colonel of a regiment of militia two or three years before the commencement of the war. This was his only military position. He was in command of a few home guards when captured in his own county. His command was made up of old men and boys who had come out to resist a raid of General Kilpatrick. His little force was scattered and the Colonel was captured at his home the same night, and but for his militia commission would have been hung for a bushwacker. He was first sent to the old capitol at Washington, then to Johnson's Island, and but a few days before his death, landed at Fort Delaware, where he was murdered. No promenade was allowed in the pen after dusk, the prisoners were told to go to their quarters and no lights must be seen or talking heard during the night, otherwise the guards were ordered to fire through the building. The Yankees had no cause for shooting anyone that night. The outlaw who shot Col. Jones was commended for the gallant deed, and the next day, made a corporal by Capt. Ahl with the consent and approval of General Schoeff, who visited the pen that day, accompanied by Capt. Ahl. They both seemed nervous, and spoke of repeated attempts of the prisoners to escape and the guards should shoot down any man who tried to get away. The sentinel who murdered Col. Edward Poe Jones was a boy about 20 years of age by the name of William Duglas, was a member of Co. C 157th Regiment, Ohio one hundred day men.

The Yankees, no doubt, feared an uprising of the prisoners because of this dastardly act. For several days the hurried manner in which they called the roll or entered the pen for other purposes and hastened out again with a quick nervous step, as though they feared a volcano might be smouldering under their feet and might break out at any moment. At least from some cause they seemed to think the pen was not a safe place for them and got out as quick as possible. At the end of a week things were back in about the same channel, and we were allowed to exercise in the pen and burn our lamps in our quarters until 9 o'clock. The prisoners made their own lamps, which answered the purpose fairly well. They were made by fitting a board in the top of a tin cup or can through which a tin tube was placed of proper size to receive the wick, chimneys were not used on lamps of this pattern. No lights were allowed after taps, otherwise a musket ball was sure to pass through a window in the division where the light was seen. A preemptive order by a leaden messenger was not often disregarded, but to the contrary quickly obeyed.

The Yankees celebrated the Fourth of July with a dress parade, martial music and the firing of thirty-five heavy guns from the fort down the bay. From the uproar on the outside of the pen they were having a jolly good time. The guard at the gate seemed to have had an extra dose of tanglefoot, which so confuddled the brain that several Confeds, who had succeeded in providing themselves with a suit of blue were passed out at the gate without being suspected. A goodly number of visitors rowed over to the island to take part in the celebration, also a supper and dance at the fort. It was late at night when the visitors left the island.

The Confeds who had escaped from the pen had prepared counterfeit or bogus passes. Without a pass signed by the commandant no one could leave the island. They all succeeded in getting away that night along with the returning visitors. I knew one of the prisoners who escaped that time, become acquainted with him while in prison at Johnson's Island. His parents resided in Delaware City, in sight of their son's prison; but this fact was unknown to them. He had gone to Texas two years before the war, volunteered in the 1st Texas Robert's Brigade of Hood's Division. Whether they succeeded in reaching Dixie or not I cannot say.

Every religious denomination seemed to be well represented by able, earnest, eloquent workers in the Master's cause of whom the High Priest or Chief was Isaac W. K. Handy, a Presbyterian by profession, a devout Christian gentleman. Dr. Handy had been a prisoner at the fort about 13 months, when our squad entered that prison in June, 1864. There was much missionary work done in the prison, preaching almost every day in one or more of the divisions, also at night. Those religious exercises were always listened to with much interest. Although there were always a few, I am ashamed to say, back on the upper bunks who ceased not to shuffle the pasteboard, whilst their brother prisoners bowed in humble submission, listened, many with groans and in tears, to the earnest prayerful plea for mercy and deliverance from a far worse imprisonment than that of Fort Delaware; that of sin from which many believing that they had been delivered, were baptized, some by sprinkling others by immersion; for which purpose they were permitted to go out into the bay, usually several at a time with Parson Thomas (an old hardshell Baptist, a Tennessee Lieutenant in the lead.

The old man was low in statue, I would think but little over five feet. He never led them far from shore to administer the ordinance of baptism by immersion; in which mode he had great faith. I became very well acquainted with him, he was a very plain man with but little education, called things by their first name, was pastor of four churches in the mountains of East Tennessee, in each of which he preached once a month, services conducted in log schoolhouses with dirt floors. He never had a connection and got no salary for preaching and usually walking his appointments, the furthest being about 25 miles. He was about 50 years of age had a wife and 12 children. Parson seemed to be a good christian man, honest and sincere in his belief, that baptism by immersion is the only true baptism.

Capt. Samford, a Methodist preacher, was an able speaker and earnest worker in the Master's cause, besides many others (twenty or more perhaps) ministers of different denominations, who did not hide their light under a bushel but were faithful workers. Lined up with these was Rev. G. W. Finley, who in after years became so well and favorable known to the people of Hampshire county, while pastor of the Presbyterian church at Romney and also at Springfield. From the pulpit and at the family altar for twenty years or more he never failed to point out the way of salvation to sinful mortals with an earnest eloquence attained by few, and seldom if ever surpassed by any. It was the same devotion to duty which lost to the South on the heights of Gettysburg a gallant and faithful soldier. In his zeal, he, with a few others having forged ahead of their companions, when the order to fall back reached them it was too late, their retreat was cut off; it was death or surrender; they chose the latter and were sent prisoners of war to Fort Delaware, where Lieut. G. W. Finley remained only a short period of time when with several hundred other prisoners, he was sent to Johnson's Island. In the latter part of April, 1864, he in company with about 75 sick and wounded reached Point Lookout, and on the 4th of July one year and one day from the date of his capture I heard him for the first time urge upon the impenitent sinner the necessity of repentance and the danger of delay.

The Kentucky boys received a visit from Dr. Breckenridge of Kentucky. He was accompanied by Gen. Schoeff and several other officers. The Doctor expressed a desire to see the officers from his State, of at least those who had a wish to see him. The Kentuckians were mostly quartered in No. 27, where the Doctor, no doubt, expected to see a hearty welcome from them, but he was doomed to disappointment, and the party soon took their departure; but before doing so the Doctor remarked that from their appearance the prisoners must be well fed and well cared for. When one of the prisoners held up his rations of bread and meat, his allowance at the last meal, the Doctor seemed surprised, and the General directed the prisoner to have them weighed at the Sutlers, and that the matter should be attended to without delay. But alas, our rations are shorter today than ever before; we have a cup of soup but no spoons, our knives and forks are absent. It all looks like a little spite work for yesterday's exhibition of rations before the company.

Capt. Harris delivered a sermon in our division tonight, which seemed to interest almost every one. The room was filled to the uttermost, but before he had closed a Sergeant stuck his head through the doorway and ordered lights out. A moment later all was darkness; we knew the penalty for disobeying this order. Next day the officers were all driven like a flock of sheep to a small unoccupied space at the rear and the quarters searched to see that all were out. When the Yankees had satisfied themselves that none had been left behind we were allowed to pass again in single file and carefully counted. There were found to be six absent without leave. The Yankees seemed to be a good deal vexed at the result of the count. Next day we were hacked out again and kept out in the broiling hot sun nearly all day. After having been huddled on a small space which allowed scarcely standing room for the prisoners many of them were so weak from diarrhoea that they were unable to walk without assistance. For a greater portion of the day the heat was almost unbearable.

The object of the last hackout was for the purpose of making a thorough search of the Barracks and if possible learn how the prisoners managed to escape from the pen. The floors in each division were taken up. Among other things a large number of canteens were found. These were used as substitutes for life preservers by the prisoners on their voyage, either to the Delaware shore or the bottom of the bay. After all the weak places had been strengthened and the floor spiked down securely we were allowed to enter the pen. At roll call that morning the Sergeant had ordered the chief of each division to have his men in line in front of their quarters with all their baggage, at 9 o'clock sharp. Capt. James McSherry, now Dr. James McSherry of Martinsburg, was chief of our Division at that time. The Captain said, "boys, all who have more than one blanket or change of underclothing, pocket knife or anything you don't care about losing had better get rid of them, there will be a search made of ourselves and our baggage as well as our quarters before we get in here again. Many of the prisoners had two, three or more blankets left behind by friends, which had either escaped from the prison or gone to the hospital, and had not returned. How to secrete these extras was the question. Under the floor seemed the only place so under the floor the extras all went. But it was evident in each division a spy had been taking notes. In short when we returned our quarters the man who had a blanket and extra shirt was fortunate; more fortunate was he who succeeded in saving his pocket knife or comb. But he who had greenbacks to his credit on the outside or Sutler checks on the inside of the pen would have no trouble replacing any or all his losses. Those who lost the heaviest by this unexpected raid were the jewelers. There were several of these in the pen, who were experts in the art of manufacturing from Guttapercha[2] rings, bracelets and watchchains, besides many other fancy ornaments.

---

[2] Purchased from the Sutler stores, this sap-like material, after being boiled, hardened and was used by prisoners to make jewelry.

CHAPTER XXI

More Glimpses of Prison

A few of these workmen had quite a stock on hand, much of which they hoped to carry with them back to Dixie some day; but most of these trinkets were destined to bedeck the Blue instead of the Gray.

By reference to my diary I find that it had been nearly six weeks since our batch of prisoners arrived at Fort Delaware. It is now August 1st, 1864; the weather is intensely hot, shut up as we are by buildings which exclude almost every breath of air, with a temperature of perhaps 100 degrees for several hours each day with but little variation. Our drinking water was about the same temperature as the air. A few of the Divisions or a portion of them bought of the Sutler a molasses barrel, filled it nearly with water from the tank, bought ice from the Sutler for what he claimed to be a very moderate price, 5 cts. per pound. It did not take many pounds of this 5 cent ice to cool a barrel of warm water, until it cost a 5-cent Sutler check to get a pint of it from the ice trust. By wrapping a half dozen wet blankets closely around a barrel with a few pounds of ice in it the water kept in fair drinking condition until it was gone. Then we had several beer stands where a mug of beer could be had for 5 cents. Mugs held about two-thirds of a pint. The beer was manufactured in this way: A molasses barrel was usually procured from the Sutler, and usually set behind the door of the Division; then after dark filled with water then usually a half gallon of blackstrap molasses was well dissolved in the water, then add a half gallon corn meal tied up in an old shirt sleeve or the leg of a pair old drawers and sunk in the barrel, which soon caused a kind of fermentation to set in, which, in about three days, gave the stuff a kind of a sharp, sour taste. With a little ice added to this rendered it far more thirst quenching than the water from the tank. Those who had the checks spent them freely, hoping to relieve the burning thirst within. Those who were not so fortunate as to have the checks looked on with envy, then turned with a sigh and walked to the tank, where they had often gone before in order to get a few moments of relief from their burning thirst. Then we had a barber, where those who had the checks could get a shave or hair cut. Also a guttapercha jeweler or two. Faro and Keno tables seemed to attract more notice than any other amusement; fighting the Tiger, as they called it, seemed to have a fascination or irresistible charm for some which they could not resist until the last check had been gobbled by the Tiger, which he was almost sure to do soon or later, though not always. This game was always a riddle to me. I watched it for hours and was only able to learn who was the winner by seeing who pocketed the money. Chess and checkers were about the only games understood by me well enough to play, but I was no amusement for anything of an expert. David Bean, of Romney, and I spent many hours laying on our bunks playing chess. It was difficult to say which knew least about playing the game. These places of business had to be sheltered in some way. Boards were gotten from the Sutler six or seven feet in length and split into narrow strips; four of these were driven into the ground a short distance apart, then a railing of the same material nailed around the top of the upright pieces, a blanket stretched over the top and tied down at the four corners; then four pieces driven in the ground at the proper height, on which a kind of table was constructed and the building was ready for business. Card playing was an everyday pasttime with many of the prisoners; although I am ashamed to say it, even the Sabbath day was not regarded by many. At the same time we had men among the prisoners of the highest type of manhood and second to none in intelligence, and who stood high in their chosen profession, as ministers or the Gospel, military men, noted for strategic, skill and heroism, lawyers, second in legal, lore and tricks of the profession to none in the land; physicians, who had attained a high standard of excellence in their profession. We had a circuit court conducted in almost every respect as any other circuit court on the bench or rather box, a judge of age and experience presided, a sheriff clerk and jury were present. The bar was filled in part by men of unquestioned ability, and in part in ability was almost entirely imaginary. This court was arraigned for the benefit of a class of young men who were reading law, striving to prepare themselves for the bar, should kind fortune avail itself to set them free. Rev. Dr. Handy had a theological class of perhaps a dozen or more young men, who were striving to prepare themselves for the ministry. Then we had a Captain from Louisiana, I can not remember his name, who was said to be a fine scholar and had classes in French, Latin and Greek, that recited to him each day. The Captain was kept quite busy, and although the tuition was moderate it was thought by many that he had several hundred dollars in Sutler checks. Dancing was also taught by a Lieut. Johnson, one of Morgan's men, who, it was said, understood the art by those who professed to know.

I was very much surprised one morning, when on hearing the not unusual cry of "fresh fish!, fresh fish!" I walked over to the gate to see if there was any one of the squad that I knew, and soon recognized the well known form and face of Capt. Shearer. I was glad to see him and learn from his lips the history of his escape from Washington, after having been lowered from the third story of the old Capitol. When near and in the act of accosting him he recognized me, and with a frown and shake of the head, turned from me. I saw at once that he did not wish to be known for some cause, and left him for the time being. The next evening whilst Capt.

Kuykendall, Lieut. Parrin and myself were taking some exercise by promenading up and down through the pen, I observed Tibets and Shearer coming to meet us. Tibet introduced Shearer as Capt. Thompson of Georgia, and we passed on. Next day he came into our division and inquired for me. I was not in, but met him at the door. We walked for an hour or more when he related to me the manner of his escape from the city, and how he came to be a prisoner again. He said a short distance from the corner where he had turned and passed away from our sight, there lived a family who had from his earliest recollection been very intimate with his father's family. Here he had spent many happy hours, and always received a hearty welcome. Although the old gentleman was considered a staunch Union man he had no choice; a hiding place must be had, and very quickly. He ran up to the door and rang the bell, the door was locked or he would have gone in at once, fearful of being detected by the police. The old gentleman came to the door and asked, who was there. Shearer gave his name without hesitation. The old gentleman said, "Your voice is familiar, but Capt. Shearer is a prisoner at this moment in the old Capitol." Shearer said, "I only escaped five minutes ago, for G—d sake let me in or I may be recaptured at any moment." Still he hesitated, but in a moment turned the key and opened the door; Shearer stepped in; at the same moment heard the click of a revolver; and felt its cold muzzle pressed against his cheek, exclaimed. "For Heaven's sake, mister, don't shoot, I am not armed." "So I see," said the gentleman, "and not well clad either. But why in the name of common sense did you come here?" Shearer said, "I came to you because I knew of no other place to go." "Come with me," said he, and he led the way to an upper chamber.

Shearer was handed a chair, and his host said he would go down and see what could be done toward fitting him up with a suit of clothes, as there was not much difference in their size; thought he could loan him a suit for a short time. Shearer said he was not altogether satisfied for fear his old time friend might return with a policeman instead of a suit of clothes, but his fears proved groundless for the time being. He was soon neatly attired in a suit, which, to all appearance, was made to order. Capt. Shearer would not give his friend's real name said he had pledged himself not do to so under any circumstances. I shall, in speaking of him, call him Mr. J. A gentle tap on the door and an invitation to enter by his host brought Mrs. J. into the room. Shearer said the old lady seemed very glad to see him, but under the circumstances was very sorry that he was there. They then wish to know how he came to be a prisoner at the old Capitol, and how he came to be there. "I gave them as correct an account of my capture and subsequent escape," said Shearer. "Also the grave charge brought against him of having been caught recruiting for the Rebel army, in charge according to the laws of war was a very serious one, which

Shearer told them was the great reason why he was taking such desperate chances to make his escape. "Well," said Mr. J. "my duty to my country is a plain one, that is to send you back to prison." Mrs. J. who was a Virginia lady before the marriage, said, "No, Mr. J. you surely will not send George back to prison and perhaps cause him to endure a long and loathsome imprisonment, or it might be, pay the penalty of youthful imprudence with his life; you surely cannot do this thing if you will stop and think of the time when you and George's father attended the same school, and later when you both graduated at the same time, from the same college: with pride to your friends and honor to yourselves, and yet, later, think of the hearty welcome you have ever received, and of the many pleasant hours spent beneath the father's roof, and then return that father's son to a prison from which he has so lately escaped at the risk of his life." "Mr. J.," said she, "you cannot, you shall not do this." "But my dear, " said he, "you have not thought of the consequence to us if it was known that we were hiding a Rebel, and one against whom serious charges rested." "You shall not send this young man back to prison," Mrs. J. said in a very calm determined manner. Shearer said he felt sure his case was in safe hands and kept mum. After a moments thought Mr. J. said, "I hardly think under the circumstances that it would be the thing to do, to send George back to prison, but we must get rid of him in some way; the children may be home at any moment, and it would never do for them to know that he is here, he must leave the house at once and take chances in making his escape from the city." "That would be a very difficult thing to do even by a person far better acquainted with the city than he is, I would say almost an impossible with every outlet so well guarded," said Mrs. J. Mr. J. said, "I am well aware that all you say is true, and turn him out now would be but little better than sending him back to prison, where he will be with twenty-four hours, but, my dear, think for a moment what would be the result of it should it ever become known that I, who have the confidence and hold an office under the government, had sheltered a traitor in my house and aided him to escape the penalty due his crime. Tomorrow I must go to New York on important business and will be absent for several days. George must leave the house at once.

"Which," said Mrs. J., "will be the same as sending him back to prison; guards have been stationed on every corner; it is getting late; before his escape is discovered you will be in New York, then no blame can rest on you. Then trust this matter to me, I have a plan by which George can be freed, and no suspicion rest on us."

The door bell rang at that moment. "The children have returned," said she, to Mr. J, "go down and let them in and go to the sitting room, I will be down in a few minutes; and when the children have retired I will explain my plan of escape to you." Without another word Mr. J left the room; when, Mrs. J said, "George, I will leave you now. The key is on the inside, lock the door and lie down on that lounge and try to sleep, you will not be disturbed; don't fret I will land you in Virginia ll right when the time comes; good night."

"When she had left the room I locked the door," said Shearer, and lay down, but not to sleep. I had not spoken a word while my case was being discussed; but was a very interested listener; was a little shaky at the idea of being turned out with perhaps one chance in a thousand of escape. I soon became convinced that Mrs. J was my friends and would have her way, not with the opposition of Mr. J, but how she would contrive to get me safe on Virginia soil was the problem I could not solve. Somehow I felt that she would prove herself equal to the emergency, when the time came, yet alternate hope and fear chased sleep away. The measured tread of the patrol could be heard at short intervals on the pavement below. Roll call was sounded from the fort, which meant for the prisoners to line up in front of their respective divisions, and answer to their names when the Sergeant entered to call the roll."

Shearer said he would finish his story next day. But next morning he was reported sick by the chief of his division. A few days later was sent to hospital and I did not see him again for several months.

Last night was very dark and rainy; the Sentinels seemed to be unusually watchful, seemed to anticipate trouble fo some kind, and appeared to challenge some one every few minutes. About the middle of the night the report of a musket was heard followed by four or five others in quick succession. "Turn out the guards!" "Turn out the guards!" was quickly heard. "What number?" "Post No. 86, double quick." In a very short time every soldier on the island seemed to be racing in the direction of No. 86. "Shoot them!" "Shoot them, don't let them escape," came from every direction. The guard soon returned and reported one "Reb" shot. The body of a man was found next morning on the Western shore of the Island. He had provided himself with a life-preserver and several canteens, but a stray shot ended his voyage in search of freedom, which death had brought him at last. But many others had gained their freedom in the same manner, and many others followed later.

We had a Sabbath school or rather several, and Bible classes. Among the teachers were Gen. Vance, Rev. Thomas W. Harris, Maj. John D. Richardson, Major Bullock, if I remember right there were about a hundred and fifty on the Bible class roll.

My diary of July 12th, 1864 reads: Last grape, 600 officers will be shipped tomorrow for Hilton Head, South Carolina; names of those to go will be drawn. We had all sorts of reports during the day as to the destination of the 600 officers. Some said that they had been resumed and that the 600 would go direct to City Point, and others would follow as fast as they could be gotten away. Gen. Schoeff was present this morning at roll call, something he has not done before since I have been here. Before he left the pen he informed two officers that they would all be exchanged in a very few days. This assertion, connected with some conversation between some Yankee officers at the Sutler store, went far toward confirming the report of an immediate exchange.

The consequences of this news was a continuous stir in the pen through the day; nothing else was discussed until long after taps. I feel sure that many failed to close their eyes in sleep that night in anticipation of what would occur on the morrow, August 18th. At an unusual early hour a Sergeant came to each division and announced that the names of those to be sent away would soon be called. In a very few moments every bunk was empty; no sick this morning remaining in their bunks, all stood up in line in front of the division to which they belonged. Soon Gen. Schoeff, Capt. Ahl, several clerks, Sergeants and Guards made their appearance. The prisoners were ordered to line up on the left of the plank walk which ran through the entire length of the pen. Field officers were first called, then Captains and Lieutenants. We understood that on the day before the Yankees had made up the list of six hundred in this way: a number of white beans equal to the number of officers in the pen, less six hundred. These six hundred were supplied by mixing six hundred black beans. All were then placed in a box and well mixed; when a name was called a bean was taken from the box; if it was black the prisoner answering, was ordered to cross over to the other side of the walk. In this way the six hundred officers were selected to go, they knew not where; General Schoeff said for exchange. But it had leaked out that they would be sent to Morris Island, S. C., and there placed under fire of the Confederate batteries, which were making it warm for the Yankees, who were endeavoring to erect batteries at that place.

The heat is almost unbearable here. Although it is Sunday Capt. Ahl has had part of the galvanized prisoners, nearly all day, sprinkling the enclosure or pen, which renders it far more pleasant, and if the mosquitos and bed bugs will only cease their attacks and be neutral for one night we may get a fair night's sleep. It has now been several days since the roll of six hundred was completed; we have nothing reliable as to the cause of the delay in moving them. Today the "Osceola", a small steam boat used for carrying water, wood, provisions, &c., brought over from New Castle a top load of boxes for the prisoners, which had been laying piled on the wharf at New Castle for several days. These boxes were sent to prisoners, usually by friends living inside the Yankee lines and contained clothing and meats, such as ham, turkeys, chickens, vegetables. Most of the boxes should have reached their destination within twenty four hours, but were detained at New Castle until the eatables were spoiled, another scheme to

298

enrich the Sutler. On the morning of August 20th a Sergeant entered the pen and said, "All whose names were down in the six hundred lot be ready to move out at 12 o'clock sharp. Until that time the prisoners whose names where on the roll were busily engaged in getting their baggage in the best possible way for convenience. Those to be left behind, many of them at least, were preparing letters to go on exchange without being inspected until they had reached their destination. Many were giving goodby to friends, whom they may never see again, although we were glad to see them go, hoping that the days of imprisonment were about over, and that those who were left behind would soon follow them, yet many had friends with whom they loathed to part.

Hampshire County was well represented in the six hundred, among them were Capt. Isaac Kuykendall, now of Romney, Captain J. M. Lovett, of Capon Bridge, Lt. C. P. Johnson, of Headsville, (a brother of George H.). C. P. Johnson has for many years been a citizen of the State of Kansas. I had known these from their early youth to the present time. They were valued friends, and the vacancy thus caused was felt for many days and weeks. Lieut. James T. Parker and myself were now the only Hampshire county men left in the pen. That evening a kind of reorganization was held. All the divisions above 30 were ordered to be vacated which caused a good deal of stir during the remainder of the evening. Lieut. Jas. T. Parker and myself concluded as we were the only officers representing Hampshire county in our pen, that we would set up house keeping on the 1st floor of division 28. We had but little time to muse over the absent friends who were with us only a few hours before, but now gone from our sight, it might be forever. The stir in the pen seemed to cease much earlier than usual; it may have been to commune with their own thoughts and feelings. Be that as it may.

The Sun arose next morning just the same as it has done ever since the fourth day of the creation, although a feeling of sadness seemed to overshadow the pen for a time, but at length passed away and the same routine prevailed. A few nights after the departure of the six hundred prisoners. The Yankees who had seemed somewhat nervous in anticipation of an insurrection or outbreak on the part of the prisoner. On the night referred to the guard was called out and marched to the gate or entrance to the pen; here they halted, unwilling to enter, but they were commanded by an officer brave and loyal who proved himself equal to the occasion. With drawn sword he sprang through the gate; at the same time exclaimed, "Come on boys they are not armed, they cannot hurt us." His men encouraged to think that they were called on to face an unarmed foe sprang through the gate, formed in a hollow square and stood ready to receive from every point of the compass the attack of the seven hundred unarmed prisoners who remained in the pen. After standing in this position for some fifteen minutes without being assaulted they ventured to send out a patrol who visited each division quietly and cautiously, listening in front of each for any unusual sound from within that would indicate danger. But no thing having been discovered of an alarming nature. On the return of the patrol a short consultation was held among the officers of the guard, when they all passed quietly out of the pen without one in an hundred of the prisoners knowing anything of their visit of the night, when they arose next morning. The Yankees were mum, had nothing to say. But a few of the prisoners quartered in Division 1, at the entrance to the pen were awakened from their sleep by the gathering of the guard in the rear and in close proximity to their division. Several prisoners who had been disturbed and whose curiosity had been aroused reported next morning to those of their comrades who had not been awakened by the movements of the guard during the night.

Dr. Handy, backed by many other ministers of the Gospel, had been for several weeks soliciting permission from General Schoeff to erect an awning at a convenient point in the pen, where services could be held without so much exposure to the rays of an almost torrid sun. Money had been subscribed to pay for the awning by those who had greenbacks to their credit on the outside, at a cost of fifty dollars. Gen. Schoeff had promised Dr. Handy that he would have the awning properly erected as soon as it came. But a few days after, Dr. Handy received notice that the awning had arrived and that he could not give it further attention, and that he (Dr. Handy) would have to look after the matter himself. So the old Doctor hustled around and found lots of carpenters, but no tools, except one old spade and one shovel. No timber or stay ropes of any kind could be found. The only resort was a requisition on the Sutler, which was promptly filled, provided the required amount of Sutler checks always accompanied the order.

We now had several days of very disagreeable rainy, foggy weather, with a strong cool wind blowing from the east. Most of prisoners remained in their quarters, wrapped in their blankets. We had no fire, stoves had not yet been furnished us. The yard or pen was a lake of water; the floor of our barracks was kept damp and muddy during the continuance of the rainy season. Here I first felt the numb, aching or at times, sharp piercing pain known as rheumatism, to those who have had the misfortune at any time of being locked in its embrace. No description will be necessary to understand what a bad attack of rheumatism means, a person must experience it, it cannot be described. My friends advised me to go to the Hospital, but I had a kind of horror of the Hospital, considering it only one short step from the graveyard. After a few days the weather cleared, the sun shone bright and warm, the water was drained from the pen into the ditches, when the pen was soon dry again. Dr. McSherry, who was chief of our division at the time, advised me to take all the exercise I could on every bright day, either walking, sitting or laying in the sun, which I did and soon felt much better. On account of the stormy weather no religious services were held outside of the divisions, in each of which a sermon was preached almost every night. But when the pen had dried services were resumed again, under the awning; to the great satisfaction of all who took an interest in Divine Worship. One morning the Philadelphia Inquirer came in with a glowing account of Sheridan's glorious victory over Early in the Valley. The first column was headed in large letters something like this. "Victory: Glorious news from Gen. Sheridan! Great battle of Monday fighting from morning till evening; complete rout of Early; 5,000 Rebels killed and wounded Sheridan in possession of the field—3000 prisoners fall into his hands—Roades and Gordon killed." In short the first page of the paper was taken up with this kind of stuff. One half at least was not believed by the prisoners until next day when a batch of Early's officers, fresh from that ill fated field, verified the Confederate defeat and retreat from the Valley. This was by no means encouraging to us, though many refused to believe the defeat of Early as bad as reported. For some time we have only been allowed to write ten lines at one time and only to near relatives. Old Welch, the Sutler, received a load of apples one day which he sold at one dollar per peck. Lieutenant Wolf, who, as usual, was full of whiskey, made his appearance on the sentinels platform near the middle and said to Col. Hardeman, "Colonel you'll be off soon now. Richmond and Petersburg have both been captured." Almost at the same moment cannons commenced booming on the Delaware side of the river. Much of the booming being so distant that it could scarcely be heard but created quite an excitement. Some declared that Washington was being attacked, others were confident that either Richmond or Petersburg or it might be that both had fallen, and that Lieut. Wolf though drunk, might have spoken the truth. We soon learned the whole Yankee nation was burning powder in the honor of what they claimed was a second and greater victory for Sheridan over Early, in which that General had lost everything. This was very sad news to us prisoners. Whilst many sought consolation in prayer, others expressed their dissatisfaction in an opposite direction far more emphatic than Divine. The firing of 100 heavy guns on the wall of Fort Delaware, was a somewhat interesting spectacle to many of the prisoners, although it proclaimed a victory for our foes. The Philadelphia Inquirer was the only newspaper allowed in the pen and was our source of information, which was always read without giving it credit for what little truth it might contain. However, we learned soon enough that defeat had over taken Gen. Early in the Valley, but that the disaster had not been as bad as reported. The next news was very encouraging over the grapevine telegraph line. That Gen. Butler's whole command had been captured, and Grant repulsed before Petersburg, with heavy losses, we hoped it might be true but had our doubts. About one hundred and fifty officers from Early's disaster in the Valley was added to our number. Different causes were ascribed by different officers, who ought to have known, something of the cause of their defeat. The general opinion was that they lacked a Jackson to take advantage of their victory that morning, hence their defeat later in the day. Some said overwhelming numbers, others said overwhelming whiskey, found in the Yankee camp, caused the defeat. There were some of the prisoners in the pen who believed that Gen. Early would capture Washington City and release all the prisoners in reach when we first heard of his advance into Maryland. Vain hope, nothing of importance, or unusual occurrence for several days, except a visible shrinkage in our rations, which had long before been figured down to the starvation point.

There were officers in each division who had friends outside, who supplied them with money. These bought hams and bread from the Sutler, crust of bread and meat rines were thrown on the floor of the barracks and well mixed with tobacco juice and other filth carried in on the feet of the prisoners. A detail was made (by the chief of each division) whose duty it was to sweep out the quarters before prisoners had left their bunks each morning generally something near a bushel of filth was piled in front of the door and hauled away by the police and dumped into the river. But before this filth had been five minutes outside, it was thoroughly analyzed and every crust of bread or rind of meat was picked out and eaten with apparent satisfaction by the poor starving human beings, whom the fortunes of war had for the time being placed within the power of those far beneath them. Many of these starving sons of the South had been brought up in luxury and never knew what a starving man could stoop to in order to relieve the gnawing pangs of an empty stomach.

Rats were quite plentiful, from the dusk of evening until taps. Men with a blanket drawn over their heads and a paddle in their hand ready to strike could be seen squatted over the pen patiently waiting for a rat to make his appearance from beneath the plank walks or from their hiding places along ditch banks. The meat after being dressed, looked like and might easily have been taken for a young squirrel, and was said to be equal in flavor by those who had tasted each. Occasionally a little dog trotted into the pen at some visitors heels, but he was a very lucky pup if he ever trotted out again. Yet these men professed the crust of bread, the rind of meat, rat, pup and starvation, rather than the oath of allegiance to the United States which was offered them almost daily. Yet I am proud to say but few accepted the invitation, rather starve with honor than live a traitor and in disgrace. These men were patrons and have left a name without a state, which future generations will ever remember with pride and reverence.

The latest reliable news from the six hundred officers sent south to be placed under fire, was that they were aboard the "Crescent" in Charleston harbor awaiting their doom. One evening early in October several penitents, who had confessed their sins, were baptized by immersion having been granted by Lieut. Wolf. The procession formed at the appointment hour near the gate. Drs. Hardy and Harris walked in front, followed by Parson Thomas and the applicants for baptism followed. On the outside of the gate two lines of guards stood ready to escort them to the waters edge. The gate closed and the procession was lost from view from those within the pen.

Dr. Woolsey spent several hours examining the sick and crippled with a view to exchanging this class of prisoners, although I was much better of my rheumatism. I thought perhaps this was my opportunity and crawled into my bunk, and left the case in charge of Lieut. Parker, who stated the case to the Dr. in its worst form. I did the grunting, the Dr. did the listening. When Parker had concluded the Dr. remarked "your friend is in no condition to go on exchange, better send him to the hospital." He then turned and walked out. Parker, after a moment remarked, "jes over done it didn't we?" Well I felt disappointed, but there was no help for it. Several prisoners who suffered less but had money were named on the Doctors list as fit persons to go on exchange. My valued friend, Major Chin, who was quartered in the fort, got permission to visit the pen for the purpose of giving his friends good bye. Although the Major was in robust health a two hundred dollar watch and a one hundred dollar check did the work. His name was entered on the list of sick, to go on exchange with the next batch. At parting the Major handed me a hand full of sutler checks, amounting to about five dollars. I never heard from him again, felt sad at parting, although a stranger. He was a true friend in time of need. A day or two later the exchange boat, New York, was reported at anchor opposite the fort, soon the names of those for exchange were called to the gate. Having held themselves in readiness they soon made their appearance and were hurried through the gate, their friends, who accompanied them thus far, slowly and silently returned to their quarters. The weather was quite cool. Many of the prisoners were scantly clad. And especially those from the far South, who now for the first time experiencing the chilling winds of the northern clime, found comfort in wrapping their blankets around them when ever they had occasion to leave their quarters, although the freezing point had scarcely yet been reached. My own outfit was very much racked, how to replenish it was a problem I had not been able to solve Lieut. Luther Ashby came to my rescue, when informed of my trouble. Said he would send me anything in clothing that I was in need of. Ashby gave me the address. I wrote Miss Hoffman and within a week received a very respectable suit of clothing including hat and shoes. Who Miss Dora Hoffman was, I never learned, but I do know that she lightened the burden and received the blessings of hundreds of ragged prisoners who were suffering from cold for want of clothing. The weather had now become rather cool for preaching or evening prayers, under the awning. A vote was taken in each division for the purpose of ascertaining their sentiments in regard to evening prayers, our division (No. 28) voted unanimous in favor of evening worship. This move interfered some what with the different kinds of games which usually ceased, only when "taps" sounded lights out. Gen. R. B. Vance, of North Carolina was chief of our division. He was in the prime of life, a good christian, a member of the Methodist Church, although he sprung from Presbyterians. He was a very quiet man and was much respected not only by his division but by all in the pen. Being a good talker with talent superior to the ordinary man, he was always listened to with attention and interest. The General usually conducted services in our division at night his lectures singing and prayers generally consumed the time until taps. The General evidently did not approve of dividing time with those who preferred gaming to praying, which ended in the class seeking a more congenial clime, Oct. 12th, 1864.

Dr. Handy left Fort Delaware for Richmond after having been an inmate of this prison since June 1863, I believe all were glad that the old man had at length after so many vain efforts succeeded in getting away with a fair prospect of being united within a few hours with his family once more. While all seemed to rejoice for his sake, at the same time very many loathed to part with him. He was considered the pioneer preacher of our pen. News for several days past has been very scarce the news collector seem to be taking an outing or on a strike. Or it may be that the armies on either side have gone into winter quarters and hence the lack of news from the front. About the middle of November I received a second attack of rheumatism and was compelled this time to go to the hospital is where the prisoner usually graduates.

On entering the hospital I was carried into a long hall into which were the different wards, and offices opened. Here I was seated on the floor by my attendants to walk along with several others, the convenience of those who had control of the hospital. In about a half hour a door opened near the farther end of the hall. Quite a youth in appearance stepped out and clattered towards us on a pair of wooden legs, asked a few questions and returned from whence he came, after another half hour had elapsed two nurses made their appearance. They were what we called galvanized rebs. I could not walk without assistance, but with a helper on each side, I was waltzed to the far end of the hall and entered a bath room, stripped of every vestige of clothing, which was rolled together and securely tied. A card with my name was attached to the bundle which was then pitched into a room adjoining the bathing apartment. If the patient recovered he recovered his clothing. After a thorough renovating I was attired in a brown cotton shirt with drawers to match and escorted toward No. 2 and placed between two sheets on a shuck mattress, supported by an iron cot. In a short time the Doctor in charge of the ward entered on his regular morning visit, accompanied by the chief or head nurse of the ward. On reaching my cot he turned to the ward master asked a few question of me in regard to my ailment, looked at my tongue, felt my pulse, wrote a prescription on a card and stuck up over the head of my cot, then passed to the next patient and so on up on one side of the ward and back on the other. I was now for the first time a regularly admitted inmate of a hospital and had ample time and opportunity to have indelibly impress on my mind the inside working of an institution of this kind. For the benefit of those who have never had a like experience a short description here may not be out of place. Ward No. 2 was as near as I could guess about twenty feet in width by one hundred in length. Cots stood on each side of the ward with a space between not exceeding three feet between each cot was a window. Beneath each window stood a small stand on which the patient's food and medicine were placed. On the wall over the head of each cot hung a small wooden paddle, on which was written the patient's name and post office address in full, also grade of office, company, regiment, brigade and division to which he belonged, and disease for which he was being treated. Across the face of this paddle was stretched a small gum cord where prescriptions for the patient were struck by the Doctor who visited the ward about 9 o'clock in the morning, often about the same hour at night and was always attended by the steward or head nurse of the ward, of whom he made inquiry concerning those who were no longer conscious, or too weak to answer questions. After the head nurse had attended the Doctor on his rounds, he then came around and took up all the prescriptions left the Dr. and carried then to the dispensary, had them properly filled by those in charge of that department, then administered by the stewart according to corresponding number, each patient and each prescription being numbered. A passage way of about eight feet was left between the cots or beds, three large stoves with equally large drums were used for heating the ward to such a degree that a sheet was all that was necessary for a covering. When a patient died his remains were placed in a pine coffin and conveyed to the Jersey side of the island and piled up ready for shipment to the Jersey shore for burial. From twenty-five to thirty of these boxes left the hospital every day. With few exceptions everything about the ward was kept in the best possible order, neat and clean. I must say that I was agreeably surprised to find the

305

patients were so well cared for in respect to comfort. The Doctor said I had an attack of acute rheumatism and might expect to experience considerable pain. In this particular I found he was right my joints were very much swollen and drawn. My suffering was great. The head nurse in ward No. 2 was from Louisiana had been Captain of a steamboat and seemed to take a liking to me from the first, a brother could not have been more kind. About 10 o'clock the lights were turned down to low that the nurses in passing through the ward seemed to be more shadows. In about two weeks I was able to sit up and soon began to shuffle about the ward, doing what I could to cheer and comfort those less fortunate. Some were too weak to reach their food, which was placed on the stand by their cot many of these I helped to get a little nourishment, many of them were too sick to eat more than a few mouths fulls. At this time I had a very fine appetite, which had been dieted, since I had been in the hospital. When the patient could not take his food I was always ready to help out. After having been in the hospital about six weeks the ward master on entering the ward one morning gave notice that Dr. Woolsey would visit the ward sometime during the day for the purpose of taking a list of those who were in a condition to go on exchange and when the Doctor entered the ward all those who were able would be expected to rise and stand by their cot. About 11 o'clock the ward master announced Dr. Woolsey whose gaunt form now entered. Instantly every patient who was able to stand was on his feet, although several poor fellows who were anxious to go on exchange but too weak to stand, sank back with a groan, on their cots before the Doctor had reached them and were passed by without notice. When my cot was reached I was standing as erect as, I thought, a bean pole. He took the little sign board from over my head of my cot and read, "acute rheumatism," asked me a few questions, then said walk down the aisle and back again. I did so, but having been on my feet for at least a half hour my limbs didn't perform first class. The Doctor thought I had better remain where I was until the next lot was sent away. I pled with him to let me go with the lot row being made up. Finally he said, well if you are determined to bring trouble on your self I will have you discharged from the barracks, it will probably be ten days yet before this batch gets off; if you are not back here within a week I will be disappointed. That evening about fifty of us marched back to the pen, I soon found Lieut. Parker. He held the same position on the upper tier of bunks, but to my surprise I could not climb the ladder or rather short pieces of lath nailed across a post to enable those who occupied an upper berth to reach the same. I was about to despair of reaching my old roasting place, when Lieut. Blankenship came to my assistance and hoisted me up. Lieut. Blankenship was certainly the largest man I ever saw. He was, if I remember right, six feet eight inches in height, and well proportioned, weighing about 275 pounds with not an ounce of surplus flesh, a giant in strength and one of the best natured men I ever saw. It was told of him that on one occasion his horse was wounded and that Blankenship carried him off the field. This story I don't think could be vouched for. Blankenship was a West Virginian. His lodging place was opposite mine. He was always ready to either elevate me of lower me. I soon found that I would have to change my sleeping place from the top to the lowermost tier of bunks. We soon found a man who, was willing to exchange places, his being behind the door and planked off to its self. Parker and I moved down, spread an old blanket for a carpet, pasted paper overhead and on the walls, hung a blanket for a door and felt that we were more comfortable by the change.

I took the best care of myself possible, hoping every day to get away on exchange. In three or four days I was convinced that I was not improving. At the end of a week I was again flat on my back in the hospital in a much worse shape than before. For six weeks I lay on my back most of this time unable to move, my joints were drawn and swollen to twice their natural size. If for ten days, I slept in all one hour, I did not know it, could only be moved in a sheet, then with great care. My suffering was almost more than I could bear. It seemed to me that I was billed for the Jersey shore this time for sure, but He who numberth the hairs of our heads ordered it otherwise and I am yet spared, after having suffered more than any except the experienced could tell. With one or more deaths every day, more passed over during the night than during the day. It was sad indeed to listen to the prayers, and supplications of the dying, not only in their own behalf but in behalf of their families whom they would never see again on earth. After a wrestle of about two months I was able to stand on my feet, with an appetite like a crosscut saw or half starved hound. I was soon shuffling around dividing rations with those who had more than they could eat. In this way I managed to get from five to ten rations daily and soon began to improve rapidly. In the meantime about four hundred of the six hundred officers who had been sent south and placed on Morris Island under fire of the Confederate guns on Fort Anderson and Battery Wagoner, were returned to Fort Delaware, the remainder who were living were on sick list and paroled.

Of those who returned to the Fort many were in a bad shape and were sent to the hospital almost dead with scurvy or diarrheoa, or both, but few of those cases recovered. Those who did or most of them were compelled to get false teeth or gum it for the remainder of their earthly pilgrimage. I. T. Brady whose parents resided at Brady's Mills, Md. often received nice boxes of eatables from home and often visited me while in the hospital, generally, with his pockets well filled with good things from his home, which was always appreciated. Brady and I belonged to the same Company. It was now near the last of March 1865. Smallpox was raging rather more than usual, the pest house for smallpox was only a short distance away from the window at the head of my cot. I had a good view of it, and if I remember right from twenty-five to thirty-five boxes containing a smallpox corpse, were taken away each day; several patients had broken out in our ward, and had been removed to the pest house. One of these was on the cot next to me, I concluded that I would prefer taking my chances in the pen. Although still somewhat stiff in my joints I was suffering no pain. I concluded to ask the Doctor for a discharge from the hospital. That morning Brady came in to see me. I told him of my determination to go back to the pen. Brady thought that while I would be less apt to take smallpox in there I was far more comfortable situated where I was but when considering the rapidity of increase in the hospital of cases developing smallpox it might be safer place in the pen. Brady now informed me that my schoolmate and nearest neighbor, David Fox, was in Ward 4, in a very bad shape and if I ever wished to see him again I had better do so before going back to the pen. Patients were not allowed to enter any ward except the one they occupy without a pass, this I did not have. Brady said, "d—n the pass, come with me." I did so and soon at David's side had I been alone should have passed him by without recognition, so changed, he could hardly have been considered a well developed skeleton, on taking his hand I was preparing, for what I really believed to be the last time, "with a smile on my lips and a lie in the heart." I did what I could to encourage him to believe that he would soon be up again at the same time feeling in my heart that this was our last parting, and that in a short time, all that was mortal of David would lay beneath the sod on the Jersey shore. That evening I returned to my quarters in the pen, found Lieut. Parker still holding our old position reinforced by Lieut. C. P. Johnson, who was one of the six hundred sent south in August of 1864 and returned again.

Next day after my return to the pen I met Capt. Shearer and learned the manner of his escape from Washington City. After remaining at the house for a few days his hostess informed him one morning that she had heard from her husband and expected him home next day, and that it would be necessary for him to make an effort to leave the city that day; at the same time submitted her plan of proceedings in order to accomplish the desired end. Her plan was this: she had two grown daughters, who were rather above the medium height. Accompanied by her daughters, on pleasant evenings, they were in the habit of taking a drive across the chain bridge to the Virginia side. The husband being in the confidence of the government, they had no trouble in getting a pass, which was required of every one crossing. On the evening of the day named a carriage containing three ladies crossed the bridge and drove several miles into the country. When passing through a pine thicket which skirted the road on either side one of the ladies leaped from the carriage with a bundle under her arm and disappeared in the thick brush. When she had reached a secluded spot she halted took from her bundle a suit of citizen's clothing which quickly took the place of the female attire, and Captain Shearer was himself again. Being somewhat acquainted with the surrounding country he got his bearing, and when the shades of evening made it safe, with a fixed star for his guide, he traveled all night and lay in a thicket next day. After he had eaten of a beautiful lunch prepared for the occasion, by his kind friends and satisfying his appetite he stretched himself on the leaves and slept until the sun was low in the western sky. Eating the remainder of his rations, and his guiding star appearing again, he started on his journey, which necessitated considerable caution because of his near approach to the advanced line of the Yankee army through which he had to make his way in order to reach the Confederate lines, which he did next morning in this manner: about four o'clock in the morning while crossing a highway he came on a picket and he was promptly halted. Supposing it to be a Yankee he fell back in double quick, hastened, somewhat by the report of a musket and the whistle of a minnie ball. Running with more speed than caution through an old field skirted by a body of timber; on reaching it a bayonet was almost thrust in his face and the command rang in his ears in a tone which seemed to mean business. He was too close to do otherwise than obey, which he did. To his great joy he learned that he had been captured by a Confederate picket, and breakfasted with friends that morning.

"Now," said I, "your story so far is satisfactory, but I still want to know how you became a prisoner again?" I will, said he, that is part of my history told in a very few words. There lives not far from Frederick City, Md., a man who was the chief cause of my capture and imprisonment at Old Capitol. I determined to take possession of this man, if ever an opportunity ever occurred. When Gen. Johnson and McCausland, on their raid into Pennsylvania, burned Chambersburg, I was with them, with a pair of handcuffs to be used in case I found my man.

"When our raiders recrossed the Potomac I had not found my man, but had procured a supply of whiskey and taken an overdose. I camped in a fence corner, and was surprised while sleeping by Yankee troops in pursuit of the Confederate column and here I am."

I had not been in my old quarters but a few days until it seemed to me that it was only a question of time when death by starvation would end my earthly career. I seriously contemplated an attempt to reach the Delaware shore or drown in preference to starving, which it seemed to me I certainly would do. While walking in the yard one morning feeling rather blue, I was accosted by Luther Ashby who said, "Blue, loan me a fifty cent check, I want to fight the tiger. I have been watching the game for some time, and see where I can win. Loan me the check and I will divide if I win anything." I had two fifty cent sutler checks left of what Major Chinn had given me. I hesitated a moment. He had done me several favors and was an all round good fellow and seemed so anxious. I handed him the check. That evening about dark Ashby crawled into our den and exclaimed, "Blue, in another hour I would have busted the game; see what I have won," and proceeded to empty his pockets of checks dividing then into two lots. He then handed me a fifty cent check and remarked, "that is the amount of capital invested, and here are the profits; one lot is yours, the other mine, take your choice of piles." I loaned you fifty cents, you paid me back, that is all I am entitled too. "No," said Ashby, "you furnished the capital and must share in the profits," at same time gathered one pile, put them in his pocket and left. Parker and I counted our pile and found that we had something over five dollars in Sulter checks. That night I lay awake several hours trying to devise some method by which we could spend our funds for something to eat, at the same time retain our capital. I gave it up and tried to sleep but could not. There were several Beer stands in the pen. Finally it occurred to me, that these institutions must make a good profit on their investment, selling their beer at five cents a mug, containing about a half pint each. I figured the cost of starting a business of this kind: One molasses barrel, $1.50; one gallon of black strap molasses, $2.50; five pounds of corn meal, 50 cents; a half dozen lemons, 10 cents each, 60 cents. The process of manufacturing the beverage was first fill the barrel with water, stir in the molasses, tie or sew 5 pounds of corn meal in a sack and sink it in the barrel. In about three days the stuff will be ready for use. The lemons were then shaved thin for a kind of seasoning, but really as an advertisement as the pieces floated over the top of the mixture.

Next morning I explained to Parker my plan of investing our capital. He thought it would be a risky business as there was already several tanks of this kind in full blast. Each had regular customers we would have to build up a trade; before this could be done our beverage would be vinegar and all we could do would be to empty it in the ditch. While we were discussing matter, Lieut. Johnson came in. Parker and I agreed to leave the question with him. He sided with me and said if you want a salesman, he would take the job for one third interest in the business." This we agreed to. The firm now consisted of three members, each had a separate duty assigned him. My duty was to see to the manufacturing department, Johnson salesman, Parker, was to run the keno table in connection with the beer stand in order to draw customers. At this moment Lt. Ashby rushed into our quarters, hat in hand and hair on end. (Luther had a way of jerking off his hat and running his fingers through his hair when excited standing it on end.) "Boys," exclaimed he, "She is gone up, and so are we."

What has gone up came from different directions. "The Confederacy, Old Uncle Bob, has surrendered everything, his whole army, Richmond, Petersburg, everything every Confederate soldier to be banished. If they ever return the penalty will be death. Every man who can swim must take water to night or it will be too late." Some one said how about those who can't swim. "Get a board," said Ashby and dashed out again to spread the news. Well, said Parker we will not take all this news for Gospel, until we hear from Bill Cayener. Bill and Luther were rival news gather's of the pen, either could give you the very latest whenever called on. One would promptly refer you to the other, whenever his report was doubted. It was not often that their reports agreed. Inside of ten minutes Cayener stuck his head through the doorway and said, "boys were gone up and passed on." A little later the Philadelphia Press was scattered all over the pen by a Yankee Sergeant, the headlines were a sight to see. Although the Press was considered a very unreliable paper many believed that the end had really come. After four long years through the heat and cold, through sunshine and storm, on the blood stained battlefield, or between prison walls, no hardships, privation or suffering had ever caused the lip to quiver, or tears to trace each other over the weather beaten and scarred visage of many a veteran; as did the news of Gen. Lee's surrender. It was the death knell to all their hopes. Strong men wept, a gloom seemed to settle over the crowd, which had thronged the pen a half hour before, but was now almost deserted. The prisoners having gone to their quarters in sadness and sorrow. Soon the heavy guns on the walls of the fort began to boom. Great was the rejoicing among the Yankees.

A few days later news of the assassination of President Lincoln was circulated throughout the pen, though at first not believed but was soon confirmed. The sutler closed his window on our side and was not opened again for three days. The prisoners were not allowed together in group or to talk outside of the barracks. The guards were unusually watchful, the prisoners had to be very cautious to not show any signs of rejoicing. For a few days it was hardly safe to talk above a whisper. The old dutch Sergeant, who called our roll, said he thought the General was too hard on you boys, for said he, "I know it was none of you kill Mr. Lincoln just soon as I heard it." In a few days the sutler store was again in full blast. We procured a barrel and necessary ingredients for manufacturing a barrel of beer. Three days later Johnson was in position with his barrel near the center of the pen close on to the main wall. Parker held a position on Johnson's right. I had a position some distance in the rear in the shadow of the barracks, where I watched the battle from afar. Johnson knew at least one half the men in the pen, but made slow progress. Parker did better and closed the day a little a head. "Just as I expected" said he knew we would have beer to pour in the ditch. We were all discouraged over the outlook, knowing that our beer would not keep another day. Next morning early Parker and Johnson had the position as the day before. From my post of observation it was easy to see the battle was against us, and that our enterprise was about to end in dismal failure. His voice was growing hoarse from his fruitless endeavors to draw custom. "Why" said he, "will you die of thirst on an Island surrounded by the briny deep or burst yourselves by drinking from the briny tank, when a fresh, sparkling thirst quencher can be had for only five cents a mug, come up gentleman and try a mug." *The prisoners could not be diverted from their former haunts, and the Blue, Parker and Johnson partnership failed.*

On May 27, 1865, the partners then joined ninety of their fellow officers in a petition addressed to Senator Waitman T. Willey of West Virginia, asking his assistance in procuring their release from prison. At the same time and in the same manner they indicated their willingness, "the Confederate cause having failed," to take oaths of allegiance to the United States. In their petition they expressed themselves as not unmindful of the difficulties before them, but they were, nevertheless, eager to try "to make their own livings" and help their friends and families.

The request was granted and in compliance with an order of the Adjutant General of the United States, on June 12, 1865, Lieutenant Blue took an oath of allegiance to and again became a loyal citizen of the United States of America. His subsequent life was proof abundant of the sincerity of his formal surrender and his request for another opportunity. The bitterness of the Lost Cause was soon forgotten and memories of it lingered only as pleasant and inspiring reminders of what Americans imbued with principles and sincerity, can accomplish in pursuit of a cause.[3]

---

[3] Italized text from "The Huckleberry Rangers" by Charles Ambler from the West Virginia University Archives.

Postscript

M r. Editor, in my reminiscence I have related things as I saw them, truthfully and conscientiously, and have no apologies to make to any one. After thanking you for the space accorded me in the columns of the REVIEW, which might have been filled with far more interesting matter to your readers, I will now close my reminiscence as a soldier in the field with the request that you publish in the columns of the REVIEW, the following lines written by Lieut. Col. Ball, of the 11th Virginia Cavalry, and dedicated to the ladies of Charlottsville, who, early in the war, presented the Eleventh with a flag; but later when it had become "battle worn and bullet torn" the ladies of the same town replaced it with a new one. It was this occasion that drew from the pen of the gallant Colonel this tribute to the fair. Colonel Ball was a cousin of the Rev. Ball, of this place, who was also a soldier of the Lost cause if I am not mistaken, was a follower of the daring Mosby.

To Ephriam Herriott, of this vicinity, who was a member of Company D. of the Eleventh, I am indebted for a copy of the poem, which was presented to him by the Colonel, and has been preserved by that gentleman with pride and jealous care to the present time; and, may be the only copy in existence today.

The Eleventh was the banner regiment of the Laurel Brigade.

Some errors have been made, either by the writer or the type setter, of names and places, which are not material.

Respectfully, John Blue,
Lieu. Co. D., 11th Regiment,
5th Brigade Virginia, Confederate Cavalry.
Romney, Hampshire Co., W. Va.

DEDICATED
To the Ladies who presented the 11th Virginia Regiment of Cavalry With a Flag While passing through Charlottsville.

Dear Ladies: a battle-flag, stainless and new,
Supplants now the one wrought and hallowed by you;
And on us-as once on the war-path we rode
All cheerless and bannerless-kindly bestowed
Bright and pure we received it, now faded and torn,
By battles and time its beauty 'tis shorn.
But blush not to take it-the tale written there

313

In as splendid as e're won the praise of the fair;
    Where the sons of Virginia, the battle storm braved.
Your gift has still ever triumphantly waved,
When the dashing "Eleventh" its summons obeyed.
And charged in the vain of the "Laurel Brigade."
While Rosser raised high his encouraging voice,
And felt, as he watched it, his spirit rejoice;
For Where it was waving and pointing he knew
The fight must be fierce and the foe must rue!
    Where'er in the smoke of combat it glowed,
The blood of our comrades beneath it had flowed.
Had its worn threads a voice they could feelingly tell
How Kirby, and Spiker, and Pendleton fell;
How Bonner went down, and the glorious dead,
Who had rushed to the charge where they gallantly led;
They could speak of the Wilderness, crimson with gore,
And the four bloody conflicts it there floated o'er,
Of Ashland's hot race and the foe's rapid flight,
Of Hawk's Shop, renowned for its long, weary fight;
Of Trevillian's we harder and better we fought
As we looked at our flag and of your safety thought;
Of Salem, not least in the roll of success,
And Sappony, the scene of the "raiders" distress.
    Oh, will you not cherish the battle-worn rag,
Which is all that remains of your beautiful flag,
For the sake of the deeds its defenders have done,
The blood they have shed, and the triumphs they've won!
Not a rent that it shows, not a stain that it wears,
But reminds of the anguish some stricken heart bears,
Which is mourning the loss of a loved one whole form
Sunk down in the wrath of the red battle's storm,
    Your gift was a god-send. His angels you gave
The hope of the fair to the hands of the brave;
That hope has a valor undaunted, inspired,
And their bosoms, with triumphs unbroken, have fired
The "talent"—its mission accomplished—again
is yours, how the type of a splendid campaign.
The credit upon it bestowed is your own;
In future let peril to either be known,
And we'll rally, with hearts to its memories true,
And save it or die for your flag and for you.

                                          "ELEVENTH"

314

Index

REGIMENTAL INDEX

GENERAL INDEX

316

Heiskell, D.H. 66
Heiskell, J.C. 66
Heiskell, Mrs. John O. 61, 64
Henson, Mr. 84, 85, 87-91
Herriott, Capt. Ephraim 41-43, 53,
  195, 212, 213, 216, 219, 222, 234,
  313
Herriott, Miss 155
Herriott, W. V. 33, 37, 39, 42, 78,
  197
High, Samuel 28
Hill, Col. A. P. 3, 4, 117, 121, 122,
  124, 130, 134, 137, 146, 241
Hilton Head, SC 297
Hines, James 5, 6
Hines, Mr. 41, 43
Hinkle, Dr. 185
Hoffman, Criss 217, 218, 223, 304
Hood, Gen. 288
Hooker, Gen. 147, 148
Hott, George 151, 158, 190
Hott, Mr. 73, 75
Houston, Dr. 211
Howard's Lick 164, 215, 217, 220,
  221
Huckleberry Ranger 1, 6, 13, 48, 55.
  105
Hulver Settlement 87
Humbaugh, Mr. 73, 92
Hunter, Gen. 265

Imboden, Gen. George 152, 155,
  157, 158, 162, 164, 165, 169, 171,
  195, 196, 204, 207, 210, 264, 265
Independent Greys 1
Inskeep, Foreman 25, 27, 29, 31
Inskeep, J. F. 104
Inskeep, John J. 212-214, 222, 282
Inskeep, Joseph 93, 186
Inskeep, Mrs. 216
Inskeep, W. V. 4, 24, 26, 34-36, 40
Inskeep, William 104
Intelligencer (South Branch) 3

Jackson, Sam 276

Jackson, Gen. T.J. "Stonewall" 22,
  32, 39, 43, 45, 4 8, 50, 56, 91, 93,
  94, 96, 97, 100, 103-105, 110,
  117-124, 126, 128-131, 135, 137-
  143, 145-149, 163, 166, 186, 187,
  232, 265, 302
Jack's Shop, VA 229, 231
James City, VA 233
Jarboe, Capt. 212
Jefferson Co., VA (WV) 278
Jersey Mountain 6, 17, 21, 26, 27,
  33, 264
Johnson, Abraham 11, 24, 25
Johnson, Lt. Chas. P. 109, 110, 282,
  299, 308, 310-312
Johnson, Gen. 309
Johnson, Gen. Edward 93, 94
Johnson, George 76
Johnson, George H. 109, 299
Johnson, Greenwell 10, 43
Johnson, Jim 27
Johnson, Joseph E. 142
Johnson, Lt. 294
Johnson, Okey 12, 282
Johnson, Z.H. 282
Johnson's Island, OH 247, 248, 250,
  261, 263, 266, 270, 287-289
Jones, Col. William E. 110, 111, 113,
  115, 134, 171-173, 181, 183, 184,
  195, 198, 199, 203, 206, 263, 265,
Col. Edward Poe Jones 287

Keller House 20, 66
Kelley, Gen. 158, 160 168, 169
Kelley's Ford 199
Kemper, Gen. 203
Kercheval Ford 155
Kerney, Gen. 147
Kernstown, VA 56
Keys, Capt. 19
Keyser, WV 1, 4, 11, 48
Kilpatrick, Gen. 233, 235, 287
Kingwood, VA (WV) 178, 179
Kirby, VA (WV) 91
Kirkpatrick, Gen. 227
Knobley Gap 24
Knobley Mountain 10, 11, 24
Krotzer Springs, VA 175, 177

319